Lecture Notes in Computer Science 5953

Commenced Publication in 1973
Founding and Former Series Editors:
Gerhard Goos, Juris Hartmanis, and Jan van Leeuwen

T0224103

José Monteiro   René van Leuken (Eds.)

Integrated Circuit and System Design

Power and Timing Modeling,
Optimization and Simulation

19th International Workshop, PATMOS 2009
Delft, The Netherlands, September 9-11, 2009
Revised Selected Papers

 Springer

Volume Editors

José Monteiro
INESC-ID / IST, TU Lisbon
1000-029 Lisbon, Portugal
E-mail: jcm@inesc-id.pt

René van Leuken
Delft University of Technology, EEMCS/MECE/CAS
Mekelweg 4, H17 CAS, 2628 CD Delft, The Netherlands
E-mail: rene@dimes.tudelft.nl

Library of Congress Control Number: 2009943912

CR Subject Classification (1998): J.2, B.7, B.2, B.1, B.3, B.6, B.5, B.4

LNCS Sublibrary: SL 1 – Theoretical Computer Science and General Issues

ISSN   0302-9743
ISBN-10   3-642-11801-1 Springer Berlin Heidelberg New York
ISBN-13   978-3-642-11801-2 Springer Berlin Heidelberg New York

springer.com

© Springer-Verlag Berlin Heidelberg 2010
Printed in Germany

Typesetting: Camera-ready by author, data conversion by Scientific Publishing Services, Chennai, India
Printed on acid-free paper   SPIN: 12844012   06/3180   5 4 3 2 1 0

Preface

Welcome to the proceedings of the 19th International Workshop on Power and Timing Modeling, Optimization and Simulation, PATMOS 2009. Over the years, PATMOS has evolved into an important European event, where researchers from both industry and academia discuss and investigate the emerging challenges in future and contemporary applications, design methodologies, and tools required for the development of the upcoming generations of integrated circuits and systems. PATMOS 2009 was organized by TU Delft, The Netherlands, with sponsorship by the NIRICT Design Lab and Cadence Design Systems, and technical co-sponsorship by the IEEE. Further information about the workshop is available at http://ens.ewi.tudelft.nl/patmos09.

The technical program of PATMOS 2009 contained state-of-the-art technical contributions, three invited keynotes, and a special session on SystemC-AMS Extensions. The technical program focused on timing, performance, and power consumption, as well as architectural aspects with particular emphasis on modeling, design, characterization, analysis, and optimization in the nanometer era. The Technical Program Committee, with the assistance of additional expert reviewers, selected the 36 papers presented at PATMOS. The papers were organized into 7 oral sessions (with a total of 26 papers) and 2 poster sessions (with a total of 10 papers). As is customary for the PATMOS workshops, full papers were required for review, and a minimum of three reviews were received per manuscript.

Beyond the presentations of the papers, the PATMOS technical program was enriched by a series of talks offered by world-class experts, on important emerging research issues of industrial relevance. Toby Doorn of NXP Semiconductors spoke about "Robust Low-Power Embedded SRAM Design: From System to Memory Cell," Davide Pandini of ST Microelectronics spoke about "Variability in Advanced Nanometer Technologies: Challenges and Solutions," and Yusuf Leblebici of Ecole Polytechnique Federale de Lausanne spoke about "Subthreshold Circuit Design for Ultra-Low-Power Applications."

We would like to thank our colleagues who voluntarily worked to make this edition of PATMOS possible: the expert reviewers; the members of the Technical Program and Steering Committees; the invited speakers; and last but not least, the local personnel who offered their skill, time, and extensive knowledge to make PATMOS 2009 a memorable event.

September 2009

José Monteiro
René van Leuken

Organization

Organizing Committee

René van Leuken	TU Delft (General Chair)
Alexander de Graaf	TU Delft
Laura Bruns	TU Delft
José Monteiro	INESC-ID / IST, TU Lisbon (Technical Program Chair)

Technical Program Committee

Atila Alvandpour	Linköping University, Sweden
David Atienza	EPFL, Switzerland
Nadine Azemard	University of Montpellier, France
Peter Beerel	USC, USA
Naehyuck Chang	Seoul University, Korea
Jorge Juan Chico	University of Seville, Spain
Joan Figueras	University of Catalonia, Spain
Eby Friedman	University of Rochester, USA
Costas Goutis	University of Patras, Greece
Eckhard Grass	IHP, Germany
José Güntzel	University of Santa Catarina, Brazil
Oscar Gustafsson	Linköping University, Sweden
Shiyan Hu	Michigan Technical University, USA
Nathalie Julien	University of Bretagne-Sud, France
Philippe Maurine	University of Montpellier, France
Vasily Moshnyaga	University of Fukuoka, Japan
Tudor Murgan	Infineon, Germany
Wolfgang Nebel	University of Oldenburg, Germany
Dimitris Nikolos	University of Patras, Greece
Antonio Nunez	University of Las Palmas, Spain
Vojin Oklobdzija	University of Texas at Dallas, USA
Vassilis Paliouras	University of Patras, Greece
Davide Pandini	ST Microelectronics, Italy
Antonis Papanikolaou	NTUA, Greece
Christian Piguet	CSEM, Switzerland
Massimo Poncino	Politecnico di Torino, Italy
Ricardo Reis	University of Porto Alegre, Brazil
Donatella Sciuto	Politecnico di Milano, Italy
Dimitrios Soudris	NTUA, Greece
Zuochang Ye	Tsinghua University, China
Robin Wilson	ST Microelectronics, France

Steering Committee

Antonio Acosta	University of Seville, Spain
Nadine Azemard	University of Montpellier, France
Jorge Juan Chico	University of Seville, Spain
Joan Figueras	University of Catalonia, Spain
Reiner Hartenstein	TU Kaiserslautern, Germany
Enrico Macii	Politecnico di Torino, Italy
Philippe Maurine	University of Montpellier, France
José Monteiro	INESC-ID / IST, TU Lisbon, Portugal
Wolfgang Nebel	University of Oldenburg, Germany
Vassilis Paliouras	University of Patras, Greece
Christian Piguet	CSEM, Switzerland
Dimitrios Soudris	NTUA, Greece
Diederik Verkest	IMEC, Belgium
Roberto Zafalon	ST Microelectronics, Italy

Table of Contents

Session 2: Power Management

Session 3: Low Power Circuits & Technology

Poster Session 2: System Level Techniques

Session 4: Power & Timing Optimization Techniques

Session 5: Self-timed Circuits

Session 6: Low Power Circuit Analysis & Optimization

Session 7: Low Power Design Studies

Robust Low Power Embedded SRAM Design: From System to Memory Cell

Toby Doorn and Roelof Salters

NXP Semiconductors

Abstract. Low power memories continue to be an important topic for low power digital design, especially in light of the recent focus on green products. Voltage scaling for some time was a natural part of technology scaling, which automatically resulted in power reduction. For sub-100nm technologies it has been difficult to reduce active power consumption for SRAMs, because the amount of memory in digital ICs is still increasing and the memory bit cell does not allow a lower supply voltage without a severe area penalty. However, voltage scaling is not a goal in itself, and a variety of techniques exist to achieve low power. This paper gives an overview of the trends in technology scaling and its impact on low power memory design. The most important techniques that are used to make low power SRAM are discussed, and system level considerations are given, including trade-offs on the selection of SRAM and DRAM. For advanced technologies, SRAM variability is an important topic. Lowering the supply voltage to save power increases the sensitivity of SRAM to variability and reduces its robustness. Simulation approaches used to guarantee high yield even for large amounts of SRAM are discussed. A combination of these methods and techniques helps to achieve low power, yet robust systems.

J. Monteiro and R. van Leuken (Eds.): PATMOS 2009, LNCS 5953, p. 1, 2010.
© Springer-Verlag Berlin Heidelberg 2010

Variability in Advanced Nanometer Technologies: Challenges and Solutions

Davide Pandini

STMicroelectronics

Abstract. As process parameter dimensions continue to scale down, the gap between the designed layout and what is really manufactured on silicon is increasing. Due to the difficulty in process control in advanced nanometer technologies, manufacturing-induced variations are growing both in number and as a percentage of device feature sizes, and a deep understanding of the different sources of variation, along with their characterization and modeling, has become mandatory.

Furthermore, process variability makes the prediction of digital circuit performance an extremely challenging task. Traditionally, the methodology adopted to determine the performance spread of a design in presence of variability is to run multiple Static Timing Analyses at different process corners, where standard cells and interconnects have the worst/best combinations of delay. Unfortunately, as the number of variability sources increases, the corner-based method is becoming computationally very expensive. Moreover, with a larger parameter spread this approach results in overly conservative and suboptimal designs, leaving most of the advantages offered by the new technologies on the table. Statistical Static Timing Analysis (SSTA) is a promising approach to deal with nanometer process variations, especially the intra-die variations that cannot be handled properly by existing corner-based techniques, in the digital design flow.

Finally, the complexity and the impact of the variability problem on design productivity and profitability require innovative design solutions at the circuit and architectural level, and some of the most promising techniques for variability-aware design will be presented.

J. Monteiro and R. van Leuken (Eds.): PATMOS 2009, LNCS 5953, p. 2, 2010.

Subthreshold Circuit Design for
Ultra-Low-Power Applications

Yusuf Leblebici

Ecole Polytechnique Federale de Lausanne

Abstract. A novel approach is presented for implementing ultra-low-power digital components and systems using source-coupled logic (SCL) circuit topology, operating in weak inversion (subthreshold) regime. Minimum size pMOS transistors with shorted drain-substrate contacts are used as gate-controlled, very high resistivity load devices. Based on the proposed approach, the power consumption and the operation frequency of logic circuits can be scaled down linearly by changing the tail bias current of SCL gates over a very wide range spanning several orders of magnitude, which is not achievable in subthreshold CMOS circuits. Measurements in conventional 0.18um CMOS technology show that the tail bias current of each gate can be set as low as 10 pA, with a supply voltage of 300 mV, resulting in a power-delay product of less than 1 fJ (Femto-Joule = 10E-15 J) per gate. Fundamental circuits such as ring oscillators and frequency dividers, as well as more complex digital blocks such as parallel multipliers designed by using the STSCL topology were presented.

J. Monteiro and R. van Leuken (Eds.): PATMOS 2009, LNCS 5953, p. 3, 2010.
© Springer-Verlag Berlin Heidelberg 2010

SystemC AMS Extensions:
New Language – New Methods – New Applications

Martin Barnasconi[1], Markus Damm[2], and Karsten Einwich[3]

[1] NXP Semiconductors
[2] TU Vienna
[3] Fraunhofer IIS/EAS

Abstract. This special session at the PATMOS 2009 conference presented the emerging system-level modeling language for embedded analog/mixed-signal systems: the SystemC AMS extensions. The AMS extensions target system-level design at architecture level, enabling true analog/digital co-design where AMS and digital HW/SW subsystems can be simulated together in an efficient manner. The first talk, presented by Martin Barnasconi from NXP Semiconductors, addressed the standardization effort in the Open SystemC Initiative (OSCI) AMS Working Group to formally define the language constructs, syntax and execution semantics for this new language. Due to the open source nature of the SystemC language and AMS extensions, it allows the creation of new design and modeling methodologies. In the second talk, presented by Markus Damm from the Technical University of Vienna, the usage of SystemC-AMS for the design of run-time reconfigurable, heterogeneous systems was explained. The various AMS application domains where SystemC-AMS modeling can be applied were presented in the third talk, by Karsten Einwich from Fraunhofer IIS/EAS. The use of SystemC-AMS for the design and verification of Complex Analog/Mixed-signal Systems-on-a-chip has been motivated, showing the benefits of this new AMS modeling language.

J. Monteiro and R. van Leuken (Eds.): PATMOS 2009, LNCS 5953, p. 4, 2010.
© Springer-Verlag Berlin Heidelberg 2010

Process Variation Aware Performance Analysis of Asynchronous Circuits Considering Spatial Correlation

Mohsen Raji, Behnam Ghavami, Hamid R. Zarandi, and Hossein Pedram

Amirkabir University of Technology, Department of Computer Engineering and
Information Technology
Tehran, I.R. Iran
{raji,ghavamib,h_zarandi,pedram}@aut.ac.ir

Abstract. Current technology trends have led to the growing impact of process variations on performance of asynchronous circuits. As it is imperative to model process parameter variations for sub-100nm technologies to produce a more real performance metric, it is equally important to consider the correlation of these variations to increase the accuracy of the performance computation. In this paper, we present an efficient method for performance evaluation of asynchronous circuits considering inter and intra-die process variation. The proposed method includes both statistical static timing analysis (SSTA) and statistical Timed Petri-Net based simulation. Template-based asynchronous circuit has been modeled using Variant-Timed Petri-Net. Based on this model, the proposed SSTA calculates the probability density function of the delay of global critical cycle. The efficiency for the proposed SSTA is obtained from a technique that is derived from the principal component analysis (PCA) method. This technique simplifies the computation of mean, variance and covariance values of a set of correlated random variables. In order to consider spatial correlation in the Petri-Net based simulation, we also include a correlation coefficient to the proposed Variant-Timed Petri-Net which is obtained from partitioning the circuit. We also present a simulation tool of Variant-Timed Petri-Net and the results of the experiments are compared with Monte-Carlo simulation-based method.

1 Introduction

In asynchronous circuits, local signaling eliminates the need for global synchronization which exploits some potential advantages in comparison with synchronous ones [1] [2], [3], [4], [5]. They have shown potential specifications in low power consumption, design reuse, improved noise immunity and electromagnetic compatibility. Asynchronous circuits are more tolerant to process parameter variations [1].

One of the interesting features of asynchronous circuits comparing with their clocked counterparts is better average-case performance [4][5]. However, the performance analysis of asynchronous circuits is a complicated problem and without an effective performance analysis method, one cannot easily take advantage of the properties of asynchronous systems to achieve optimal performance [6]. There are two

J. Monteiro and R. van Leuken (Eds.): PATMOS 2009, LNCS 5953, pp. 5–15, 2010.

major technical difficulties involved in the performance analysis of asynchronous systems. First, unlike clocked circuits where clock boundaries form natural partitions for logic between stages to be analyzed individually, an asynchronous circuit is inherently nonlinear, meaning there is no easy way to partition the system into independent sub-systems. The systems have to be analyzed as a whole. Second, as the functionality of the system is dependent on the concurrent events, variations in delays mostly caused by process variation in individual components can have considerable effect on the performance of the system. As a result, performance analysis based on the average delay is not accurate. As process variations become a significant problem in deep sub-micron technology, it is really necessary to shift from deterministic timing analysis to statistical timing analysis for high-performance asynchronous circuit designs similarly to what is done in synchronous ones [7][8].

Basically, process variations can be classified into inter-die (also called chip-to-chip) variations and intra-die (also called within-chip) variations. Process parameters that change from die to die are called inter-die variations while process parameters that have different values at different points on a die are called intra-die variations. It is noticeable that the intra-die process variations of a gate are spatially correlated with other gates found in its neighborhood [31]. In order to have a more accurate analysis, it is important to consider the spatial correlation of intra-die parameter variations in addition of incorporating the process variation issue into the analysis.

This paper introduces a novel and efficient performance analysis method for asynchronous circuits considering process variation and also incorporating the correlation between process parameters into the analysis. In our approach, a synthesized template-base asynchronous circuit is modeled as a Variant-Timed Petri-Net that captures concurrency between interactive components in decision-free systems [13]. Delay variations in component delays caused by process variations are captured in a probabilistic delay model. As the variability of process parameters is naturally random, in order to analyze the effect of the process variation, we applied a statistical approach to the proposed timing analysis.

The main goal of the proposed statistical timing analysis is to calculate the probabilistic density function of a performance metric. The random variables for each process parameter are correlated to each other with different amounts of correlation. Principal Component Analysis (PCA) is used to make the analysis tractable [32]. PCA transforms a set of correlated variables into a smaller set of principal components that are independent and orthogonal. Both the proposed SSTA and Petri-Net simulation-based method are implemented and tested on the benchmark circuits modeled in Variant-Timed Petri-Net and its results are compared with the Monte-Carlo simulation-based results. The difference between the proposed methods and MC simulation results was shown to be small, ranging from 0.6% to 5.5%.

The remaining part of the paper is organized as follows; Section 2 provides a survey of previous works. Section 3 describes Variant-Timed Petri-Nets as the dominant performance analysis model. Section 4 discusses the proposed statistical static performance evaluation framework in detail. Section 6 gets on with the results and analysis. In the last section, we conclude the paper.

2 Previous Works

There are few works that consider probabilistic delay models in the performance analysis of asynchronous systems [6], [7], [10], [11]. In [6], a method for analyzing the asymptotic performance of asynchronous systems considering delay variation was presented. However, it focused on modeling at system architecture level and did not consider circuit modeling issues such as delay variations due to the process variation. Recently Yahya [12] proposed a performance model for asynchronous linear-pipeline with time variable delays. But in practical designs, asynchronous pipelines can be linear or non-linear and their method cannot be applied to non-linear models easily.

Newly in [30], we introduced a method to analyze the performance of asynchronous circuits statistically. The asynchronous circuit has been modeled using Timed Petri-Net. Based on this model, the probability density function of the delay of global critical cycle is calculated.

None of the above approaches considered the correlation of parameters variation. However, to realize the full benefit of variation-aware performance analysis, one must solve a difficult problem that timing variables in a circuit could be correlated due to inter-parameter dependency, chip-to-chip variation, and within chip spatial dependency.

3 A Performance Model Using Variant-Timed Petri-Net (VTPN) Model

Asynchronous circuits after decomposition can be considered as a set of fine grained concurrent modules each one is responsible for producing a single variable. We model the network of templates with a novel Variant-Timed Petri-Net model. The main advantage of this model is that it can be used for simulation of circuits in addition to static performance analysis. In this model, the detailed structures of the original circuit including the handshaking channels are preserved. We have developed a class of models that fully supports full buffer templates [21].

The simplest form of a full buffer is a simple buffer that only reads a value from its input and writes it to its output. Transition tW is analogous to the write statement while place pWa emulates the write acknowledge. Similarly pF can be seen as the dual for read statement while tRa is the corresponding acknowledge. This model is very similar to FCBN model presented in [23] and the only difference is that we added tRa. The reason for this is that the used definition of the hierarchical Petri-Nets has a restriction on the input and output ports; all outputs must be transitions and all inputs must be places. This convention ensures that unwanted choices or merge constructs cannot be formed when connecting Petri-Net modules to each other.

We have considered delays on the places, therefore forward delay and backward delay can be put on pF and pB. In this model, the $d(f)$ represents the forward latency of a channel, while the corresponding $d(p)$ represents the backward latency of channel.

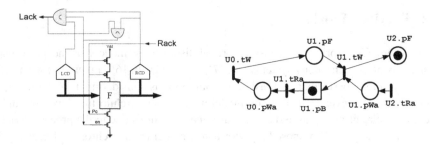

Fig. 1. A Simple Full Buffer Template and Its Corresponding Timed Petri-Nets model

The values of these parameters are the normalized delays which are back annotated from the associated cell layout. In other words, the proposed template model exploits the normalized delays model for the sake of accurate performance estimation. Considering process variation in timing modeling necessitate applying probability distribution functions as delay models which will be more explained in further sections.

Performance of any computation modeled with a VTPN is dictated by the cycle time of the VTPN and thus the largest cycle metric. A cycle C in a VTPN is a sequence of places P_1, P_2,..., P_l connected by arcs and transitions whose the first and the last place are the same. The statistical cycle metric, $(SCM(c))$, is the statistical sum of the delays of all associated places along the cycle C, $d(c)$, divided by the number of tokens that reside in the cycle, $m_0(c)$, defined as:

$$SCM(c) = d(c)/m_0(c) \tag{1}$$

The cycle time of a VTPN is defined as the largest cycle metric among all cycles in the Variant-TPN which must be computed statistically, i.e. $max(SCM(c)) \forall c \in C$, where C is the set of all cycles in the Variant-TPN.

4 The Proposed Statistical Performance Analysis Method

In this section, we define the modeling assumptions and our proposed SSTA method and also the required operations used in the method.

As mentioned, the delays must be modeled statistically. We model the delays as random variables with normal distributions. So each place in VTPN has a mean delay value, μ, and a set of parameter variation. The linear model used to approximate delay in the analysis is as follows:

$$d = \mu + \sum_{i=1}^{m} s_i \, \Delta p_i \tag{2}$$

Where d is the delay of a gate, μ is the mean value for the delay; s_i is the delay sensitivity of process parameter p_i, Δp_i is the parameter variation in p_i for this gate, and m is the number of process parameters.

As mentioned earlier, the process parameters are correlated. To model the intra-die spatial correlations of parameters, we partition the die into a number of grids. Gates placed in close proximity of each other will have many common intra-die variation components resulting in a strong intra-die parameter variation correlation. Gates that lie far apart on a die share few common components and therefore have weaker correlation.

Under this model, a parameter variation in a single grid at location (x_0, y_0) can be modeled using a single random variable $p(x_0, y_0)$. In addition, we assume that correlation exists only among the same type of parameters and there is no correlation between different types of parameters.

Correlation is a challenging problem for statistical timing analysis. When these relationships among process parameters are taken into consideration, the correlation structure becomes even more complicated. To make the problem tractable, we use the Principal Component Analysis (PCA) technique [37] to transform the set of correlated parameters into an uncorrelated set.

Given N process parameters $X = [x_1, x_2, \dots x_N]^T$, the process variation $\Delta X = X - \mu_x$, where μ_x is the mean value of X, is often approximated as a zero-mean *multivariate Normal distribution*. The correlation of ΔX can be represented by a symmetric, positive semi-definite covariance matrix R. PCA decomposes R as follows:

$$R = V.\tau.V^T ,\tag{3}$$

where $\tau = diag(\lambda_i) \ \forall i = 1, 2, \dots N$, contains the eigenvalues of R, and $V = [V_1, V_2, \dots V_N]$ contains the corresponding eigenvectors that are orthonormal, i.e., $V^T.V = I$ (I is the identity matrix). Based on τ and V, PCA defines a set of new random variables:

$$\Delta Y = \tau^{-0.5}.V^T.\Delta X \tag{4}$$

These new random variables in ΔY are called the principal components. It is easy to show that all elements in $\Delta Y = [\Delta y_1, \Delta y_2, \dots, \Delta y_N]^T$ are uncorrelated and satisfy the standard Normal distribution $N(0,1)$33].

Superposing the set of uncorrelated random variables of parameters on the random variables in gate delay as in equation (1), the expression of gate delay is then changed to the linear combination of principal components of all parameters:

$$d = \mu + \sum_{i=1}^m a_i.pc_i ,\tag{5}$$

while pc_i are the principle components or factors of the delay. The variance of d can be calculated as the sum of the squares of the coefficients, i.e.

$$\sigma^2 = \sum_{i=1}^m a_i^2 \tag{6}$$

It is interesting to notice that the covariance between paths (here between path 1 and 2) can be calculated easily through the equation below:

$$d_1 = \mu_1 + \sum_{i=1}^m a_{1,i} pc_{1,i}$$
$$d_2 = \mu_2 + \sum_{i=1}^m a_{2,i} pc_{2,i}$$
$$cov(1,2) = \sum_{i=1}^m a_{i,1} a_{i,2} \tag{7}$$

As each delay is modeled as a random variable with normal distribution, it is noteworthy to explain about the statistical operations first. The three operations used in our method are SUM, DIV and MAX.

4.1 SUM Operation

The sum of two random variables with normal distribution results in a random variable with normal distribution. The SUM operation along each cycle $(d_{sum}=d_1+d_2)$ is computed as follows:

$$d_1 = \mu_1 + \sum_{i=1}^{m} a_{1,i} pc_{1,i}$$
$$d_2 = \mu_2 + \sum_{i=1}^{m} a_{2,i} pc_{2,i}$$
$$d_{sum} = \mu_{sum} + \sum_{i=1}^{m} a_{sum,i} pc_{sum,i} , \qquad (8)$$

where $\mu_{sum}= \mu_1+\mu_2$, $a_{sum,i}=a_{1,i}+a_{i,2} \forall i=1,2,...m$. The standard deviation of d_{sum} can be calculated using Equation (6) on the new set of coefficients.

4.2 DIV Operation

In calculating the SCM of a cycle, the sum of delay values of the cycle will be divided by the number of the tokens in the cycle. As the sum of the delays modeled by normal random variable is still a normal random variable, the parameters of the division   are calculated as follows:

$$\mu_{\frac{A}{n}} = \frac{\mu_A}{n}$$
$$\sigma^2_{\frac{A}{n}} = \frac{\sigma^2_A}{n^2}$$
$$a_{\frac{A}{n},i} = \frac{a_{A,i}}{n} \qquad (9)$$

4.3 MAX Operation

The maximum distribution (μ_{max}, max) of two normal distributions with means (μ_A, μ_B) and standard deviations (σ_A, σ_B) and a correlation factor of $(\rho_{A,B})$ between the distributions is calculated as follows:

The maximum distribution takes the form:

$$d_{max} = \mu_{max} + \sum_{i=1}^{m} a_{max,i} pc_{max,i} \qquad (10)$$

where a_i's are the coefficients of principal components pc_i's respectively.

Case 1: Standard deviations are equal $(\sigma_A = \sigma_B)$ and correlation factor is 0 $(\rho_{A,B}=0)$,

$$d_{max} = \begin{cases} \mu_A, if \ \mu_A \geq \mu_B \\ \mu_B \qquad else \end{cases} \qquad (11)$$

Case 2: Standard deviations are not equal ($\sigma_A \neq \sigma_B$) or correlation factor is not equal to 0 ($\rho_{A,B} \neq 0$), We define two constants (α and β) as follows:

$$\alpha = \frac{\mu_A - \mu_B}{2}$$
$$\beta^2 = \sigma_A^2 + \sigma_B^2 - 2\sigma_A\sigma_B\rho_{A,B} \tag{12}$$

The first moment (d'_{max} or $E(d_{max})$) and the second moment (d''_{max} or $E(d^2_{max})$) of the max distribution are calculated as follows:

$$E(d_{max}) = \mu_A\phi(\alpha) + \mu_B\phi(-\alpha) + \beta\varphi(\alpha)$$
$$E(d^2_{max}) = (\mu_A^2+\sigma_A^2)\phi(\alpha) + (\mu_B^2+\sigma_B^2)\phi(-\alpha) + (\mu_A + \mu_B)\beta\varphi(\alpha) \tag{13}$$

Here, φ and ϕ are the cumulative density function, CDF, and the probability density function, PDF, of a standard normal (i.e., mean 0, STD 1) distribution, respectively. We know that the mean and the standard deviation of the distribution can be calculated using the first and second moments as follows:

$$\mu_{max} = E(d^2_{max})$$
$$\sigma^2_{max} = E(d^2_{max}) - E(d_{max})^2 \tag{14}$$

The coefficients of the principal components of the new normal distribution are calculated as follows:

$$a_{max,i} = \frac{\sigma_A \cdot a_{A,i} \cdot \phi(\alpha) + \sigma_B \cdot a_{B,i} \cdot \phi(-\alpha)}{\sigma_{max}} \tag{15}$$

But as there is a potential for mismatch between the standard deviation calculated using the coefficients and the standard deviation calculated using the closed-form formulae in Equation 12, the coefficients (a_r) are normalized to reduce the standard deviation potential errors in further calculations using the coefficients and standard deviation:

$$s_0 = \sqrt{\sum_{i=1}^{m} a_{max,i}^2}$$
$$a_{max,i} = a_{max,i} \cdot \frac{\sigma_{max}}{s_0} \tag{16}$$

5 Evaluation and Experimental Results

The proposed SSTA method has been implemented in C++, and has been tested on a set of benchmark circuits. An asynchronous synthesis toolset (PERSIA [36]) is employed to synthesis benchmarks. Then the developed tool automatically translates the decomposed circuits to its Variant-Timed Petri-Net equivalents. Inputs and outputs of the circuit are connected to each other in Petri-Net structure to form a closed loop system. Initially, all tokens are placed in input nodes. Variability of process parameters (L, Vth, and Tox) and the environmental fluctuation (Vdd) are taken into account.

Table 1. Comparison Results of the Proposed Method and Monte-Carlo Simulation Method

The circuit	# of the Nodes	# of the Cycles	The proposed SSTA		Monte-Carlo		Error (SSTA-MC)/MC%	
			Mu (μ)	Sigma (σ)	Mu (μ)	Sigma (σ)	Mu (μ)	Sigma (σ)
A	6	17	15.5771	0.5857	14.9887	0.5359	3.93	17.08
B	10	51	17.3944	0.1714	16.9978	0.3947	2.33	8.50
C	16	1389	22.1605	1.0181	21.9924	0.6378	3.62	59.61
D	26	1864	29.2346	1.2150	29.300	0.662	0.22	83.5
E	35	7369	20.1775	0.2685	19.6868	0.2415	2.49	11.22
F	20	276	17.7016	0.1921	17.2629	0.2715	2.54	-29.22
G	22	5605	20.7108	0.1125	20.4993	0.0823	1.03	36.64
I	56	812	24.0003	1.1996	23.9898	0.7016	0.08	70.9

The 3σ values for process parameters are set at 20% of the mean. The standard deviation of Vdd is 4% of the maximum, the mean is 96% of the maximum, and the range is 84-100% of the maximum value. In the experiments, Vth, Tox and Vdd are modeled as probabilistic interval variables. The range of Vth and Tox is 80-120% of the mean. Sensitivities of parameters are from SPICE simulations for a cell library of BPTM 0.06um technology [29]. The runtime for our benchmark ranges from 5s to 400s, depending on circuit sizes and the structure of VTPN model of circuit.

To verify the results of our statistical method, we used Monte Carlo (MC) simulation for comparison. To balance the accuracy, we chose to run 1,000 iterations for the Monte Carlo simulation. A comparison of these results with those from statistical approach is shown in Table I. For each test case, the mean and standard deviation (SD) values for both methods are listed. The results of SSTA can be seen to be close to the MC results: the average error is %2.8 for the mean value of the delays.

In Figure 2 and 3, for the test case named C, we show the plots of the PDF and CDF of the circuit delay for both SSTA and MC methods. It is observable that the curves almost match each other and the main source of the difference between them is the correlation of the process parameters which are considered inn SSTA but not in

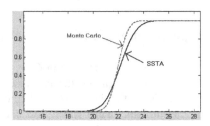

Fig. 2. Comparison of SSTA and MC Methods: CDF Curves

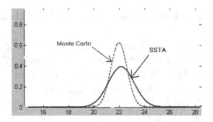

Fig. 3. Comparison of SSTA and MC Methods: PDF Curves

the Monte Carlo simulation. Since the samples in the Monte Carlo simulation are created randomly, the correlation between the samples cannot be considered and the error appears in the comparison stage, especially in the variance part of the results as the correlation is applied in calculating the variance value of the delay more than calculating the mean value.

6 Conclusion

Even though asynchronous circuits are highly tolerant to process variation, it seemed to be necessary to present a method to analyze the performance of asynchronous circuits considering the variation in process parameters. This view has facilitated us to derive an efficient method to analyze system performance, and to define meaningful performance metrics for optimization. In this paper, we present a method to analyze the performance of template-based asynchronous circuits statistically. The results of the experiments are compared with Mont Carlo simulation results. We demonstrated our method via a tool. Results show that it is possible to consider the process variation and analyze the performance while there is ignorable error between the results of the proposed method and the general Monte Carlo simulation method.

References

1. Tang, Lin, C.Y., Lu, Y.C.: An Asynchronous Circuit Design with Fast Forwarding Technique at Advanced Technology Node. In: Proceedings of ISQED 2008. IEEE Computer Society, Los Alamitos (2008)
2. Beerel, P.A.: Asynchronous Circuits: An Increasingly Practical Design Solution. In: Proceedings of ISQED 2002. IEEE Computer Society, Los Alamitos (2002)
3. Martin, A.J., et al.: The Lutonium: A Sub-Nanojoule Asynchronous 8051 Microcontroller. In: ASYNC 2003 (2003)
4. Yun, K.Y., Beerel, P.A., Vakilotojar, V., Dooply, A.E., Arceo, J.: A low-control-overhead asynchronous differential equation solver. In: Proceedings of ASYNC (1997)
5. Garnica, O., Lanchares, J., Hermida, R.: Fine-grain asynchronous circuits for low-power high performance DSP implementations. In: SiPS 2000 (2000)
6. McGee, P.B., Nowick, S.M., Coffman Jr., E.G.: Efficient performance analysis of asynchronous systems based on periodicity. In: Proceedings of the 3rd IEEE/ACM/IFIP international conference on Hardware/software codesign and system synthesis (2005)

7. Visweswariah, C., et al.: First-order incremental block-based statistical timing analysis. In: Proc. of DAC (2004)
8. Wang, W.-S., Kreinovich, V., Orshansky, M.: Statistical timing based on incomplete probabilistic descriptions of parameter uncertainty. In: Proc. of DAC (2006)
9. Pang, P.B., Greenstreet, M.: Self-timed meshesare faster than synchronous
10. Xie, A., Kim, S., Beerel, P.A.: Bounding average time separationsof events in stochastic-timed petrinets with choice. In: Proceedings of ASYNC (1999)
11. Pang, P.B., Greenstreet, M.: Self-timed meshesare faster than synchronous. In: Proceedings of ASYNC (1997)
12. Yahya, E., Renaudin, M.: Performance Modeling and Analysis of Asynchronous Linear-Pipeline with Time Variable Delays. In: ICECS 2007 (2007)
13. Commoner, F., Holt, A., Even, S., Pnueli, A.: Marked directed graphs. Journal of Computer and System Sciences 5, 511–523 (1971)
14. Wong, C.G., Martin, A.J.: High-Level Synthesis of Asynchronous Systems by Data Driven Decomposition. In: Proc. of 40th DAC, Anneheim, CA, USA (June 2003)
15. Dinh Duc, A.V., Rigaud, J.B., Rezzag, A., Sirianni, A., Fragoso, J., Fesquet, L., Renaudin, M.: TASTCAD Tools: Tutorial. In: Proc. of Advanced Research in Asynchronous Circuits and Systems, ASYNC 2002 (2002)
16. Ghavami, B., Pedram, H.: Design of Dual Threshold Voltages Asynchronous Circuits. In: ISLPED 2008, pp. 185–188 (2008)
17. Prakash, P., Martin, A.J.: Slack Matching Quasi Delay-Insensitive Circuits. In: ASYNC 2006, pp. 195–204 (2006)
18. Xie, A., Kim, S., Beerel, P.A.: Bounding average time separations of events in stochastic timed Petri nets with choice. In: ASYNC, pp. 94–107 (1999)
19. Burns, S.M., Martin, A.J.: Performance Analysis and Optimization of Asynchronous circuits. In: Advanced Research in VLSI conference, Santa Cruz, CA (March 1991)
20. Kim, S.: Pipeline Optimization for Asynchronous circuits. PHD Thesis, University of Southern California (August 2003)
21. Orshansky, M., Nassif, S.R., Boning, D.: Design for Manufacturability and Statistical Design, A Constructive Approach, pp. 11–15. Springer, Heidelberg (2008)
22. Lines, A.M.: Pipelined asynchronous circuits. Master's thesis, California Institute of Technology, Computer Science Department, 1995 CS-TR-95-21 (1995)
23. Beerel, P.A., Kim, N.-H., Lines, A., Davies, M.: Slack Matching Asynchronous Designs. In: Proceedings of the 12th IEEE International Symposium on Asynchronous Circuits and Systems, Washington, DC, USA (2006)
24. Karp, R.M.: A characterization of the minimum cycle mean in a diagraph. Discrete Mathematics 23, 309–311 (1978)
25. Dasdan, A., Gupta, R.K.: Faster maximum and minimum mean cycle algorithms for system performance analysis. IEEE Trans. on Computer-Aided Design of Integrated Circuits and Systems 17(10), 889–899 (1998)
26. Liu, H., Wang, J.: A new way to enumerate cycles in graph. In: Proceedings of the Advanced International Conference on Telecommunications and International Conference on Internet and Web Applications and Services, AICT/ICIW (2006)
27. Clark, C.E.: The Greatest of a Finite Set of Random Variable. Operations Research 9, 85–91 (1961)
28. Lane, B.: SystemC Language Reference Manual. Copyright © 2003 Open SystemC Initiative,San Jose, CA
29. PTM: http://www.eas.asu.edu/~ptm

30. Raji, M., Ghavami, B., Pedram, H.: Statistical Static Performance Analysis of Asynchronous Circuits Considering Process Variation. In: Proceedings of ISQED 2009. IEEE Computer Society, Los Alamitos (2009)
31. Agarwal, A., Blaauw, D., Zolotov, V.: Statistical timing analysis forintra - die process variations with spatial correlations. In: IEEE International Conference on Computer Aided Design, pp. 900–907 (2003)
32. Seber, G.: MultivariateObservations. Wiley Series (1984)
33. Li, X., Le, J., Pileggi, L.T.: Statistical Performance Modeling and Optimization. Foundation and Trends in Electronic Design Automation 1(4) (2003)
34. Nassif, S.R.: Modeling and Analysis of Manufacturing Variations. In: IEEE 2001 Custom Integrated Circuits Conference, pp. 223–228 (2001)
35. Chang, H., Sapatnekar, S.: Statistical timing analysis under spatial correlations. IEEE Trans. Computer-Aided Design of Integrated Circuits and Systems 24(9), 1467–1482 (2005)
36. Persia: A QDI Asynchronous Synthesis Tool. In: ASYNC 2008 (2008)
37. Morrison, D.F.: Multivariate Statistical Methods. McGraw-Hill, New York (1976)

Interpreting SSTA Results with Correlation

Zeqin Wu[1], Philippe Maurine[1], Nadine Azemard[1], and Gille Ducharme[2]

[1] LIRMM, UMR CNRS/University of Montpellier II, (C5506),
161 rue Ada, 34392 Montpellier, France
{azemard,pmaurine,wu}@lirmm.fr
[2] Dept. Math University of Montpellier II
Place Eugène Bataillon, 34095 Montpellier, France
ducharme@math.univ-montp2.fr

Abstract. *Statistical Static Timing Analysis* (SSTA) is becoming necessary; but has not been widely adopted. One of those arguments against the use is that results of SSTA are difficult to make use of for circuit design. In this paper, by introducing conditional moments, we propose a path-based statistical timing approach, which permits us to consider gate topology and switching process induced correlations. With the help of this gate-to-gate delay correlation, differences between results of SSTA and those of *Worst-case Timing Analysis* (WTA) are interpreted. Numerical results demonstrate that path delay means and standard deviations estimated by the proposed approach have absolute values of relative errors respectively less than 5% and 10%.

Keywords: Conditional Moment, Worst-case Timing Analysis (WTA), Statistical Static Timing Analysis (SSTA), Gate-to-gate Delay Correlation (GDC).

1   Introduction

Traditional *Worst-case Timing Analysis* (WTA) assumes that all physical and environmental parameters are at their worst or best conditions simultaneously. From the point of view of probability theory, this conservative case is next to impossible to appear in reality. Consequently, such an assumption induces pessimism in delay estimation, and thereby in circuit design. As the magnitude of process variations grows, this pessimism increases significantly, leading to the understanding that traditional corner-based design methodologies will not meet the needs of designers in the near future. Thus, *Statistical Static Timing Analysis* (SSTA), where process variations and timing characteristics are considered as *Random Variables* (RV), has gained favor in the past six years.

The authors of [1]-[2] propose non-linear parametric models handling Gaussian and non-Gaussian process variations, which is a significant progress relative to the linear dependency on Gaussian process parameters presented in [3]-[4]. These approaches are based on first or second order approximation of Taylor expansion, which describes gate-level timing behavior, and is capable of capturing process variations. Then, SUM and MAX operations corresponding to each proposed parametric model are performed on the random timing variables, such as arrival time and gate delay.

J. Monteiro and R. van Leuken (Eds.): PATMOS 2009, LNCS 5953, pp. 16–25, 2010.

It seems that SSTA is becoming a promising alternative by introducing more and more advanced elements from probability theory and statistics, such as Reduced Rank Regression (RRR) [1], Fourier series [2], etc. However, statistical timing techniques have not been widely adopted. First, as suggested in [5], the accuracy of published approaches is not clear due to the fact that *Monte-Carlo* (MC) simulations used for validations are based on the same assumptions used in SSTA. Next, the dependency of gate delay on input slope and output load has not received much attention [5]. In fact, most of the proposed approaches either make a worst-case estimate of slope, or propagate the latest arriving slope, each of which can lead to significant error of estimation [6]. At last, it takes time to understand and make use of statistical terms, like correlation, for circuit design.

In this paper, we propose a path-based statistical timing engine to propagate iteratively means and variances of gate delays with the help of conditional moments. These moments conditioning on input slope and output load are pre-characterized by MC simulation, and organized as a tree of lookup tables, called statistical timing library. This timing engine may: a) avoid gate delay modeling errors, b) take into account the effects on gate delay: input pin, output edge, input slope, and output load, and c) deal with a large number of process parameters. Moreover, in a first attempt, we propose an empirical technique to estimate *Gate-to-gate Delay Correlation* (GDC). With this statistical term, we explain the incoherence between the critical paths arrangement of SSTA and that of WTA.

Figure 1 gives us an overview on the flow of the approach. First, given a statistical process model, we characterized conditional moments of timing variables with HSPICE [7] under certain power supply voltage (1.1V, 1.2V, 1.3V) and temperature (-45C°, 25C°, 125C°) conditions. Then statistical timing library is constructed as a tree of lookup tables with the statistical computing tool R [8]. Each of these lookup tables contains conditional moments of timing variables with input slope and output load as indices. In the second step, a certain number of critical paths were extracted from the considered circuits using WTA under the software RTL Compiler [9]. Once the two steps above are finished, we can perform an analysis and generate a statistical timing:

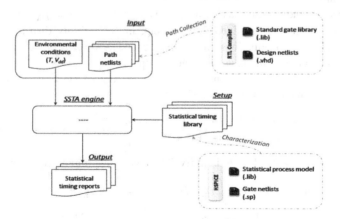

Fig. 1. Flow of the proposed approach

The rest of the paper is organized as follows. Section 2 presents the path-based timing approach, especially the skills to estimate GDC. Section 3 explains why results of SSTA and those of WTA are incoherent. The validation of the approach is given in Section 4. At last, the paper is concluded in Section 5.

2   Statistical Timing Engine

This section introduces the statistical timing engine basing on moment propagation. For gate-level delays, we make no assumption on their distributions, and just propagate means and variances; whereas path delays are assumed to be Gaussian distributed. Such an assumption is somewhat reasonable according to the Central Limit Theorem.

2.1   Conditional Moments

The mean and variance of a random variable, if they exist, are respectively the first and second central moment. A *conditional moment* is the moment of one random variable conditioning on another random variable. If X and Y are two random variables, then the *conditional mean* $E(X|Y = y)$ is the mean of X given the value $Y = y$. Unlike the conventional mean, which is a constant for a specific probability distribution, $E(X|Y = y)$ is a function of y, that is to say, the conditional mean varies along with the condition Y. Similarly, the *conditional variance* $Var(X|Y = y)$ is the variance of X given the value $Y = y$. If Y follows a continuous distribution with *Probability Density Function* (PDF) $f(y)$, then we have:

$$\mu_X = E(X) = E[E(X|Y)] = \int E(X|Y = y) \cdot f(y)dy \tag{1}$$

$$\sigma_X^2 = Var(X) = E[Var(X|Y)] + Var[E(X|Y)]$$
$$= \int \{Var(X|Y = y) + [E(X|Y = y) - \mu]^2\} \cdot f(y)dy \tag{2}$$

where μ_X and σ_X^2 are respectively the mean and variance of X.

Equations (1) and (2) give us an alternative way to calculate μ_X and σ_X^2 if these two moments cannot be obtained directly (e.g. the probability distribution of X is unknown). These two equations imply the dependency between X and Y, which permits us to implement the idea of moment propagation.

In (1) and (2), if X, Y represent respectively the output slope τ_{out} and the input slope τ_{in} of a considered gate, given (3) – (4):

$$E(\tau_{out}|\tau_{in}) = a_1 + a_2 \cdot \tau_{in} \tag{3}$$

$$Var(\tau_{out}|\tau_{in}) = b_1 + b_2 \cdot \tau_{in} \tag{4}$$

where a_1, a_2, b_1, b_2 are values to identify. Then, we can compute $\mu_{\tau_{out}}, \sigma_{\tau_{out}}^2$ with:

$$\mu_{\tau_{out}} = a_1 + a_2 \cdot \int \tau_{in} \cdot f(\tau_{in})d\tau_{in} = a_1 + a_2 \cdot \mu_{\tau_{in}} \tag{5}$$

$$\sigma_{\tau_{out}}^2 = \int \left[b_3 + b_4 \cdot \tau_{in} + \left(a_2 \cdot \tau_{in} - a_2 \cdot \mu_{\tau_{in}} \right)^2 \right] \cdot f(\tau_{in})d\tau_{in}$$

$$= \left(b_1 + b_2 \cdot \mu_{\tau_{in}} \right) + \left(a_2 \cdot \sigma_{\tau_{in}} \right)^2 \tag{6}$$

where $f(\tau_{in})$ is the PDF of τ_{in}. Note that in Equations (5) – (6), $f(\tau_{in})$ is not explicitly known, while $\mu_{\tau_{in}}$ and $\sigma^2_{\tau_{in}}$ are required.

2.2   Moment Propagation

This subsection presents the technique to propagate moments of timing variables iteratively along a timing path. First of all, we assume that all timing variables follow continuous distributions.

Let us define the problem of moment propagation: for the considered gate, given mean $\mu_{\tau_{in}}$ and variance $\sigma^2_{\tau_{in}}$ of input slope, and the output load $C_{out} = K$, we expect to get the output slope moments $\mu_{\tau_{out}}$, $\sigma^2_{\tau_{out}}$ and the gate delay moments μ_{gd}, σ^2_{gd}. Note that K represents the nominal value of output load. Its variations have been captured during timing characterization [10]. Besides, only the moments of timing variables instead of distributions are known, i.e. slope and gate delay may follow any distribution.

After the timing characterization presented in [10], we construct the lookup tables in the statistical timing library with the structure as follow: (a) input slope index T_i ($i = 1, ..., I$), (b) output load index C_j ($j = 1, ..., J$), and (c) lookup values including conditional moments: $E(\tau_{out}|\tau_{in} = T_i, C_{out} = C_j)$, $Var(\tau_{out}|\tau_{in} = T_i, C_{out} = C_j)$, $E(d|\tau_{in} = T_i, C_{out} = C_j)$, and $Var(d|\tau_{in} = T_i, C_{out} = C_j)$.

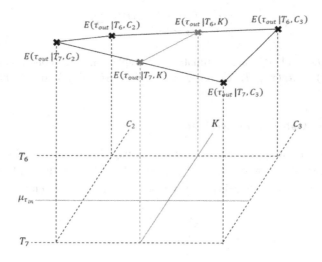

Fig. 2. Estimating $\mu_{\tau_{out}}$ with bilinear interpolation

For simplicity, $E(\tau_{out}|\tau_{in} = T_i, C_{out} = C_j)$ will be denoted as $E(\tau_{out}|T_i, C_j)$ in the rest of this paper, and the other three conditional moments will use the similar notation. Typically, suppose $\mu_{\tau_{in}} \in (T_6, T_7)$ and $K \in (C_2, C_3)$, then as shown in Figure 2, the estimation is done using the bilinear interpolation technique, which is an extension of linear interpolation for interpolating functions of two variables on a regular grid. First, in terms of the output load $C_{out} = K$, the interpolation gives:

$$E(\tau_{out}|T_i, K) = \frac{K - C_2}{C_3 - C_2} \cdot [E(\tau_{out}|T_i, C_3) - E(\tau_{out}|T_i, C_2)] + E(\tau_{out}|T_i, C_2) \tag{7}$$

$$Var(\tau_{out}|T_i, K) = \frac{K - C_2}{C_3 - C_2} \cdot [Var(\tau_{out}|T_i, C_3) - Var(\tau_{out}|T_i, C_2)]$$
$$+ Var(\tau_{out}|T_i, C_2) \qquad (i = 6, 7) \tag{8}$$

With equations (7) – (8), we can further interpolate in the direction of τ_{in} as:

$$E(\tau_{out}|\tau_{in}, K) = \frac{\tau_{in} - T_6}{T_7 - T_6} \cdot [E(\tau_{out}|T_7, K) - E(\tau_{out}|T_6, K)] + E(\tau_{out}|T_6, K) \tag{9}$$

$$Var(\tau_{out}|\tau_{in}, K) = \frac{\tau_{in} - T_6}{T_7 - T_6} \cdot [Var(\tau_{out}|T_7, K) - Var(\tau_{out}|T_6, K)] + Var(\tau_{out}|T_6, K) \tag{10}$$

Combining equations (3) – (4) with (9) – (10), we have:

$$\begin{cases} a_1 = \dfrac{T_7 \cdot E(\tau_{out}|T_6, K) - T_6 \cdot E(\tau_{out}|T_7, K)}{T_7 - T_6} \\[2mm] a_2 = \dfrac{E(\tau_{out}|T_7, K) - E(\tau_{out}|T_6, K)}{T_7 - T_6} \\[2mm] b_1 = \dfrac{T_7 \cdot Var(\tau_{out}|T_6, K) - T_6 \cdot Var(\tau_{out}|T_7, K)}{T_7 - T_6} \\[2mm] b_2 = \dfrac{Var(\tau_{out}|T_7, K) - Var(\tau_{out}|T_6, K)}{T_7 - T_6} \end{cases} \tag{11}$$

Similarly, μ_d and σ_d^2 are estimated by replacing the conditional moments $E(\tau_{out}|T_i, K)$, $Var(\tau_{out}|T_i, K)$ respectively with $E(d|T_i, K)$ and $Var(d|T_i, K)$ in equation (11).

2.3   Gate-to-Gate Delay Correlation

For a timing path of L gates, if the moment propagation technique allows iteratively computing gate delay moments $\mu_{d_l}, \sigma_{d_l}^2, (l = 1, 2, \dots, L)$, then the path delay d_{path}, which is the sum of all gate delays, has the mean and variance given by:

$$\begin{cases} \mu_{d_{path}} = \displaystyle\sum_{l=1}^{L} \mu_{d_l} \\[3mm] \sigma_{d_{path}}^2 = \displaystyle\sum_{l=1}^{L} \sum_{k=1}^{L} \rho_{kl} \cdot \sigma_{d_k} \sigma_{d_l} \end{cases} \tag{12}$$

where ρ_{kl} is the correlation $cor(d_k, d_l)$. Assuming that path delay is a Gaussian RV, then to get the distribution $N\left(\mu_{d_{path}}, \sigma_{d_{path}}^2\right)$, all that remains is to estimate ρ_{kl}.

A common way to estimate **Gate-to-gate Delay Correlation** (GDC) is to approximate the dependency of gate delay on process parameters with Taylor expansion, and then to translate the parameter-space correlation to the performance-space correlation. Theoretically, apart from process parameters, all factors that affect gate delay, like gate type, output load, etc., should be considered. Table 1 demonstrates that GDC varies with gate type, output load ($1fF$, $10fF$, $100fF$) and input/output edge ($R \rightarrow F$, $F \rightarrow R$, $R \rightarrow R$, $F \rightarrow F$). The CDC coefficients are estimated with data from MC simulations. As shown in Table 1, the effects of gate type and input/output edge on CDC are obvious. In addition, it seems that coefficients are brought down by increasing output load. Thus, GDC is impacted by several parameters that can be classified in four categories: (a) switching induced parameters such as input slope, output load and edge applied on gate inputs; (b) gate topology parameters such as width of transistors, gate polarity (inverting or non-inverting gate) etc; (c) environmental parameters power supply voltage and temperature; and (d) distance separating gates. In the rest of the paper, spatial correlation is neglected because of the lack of data from industry to construct statistical process model.

Table 1. GDC varying with gate type, output load and input/output edge

			F_IVLL		CTBUFLLP	
			$10fF$	$10fF$	$10fF$	$10fF$
			$R \rightarrow F$	$F \rightarrow R$	$R \rightarrow R$	$F \rightarrow F$
AN2LLX05	$1fF$	$R \rightarrow R$	0.88	0.93	0.99	0.99
		$F \rightarrow F$	0.81	0.92	0.99	0.98
	$10fF$	$R \rightarrow R$	0.91	0.82	0.98	0.99
		$F \rightarrow F$	0.90	0.86	0.97	0.97
	$100fF$	$R \rightarrow R$	0.86	0.58	0.85	0.84
		$F \rightarrow F$	0.96	0.59	0.78	0.83
NR2LLX05	$1fF$	$R \rightarrow F$	0.97	0.76	0.90	0.94
		$F \rightarrow R$	0.61	0.97	0.94	0.90
	$10fF$	$R \rightarrow F$	0.99	0.75	0.91	0.95
		$F \rightarrow R$	0.66	0.99	0.95	0.92
	$100fF$	$R \rightarrow F$	0.99	0.62	0.89	0.88
		$F \rightarrow R$	0.64	0.99	0.89	0.87

As gate delay depends on a number of factors, which affects GDC as well, we propose a technique to estimate directly GDC instead of translating parameter-space correlation. Suppose that process parameters $X_1, \dots, X_n$ are classified into three groups: $\{X_1^N, \dots, X_{n_1}^N\}$ are parameters describing only N-transistors; $\{X_1^P, \dots, X_{n_2}^P\}$ are those only for P-transistors; and $\{X_1^S, \dots, X_{n_3}^S\}$ characterizing behaviors of both N- and P-transistors. Note that $n = n_1 + n_2 + n_3$. Adopting this classification, each process parameter X_i is further divided into a global component $X_{g,i}$ and a local component $X_{l,i}$, which are independent to each other.

Once this dichotomy achieved, variability of timing metrics is computed for each gate considering separately the three groups of process parameters, and at the same time global and local variations, as illustrated by:

$$\begin{cases} \left(\sigma_d^N\right)^2 = \left(\sigma_{g,d}^N\right)^2 + \left(\sigma_{l,d}^N\right)^2 \\ \left(\sigma_d^P\right)^2 = \left(\sigma_{g,d}^P\right)^2 + \left(\sigma_{l,d}^P\right)^2 \\ \left(\sigma_d^S\right)^2 = \left(\sigma_{g,d}^S\right)^2 + \left(\sigma_{l,d}^S\right)^2 \end{cases} \tag{13}$$

With such definitions, the total variance σ_d^2 of gate delay can be decomposed as:

$$\sigma_d^2 = (\sigma_d^N)^2 + (\sigma_d^P)^2 + (\sigma_d^S)^2 \tag{14}$$

Owing to this decomposition, correlation can then be estimated according to:

$$\rho_{kl} = \frac{cov(d_k, d_l)}{\sigma_{d_k} \cdot \sigma_{d_l}} \tag{15}$$

where

$$cov(d_k, d_l) \approx \sigma_{g,d_k}^N \cdot \sigma_{g,d_l}^N + \sigma_{g,d_k}^P \cdot \sigma_{g,d_l}^P + \sigma_{g,d_k}^S \cdot \sigma_{g,d_l}^S \tag{16}$$

From the above formulas, an immediate drawback appears: $\sigma_{g,d}^N$, $\sigma_{g,d}^P$, $\sigma_{g,d}^S$ must be characterized. However, the characterization step is only a one-off job, i.e. the high time-cost simulation is only needed to build the statistical timing library.

3   Application and Interpretation

In this section, we address the problem on arrangement of critical paths. Given a circuit block and the desired cycled time, we collect the top 100 paths in decreasing order of worst path delays under the 1.1V (supply voltage) and 125C° (temperature) operating conditions. As shown in Figure 3, the dashed line is the result ordered by worst path delays. Next, under the same environmental conditions, for each critical path, we calculate the corresponding statistical 3σ corners with the proposed timing engine, which is plotted with the continuous line in Figure 3.

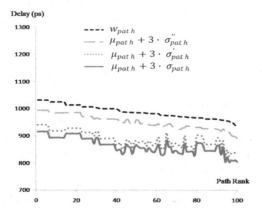

Fig. 3. Arrangement of critical paths

Obviously, the two arrangements obtained respectively by SSTA and WTA are not coherent. To interpret the difference, we suppose a timing path of N gates, each of which has his corresponding gate delay mean μ_i and variance σ_i^2, and define the worst gate delay w_i by:

$$w_i = \mu_i + \theta_i \cdot \sigma_i \qquad (i = 1, ..., N) \qquad (17)$$

where θ_i are parameters to identify. Then, according to (12) and (17), path delay 3σ corner from SSTA and worst path delay w_{path} using WTA can be decomposed as:

$$\mu_{path} + 3 \cdot \sigma_{path} = \sum_{i=1}^{N} \mu_i + 3 \cdot \sqrt{\sum_{i=1}^{N} \sum_{j=1}^{N} \rho_{ij} \cdot \sigma_i \sigma_j} \qquad (18)$$

$$w_{path} = \sum_{i=1}^{N} w_i = \sum_{i=1}^{N} \mu_i + 3 \cdot \left(\sum_{i=1}^{N} \frac{\theta_i \cdot \sigma_i}{3} \right)$$

$$= \sum_{i=1}^{N} \mu_i + 3 \cdot \sqrt{\sum_{i=1}^{N} \sum_{j=1}^{N} 1 \cdot \left(\frac{\theta_i \cdot \sigma_i}{3} \right) \cdot \left(\frac{\theta_j \cdot \sigma_j}{3} \right)} \qquad (19)$$

Comparing (18) with (19), we can find that the incoherence between the arrangement of SSTA and that of WTA comes from two factors: (a) GDC coefficients, in other words, $\rho_{ij} \neq 1$ if $i \neq j$ in (18) while the corresponding value in (19) is set to a constant "1"; and (b) standard deviation of gate delay, to be more precise, there exists at least one indicator i so that $\theta_i \cdot \sigma_i / 3 \neq \sigma_i$.

In order to eliminate respectively one of the two factors for more detailed comparison, we compute σ'_{path} and σ''_{path} with:

$$\sigma'_{path} = \sqrt{\sum_{i=1}^{N} \sum_{j=1}^{N} 1 \cdot \sigma_i \sigma_j} \qquad (20)$$

$$\sigma''_{path} = \sqrt{\sum_{i=1}^{N} \sum_{j=1}^{N} \rho_{ij} \cdot \left(\frac{\theta_i \cdot \sigma_i}{3} \right) \cdot \left(\frac{\theta_j \cdot \sigma_j}{3} \right)} \qquad (21)$$

According to Figure 3, we can conclude that: (a) the violation of path ranks is mainly from the way with which we estimate standard deviation of gate delay, in other words, from the gaps $\sigma_i \cdot (\theta_i / 3 - 1)$; (b) it is feasible to attack problems like yield analysis and statistical optimization in terms of gate-level delay correlation. For example, the continuous line will move closer to the dotted line if we can propose techniques to increase ρ_{ij}, such as the use of low process sensitivity gates.

4   Validation

For the validation, we apply the path-based SSTA flow to the ITC99 benchmark circuits implemented respectively in 130nm and 65nm process. Results from the statistical timing engine were compared to those delivered by MC simulations which are performed using the same statistical process model under the typical operating conditions (1.2V and 25C°).

In Figure 4, points above the 45° straight line indicate that values are overestimated; and those below the line are underestimated. To sum up, for mean of path delay, relative errors $|(\hat{\mu} - \mu)/\mu| \times 100\%$ are less than 5%; and as regards standard deviation, less than 10%. These errors are acceptable in the context of timing analysis. Moreover, most of the standard deviations are a little overestimated, which reduces the probability of the violations of the setup and hold time constraints.

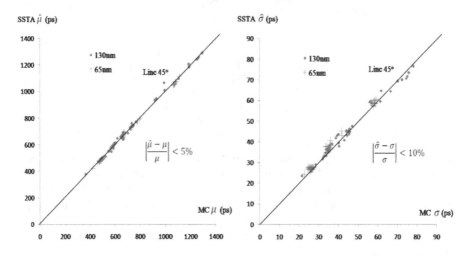

Fig. 4. Validation on estimating path delay probability distribution

In addition to accuracy, Table 2 gives some examples to demonstrate the significant CPU time gain of the SSTA engine compared to MC simulation. The ratio st/et means that the time needed to simulate one path is enough for us to perform SSTA on over 10^5 paths of the same length with the engine.

Table 2. Computational cost of MC simulation and the SSTA engine

path	logical depth	CPU time (s)		st/et (simulation time : st SSTA time : et)
		simulation (1500 runs)	SSTA	
1	5	2794.02	0.02	1.40×10^5
2	10	5245.12	0.03	1.75×10^5
3	15	6914.28	0.06	1.15×10^5
4	20	9881.50	0.08	1.24×10^5
5	25	12020.70	0.11	1.09×10^5

5   Conclusions

In this paper, we present a statistical timing engine considering effects of gate topology and switching induced correlation. A procedure to estimate gate-to-gate delay correlation along path has been introduced for this purpose. What is more, with the help of this statistical dependency "gate-level correlation", differences between results of SSTA and those of WTA can be reasonably interpreted. The proposed SSTA flow gives us acceptable estimates of path delay distributions with absolute values of relative errors 5% and 10% respectively on mean and on standard deviation.

References

[1] Feng, Z., Li, P., Zhan, Y.: Fast second-order statistical static timing analysis using parameter dimension reduction. In: DAC 2007 (2007)
[2] Cheng, L., Xiong, J., He, L.: Non-linear statistical static timing analysis for non-Gaussian variation sources. In: DAC 2007 (2007)
[3] Chang, H., Sapatnekar, S.S.: Statistical timing analysis considering spatial correlations using a single PERT-like traversal. In: ICCAD 2003 (2003)
[4] Visweswariah, C., Ravindran, K., Kalafala, K.: First-order parameterized block-based statistical timing analysis. In: DAC 2004 (2004)
[5] Ripp, A., et al.: Design for Manufacturability and Yield – influence of process variations in digital, analog and mixed-signal circuit design. In: DATE 2006 (2006)
[6] Ramalingam, A., Singh, A.K., et al.: An Accurate Sparse Matrix Based Framework for Statistical Static Timing Analysis. In: ICCAD 2006 (2006)
[7] http://www.synopsys.com/home.aspx
[8] http://www.r-project.org002F
[9] http://www.cadence.com/
[10] Wu, Z., Maurine, P., Azémard, N., Ducharme, G.: SSTA with Correlations Considering Input Slope and Output Load Variations. In: VLSI-SOC 2008 (2008)

Residue Arithmetic for Variation-Tolerant Design of Multiply-Add Units

Ioannis Kouretas and Vassilis Paliouras

Electrical and Computer Engineering Dept.,
University of Patras, Greece

Abstract. This paper investigates the residue arithmetic as a solution for the design of variation-tolerant circuits. Motivated by the modular organization of residue processors, we comparatively study the sensitivity of residue arithmetic-based and binary processors to delay variations, and in particular the impact of delay variations onto the maximum critical path. Experiments are performed on two multiply-add (MAC) circuits based on residue and binary arithmetic. Results reveal that residue arithmetic-based circuits are up to 94% less sensitive to delay variation than binary circuits, thus leading to increased timing yield.

1 Introduction

As integration technology scales down, the physical features and parameters of integrated circuits exhibit severe fluctuations due to the manufacturing process. The process-induced variations are classified as intra-die and intra-die variations. The term inter-die characterizes variations of devices parameters that are manifested from die-to-die and, therefore, affect all the devices on the die in a similar way. The term intra-die characterizes variations that occur among the elements of a single chip [1,2,3].

As manufacturing processes move below 90nm, the traditional static time analysis (STA) becomes incapable of accurately capturing the timing behavior of a system, due to the severe effects of the intra- and inter-die variations on the delay. Corner-based analysis becomes impractical, due to the large number of corners. As a remedy, statistical time analysis (SSTA) has been developed to deal with the impact of process variations [4]. While STA analysis perceives delays as fixed numbers, SSTA considers delays as random values that assume particular probability density functions (PDF's) for the circuit analysis [1]. In the last decade many SSTA-based tools and methods have been proposed in the literature to overcome the difficulty of the statistical time analysis problem [5,6,7,8,9,10,11,4,12,13]. Monte-Carlo simulation is the most usual method for performing SSTA. The particular method generates random samples in the process domain and then runs analysis for each sample to find the delay distribution [8,7,14]. The main disadvantage of this approach is the increased computational cost [2].

Since process variations generate delay variations, critical path identification emerges as a crucial issue for the SSTA. By identifying the critical path, or a

J. Monteiro and R. van Leuken (Eds.): PATMOS 2009, LNCS 5953, pp. 26–35, 2010.

small number of paths that are likely to be critical in a circuit, the designer is able to meet the timing specifications by applying simpler critical-path optimization procedures, such as the utilization of low-threshold voltage cells, or by varying clock frequency to provide acceptable timing yield.

Since the optimization techniques applied on the candidate critical paths have associated cost in terms of area and/or power, it is of interest to use circuits where the number of candidate critical paths is small.

In this paper we investigate the use of an alternative number representations, called Residue Number System (RNS) and comparatively study its performance in the presence of process variations using SSTA techniques. RNS architectures process the remainders of values modulo a set of relatively coprime integers, called moduli. In RNS architectures, complexity reduction has been sought by resorting to the use of moduli that lead to simpler circuits. In particular, common choices are moduli of the form $2^n - 1$[15], 2^n, and $2^n + 1$ [15,16,17]. Moduli of the form $2^n - 1$ and $2^n + 1$ offer low-complexity circuits for arithmetic operations due to the end-around carry property, while moduli of the form 2^n lead to simple and regular architectures due to the carry-ignore property. Furthermore, recent works [18,19] have demonstrated the low-power properties of RNS circuits in comparison to two's complement-based circuits, for the implementation of FIR digital filters.

The remainder of the paper is organized as follows: Section 2 reviews basics of RNS. Section 3 discusses the organization of the RNS and binary multiply-add units. In section 4 the delay model used in this paper is described. Results are analyzed in section 5 and, finally, some conclusions are discussed in section 6.

2   Review of RNS Basics

The RNS maps an integer X to a N-tuple of *residues* x_i, as follows

$$X \xrightarrow{\text{RNS}} \{x_1, x_2, \ldots, x_N\}, \tag{1}$$

where $x_i = \langle X \rangle_{m_i}$, $\langle \cdot \rangle_{m_i}$ denotes the mod m_i operation, and m_i is a member of a set of pair-wise co-prime integers $\{m_1, m_2, \ldots, m_M\}$, called *base*. Co-prime integers have the property that $\gcd(m_i, m_j) = 1$, $i \neq j$. The modulo operation $\langle X \rangle_m$ returns the integer remainder of the integer division x div m, i.e., a number k such that $x = m \cdot l + k$, where l is an integer. Mapping (1) offers a unique representation of integer X, when $0 \leq X < \prod_{i=1}^{N} m_i$.

RNS is of interest because basic arithmetic operations can be performed in a carry-free manner. In particular the operation $Z = X \circ Y$, where $Y \xrightarrow{\text{RNS}} \{y_1, y_2, \ldots, y_N\}$, $Z \xrightarrow{\text{RNS}} \{z_1, z_2, \ldots, z_N\}$, and the symbol $\circ$ stands for addition, subtraction, or multiplication, can be implemented in RNS as $z_i = \langle x_i \circ y_i \rangle_{m_i}$, for $i = 1, 2, \ldots, M$. According to the above, each residue result z_i does not depend on any of the $x_i, y_i, j \neq i$, thus allowing fast data processing in N parallel independent residue channels. Inverse conversion is accomplished by means of the Chinese Remainder Theorem (CRT) or mixed-radix conversion [20].

3   RNS and Binary Multiply-Add Units

This section describes the organization of the RNS and binary multiply-add units. In the case of RNS, in the following bases of the form $\{2^n - 1, 2^n, 2^n + 1\}$ are used, while the binary MAC unit comprises a Wallace multiplier augmented by a step for the addition of a third operand. Fig. 1 and Fig. 3 depict the organization of a binary and an RNS-based MAC respectively, while Fig. 4 shows possible 4-bit implementations for modulo-$(2^n - 1)$ MAC (Fig. 4(a)), modulo-2^n (Fig. 4(c)) and binary MAC (Fig. 4(b)).
Both architectures implement the multiply-add operation $a * b + c$. It is noted that in the case of RNS, binary-to-RNS and RNS-to-binary converters are required. Forward conversion is required at the start and reverse conversion at the end of a MAC-intensive operation, such as the computation of an N-point Fourier transform [21]. For sufficiently large amount of processing, the conversion cost can be compensated by savings achieved due to more efficient

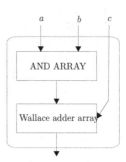

Fig. 1. Organization of binary MAC

processing. Due to the conversion overhead, applications suitable for RNS include MAC-intensive kernels such as digital filtering or discrete transforms.

4   Delay Model

In this section the delay variation of a multiply-add (MAC) unit is quantified for both RNS and binary implementations. The logic elements that compose each circuit are characterized by a nominal delay value d_{nom}, and two independent gaussian random variables, namely d_{intra} and d_{inter}. The d_{intra} and d_{inter} values model the intra-die variation component and inter-die variation component of the delay respectively [6,22].

It is noted that the delay model used does not explicitly take into consideration the impact of variation on wiring delay. Since for the RNS-based MAC, bases of the form $\{2^n - 1, 2^n, 2^n + 1\}$ are used, which lead to structures (cf. Fig. 4) that closely resemble the bit-level organization of binary MAC, the consideration of the particular delay model does not bias the results.

For the ith logic element at the jth chip, delay D_{ij} is given by

$$D_{ij} = d_{\text{nom}}(i) + d_{\text{intra}}(i, j) + d_{\text{inter}}(j), \tag{2}$$

where $d_{\text{nom}}(i)$ is the nominal delay of the element, $d_{\text{intra}}(i, j)$ is the component due to the intra-die variation, and $d_{\text{inter}}(j)$ is the delay component due to inter-die variation.

Based on complexities taken from a standard-cell library, a full adder (FA) is assumed to have a delay from input to carry output of $t_{FA,s_i \to c_o} = 2t_g$ and from input to sum output of $t_{FA,s_i \to s_o} = 2.5t_g$, where t_g is the unit delay. Besides, both XOR and AND-OR gates are assumed to have a delay of $t_{XOR} = t_{AND\text{-}OR} = 1t_g$, while AND gates demonstrate a delay of $t_{AND} = 0.5t_g$. Half adder (HA) is assumed to have a nominal delay of $t_{HA} = 1t_g$.

The delay of RNS MAC and binary MAC circuits is measured for a thousand instances. It is assumed that $d_{intra}(i,j)$ is independent gaussian for each logic element, while $d_{inter}(i,j)$ is the same for logic gates located on the same die. The delay of a path of elements is computed utilizing (2). For example, assume the circuit of Fig. 2. The maximum delay is obtained as $T = \max(T_1, T_2)$, where $T_1 = D_{31} + \max(D_{11}, D_{21})$ and $T_2 = D_{41} + \max(D_{11}, D_{21})$. Notice that due to variation, not all circuit instances may have the same critical path.

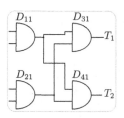

Fig. 2. Delay model example circuit

For each circuit the variation is normalized with the mean value of the delays. In this way, it is possible to compare the sensitivity to variations of different circuits, that exhibit different nominal delay. In particular let T_{RNS} and T_{binary} denote the delay and mT_{RNS} and mT_{binary} denote the mean delay for the RNS and binary MAC, respectively. Then $T'_{RNS} = \frac{T_{RNS}}{mT_{RNS}}$ and $T'_{binary} = \frac{T_{binary}}{mT_{binary}}$

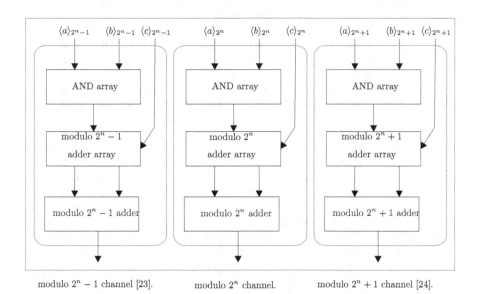

Fig. 3. Organization of RNS-based MAC

denote the corresponding normalized delays. Since D_{ij} is a random variable, T'_{RNS} and T'_{binary} are also random variables, with mean value equal to one, due to their construction. In the following, the behavior of delay variation is studied for both circuits and a quantitative discussion is offered.

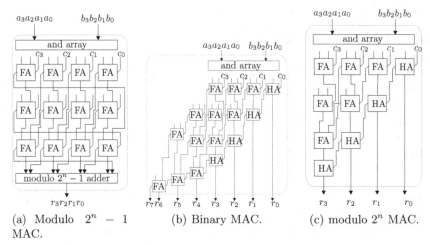

(a) Modulo $2^n - 1$ MAC.   (b) Binary MAC.   (c) modulo 2^n MAC.

Fig. 4. Implementations of RNS and binary MAC units

Table 1. T''_{RNS} and T''_{binary} variations

intra-die	inter-die	T''_{RNS}	T''_{binary}	reduction	—	—	—	—	—
5%	5%	0.000177	0.002268	92.21%	20%	5%	0.000317	0.001849	82.87%
5%	10%	0.000745	0.007936	90.61%	20%	10%	0.000765	0.007136	89.28%
5%	15%	0.001537	0.020021	92.32%	20%	15%	0.001296	0.016611	92.20%
5%	20%	0.002270	0.033000	93.12%	20%	20%	0.002101	0.028892	92.73%
5%	25%	0.005341	0.054417	90.19%	20%	25%	0.004065	0.046355	91.23%
5%	30%	0.007051	0.084647	91.67%	20%	30%	0.003982	0.075126	94.70%
10%	5%	0.000184	0.002004	90.83%	25%	5%	0.000327	0.001750	81.32%
10%	10%	0.000643	0.008361	92.32%	25%	10%	0.000805	0.006464	87.55%
10%	15%	0.001567	0.018560	91.56%	25%	15%	0.001623	0.014537	88.84%
10%	20%	0.002841	0.033584	91.54%	25%	20%	0.002566	0.026806	90.43%
10%	25%	0.003049	0.053872	94.34%	25%	25%	0.002979	0.044449	93.30%
10%	30%	0.004244	0.070923	94.02%	25%	30%	0.005898	0.061970	90.48%
15%	5%	0.000245	0.002025	87.89%	30%	5%	0.000566	0.001908	70.31%
15%	10%	0.000768	0.007682	90.00%	30%	10%	0.000991	0.006595	84.97%
15%	15%	0.001658	0.018621	91.10%	30%	15%	0.001389	0.013793	89.93%
15%	20%	0.002380	0.030261	92.13%	30%	20%	0.002133	0.026074	91.82%
15%	25%	0.003228	0.053310	93.95%	30%	25%	0.003415	0.040347	91.53%
15%	30%	0.004112	0.068989	94.04%	30%	30%	0.004793	0.059318	91.92%

5   Sensitivity of Multiply-Add Units to Delay Variation

In this section the behavior of delay under different severities of intra- and inter-die variation is studied. Both RNS and binary implementations are compared in terms of their sensitivity to delay variation. In the case of RNS, measurements

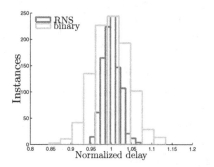

(a) 25% intra-die and 5% inter-die variation.

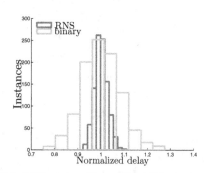

(b) 25% intra-die and 10% inter-die variation.

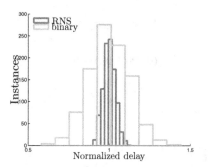

(c) 25% intra-die and 15% inter-die variation.

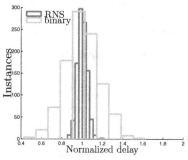

(d) 25% intra-die and 20% inter-die variation.

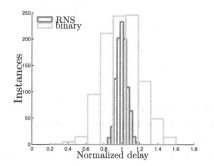

(e) 25% intra-die and 25% inter-die variation.

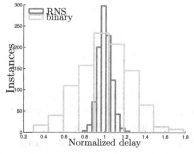

(f) 25% intra-die and 30% inter-die variation.

Fig. 5. Delay variation histograms for 30-bit wordlength for 25% intra-die variation

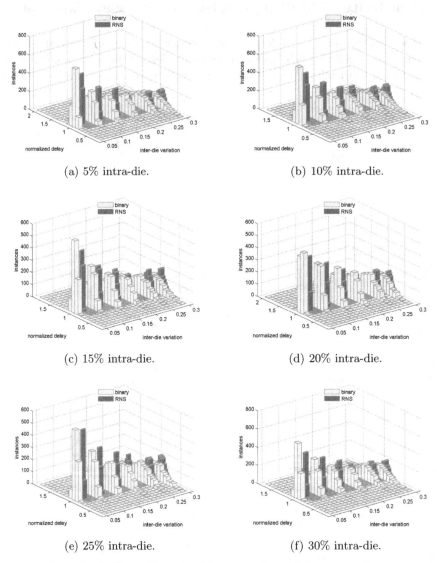

(a) 5% intra-die.

(b) 10% intra-die.

(c) 15% intra-die.

(d) 20% intra-die.

(e) 25% intra-die.

(f) 30% intra-die.

Fig. 6. Three dimension histograms for 30-bit wordlength

have been performed for all possible bases of the form $\{2^n - 1, 2^n, 2^n + 1\}$ and the case $\{2^{10} - 1, 2^{10}, 2^{10} + 1\}$ is presented. The particular base provides equivalent dynamic range of 30 bits in a binary system.

The obtained delay histograms are shown in Fig. 5, in case of 30-bit wordlength and for 25% intra-die delay variation. Fig. 5 depicts the number of critical instances that demonstrate a particular maximum delay. Corresponding three-dimensional histograms are shown in Fig. 6 for intra-die and inter-die delay variation in $\{5\%, 10\%, 15\%, 20\%, 25\%, 30\%\}$. For example, Fig. 6(d) depicts

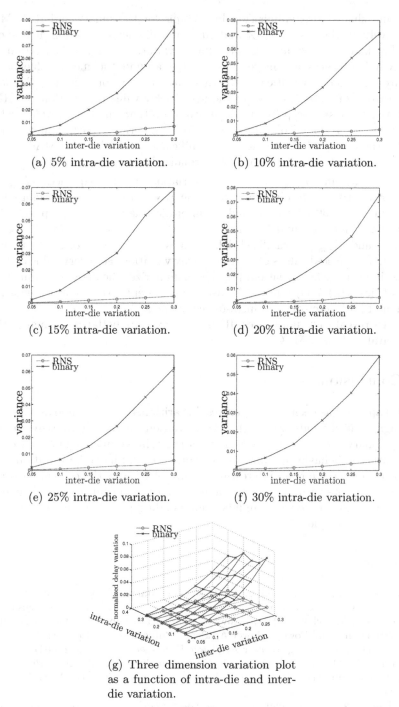

(a) 5% intra-die variation.

(b) 10% intra-die variation.

(c) 15% intra-die variation.

(d) 20% intra-die variation.

(e) 25% intra-die variation.

(f) 30% intra-die variation.

(g) Three dimension variation plot as a function of intra-die and inter-die variation.

Fig. 7.

white and shaded three-dimension histograms for the binary and RNS MAC respectively. In the cases of 15% and 20% inter-die delay variation, it is shown that the shaded histograms exhibit smaller variations. Fig. 6 depict that the RNS MAC instances are more concentrated around the mean value of the measured delays of the critical paths than their binary counterparts. The large concentration of instances close to the mean delay value reveals that the RNS-based MAC is less susceptible to delay variation than the binary MAC, which exhibits a larger spread of values. Therefore, the critical path definition may vary for the binary MAC circuit more significantly than the RNS MAC.

Table 1 depicts the variations of normalized delays T'_{RNS} and T'_{binary}. In Table 1, T''_{RNS} and T''_{binary} denote the variations of the sequences T'_{RNS} and T'_{binary} respectively. Results show that the RNS MAC exhibits savings from 70.31% in case of 30% intra-die and 5% inter-die delay variations, up to 94.70% in case of 20% intra-die and 30% inter-die delay variations. Figs. 7(a)–7(f) depict the T''_{RNS} and T''_{binary} normalized delay values as a function of inter-die delay variation, for selected values of intra-die delay variation. For every value of intra-die and inter-die delay variation, Fig. 7(g) summarizes the above two-dimension figures (Figs. 7(a)–7(f)) into a 3-D histogram to depict variation behavior as a function of both inter-die and intra-die components.

Results reveal that in all cases, RNS MAC exhibits better performance than the equivalent binary MAC.

6   Conclusions

In this paper, it has been shown that residue arithmetic can be used as a solution to design multiply-add circuits that are variation-tolerant. Two MAC circuits namely binary and RNS have been experimentally compared in terms of the delay variation behavior for various cases of inter- and intra-die variation.

This characteristic is an interesting feature of RNS as the critical path may be predicted more accurately, thus leading to increased timing yields. Therefore RNS may be an interesting candidate for building processing circuits in deep nanoscale technologies.

References

1. Michael, O., Sani, N., Boning, D.: Design for Manufacturability and Statistical Design: A Constructive Approach. Springer-Verlag New York, Inc., Secaucus (2006)
2. Srivastava, A., Sylvester, D., Blaauw, D.: Statistical Analysis and Optimization for VLSI: Timing and Power. Kluwer Academic Publishers, Dordrecht (2005)
3. Sapatnekar, S.: Timing. Kluwer Academic Publishers, Dordrecht (2004)
4. Najm, F.N.: On the need for statistical timing analysis. In: DAC 2005: Proceedings of the 42nd annual conference on Design automation, pp. 764–765. ACM, New York (2005)
5. Rubanov, N.: An information theoretic framework to compute the MAX/MIN operations in parameterized statistical timing analysis. In: International Symposium on Quality Electronic Design, pp. 728–733 (2009)

6. Viswanath, P., Murthy, P., Das, D., Venkatraman, R., Mandal, A., Veeravalli, A.: Optimization strategies to improve statistical timing. In: International Symposium on Quality Electronic Design, pp. 476–481 (2009)
7. Singhee, A., Singhal, S., Rutenbar, R.A.: Practical, fast monte carlo statistical static timing analysis: Why and how. In: International Conference on Computer-Aided Design, pp. 190–195 (2008)
8. Jaffari, J., Anis, M.: On efficient monte carlo-based statistical static timing analysis of digital circuits. In: International Conference on Computer-Aided Design, pp. 196–203 (2008)
9. Liu, J.H., Zeng, J.K., Hong, A.S., Chen, L., Chen, C.C.P.: Process-variation statistical modeling for VLSI timing analysis. In: International Symposium on Quality Electronic Design, pp. 730–733 (2008)
10. Mutlu, A., Le, K.J., Celik, M., sun Tsien, D., Shyu, G., Yeh, L.C.: An exploratory study on statistical timing analysis and parametric yield optimization. In: International Symposium on Quality Electronic Design, pp. 677–684 (2007)
11. Mangassarian, H., Anis, M.: On statistical timing analysis with inter- and intra-die variations. In: Design, Automation and Test in Europe Conference and Exhibition, pp. 132–137 (2005)
12. Najm, F.N., Menezes, N.: Statistical timing analysis based on a timing yield model. In: Design Automation Conference, pp. 460–465 (2004)
13. Liou, J.J., Cheng, K.T., Mukherjee, D.A.: Path selection for delay testing of deep sub-micron devices using statistical performance sensitivity analysis. In: VLSI Test Symposium, p. 97. IEEE, Los Alamitos (2000)
14. Huang, J.F., Chang, V.C., Liu, S., Doong, K.Y., Chang, K.J.: Modeling sub-90nm on-chip variation using monte carlo method for DFM. In: Asia and South Pacific Design Automation Conference, pp. 221–225 (2007)
15. Efstathiou, C., Vergos, H.T., Nikolos, D.: Modulo $2^n \pm 1$ adder design using select-prefix blocks. IEEE Transactions on Computers 52(11) (November 2003)
16. Hiasat, A.A.: High-speed and reduced area modular adder structures for RNS. IEEE Transactions on Computers 51(1), 84–89 (2002)
17. Wang, Z., Jullien, G.A., Miller, W.C.: An algorithm for multiplication modulo $(2^n + 1)$. In: Proceedings of 29th Asilomar Conference on Signals, Systems and Computers, Pacific Grove, CA, pp. 956–960 (1996)
18. Bernocchi, G.L., Cardarilli, G.C., Re, A.D., Nannarelli, A., Re, M.: Low-power adaptive filter based on rns components. In: ISCAS, pp. 3211–3214 (2007)
19. Nannarelli, A., Re, M., Cardarilli, G.C.: Tradeoffs Between Residue Number System and Traditional FIR Filters. In: Proceedings of the 2001 IEEE International Symposium on Circuits and Systems (ISCAS), vol. II, pp. 305–308 (2001)
20. Soderstrand, M.A., Jenkins, W.K., Jullien, G.A., Taylor, F.J.: Residue Number System Arithmetic: Modern Applications in Digital Signal Processing. IEEE Press, Los Alamitos (1986)
21. Kouretas, I., Paliouras, V.: Mixed radix-2 and high-radix RNS bases for low-power multiplication. In: Svensson, L., Monteiro, J. (eds.) PATMOS 2008. LNCS, vol. 5349, pp. 93–102. Springer, Heidelberg (2009)
22. Bowman, K., Duvall, S., Meindl, J.: Impact of die-to-die and within-die parameter fluctuations on the maximum clock frequency distribution for gigascale integration. IEEE Journal of Solid-State Circuits 37(2), 183–190 (2002)
23. Zimmermann, R.: Efficient VLSI implementation of modulo $(2^n \pm 1)$ addition and multiplication. In: ARITH 1999: Proceedings of the 14th IEEE Symposium on Computer Arithmetic, p. 158 (1999)
24. Efstathiou, C., Vergos, H.T., Dimitrakopoulos, G., Nikolos, D.: Efficient diminished-1 modulo $2^n + 1$ multipliers. IEEE Transactions on Computers 54(4), 491–496 (2005)

Exponent Monte Carlo for Quick Statistical Circuit Simulation

Paul Zuber[1], Vladimir Matvejev[2], Philippe Roussel[1],
Petr Dobrovolný[1], and Miguel Miranda[1]

[1] Smart Systems and Energy Technology, IMEC, 3001 Heverlee, Belgium
[2] Dept. of Electronics and Informatics, Vrije Universiteit Brussel, Belgium

Abstract. The main goals of this article are to report an implementation and a quantitative study of Exponent Monte Carlo, an enhanced version of Monte Carlo for verifying high circuit yield in the presence of random process variations. Results on industry-grade standard cell netlists and compact models in 45nm show that EMC predicts reasonable results at least 1,000 times faster than MC.

1 Introduction

Conservative design margins have been the traditional way to working SoCs under random process variability. However, with decreasing physical device dimensions those margins increase and with them the risk of over-design and profit loss. Statistical methods are getting inevitable in more and more domains of SoC design such as logic gate characterisation [2].

1.1 Random Variability

Suppose $\xi = (V_{\text{th},1}, \beta_1, \cdots, V_{\text{th},n}, \beta_n)$ denotes those transistor parameters of a circuit that are subject to independent process fluctuations. While ξ was seen as constant in the past, any circuit metric $y = h(\xi)$ was constant too, and its value could be determined by a single Spice run and used to characterise the circuit. Since now ξ is statistical with a probability distribution $f_{\text{i}}(\xi)$, the possibly multi-valued $y = h(\xi)$ becomes statistical too. The way the circuit is characterised now is typically by a possibly multi-variate probability distribution $f_{\text{o}}(y)$ or by guarantee bounds, such as 99% of the manufactured circuits are faster than 1 ns and consume less than 1 nW. Sometimes, this fraction is referred to as (parametric) yield and mathematically expressed as

$$Y = \int_{V_{\text{th},1}} \int_{\beta_1} \cdots \int_{V_{\text{th},n}} \int_{\beta_n} f_{\text{i}}(\xi) C(h(\xi)) \mathrm{d}V_{\text{th},1} \cdots \mathrm{d}\beta_n \ .$$

The constraint function C is defined as 1 for circuits that are considered to be working, and 0 otherwise. In the example, $C(h) = 1$ for $h_1(\xi) < 10^{-9}\,\text{s} \wedge h_2(\xi) < 10^{-9}\,\text{W}$. Eventually, ξ contains transistor outliers that render the circuit non-functional, e.g. a storage element that never flips due to an extreme threshold voltage variation in one of the transistors. In these cases $C = 0$ if the evaluation of h fails and Y denotes functional yield. In either case, there is no analytical approach, as $h(\xi)$ does not have a closed expression but is evaluated in Spice.

J. Monteiro and R. van Leuken (Eds.): PATMOS 2009, LNCS 5953, pp. 36–45, 2010.

1.2   Monte Carlo

Monte Carlo simulation is known as a very flexible numerical solution from two points of view. A random N-sized sample $x_1 \ldots x_N$ from the statistical transistor domain, which follows the PDF $f_i(\xi)$ and repeated evaluation of $h(x_i)$, give a picture of the distribution $f_o(h(\xi))$. Less obvious, though at least equally valuable, Monte Carlo is the only general way to numerically solve multi-dimensional integrals, such as the expression for Y above. The calculation reduces to a summation: $Y \approx \frac{1}{N} \sum C(h(x_i))$. This is binary GO versus NOGO counting is a crude approximation of Y. It can be shown that interpolating points $h(x_i)$ to a continuous approximation of the output CDF $F_o(h(\xi))$ and reading the yield value at the desired constraint can give more confident results. In any case, in order to be reasonably accurate in terms of low confidence intervals of Y, the number of repetitions N can grow prohibitively high. See top chart of Figure 1. 100 Monte Carlo runs cover little of the spread in the output domain of a small gate. To explore about twice the range in timing, the required number of simulations squares.

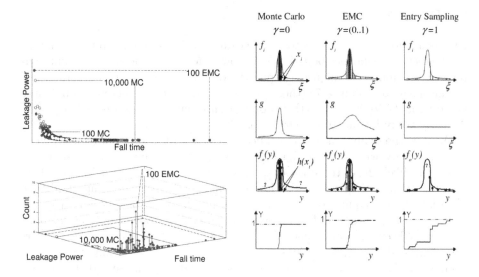

Fig. 1. Exponent Monte Carlo covers the same output domain as Monte Carlo in 100 times less runs

Fig. 2. Exponent Monte Carlo falls between Monte Carlo and entry sampling

1.3   Exponent Monte Carlo

Exponent Monte Carlo (EMC) is a statistical enhancement to Monte Carlo and was conceptually proposed in [3]. Its goal is to build a picture of the output domain $f_o(h(\xi))$ and to reduce N at constant accuracy levels of Y. See top chart of Figure 1, where about 100 EMC runs are enough to cover a larger spread than 10,000 MC runs could do, and a many-fold of that of 100 MC runs. The principle is to sample $x_1 \ldots x_N$ from $g(\xi) := f_i(\xi)^{1-\gamma}$ (hence the name Exponent MC) instead of $f_i(\xi)$. For $\gamma > 0$, EMC samples less likely observations, which define the tails of $f_o(y)$ more precisely than the bulk. This allows to verify for higher yields with increased confidence. Of course $\gamma = 0$ represents naive Monte Carlo. Another special case is $\gamma = 1$, which we refer to as entry sampling. Figure 2 summarises how Exponent Monte Carlo blends in between Monte Carlo and entry sampling.

Obviously $h(x_i)$ must be unbiased if x follows the biased distribution $g(\xi)$. The bottom chart of Figure 1 shows a tilted view of the top chart, and the distinct values $f_i(x_i)^\gamma$ at positions $h(x_i)$ become visible. This is true for EMC only, as for plain MC, every weight is equal. In the limit, sampling an input PDF $f_i(\xi)$ with Exponent Monte Carlo, propagating the resulting distribution $f(\xi)^{1-\gamma}$ through the function $h(\xi)$, and correcting the resulting output PDF with the factors $f_i(\xi)^\gamma$ indeed leads to the desired distribution $f_o(y) = \frac{f_i^{1-\gamma}(h^{-1}(y))}{|h'(h^{-1}(y))|} f_i^\gamma(h^{-1}(y))$. It is also easy to see that $Y \approx \frac{\sum C(h(x_i)) f_i(x_i)^\gamma}{\sum f_i(x_i)^\gamma}$. Again, approximating the CDF with a continuous function first and then reading the yield value provides a better result.

2   Prior Art

Exponent Monte Carlo falls under the heading variance reduction techniques as the prediction confidence bounds are narrowed. More specifically, it falls into importance sampling techniques. Despite the rather long history of such statistical enhancement techniques [7] (there existed international conferences on Monte Carlo variants 50 years ago) their application to circuit design is rather young. An early study for integrated circuits is [6].

What is the definition of importance? To stay with the example of V_{th} variations, some works consider the high (absolute) V_{th} values as important and pick more likely from those regions. This is indeed correct for delay but there are many applications where also low V_{th} values become important. Hold time violation checks require to be accurate in small delay regions, because too fast circuits cause the problem. Further examples are leakage power, differential logic, memory cells or sense amplifiers. The EMC approach presented above considers both high and low V_{th} variations. This allows for joint yield computations, i.e. compute $C(h(\xi))$ for multivariate $h(\xi)$ as correlation is preserved. For example, if the constraint is to be faster than $1\,\mathrm{ns}$ and to consume less than $1\,\mathrm{nW}$, then correlation between timing and power is required, and the important region includes both high and low V_{th} values.

One variant of importance sampling was presented in [8]. The work uses an ideal-case analytical example for $h(\xi)$ and a realistic SRAM cell's read stability as test vehicles for $C(h(\xi))$. Reported speed-ups are in the order of 10,000 and 100, respectively. Later, the same authors applied the method to DRAMs [9] using a uniform proposal function g. Other speed-up techniques such as Quasi Monte Carlo (QMC) sampling are described in [16]. A combination of several speed-up techniques has been published in [15], a paper that made it into a collection of the best papers of ten years of DATE.

Process corners are an adequate solution for global variations, but the advent of statistical static timing analysis (SSTA, [11]) tools indicates that the microelectronics economy may need to manage major changes to accommodate the increasing impact of local random device variability inherent to small device geometries. SSTA happens on a higher level of the design flow, and is not in the direct scope of this paper.

The scientific contribution of this article is to present an implementation and results of EMC optimised for standard cell circuit characterisation in an industry-strength environment. For this we organise the following part in the sections Analysis Plan, Implementation, and Results.

3   Analysis Plan

This section lays out the plan to systematically test the usefulness of the proposed technique. The main objective is to measure the speed-up of EMC as compared to MC. Formally this means $N_{MC} : N_{EMC}$, subject to a criterion to be fulfilled by either method. In this work, we target two criterions,

1. equal confidence levels of the statistical information computed with either method. Unfortunately, little is known about analytic derivation of confidence levels of importance sampling [10]. The plan is therefore to pick any N-sized sample M times with different random sequences and analyse the variance of the simulation results.
2. the possibility to verify high yield values at all. Consider for example a chance of 1:100 that C is 0. It is obvious that in 10 runs, MC cannot approximate Y, while EMC may generate rare enough circuit variants to do so.

Confer Figure 3 for an overview of the analysis plan. A set of M CDF approximations is generated for several circuits, several of their performance metrics and several combinations of N and γ. A value of $M = 200$ is a reasonable choice for obtaining good accuracy of the variance predictions. By overlaying the CDFs we extract the standard deviation of the one-dimensional constraint at several fixed yield percentiles. This is in fact a useful measure. For example, the user can learn what is the maximum delay specification in order to be 84% sure that the parametric yield will be better than 99%. A wide range of parameters is set in order to provide relevant results. In particular, one is interested in the following influence factors:

1. The sample size N. It is the main measure of simulation speed and trades off with prediction confidence. We used practical values between 10 and 10,000.
2. The value of γ is the only parameter of the method itself. It is expected that the speed-up depends much on γ. As a logical step, that value is swept among the exercises to find its optimal setting.
3. Circuits with different transistor counts are considered as listed in Figure 3. This influences the dimensionality of the integral. The post-layout netlists were taken from a partner's design flow and were simulated with HSpice using an industrial 45nm technology model.

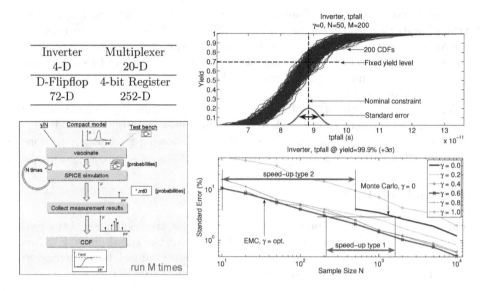

Fig. 3. Left: Analysis flow to obtain a set of M CDFs as displayed on the top right together with indication of the CDF accuracy assessment strategy. Right bottom: accuracy over sample size for EMC, MC and entry sampling to measure the speed-up.

4. Among the circuit performance measures $h(\xi)$ are propagation delay, power and leakage. Setting a constraint on one of these metrics classifies a circuit as yielding or not. We test the circuit at constant yield, and amount the prediction accuracy by estimating the variance of the constraint value. The yield level can be expressed in the equivalent σ notation, i.e. units in a probit plot, in order to avoid unhandy percentage numbers, cf. Table 1.
5. The whole article deals with local random variations. Global variations alone affect all transistors in a correlated way and are represented by a dramatically reduced dimensionality of the problem. Since in reality there is always a random component, we analyse this more difficult case, expecting and accepting smaller but realistic speed-up numbers than under ideal assumptions.

4 Implementation

4.1 Technology Input

So far, V_{th} and β were mentioned implicitly as transistor parameters under variability. One can obtain an input population of such tuples from silicon mea-

Table 1. Translation of percentile and σ notation

%	3.17e-3	0.135	2.28	15.9	50.0	84.1	97.7	99.9	99.99
σ	-4	-3	-2	-1	0	+1	+2	+3	+4

surements. In our experiments we extracted these pairs from the information contained in our partner's statistical compact model library, which uses about six different variable parameters. Comparison to our two-parameter model using 10,000 Monte Carlo runs shows excellent agreement of mean, spread and correlation of circuit performance metrics. As a note, this is not true for the model of most publications where V_{th} alone is used, which can cause some 20% difference in standard deviation of important metrics like gate leakage or delay.

4.2   Picking

Filling the $x_i = ((V_{th}, \beta)_1, \ldots (V_{th}, \beta)_n)_i$ vector requires an independent picking process of the n transistor parameter pairs under variability. The value of $f_o(h(x_i))$, i.e. the probability of a circuit observation i, is then the product of the probabilities of the n individual transistor observations. Picking is driven by the value of the γ coefficient. The correct implementation of the EMC sampling method consists of the following consecutive steps.

1. Before starting any sampling we have to apply the actual (γ dependent) value to the observations. This means that for each transistor observation j, i.e. a particular entry of a (correlated) $w_j := (V_{th}, \beta)_j$ pair, two probability values have to be computed: the cumulative probability to be sampled cumPTBS $= \sum g(w_j) = \sum f(w_j)^{1-\gamma}$ and the probability to be returned PTBR $= f(w_j)/g(w_j) = f(w_j)^\gamma$.

2. The next step of the sampling process is the picking itself. A randomly generated number r_j from the uniform distribution between 0 and 1 represents a random value of the cumulative probability to be sampled. Through the normalised cumPTBS values of a sample, r_j is mapped to a random observation index. To search for the observation with the cumPTBS value close to r_j, the bisection algorithm in the domain of observation indices is exploited. Finally the picking ends by returning the randomly picked observation index together with the observation's value of PTBR.

The EMC functionality was implemented as a JAVA library that easily links to other languages such as MATLAB.

4.3   Vaccination

Since Spice itself does not support EMC, a mechanism is required to inject variability into a nominal Spice simulation. We use the term VACCination (Variability Aware Circuit Characterisation) to denote the process of transforming a Spice level netlist with any number and type of transistors into N variants of the same. These variants differ to the original netlist in that two variability injection sources are added to every MOSFET instance. The values of these injection sources differ among the variants and obey the underlying distribution. A voltage source at the gate and a drain-current controlled current source along source-drain are used to model ΔV_{th} and $\Delta \beta$, respectively. Some features of this approach are:

1. It is independent of the MOSFET model type (BSIM, PSP, etc.) and the shape of the distribution.
2. The area-dependent variability [14] is respected by evaluating the actual width and length of each transistor instance.
3. Subcircuits are traversed, and injection happens at top level in order to make sure that each individual instance receives an individual injection. Furthermore, adding a systematic component to model global variations is supported.
4. The test bench remains identical. This is useful if a third-party cell characteriser is used.
5. Apart from the speed-up of EMC vs. MC, there are two more speed-ups as a by-product: a. Spice itself does not need to evaluate the model statistics, which can make 50% of the time for small circuits. In some cases, this overcompensates the vaccination process. For small circuits, data sweep based iterations are used. b. It is also possible to generate N independent Spice jobs for parallel execution on a server farm. This pays off for large circuits such as memory blocks.
6. Extension to other elements under process variability such as DRAM capacitors or line resistances is easy.

Vaccination was implemented as generic MATLAB script and successfully tested against a wide range of circuit classes from three different industrial partners and several academic netlists.

5   Results

One important result was already visible in Figure 3 (bottom right). The graphs correspond to the standard error over the sample size for different γ values. Their parallelity indicates that the EMC standard error decreases independent of γ when increasing N. The speed-up factor (type one) is therefore not a function of the required accuracy level.

Detailed results for the inverter are presented in Figure 4. One can see the possible speed-up of type one for all four circuit performances (for leakage, up to 16), and the required optimal γ setting. An important conclusion is that these two values barely differ among the four performance metrics. General results for other circuits are similar and were compacted into Figure 5. As expected, EMC efficiency type one increases when dealing with low number of transistors and with high yield areas of interest. This agrees with general conclusions on importance sampling [6].

It is clear that Monte Carlo is unable to give results at all in higher yield realms, since rare events are simply not produced. Speed-ups of type one beyond 3.5σ (99.98% yield) were therefore not computed, as more than 10,000 MC runs would have been required. Figure 6 shows how far in yield verification one can go. As we increase γ, we see higher possible yield ranges at constant N, but also higher standard errors in low yield ranges. The table compares the typical required runs for MC and EMC to obtain results without having to resort to

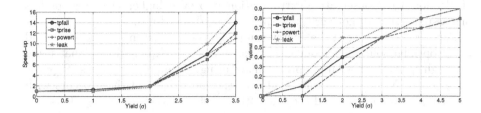

Fig. 4. Summary of inverter results showing maximum speed-up type one of EMC compared to MC for several metrics and optimal γ for several yield regions

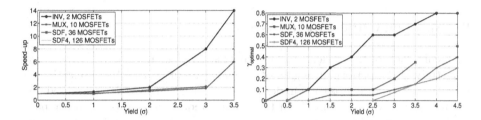

Fig. 5. Summary for different circuits showing typical speed-up type one of EMC compared to MC and optimal γ for several yield regions

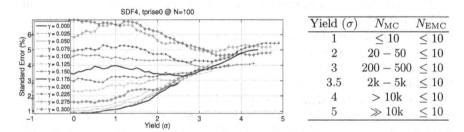

Yield (σ)	N_{MC}	N_{EMC}
1	≤ 10	≤ 10
2	$20 - 50$	≤ 10
3	$200 - 500$	≤ 10
3.5	$2k - 5k$	≤ 10
4	$> 10k$	≤ 10
5	$\gg 10k$	≤ 10

Fig. 6. Left: Accuracy of rise propagation delay specification of a 4-bit register over yield level for different values of γ. Right: Required number of simulations to be able to predict in given yield region

inaccurate PDF extrapolation. As opposed to speed-up type one, we have not seen a large influence of the circuit size on this result. The speed-up of type two can easily exceed three orders of magnitude, even for a synchronous 4-bit register with more than 100 MOSFETs.

EMC has shown its advantages over MC. Comparing to other works such as [6,8,9,15,16] is difficult from different points of view, like the circuit used, assumptions about the technology input, the definition of speed-up and the availability of an efficient implementation. We assume that higher speed-ups can be achieved if a one-dimensional transistor variation model is used as in most works. However we have seen that then the model accuracy can suffer, cf. Section 4.1. Conservative extrapolation into even higher yield regions lets one assume (though not verify) further increased speed-ups.

Further, we have seen that entry sampling as e.g. used in [9] has never lead to an optimal solution for our examples. A possible explanation is that using too high γ leads to a large spread in resulting output probabilities. Suppose for example N circuit variants, and that the most likely of those occurs with relative probability ≈ 1 and the one with lowest ≈ 0 after unbiasing. This acts like having only $N - 1$ circuits, decreasing the achievable accuracy according to Figure 3. The same explanation can be used for the decreased effectiveness (type one) of EMC for higher-dimensional problems. High probability spread forces to choose lower γ values, which in turn limit the sampling in extreme regions.

6   Summary and Future Work

The main goals of this article were to report an implementation and a quantitative study of the performance gain of Exponent Monte Carlo. Its application to statistical cell characterisation under process fluctuations was demonstrated under realistic conditions using industry-grade standard cell netlists and compact models in 45nm. Given that the user knows very well which statistical parameters are of interest, EMC enables first results at a speed gain of more than three orders of magnitude. For small circuits and constant accuracy, a factor of up to 15 at 3.5σ (99.98% yield) as compared to Monte Carlo simulation is possible.

EMC is very well suited to evaluate small and often repeated circuits such as SRAM or DRAM cells. We used this result to develop and implement MemoryVAM, a method to enable statistical timing, power and yield analysis for full memory arrays of given architecture. EMC is deployed to derive building block sensitivies and functial yield figures, which are then scaled to memory level. Joint publications with Samsung have been submitted for review.

How does the accuracy demand on system level parameters such as parametric yield loss translate into yield and PDF accuracy requirements of particular gates as described in this work? How will the optimal settings change and will one still be more economic in run time than with naive MC? The theory to answer these types of questions is currently developed.

References

1. Asenov, A., et al.: Advanced simulation of statistical variability and reliability in nano CMOS transistors. In: IEDM 2008 (2008)
2. Centurelli, F., Giancane, L., Olivieri, M., Scotti, G., Trifiletti, A.: A Statistical Model of Logic Gates for Monte Carlo Simulation Including On-Chip Variations. In: Azémard, N., Svensson, L. (eds.) PATMOS 2007. LNCS, vol. 4644, pp. 516–525. Springer, Heidelberg (2007)
3. Dierickx, B., et al.: Propagating variability from technology to system level. In: Physics of Semiconductor Devices, Mumbai, pp. 74–79 (2007)
4. Hammersley, J.M., Handscomb, D.C.: Monte Carlo methods. Chapman and Hall, London (1983)

5. Doorn, T.S., ter Maten, E.J.W., Croon, J.A., Di Bucchianico, A., Wittich, O.: Importance sampling Monte Carlo simulations for accurate estimation of SRAM yield. In: ESSCIRC 2008 (2008)
6. Hocevar, D.E., Lightner, M.R., Trick, T.N.: A Study of Variance Reduction Techniques for Estimating Circuit Yields. IEEE TCAD 2(3), 180–192 (1983)
7. Kahn, H., Marshall, A.W.: Methods of reducing sample size in Monte Carlo computations. J. Oper. Res. Soc. Amer. 1, 263 (1953)
8. Kanj, R., Joshi, R., Nassif, S.: Mixture importance sampling and its application to the analysis of SRAM designs in the presence of rare failure events. In: DAC 2006 (2006)
9. Kanj, R., Joshi, R.V., Kuang, J.B., Kim, J., Meterelliyoz, M., Reohr, W., Nassif, S.R., Nowka, K.J.: Statistical yield analysis of silicon-on-insulator embedded DRAM. In: ISQED (2009)
10. Kosbar, K.L., Chang, T.F.: Conservative confidence intervals of importance sampling estimates. In: MILCOM 1992 (1992)
11. Kukimoto, Y., Berkelaar, M., Sakallah, K.: Static timing analysis. In: Hassoun, S., Sasao, T. (eds.) Logic Synthesis and Verification. Kluwer International Series In Engineering And Computer Science Series, vol. 654. Kluwer, Dordrecht (2002)
12. Matvejev, V.: Optimal Gamma in Exponent Monte Carlo Simulation of SRAM. Master's thesis, Univ. Furtwangen (2009)
13. Mukhopadhyay, S., Mahmoodi, H., Roy, K.: Statistical design and optimization of SRAM cell for yield enhancement. In: ICCAD 2004 (2004)
14. Pelgrom, M., Duinmaijer, A., Welbers, A.: Matching properties of MOS transistors. Solid-State Circuits 24(5), 1433–1439 (1989)
15. Singhee, A., Rutenbar, R.A.: Statistical Blockade: A Novel Method for Very Fast Monte Carlo Simulation of Rare Circuit Events, and its Application. In: DATE 2007 (2007)
16. Singhee, A., Singhal, S., Rutenbar, R.A.: Practical, fast Monte Carlo statistical static timing analysis: why and how. In: ICCAD 2008 (2008)

Clock Repeater Characterization for Jitter-Aware Clock Tree Synthesis

Monica Figueiredo[1] and Rui L. Aguiar[2]

[1] Instituto Politécnico de Leiria, Escola Superior de Tecnologia e Gestão
[2] Universidade de Aveiro, Dpt. Electrónica e Telecomunicações
Instituto de Telecomunicações
Leiria, Aveiro, Portugal
monicaf@estg.ipleiria.pt, ruilaa@ua.pt

Abstract. This paper presents a simple jitter model for clock repeaters. The model is scalable and technology independent, which makes it suitable for integration in current clock tree synthesis algorithms. It is based on the timing characterization of a reference inverter, which can be performed for different process corners to account for process variability. Simulation results show that the model is accurate to within 10% for the most common inverter and NAND based repeaters.

Keywords: Jitter Model, Clock Repeaters, CTS.

1 Introduction

Clock Tree Synthesis (CTS) is a layout technique to optimally distribute repeaters along the path between clock sources and receivers with the minimum skew in clock arrival times. Skew depends on many different parameters associated with the clock distribution network: the number of stages; the repeater's size and locations; the on-chip spacial and temporal load distribution; and the interconnect structure. Various approaches to CTS have been proposed to minimize skew such as symmetric and asymmetric trees [1], optimal repeater insertion and repeater/wire sizing schemes [2] or tunable repeaters [3].

Timing uncertainties also depend on process, voltage and temperature (PVT) variations, physical and circuit noise sources. In [4], clock skew is evaluated under several variability models while a statistical methodology to compute time uncertainties under the impact of PVT, power supply noise (PSN) and crosstalk is presented in [5]. Other works focus on PSN induced jitter estimation and minimization. In [6], jitter estimation in clock trees is based on a recursive analytical expression considering sinusoidal PSN, while [7] presents analytical expressions for buffer delay variation. Jitter minimization is usually accomplished with clock buffer polarity assignment techniques [8], with intentional clock skew introduction or clock frequency modulation [9]. Due to the increasing relevance of jitter in high-speed digital designs, it is our belief that it should be accounted for as early as possible in the design flow. It is thus desirable to have jitter minimization during CTS through a proper choice of repeaters, their size and location.

J. Monteiro and R. van Leuken (Eds.): PATMOS 2009, LNCS 5953, pp. 46–55, 2010.

In this paper we present a model for jitter generated in clock repeaters based on a reference inverter timing characterization, which can be performed for different process corners to account for process variability. This pretends to be a simple and efficient tool to enable the introduction of jitter-awareness in CTS algorithms, concerning jitter generated in repeaters. Other jitter sources and accumulation models should be considered in future work to allow system level jitter modeling. The characterization and model generation flow is schematically represented in Fig. 1. The model can be based on delay parameters usually available on technology library files, but a more extensive timing characterization can also be done specifically for this purpose. Although the characterization has to be done for each technology, the model itself is technology independent and allows jitter estimation for any clock repeater, given its specific design parameters and a particular PSN model. The PSN model should be selected according to the circuit's design, as will be explained in section 2.3.

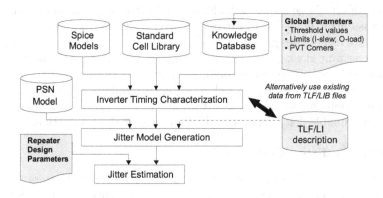

Fig. 1. Characterization and model generation flow

During CTS, repeaters are optimally sized and separated to minimize the interconnect delay and guarantee sharp clock edges at receivers. However this typically requires an increased number of large buffers, which may draw huge current from power/ground network and incur in PSN, which is a main jitter source. To identify current-hungry repeaters during CTS, we propose the usage of a simple current model based on the popular triangular approximation. Peak current information can then be used as an input parameter during the CTS decision process to minimize auto-induced jitter in clock repeaters.

The paper is organized as follows. In section 2 we describe the clock distribution cell and the noise sources that affect its precision. After, we present the inverter and buffer characterization methodology and the proposed jitter model. Model predictions are compared with simulation results in a 180nm technology, for these inverter based clock repeaters. The model applicability to other repeaters is presented in section 3. Section 4 discusses the usage of current models for auto-induced jitter prediction and conclusions are given in section 5.

2   Jitter Model

2.1   Clock Distribution Cell

The most common topology of clock distribution networks is the clock tree with repeaters. Symmetric H-trees were typically adopted in high performance designs for global clock distribution due to their intrinsic low skew characteristics. However, balanced trees with repeaters are usually preferred in the presence of obstructions or non-uniform load distribution, which is the most common situation in present designs. In both structures, a clock distribution cell is defined from the input of one clock driver to the input of the next clock driver, which includes the repeater, the interconnects and load. In this work we will only focus on the repeater's jitter model, with interconnects and load modeled as a single effective load capacitance [10].

For a given number of cascaded clock distribution cells, wire interconnects and total driving capacitance, the repeaters' sizes determine the cell's delay and transition times. These choices will also determine the jitter associated with each cell because jitter is known to directly depend on transition times [11]. Clock repeaters are usually designed to produce equal rise and fall times, propagating a nearly constant clock pulse width throughout the distribution network, but other options may contribute to minimize power consumption [12]. Regarding architecture, the most common clock repeaters are buffers and inverters. Other increasingly popular options include tristate or AND-type repeaters for clock gating, and tunable delay repeaters (TDR) to adjust delay variations.

2.2   Inverter Jitter Model

We propose a model to estimate jitter generated in clock inverters ($\Delta \hat{t}_{d,inv}$) based on a reference jitter value ($\Delta t_{d,ref}$) and scalable correction factors ($\Upsilon(r_j)$) (1). The correction factors vary according to the inverter's size ($r_s = s/s_{ref}$), fanout ($r_f = C_{out}/C_{in}$) and on the ratio between input and output transition times ($r_{io} = t_{in}/t_{out}$). The mean rising/falling transition time should be used even if the inverter is not balanced, because each distributed clock edge will be equally affected by rising and falling inverters in a repeater chain.

$$\Delta \hat{t}_{d,inv} = \Delta t_{d,ref} \cdot \prod_j \Upsilon(r_j) \ , \quad j \in \{s, f, io\}. \tag{1}$$

The first step to obtain the correction factors is to select a reference inverter, with a reference fanout and input transition time. Any drive strength can be chosen for this purpose but simpler factors result if we choose the smaller inverter available in the clock repeater's library, with $r_f = r_{io} = 1$. The second step is to characterize the inverter's output transition time (t_o) and delay (t_d) for different sizes, loads and input transition times. The timing data is usually already available in the technology library file, but can also be easily obtained from simulation. The third step is to curve/surface fit the data to analytically model t_o and t_d with r_s, r_f and r_{io} as arguments.

Having done this, empirical correction factors can be obtained from the ratios shown in (2). There are two output transition time ratios ($r_{to,s}$ and $r_{to,io}$) and one delay time ratio ($r_{td,f}$). The ratios $r_{to,s} = t_{o,r_s}/t_{o,ref}$ and $r_{td,f} = t_{d,r_f}/t_{d,ref}$ are obtained with $r_{io} = r_f = 1$, while the ratio $r_{to,io} = t_{o,r_{io}}/t_{o,ref}$ is obtained for different r_f factors and $r_s = 1$. The quadratic jitter dependence on $r_{to,io}$ results from the known significant impact of the input transition time on propagation delay. Hence, care must be taken when characterizing the reference inverter for different input transition times. It is advisable that similar inverters are used as driving gates and the slew rate measured at $30 - 90\%$ V_{dd} rising ($10 - 70\%$ V_{dd} falling), as usually recommended.

$$\Upsilon(r_s) = \sqrt{r_{to,s}} \ ; \ \Upsilon(r_f) = r_{td,f} \ ; \ \Upsilon(r_{io}) = (r_{to,io})^2 \qquad (2)$$

2.3   Buffer Jitter Model

Clock buffers are just a cascade of two inverters (with eventually different sizes). Their output jitter variance depends on the jitter introduced by each inverter and the correlations among the noise sources involved [7]. So, we can use the inverter's model to estimate jitter in clock buffers as long as adequate design parameters are inferred for each inverter and the noise sources are characterized. In (3) and (4) we present the inverter's design parameters based on the buffer's parameters $\{\Gamma_n; r_s; r_f; r_{io}\}$, where Γ_n is the buffer's tapering factor. Some of these parameters are given as approximations, but the exact values can be obtained through simulation (for a given technology) if higher accuracy is desired.

$$Inv_1 : \{r_{s,1} = r_s/\Gamma_n; \ r_{f,1} \approx \Gamma_n; \ r_{io,1} \approx r_{io}\sqrt{r_f/\Gamma_n^2}\} \qquad (3)$$

$$Inv_2 : \{r_{s,2} = r_s; \ r_{f,2} = r_f/\Gamma_n; \ r_{io,2} \approx \sqrt{\Gamma_n^2/r_f}\} \qquad (4)$$

In a clock repeater the input waveform depends on noise introduced by the previous repeater, which is usually placed in a distant location, probably with independent power/ground rails. So, the input transition levels can be considerd independent of buffer's PSN levels, as shown in Fig. 2. In this scenario, the buffer's output jitter is given by the sum of the individual inverter's standard deviations, based on the inverter's reference jitter (rms), multiplied by a PSN correction factor (Υ_{psn}), as shown in (5).

$$\Delta \hat{t}_{d,buf} = \left(\Delta \hat{t}_{d,inv1} + \Delta \hat{t}_{d,inv2}\right) \cdot \Upsilon_{psn}. \qquad (5)$$

This factor varies between 0 and 2 for different design parameters and PSN correlations inside the buffer cell. When power and ground rails have dominant common mode noise (CMN), positive jitter generated in one inverter is canceled by negative jitter generated in the other and $\Upsilon_{psn} \approx 0$, as CMN has opposite effects on rising and falling transitions. On the other hand, if differential mode noise (DMN) is dominant, jitter can be as high as 2 times the sum of jitter (rms) in the individual inverters ($\Upsilon_{psn} \approx 2$), as those values depend on $\Delta t_{d,ref}$, obtained with independent PSN sources (with 50% CMN and 50% DMN).

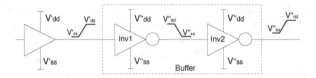

Fig. 2. PSN sources in cascaded buffer repeaters

2.4   Model Evaluation

To evaluate the proposed jitter model we used time domain noise simulation with independent power/ground noise sources, characterized by a PSN correction factor $\Upsilon_{psn} = 0.29$. Table 1 and 2 shows the model error for inverters and buffers with different r_s, r_f, r_{io} and Γ_n ratios. The inverter's jitter predictions have less than 5% error while the buffer's model error is inferior to 10%. Higher accuracy could be obtained if we have used an exact characterization of each inverter's design parameters, instead of the approximate values defined in (3) and (4).

Table 1. Inverter Model Evaluation

Parameters			$(\Delta \hat{t}_{d,inv}/\Delta t_{d,ref})$		
r_s	r_f	r_{io}	sim	model	error
40	2	1.0	1.436	1.441	0.32%
100	4	1.0	2.390	2.374	0.66%
200	6	1.0	3.477	3.387	2.59%
6	4	0.8	2.138	2.156	0.88%
60	3	1.4	2.304	2.250	2.32%
30	2	1.6	1.924	1.877	2.45%

Table 2. Buffer Model Evaluation

Parameters				$(\Delta \hat{t}_{d,buf}/\Delta t_{d,ref})$		
r_s	r_f	r_{io}	Γ_n	sim	model	error
40	16	1.0	4	1.834	1.852	0.99%
80	12	1.0	4	1.609	1.705	5.93%
3	6	1.0	3	1.260	1.313	4.22%
100	6	0.8	2	1.255	1.146	8.68%
160	16	0.6	4	1.604	1.732	7.97%
50	6	1.2	5	1.454	1.560	7.33%

To characterize the PSN sources we evaluated the ratio between the buffer's and the sum of the inverter's output jitter. This ratio is plotted in Fig. 3, for $\Gamma_n = 1$ and $\Gamma_n = 4$, using independent, filtered white gaussian noise sources in power and ground rails. Above each plot we present the mean and standard deviation of the measured values. The ratio is shown to weakly depend on the buffer's design parameters, except for the case when r_{io} is small, which is not a common situation in clock repeaters. The ratio does not depend on r_s, at least for common buffer sizes.

The data presented in Fig. 3 could be obtained for every possible Γ_n and arranged in a lookup table to fully characterize the impact of this particular set of PSN sources. However, this procedure would take intensive simulation to obtain data for every possible combination of design parameters, which is contrary to our goal of obtaining a simple jitter model. Because the ratio is shown to be almost independent of the buffer's design, we can use a simpler model based on

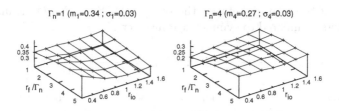

Fig. 3. Ratio between the buffer's and the total inverter's output jitter

a reference value obtained for a buffer with middle range design parameters. For a buffer with $\{\Gamma_n = 3; r_f = 3; r_{io} = 1\}$ we have obtained $\Upsilon_{psn} = 0.29$.

Other noise sources would result in a different Υ_{psn} model. In Fig. 4, we compare the Υ_{psn} factor for independent PSN sources with the factors obtained for dominant CMN and DMN sources. These plots show that Υ_{psn} is almost independent of the buffer's design parameters for independent noise sources because the CMN and DMN variations cancel out. If this is not the case, Υ_{psn} should be modeled as a linear function of the buffer's design parameters, especially if DMN sources are predominant. The predominant noise mode should be inferred from the power supply network design or from previous designs.

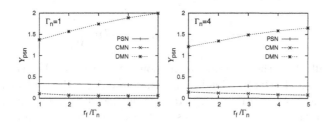

Fig. 4. Buffer's Υ_{psn} for different noise modes and design parameters

3   Applicability to Other Repeaters

3.1   Asymmetrical Inverters

In circuits with single-edge triggered flip-flops, it is possible to design asymmetrical inverters that focus the majority of their drive current on the critical clock edge. These are called single edge clock (SEC) inverters [13]. When used as clock repeaters, SEC inverters are designed to have the same size ($W_p + W_n$) as balanced symmetrical inverters so they can be used as drop-in replacements, although their $\beta = W_p/W_n$ is varied. When strong pull-up (Inv_r) and strong pull-down (Inv_f) SEC inverters are cascaded in a clock distribution network, the critical and the neglected clock edges are distributed through virtually different networks. The critical (neglected) clock edge will see bigger (smaller) transistors than in the case of symmetrical inverters, but with the same capacitive load. In

(6) we present the relation between the size of PMOS and NMOS transistors in SEC inverters, compared to symmetrical inverters.

$$W_{n,sec} = \frac{1+\beta}{1+\beta_{sec}} \cdot W_n \; ; \; W_{p,sec} = \frac{(1+\beta)\beta_{sec}}{(1+\beta_{sec})\beta} \cdot W_p \; . \tag{6}$$

Because each repeater is equivalent to two virtual ones, they must have two associated jitter models: one related to the inverter seen by the critical clock edge (fast inverter) and another for the inverter seen by the neglected edge (slow inverter). The critical clock edge sees a fast inverter because the load is smaller than what would be expected in a symmetrical inverter with that transistor's size. Likewise, the neglected clock edge sees a slow inverter because its load is bigger than expected. As long as equivalent fanouts are defined for these virtual inverters, the data obtained for the reference symmetrical inverter can be used to estimate their output jitter.

By definition, the load capacitance of a SEC inverter is the same as its equivalent symmetrical inverter $C_L = r_f(\beta+1)C_{gn} = C_{L,sec}$, where C_{gn} is the NMOS gate capacitance. On the other hand, the repeater's output transition times $t_{LH,sec}$ and $t_{HL,sec}$ depend on the output load and the transistor's resistance ($R_{p,sec}$ and $R_{n,sec}$). Using the Elmore delay model, the Inv_r transition times can be expressed as shown in (7), where t_{LH} and t_{HL} are the transition times of equivalent inverters with $r_f=1$.

$$t_{LH,sec} = t_{LH} \frac{W_p}{W_{p,sec}} \cdot r_f \; \wedge \; t_{HL,sec} = t_{HL} \frac{W_n}{W_{n,sec}} \cdot r_f \; . \tag{7}$$

The factors affecting the reference transition times can also be seen as factors affecting the virtual inverter's load. Using these relations, the equivalent r_f ratio for the fast and slow inverters in a Inv_r are defined in (8). The same could be done to obtain the equivalent r_f ratios for the virtual inverters in a Inv_f.

$$r_{f,slow} = \frac{W_n}{W_{n,sec}} \cdot r_f \; ; \; r_{f,fast} = \frac{W_p}{W_{p,sec}} \cdot r_f \; . \tag{8}$$

In table 3 we show the model error for the fast and slow virtual inverters in a strong pull-up SEC inverter (Inv_r), for which $\beta_{sec} > \beta_{ref}$. Results show the applicability of the symmetrical inverter model to SEC inverters, with an error below 10% for different combinations in design parameters.

3.2   Tunable Delay Repeaters

Various implementations of TDRs exist in literature, for different purposes and applications. Repeater chains feeding a multiplexer can be used as TDRs but have three significant drawbacks when used in clock distribution networks: 1) jitter accumulation along the chain; 2) high minimum tuning delay; and 3) high power overhead due to continuous switching of the repeaters along the chain. In this field, the most common solution is to digitally control the speed of a typical buffer or inverter. There are three basic techniques to accomplish that:

Table 3. SEC Jitter Model Evaluation   **Table 4.** NANDs Jitter Model Evaluation

Inv_r SEC Inverter					$\Delta\hat{t}_{d,sec}/\Delta t_{d,ref})$
r_s	r_f	r_{io}	β_{sec}/β	Type	error
4	1	1.2	2.00	slow	8.10%
10	4	1.0	1.66	slow	1.07%
12	2	0.8	1.33	slow	0.45%
4	1	1.2	2.00	fast	6.73%
10	4	1.0	1.66	fast	4.32%
12	2	0.8	1.33	fast	2.15%

NAND gate			$\Delta\hat{t}_{d,nand}/\Delta t_{d,ref})$
r_s	r_f	r_{io}	error
10	3	1.0	1.36%
40	3	1.0	0.86%
60	2	1.0	0.33%
100	4	0.8	1.68%
160	4	1.2	2.48%
20	1	1.4	0.51%

the variable resistor inverter (VRI), the current-starved inverter (CSI) and the shunt-capacitor inverter (SCI). The first two can be used to design asymmetric TDRs while the last technique is intrinsically symmetric.

The inverter/buffer jitter model proposed in this paper can be directly applied to TDRs. Asymmetrical VRIs and CSIs behave like SEC inverters, with different rise and fall transition times. In symmetrical VRIs and SCIs, both transitions have the same controlled delay and thus, behave similarly to balanced inverters. Jitter generated in these repeaters depends on their transition time and so, a TDR corresponds to as many virtual inverters as the possible delay increments, each of which has its own jitter model. To reduce the complexity of such approach, the model can be applied only to the virtual inverter with the higher introduced delay (worst case jitter), the lower introduced delay (worst case current consumption), or a combination of both.

3.3 NAND Gates

NAND gates are commonly used as clock gating repeaters, available with symmetrical transition times and variable drive strengths. It is known that a two-input NAND gate with the same driving strength of a CMOS inverter has a higher input capacitance and self load factor. So, we can not use the reference inverter's data to estimate jitter on NAND gate repeaters. However, the model proposed in (1) and (2) can still be applied as long as a reference NAND gate is characterized. Simulation results with a reference NAND gate with the same driving strength as the reference inverter are shown in Table 4. The model shows an error inferior to 5% for different NAND designs.

4   Auto-induced Jitter

Although PSN is usually considered an external noise source, the switching activity of large clock repeaters can itself generate sharp potential drops/surges. To reduce the on-chip PSN generation, there are some techniques which apply to clock repeaters. It is possible to reduce the repeater's peak current reducing its

Table 5. Current Model Correction Factors

	$\hat{I}_p$	$\hat{D}_p$	$\hat{P}_p$
$\Upsilon(r_s)$	$r_s/\sqrt{r_{to,s}}$	$\sqrt{r_{to,s}}$	$\sqrt{r_{to,s}}$
$\Upsilon(r_f)$	$r_{Ip,f}$	$r_{Dp,f}$	$r_{Pp,f}$
$\Upsilon(r_{io})$	$1/r_{to,io}$	$r_{to,io}$	r_{io}

drive strength or increasing the turn-on time, at the cost of increased delay and noise sensitivity. Low swing drive circuits have been proposed to reduce power consumption and noise generation but other considerations such as complexity, reliability and performance have limited their popularity. By delaying the transitions in some buffers, using intentional skews, clock modulation or multiphase clock distribution, the current consumption is more evenly distributed in time, giving lower PSN generation. Because these techniques can effectively reduce PSN generation and limit self-induced jitter in clock repeaters, the current consumption waveform should be considered part of their jitter characterization.

Several current consumption models have been proposed in literature. However, for the purpose of identifying current-hungry clock repeaters during CTS, high accuracy in waveform prediction is not essential. We propose a simple scalable model based in [14], but with lower data storage requirements. Our approach is based on the symmetrical triangular approximation for the inverter's current waveform, which can be characterized by its peak current (I_p), duration (D_p) and position (P_p). The current model depends these three values, obtained for the reference inverter, to which are applied size, fanout and input transition time correction factors (9).

$$\{\hat{I}_p; \hat{D}_p; \hat{P}_p\} = \{I_p; D_p; P_p\}_{ref} \cdot \prod_j \Upsilon(r_j) \ , \quad j \in \{s, f, io\}. \tag{9}$$

The correction factors are shown in Table 5. There are two output transition time ratios ($r_{to,s}$ and $r_{to,io}$) and three current ratios ($r_{Ip,f}$, $r_{Dp,f}$ and $r_{Pp,f}$). The transition time ratios are the same as the ones used in the jitter model, while the current ratios ($r_{kp,f} = k_{p,r_f}/k_{p,ref}$, with $k \in \{I, D, P\}$) must be obtained during the characterization phase, with $r_{io} = r_s = 1$. Simulations have shown this model to have an accuracy within 10%, which is considered to be sufficient for this purpose.

5   Conclusion

In this paper we proposed a simple model for PSN induced jitter in the most common clock repeaters. It is based on the timing and current waveform characterization of a reference repeater. The model is scalable, technology independent, and can account for process variability if the inverter is characterized in different process corners. For clock buffers, the model requires an additional characterization of the expected PSN in both ground and power rails. Results have shown that it has an accuracy within 10% for inverter and NAND based repeaters, which fulfills our goal to develop a simple yet efficient tool to introduce jitter awareness in CTS tools, with minimal changes and complexity increase.

References

1. Friedman, E.G.: Clock distribution networks in synchronous digital integrated circuits. Proceedings of the IEEE 89(5), 665–692 (2001)
2. Tsai, J.-L., et al.: Zero skew clock-tree optimization with buffer insertion/sizing and wire sizing. IEEE Trans. Computer-Aided Design of Integrated Circuits and Systems 23(4), 565–572 (2004)
3. Chakraborty, A., et al.: Dynamic Thermal Clock Skew Compensation Using Tunable Delay Buffers. IEEE Trans. on VLSI Systems 16, 639–649 (2008)
4. Hashimoto, M., et al.: Statistical analysis of clock skew variation in H-tree structure. In: 6th Int. Symp. Qual. Elect. Design, March 2005, pp. 402–407 (2005)
5. Wason, V., et al.: An Efficient Uncertainty- and Skew-aware Methodology for Clock Tree Synthesis and Analysis. In: Int. Conf. on VLSI Design, January 2007, pp. 271–277 (2007)
6. Jang, J., et al.: Period Jitter Estimation in Global Clock Trees. In: 12th IEEE Workshop on Signal Propagation on Interconnects, May 12-15, pp. 1–4 (2008)
7. Chen, L.H., et al.: Buffer delay change in the presence of power and ground noise. IEEE Trans. on VLSI Systems 11(3), 461–473 (2003)
8. Samanta, R., et al.: Clock Buffer Polarity Assignment for Power Noise Reduction. In: IEEE/ACM Int. Conf. on Computer-Aided Design, November 5-9, pp. 558–562 (2006)
9. Badaroglu, M., et al.: Digital ground bounce reduction by supply current shaping and clock frequency modulation. IEEE Trans. Computer-Aided Design of Integrated Circuits and Systems 24(1), 65–76 (2005)
10. O'Brien, P.R., Savarino, T.L.: Modeling the driving-point characteristic of resistive interconnect for accurate delay estimation. In: IEEE Int. Conf. on Computer-Aided Design - ICCAD 1989, November 1989, pp. 512–515 (1989)
11. Hajimiri, S.L.A., Lee, T.H.: Jitter and phase noise in ring oscillators. IEEE JSSC 34, 790–804 (1999)
12. Tawfik, S.A., Kursun, V.: Buffer Insertion and Sizing in Clock Distribution Networks with Gradual Transition Time Relaxation for Reduced Power Consumption. In: IEEE Int. Conf. on Electronics, Circuits and Systems, December 2007, pp. 845–848 (2007)
13. Mueller, J., Saleh, R.: Single Edge Clock Distribution for Improved Latency, Skew, and Jitter Performance. In: 21st Int. Conf. VLSI Design, January 4-8, pp. 214–219 (2008)
14. Osorio, J.F., et al.: Extraction of Circuit Elements for Macromodel-Based Estimation of Substrate Noise. In: XX Conf. Design Circ. Integrated Syst., pp. 1–6 (2005)

A Hardware Implementation of the User-Centric Display Energy Management

Vasily G. Moshnyaga, Koji Hashimoto, Tadashi Suetsugu, and Shuhei Higashi

Dept. of Electronics Engineering and Computer Science, Fukuoka University
8-19-1 Nanakuma, Jonan-ku, Fukuoka 814-0180, Japan
vasily@fukuoka-u.ac.jp

Abstract. This paper introduces a hardware system for user-centric display energy management. From the camera readings, the system detects the user presence and gaze and produces signals that control the display backlight. Experiments show that the system operates in real-time, has 88% detection accuracy and consumes less than 1W of power.

1 Introduction

In a typical personal computer, display accounts for 1/3 of the total power [1-2]. To reduce energy consumption, OS-based Advanced Configuration and Power Interface (ACPI)[3] sets display to low-power modes after specified periods of inactivity on mouse and/or keyboard. The efficiency of ACPI strongly depends on inactivity intervals, set by the user. From one hand, if the inactivity intervals are improperly short, e.g. 1 or 2 minutes, the ACPI can be quite troublesome by shutting the display off when it must be on. From another hand, if the inactivity intervals are set to be long, the ACPI's efficiency decreases. Because modifying the intervals requires system setting, a half of the world's PC users never adjust the power management of their PCs for fear that it will impede performance [4]. Those who do the adjustment, usually assign long intervals. HP inspected 183,000 monitors worldwide and found that almost a third was not set to take advantage of the energy saving features. However, enabling these features just after 20 minutes of inactivity can save up to 381 kWh for a monitor per year [5]. Evidently, to prevent such a problem the power management must employ more efficient user presence identification.

Several techniques have been proposed to improve user presence detection. Extending touch-pad function beyond pointer movement to provide user-presence identification is proposed in [6,7]. Work [8] suggests using thermal sensors placed around display screen to detect user's presence by comparing temperature fluctuation the sensors during a sample interval. When user is present, the temperature fluctuation is consistent with a normal fluctuation pattern of human breathing.

An alternative is to detect user presence from readings of video camera, placed at the display is advocated [9]. In contrast to the other techniques, which improve computer "sensing", this technique enables computer to "watch" the user through the camera. The images produced by the camera are analyzed and if

J. Monteiro and R. van Leuken (Eds.): PATMOS 2009, LNCS 5953, pp. 56–65, 2010.

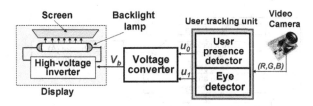

Fig. 1. System overview

the user's presence is not detected, the display is turned off to save energy. Otherwise, it tracks the user's gaze, keeping the display bright only if he or she looks at the screen. When the user detracts his or her attention from the screen, the method dims the display down or even switches it off to save energy. The technique allows fast adjustment of display power to varying requirements of the user. However, its efficiency strongly depends on energy overhead of user monitoring. As [9] shows, the software implementation has large power overhead (over 5W), which shrinks the efficiency of the method.

In this paper we present a new hardware implementation of the user-based display energy management, which works in real time, has by 5 times less power overhead than software, and adjusts the display brightness and power to user's behavior.

The paper is organized as follows. Section 2 describes related research. Section 3 presents the design and discusses its implementation features. Section 4 reports on experimental evaluation. Section 5 summarizes our findings and outlines work for the future.

2 The Display Energy Management System

2.1 An Overview

The proposed system is based on the following assumptions:

1. The display is equipped with a color video camera, which is located at the top of display. When the user looks at display it faces the camera frontally.
2. The display has a number of backlight intensity levels with the highest level corresponding to the largest power consumption and the lowest level to the smallest power, respectively. The highest level of backlight intensity is enabled either initially or whenever the user looks at the screen.

Fig.1 shows the block-diagram of the proposed hardware system. The user tracking unit receives an RGB color image and outputs two logic signals, $u1, u0$. If the user is detected in the image, the signal $u0$ is set to 1; otherwise it is 0. The zero value of $u0$ enforces the voltage converter to shrink the backlight supply voltage to 0 Volts, dimming the display off. If the detector determines that the user looks at screen, it sets $u1=1$. When both $u0$ and $u1$ are 1, the display operates as usual. If the user's gaze has been off the screen for more than N consecutive frames, $u1$ becomes 0. If $u0 = 1$ and $u1 = 0$, the input voltage (Vb) of the high-voltage

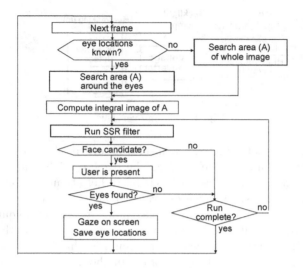

Fig. 2. Flowchart of the eye-tracking algorithm

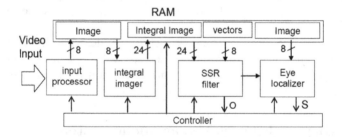

Fig. 3. Block-diagram of the eye gaze detector

inverter is decreased by ΔV. This voltage drop lowers backlight luminance and so shrinks the power consumption of the display. Any on-screen gaze in this low power mode reactivates the initial backlight luminance and moves the display onto normal mode. However, if no on-screen gaze has been detected for N consecutive frames and the backlight luminance has already reached the lowest level, the display is turned off. Returning back from the OFF mode requires pushing the ON button.

2.2   Eye-Gaze Detector

The eye-gaze detector implements the algorithm [10], which unlike other methods, tracks the between-the-eyes (BTE) point not eyes. The BTE point does not depend on illumination, face occlusion, eye closure and hence is more stable and robust. To reduce complexity, we modify the algorithm assuming that:

1. The target object is a single PC user. The user sits in front of PC at a relatively close distance (50-70cm).

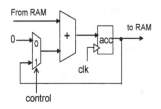

Fig. 4. Integral image unit

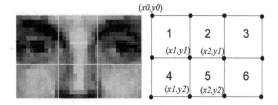

Fig. 5. Illustration of the SSR filter

2. The user's motion is slow relatively to the frame rate.
3. The background is stable and constant.

Based on the assumptions, the search for a BTE candidate is limited to a single SSR filter scan with fixed SSR filter size and 3 pixel displacement of the SSR filter during the scan. As our study shows [11], such enhancements reduce computational complexity considerably without affecting the quality of the results. Fig.2 shows the modified algorithm. For the first frame or any frame, in which the BTE point is unknown, we search the whole image to locate human eyes; otherwise only a small area (A) of ±8 pixels around the BTE point. For the chosen area, the algorithm first computes the integral image and then scans it by the Six Segment Region filter (SSR) to select the BTE candidate. If the BTE point is found, the user is considered present in front of the display. In this case, the system uses the BTE as a starting point to locate eyes. If eyes have been detected, the user is assumed to be looking at screen; else it is not. If no face candidate has been found for N consecutive frames, the user is considered not present in front of the display.

Fig.3 depicts the block-diagram of the eye-gaze detector. The input processing module implements hardware interface with video camera. It inputs from camera the (R,G,B) color image, filters the random noise and saves the green component of the image in RAM. The integral imager reads from the RAM the green component of the derived search area (A) and transforms it into the integral image representation $I(x, y)$ as follows:

$$S(x, y) = S(x, y - 1) + i(x, y) \tag{1}$$
$$I(x, y) = I(x - 1, y) + S(x, y), \tag{2}$$

where $S(x, y)$ is the cumulative row sum, $S(x, -1) = 0$, $I(-1, y) = 0$.

The integral image computation circuit includes one adder and one register-accumulator, as shown in Fig.4. To obtain the integral representation of an image, it performs two image scans: the first one reads pixels in the row-first fashion, computes the cumulative sums $S(x, y)$ and writes them into the RAM; the second scan reads $S(x, y)$ from the RAM in the column-first fashion, computes $I(x, y)$ and writes them back to the RAM. The integral image representation of $I(x, y)$ of a pixel (x, y) is 24 bit long. The SSR filter scans the integral image (pixel by pixel) by a six-segment rectangle filter (Fig.5), computing the sums of

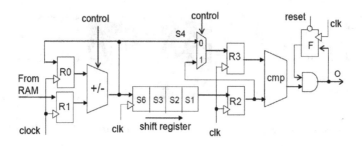

Fig. 6. Block-diagram of the SSR filtering module

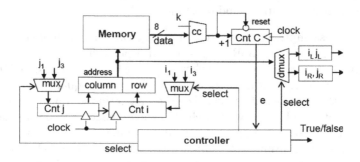

Fig. 7. The structure of eyes localization unit

pixel values in each segment. For example, the sum of pixels within segment 5 is defined as: $Sum(5) = I(x2, y2) + I(x1, y1) - I(x2, y1) - I(x1, y2)$. It requires only one addition, two subtractions and 4 lookups to compute the sum of one SSR segment; or 12 lookups, 18 add/subtract operations for all filter segments, respectively. At each location, the SSR filter compares the integral sums of the segments as follows:

$$Sum(1) < Sum(2) and Sum(1) < Sum(4) \tag{3}$$

$$Sum(3) < Sum(2) and Sum(3) < Sum(6) \tag{4}$$

If the above criteria (3)(4) are satisfied, the center location of the region 2 of the SSR is considered to be a candidate for Between-The-Eyes point.

Fig.6 shows the data-path of the SSR filter. In this figure, $S1 - S6$ are the integral sums of the corresponding SSR segments; $+/-$ is the adder-subtracter; cmp is comparator; $R0, R2$ are registers; F is flip-flop. The frequency of signal clk is one forth of that of signal clock. Therefore the left adder-subtracter feds the shift register with a sum of corresponding SSR segment every forth clock cycle. With each new clk, the shift register is shifted one step to the right. Thus, when the $S1$ reaches the output, the adder-subtracter generates $S4$. The comparison of these two signals sets the flip-flop F such that if inequalities (3)(4) are satisfied, the output $O=1$; else $O=0$. Initially F is set to 1. Each $O=1$ indicates detection of the user face.

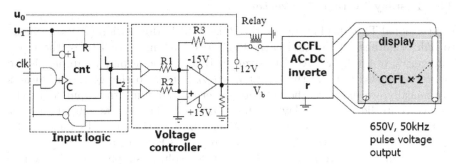

Fig. 8. The modified voltage converter

As the BTE point is found, the controller activates the eye localizer to scan rectangular regions 1 and 3 of the SSR (see Fig.5), respectively, and extract local minimum (i.e. dark) points for left and right eye candidates. Fig.6 shows the supporting architecture. To avoid effects of eyebrows, hair and beard, we ignore 2 pixels at the boarder of the areas. Also, because the eyebrows have almost the same grey level as the eyes, the search starts from the lowest positions of regions 1 and 3. Let coordinates of these positions be $(i1, j1)$ and $(i3, j3)$. At each clock cycle, the counters (cnt_j and cnt_i) generate new address and fed it to memory to read a corresponding pixel of the green plane of the original image. If the pixel data exceeds a predefined threshold k, the comparator (cc) produces 0; else 1. Any non-zero signal increments the counter, while any zero on the input resets the counter to 0. If the number of ones produced in a sequence overcomes the counting range, the counter (cnt_C) overflows, thus signaling the controller that an eye-like point is found. Otherwise the search is continued until all the pixels in the region 1 are scanned. Then the search is repeated for region 3. When found, the eye locations are represented by coordinates (i_L, j_L) and (i_R, j_R) and the signal true/false that points out whether the search was successful or not. As in [12] we assume that eyes are found if the distance between the located eyes (D_E) and the angle (A_E) at the BTE point (the center point of the area 2) satisfy the following relations: $30 < D_E < 42$ and $115° < A_E < 180°$.

If both eyes are detected, the user gaze is considered to be on screen. Otherwise, it is assumed to be off the screen. If the BTE point had not been found for more than N consecutive frames, the user is assumed to be not present in front of the camera. In this case, the system produces the signal $u0 = 0$. Otherwise, $u0 = 1$. If the BTB point has been found, but the user's gaze has been off the screen for more than N consecutive frames, $u1$ is set to 0. Else $u1$ is 1.

Finally, once we have located the positions of eyes on the first frame, we use this knowledge to reduce complexity of processing the successive frames. Since the face/eye motion of computer user is slow in practical circumstances, we limit the search in the next frame to a small region of interest, which spans by 8 pixels in vertical and horizontal direction around the BTE point of the current frame.

2.3   Display Voltage Converter

Conventional TFT displays utilize the Pulse Width Modulation (PWM) scheme to link brightness of the cold cathode fluorescent lamps (CCFL) to the input voltage, V_b, of the CCFL AC-DC inverter. Usually, the display brightness is the highest when $V_b = 0$ and the lowest when $V_b = 5V$. To change the brightness dynamically, we modified the voltage converter by adding the input logic, the voltage controller, and a relay, as shown in Fig.8. The inputs $(u0, u1)$ are set by the eye-gaze detector (see fig.2). When $u0 = 0$, the relay disconnects the 12V power supply to the display switching it OFF. Turning the display ON automatically sets $u0$ to 1, which enforces +12V voltage supply to display. When $u0=1$, the display power consumption is controlled by the output (V_b) of the voltage controller. Namely, when $u1=1$, the counter (cnt) nulls outputs L0,L1 setting V_b to 0V. When $u1=0$, the counter increments its state with each new rise of signal clk, thus setting the voltage converter to increment its output Vb by approximately 0.7V.

3   Implementation and Evaluation

We implemented the system in hardware and measured its efficiency on a number of tests. The gaze detector was synthesized in Verilog HDL using Synopsis Design Tools and realized on a single FPGA (Xilinx XC3S250E) board. The design runs at 48MHz frequency using 3.3V external voltage and provides user presence detection at 20fps rate. Due to capacity limitations of the on-chip SRAM memory, input images were 160x120 pixels in size. The SSR filter was 30x20 pixels in size. The total power consumption of the gaze detector design was 150mW, which is 35 times less than software implementation of the user presence detector on desktop PC (Pentium4@2.53GHz)[9]. Table 1 summarizes parameters of the FPGA design. The voltage converter has been implemented on discrete elements. The Logitec CCD Quick CAM PRO4000 was used as a camera.

To evaluate accuracy of the gaze detector, we ran four different tests each of each conducted by different users. The users were free to look at the camera/display, read from the materials on the table, type text, wear eyeglasses,

Table 1. FPGA design parameters

Parameter	Value
clock frequency	48MHz
External voltage	3.0V
Internal voltage	1.2V
System gate count	250000
Logic cell count	18508
Memory size	216Kb
Frame size (pixels)	160x120
Detection rate	20fps
Power	150mW

Table 2. Evaluation results

Test	Frames	True	False	Acc.(%)
1	151	133	18	88
2	240	214	26	89
3	100	90	10	90
4	180	152	28	84
Av.	167	147	20	88

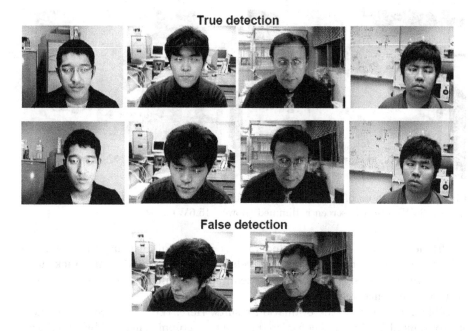

Fig. 9. Eye detection examples

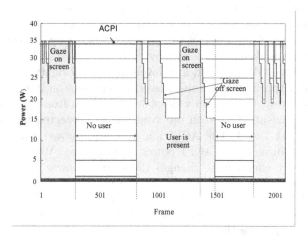

Fig. 10. Power consumption profile of the tested display

move gesticulate or even leave the PC whenever wanted. Fig.9 illustrates examples of the detection results. The + marks depict positions where the system assumes the eyes to be. As we see, even though the lighting conditions of faces vary, the results are correct. Ordinary pairs of glasses (see Fig.9) have no bad effect on the performance for frontal faces. In some face orientations, however,

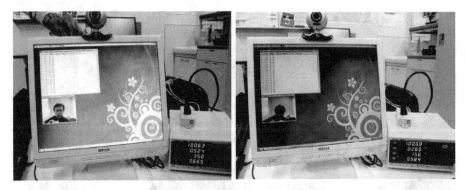

Fig. 11. Screenshots of display: when the user looks at screen, the screen is bright (power: 35W); else the screen is dimmed (power: 15.6W)

the frame of pair of glasses can hide a part of eye ball, causing the system to loose the eye. Or sometimes it takes eyebrow or hair as an eye and tracks it in the following frames. Fig.9 (bottom) exemplifies two image frames in which eye positions were incorrectly found.

Table 2 summarizes the evaluation results. Here, the second column depicts the total number of frames considered in the test; columns marked by eTruef and eFalsef reflect the number of true and false detections, respectively; the column *Acc.* shows the ratio of true decisions to the total number of all decisions made; *Av..* shows average over all tests. As we observe, the eye detection and tracking accuracy of proposed hardware is quite high (88% on average).

Next, we estimated efficiency of the proposed system by measuring the total power consumption taken from the wall by the system itself and the 17"IO-DATA TFT LCD display (35W on peak, four levels of screen brightness) controlled by the system. Fig.10 profiles the results measured per frame on 100sec (2000frames) long test. In the test, the system was set to step down from the current power level if the eye-gaze off the screen was continuously detected for more than 15 frames (i.e. almost 1 sec). The ACPI line shows the power consumption level ensured by the conventional ACPI power management. We observe that our technology is very effective. It changes the display power accordingly to the user behavior dimming the display when the user gaze is off the screen and illuminating the screen (by elevated power) when the user looks on it. Changing the brightness from one power level to another in our system takes only 20ms, which is unobservable for the user.

Fig.11 shows the brightness of the screenshots and the corresponding power consumption level (see values displayed in the down-right corner of the pictures; the second row from the bottom shows the power). The total power overhead of the system is 960mW. Even though the system takes a little more power than ACPI (see horizontal line in Fig.10) in active mode on this short test, it saves 36% of the total energy consumed by the display. In environments when users frequently detract their attention from the screen or leave computers unattended (e.g. school, university, office) the energy savings could be significant.

4   Summary

In this paper we presented a prototype hardware design for improving display power management through user monitoring. Experiments showed that the hardware is capable of monitoring PC user in real-time with 88% accuracy while consuming only 1W of power. However, this power figures can be reduced even further should custom design of both chip and board performed. We are currently working on custom hardware design.

Acknowledgement

The work was sponsored by The Ministry of Education, Culture, Sports, Science and Technology of Japan under the Knowledge Cluster Initiative (The Second Stage) Program and Grant-in-Aid for Scientific Research (C) No.21500063. The authors are thankful for the support.

References

1. Robertson, J., Homan, G.K., Mahajan, A., et al.: Energy use and power levels in new monitors and personal computers. LBNL-48581, UC Berkeley (July 2002)
2. Mahesri, A., Vardhan, V.: Power Consumption Breakdown on a Modern Laptop. In: Falsafi, B., VijayKumar, T.N. (eds.) PACS 2004. LNCS, vol. 3471, pp. 165–180. Springer, Heidelberg (2005)
3. Advanced Configuration and Power Interface Specification, Rev.3.0 (September 2004), http://www.acpi.info/spec.htm
4. Energy savings with personal computers, Fujitsu-Siemens Corp., http://www.fujitsu-siemens.nl/aboutus/sor/energysaving/profdesk_prod.html
5. 2006 Global Citizenship Report, Hewlett-Packard Co., http://www.hp.com/hpinfo/globalcitizenship/gcreport/pdf/hp2006gcreport_lowres.pdf
6. Method for laptop mouse pad user-presence detection, http://priorartdatabase.com/IPCOM/000009803/
7. Park, W.I.: Power saving in a portable computer, EU Patern, EP0949557 (1999)
8. Dai, X., Ravichandran, K.: Computer screen power management through detection of user presence, US Patent 6650322, November 18 (2003)
9. Moshnyaga, V.G., Morikawa, E.: LCD Display Energy Reduction by User Monitoring. In: Proc. Int. Conf. on Computer Design (ICCD), pp. 4–97 (2005)
10. Kawato, S., Tetsutani, N., Osaka, K.: Scale-adaptive face detection and tracking in real time with SSR filters and support vector machine. IEICE Trans.Information & Systems E88-D(12), 2857–2863 (2005)
11. Moshnyaga, V.G., Yamamoto, S.: Algorithm Optimizations for Low-Complexity Eye-Tracking. In: Proc. IEEE Int.Conf. of Systems, Man & Cybernetics (2009)
12. Kawato, S., Ohya, J.: Two-step approach for real-time eye-tracking with a new filtering technique. In: IEEE Int. Conf. of Systems, Man & Cybernetics, pp. 1366–1371 (2000)

On-chip Thermal Modeling Based on SPICE Simulation

Wei Liu[1], Andrea Calimera[2], Alberto Nannarelli[1],
Enrico Macii[2], and Massimo Poncino[2]

[1] Technical University of Denmark, Denmark
[2] Politecnico di Torino, Italy

Abstract. With technology scaled to deep submicron regime, temperature and temperature gradient have emerged as important design criteria. Elevated temperatures, spatial and temporal temperature variations
and on-chip hotspot not only affect timing in both transistors and interconnects but also degrade circuit reliability. A SPICE simulation based
thermal modeling method is proposed in this paper. Experiments on a
set of tests show the correlations between functional and spatial hotspots
in a circuit implemented in STM 65nm technologies.

1 Introduction

Growing temperature can have dramatic impacts on circuit behavior. MOS current drive capability decreases approximately 4% for every $10\,^{\circ}\mathrm{C}$ temperature
increase, and interconnect delay increases approximately 5% for every $10\,^{\circ}\mathrm{C}$
increase. Thus, temperature variations across the die can result in significant
timing uncertainties, requiring larger timing margins and lowering circuit performance. Elevated temperatures are also a major contributor to increased leakage
and reduced reliability due to effects such as electromigration [1]. Therefore, accurate yet fast on-chip temperature analysis is very important in deep submicron
VLSI design.

Solutions to reduce temperature can be either done at run time or at design
time. Many thermal management methods have been proposed to reduce power
consumption at runtime, basically to slow down or shut down some of the units
on the chip. At design time, redundancy can be for instance used to reduce
heating. If duplicate units are available we can also schedule the task on some
or all of these units and run them at a lower speed so that no single unit will
get too hot. The most classical design-time solution is however that of playing
with the placement of the different units of a design.

Full-chip thermal analysis can be performed at a coarse-grained level where
quantum-mechanical effects at small length scales can be ignored. Fourier's law
describes heat conduction which is in partial differential equations(PDE) form.
To solve the PDE numerically, one of several frameworks for PDE solution can
be employed. The work in [2][3] use the finite difference method while authors in
[4][5] proposed thermal modeling algorithms using finite element methods. An

J. Monteiro and R. van Leuken (Eds.): PATMOS 2009, LNCS 5953, pp. 66–75, 2010.

alternative to the FEM and FDM methods is a boundary element method using Green functions [6][7]. This method is particularly appropriate for coarse level modeling where the total number of heat sources is small. An improved method in [8] reduces the complexity in Green function based methods by recognizing the bottleneck corresponds to a convolution operation.

Many proposed thermal modeling algorithms target a coarse-grain model of a design, in which elements are typically large blocks (e.g., cores or caches); in some cases complex blocks like cores are broken down in smaller sub-blocks (e.g., control unit, register file, branch prediction unit, etc.) for a finer control of hotspots. Therefore, the number of sources is usually small (typically in the order of tens).

The issue of the granularity of the thermal modeling is a very debated one. For instance, the issue of thermal gradients in standard-cell designs, where the layout structure is quite regular, and the variance in the elements dimension is relatively small, has been somehow disregarded in the literature. Nevertheless, some works on thermal-aware standard-cell placement ([9],[10]) reported non-negligible gradients. In this paper, we analyze this problem by explicitly targeting the thermal analysis of standard-cell designs. More specifically, we propose a temperature estimation method based on SPICE simulation that uses the well-known equivalence between thermal and electrical networks. A SPICE netlist is constructed after all standard cells are placed and power consumption in these cells are estimated. Nodal voltages after simulation are temperatures at these points.

The main contribution of this work is trying to establish a correlation between *functional* hotspots (i.e., units or portions of a design which are intensively used) and *spatial* hotspots (i.e., the cells implementing that units and their placement on the die). The limited degrees of freedom offered by row-based, traditional standard-cell placement should give important insights on whether we should consider a standard-cell design as an iso-thermal component or not.

Our experiments are done on cicuit benchmarks implemented in STM 65nm libraries and power values are estimated based on annotated switching activities. The results show that for standard cell based design the actual maximum temperature and temperature gradient are much smaller than the values reported in other papers [9][10] where the authors performed thermal analysis on generic cell libraries and assigned randomly generated power values to the cells. On the other hand, results also show that temperature distributions are strongly dependent on functional and spatial hotspots.

The remainder of this paper is organized as follows. In Section 2, we overview heat transfer theories and thermal analysis methods. In Section 3, the SPICE model used to solve the heat equation is described and the impact of heating in interconnect on temperature distribution in the substrate is analyzed. In Section 4, we illustrate the experiment method based on STM 65nm standard cell libraries. Section 5 presents the experimental results and analysis. We draw conclusions in Section 6.

2   Overview of Thermal Analysis Methods

Heat transfer inside the chip is mainly through conduction. The rate of heat conduction is described by Fourier's law as,

$$q = -k_t \nabla T \tag{1}$$

which states that the heat flux, q (in W/m^2), is proportional to the negative gradient of the temperature, T (in K), with the constant of proportionality corresponding to the thermal conductivity of the material, k_t (in $W/(mK)$).

The divergence of q is the difference between the power generated and the time rate of change of heat as described in Equation(2),

$$\nabla \cdot q = -k_t \nabla \cdot \nabla T = -k_t \nabla^2 T = g(\mathbf{r},t) - \rho c_p \frac{\partial T(\mathbf{r},t)}{\partial t} \tag{2}$$

where $\mathbf{r}$ is the spatial coordinate of the point at which the temperature is being determined, g is the power density of the heat source (in W/m^3), c_p is the heat capacity of the material (in $J/(kgK)$) and ρ is the density of the material (in kg/m^3). Equation2 is subject to the boundary condition,

$$k_t \frac{\partial T(\mathbf{r},t)}{\partial n} = h_c(T_a - T_{\mathbf{r},t}) \tag{3}$$

which states that the heat generated inside the chip equals the heat dissipated to the ambient. At steady state, all derivatives with respect to time become zero. Therefore, steady-state analysis corresponds to solving the Poisson's equation,

$$\nabla^2 T(\mathbf{r}) = -\frac{g(\mathbf{r})}{k_t} \tag{4}$$

This equation can be approximated using Finite Difference Method as a difference equation by space discretization. Let Δx, Δy and Δz denote the lengths of the rectangles after discretization along the x, y and z axis and $T_{i,j,k}$ denote the steady state temperature at point ($i\Delta x$,$j\Delta y$ and $k\Delta z$). Then, along the x direction, we can write

$$\frac{\partial^2 T(\mathbf{r})}{\partial^2 x} \approx \frac{\frac{T_{i-1,j,k}-T_{i,j,k}}{\Delta x} - \frac{T_{i,j,k}-T_{i+1,j,k}}{\Delta x}}{\Delta x} \tag{5}$$

The thermal resistance in each discretization rectangle along the x direction is $R_{i-1,j,k} = \frac{\Delta x}{k_t A_x \Delta x}$ where $A_x = \Delta y \Delta z$ is the cross sectional area. Thus the Poisson's equation using finite difference discretization results in the following linear equation,

$$\left[\frac{T_{i-1,j,k}-T_{i,j,k}}{R_{i-1,j,k}} + \frac{T_{i+1,j,k}-T_{i,j,k}}{R_{i,j,k}} \right] +$$
$$\left[\frac{T_{i,j-1,k}-T_{i,j,k}}{R_{i,j-1,k}} + \frac{T_{i,j+1,k}-T_{i,j,k}}{R_{i,j,k}} \right] +$$
$$\left[\frac{T_{i,j,k-1}-T_{i,j,k}}{R_{i,j,k-1}} + \frac{T_{i,j,k+1}-T_{i,j,k}}{R_{i,j,k}} \right] = -G_{i,j,k} \tag{6}$$

where $G_{i,j,k} = g_{i,j,k}\Delta V$ is the total power generated within each discretization rectangle.

3   SPICE Model and Interconnect Effect

As can be seen, Equation(6) is equivalent to Kirchhoff's Current Law describing nodal voltage in circuit analysis. Therefore, by constructing a netlist of all discretization rectangles we can solve the thermal modeling problem through SPICE simulation. The substrate can be modeled as an RC equivalent circuit, the heat source can be modeled as current source, the boundary condition with constant temperature can be modeled as voltage source and the nodal temperature can be modeled as nodal voltage in the RC equivalent circuit. Fig.1 shows the RC equivalent model and the geometrical structure for one cell. The circuit is meshed into these thermal cells. Cells inside the circuit are connected to each other while cells on the boundary are connected to voltage sources which model the ambient temperature. The time constant of on-chip heat conduction is in milliseconds, which is much larger than the clock periods in nanoseconds. This means that transient currents with short time constants do not have significant effects on the temperature profile. Thus to obtain the steady state temperature profile, the average power consumption can be used. Consequently, the capacitor in the cell model in Fig.1 can be removed and the SPICE netlist becomes a netlist of resistors, current sources and voltage sources.

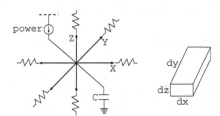

Fig. 1. Thermal cell equivalent model

The interconnect could potentially redistribute heat in the substrate layer due to the fact that metals are better in conducting heat than silicon. Table 1 compares the ability of heat conducting between a single wire in layer Metal Three(M3), typically used for interconnection between standard cells, and a piece of silicon of the same length. Copper is used in the metal layers and is sized twice wider than the minimum width.

Table 1. Comparison of heat conducting between interconnect and silicon

	Ratio(Si/Cu)
Length(um)	1
Width(um)	13
Thickness(um)	1.5
Thermal Conductivity(W/mK)	0.3
Thermal Resistance(K/W)	1/6.5

Table 1 shows that although copper is more than 3 times better in thermal conductivity than silicon, the resistance is actually much larger due to its small cross sectional area. In reality, the ratio of thermal resistance would be smaller than 1/6.5 because the effective resistance in silicon will be smaller since there are multiple paths between the two end points through adjacent cells. And most metal signal wires are sized using the minimum width, which is only half of the value used in the above comparison. Therefore, if a cool region gets 10 K rise in temperature due to heat diffusion from a hot region, the heat diffusion through interconnect only contributes less than 1 K. In other words, the substrate layer is the dominating layer of heat diffusion.

To verify the above analysis with our model, we created a grid of cells in a square shape where cells in the center have a high power consumption and all the other cells have zero power consumption. The temperature rise in the other cells is thus solely due to heat diffusion from the hot cell through the substrate. Then we create a resistor to model wires in M3 connecting the hot cell (die center) and a cool cell in the periphery. The width of the wire is twice the minimum and the length of the wire is the distance from the the center of the hot cell to the center of the cool cell (the length of ten thermal cells in our experiment). This time the temperature rise includes contributions from heat diffusion through the interconnect. Simulation results are shown in Table 2. $\triangle T$ is the temperature increase due to heat diffusion through interconnect.

Table 2. Temperature rise in the cool cell

	$T_{rise}(K)$	$\triangle T(K)$
substrate only	14.37	
substrate and 1 wire	14.63	0.26
substrate and 10 wires	16.32	1.95

The temperature rise is 23.3 K in the hot cell and 14.37 K in the cool cell when there are no wires connecting the two cells. When the metal wire is added, the temperature in the cool cell increased by another 0.26 K per wire reaching 14.63 K. For ten wires the interconnect contribution is 1.95 K, corresponding to about 12% of the total temperature rise.

However, the temperature increase due to wire is smaller than the value expected from the analysis based on Table 1 (approx 1 K) because the heat can be diffused in the substrate layer to the cool cell not only through cells in a straight line source-sink, but also through the cells in adjacent rows. Therefore, the effective resistance in the substrate layer becomes smaller than the value used in the analysis in Table 1.

In conclusion, if the wire density between thermal cells in different regions is not high, as in most cases, we can reasonably assume that the heat is mainly redistributed in the substrate layer, and the contribution of the interconnects is marginal.

4   Experimental Methods

As described in the previous two sections, the circuit is discretized into small rectangles modeled as thermal cells. Since the positions of standard cells may not align exactly with thermal cells, we group several standard cells into one thermal cell. Thus, the power value in a thermal cell is the sum of power consumptions in all the standard cells that it covers.

The temperature profile inside a chip is largely dependent on packaging. For the same total power, it is possible to have different peak temperature and temperature gradient by using cooling mechanisms with different heat removing capabilities. In our experiment, we simplified the modeling of packaging and focused on the substrate layer. The z direction is discretized into 3 layers and on each layer x and y directions are both discretized into 40 units which results in a grid of 1600 cells. For designs no larger than 16,000 standard cells which is typical in the circuits we used in the experimentation, this means a thermal cell covers no more than 10 standard cells. Table 3 shows the thermal properties of different layers.

Table 3. Thermal properties in different layers

Thickness(mm)	$R_{top}(10^3 K/W)$	$R_{sub}(10^3 K/W)$	$R_{bottom}(10^3 K/W)$
0.13	12.5	0.96	6.25

5   Experiment Setup and Results

To our knowledge, there are no circuit benchmarks specifically designed to investigate thermal properties in standard cell based design yet. There are some works in the literature that used the MCNC and ISPD standard cell placement benchmarks in their experiments. However, these circuits are composed of generic cells and information about the logic implemented inside these circuits are not available. Our motivation is to model temperature distribution in real life situations. Therefore, we first used the ISCAS benchmarks, which are described in verilog and are widely used for placement and testing. The circuits are synthesized and placed in STM 65nm libraries. Tools used are Synopsys' VSS for logic simulation, Design Compiler for logical synthesis, IC compiler for physical placement and Power Compiler for power estimation based on annotated switching activity of random generated vectors. The circuits after placement are mapped to our SPICE based thermal model. Circuit geometries and simulation results are shown in Table 4. Values reported in Table 4 are temperature rises above the ambient.

As can be seen, the ISCAS benchmark circuits are small in size and flat in power profile. Due to the heat diffusion in the substrate layer, temperature distributions in the cells are quite even. As a result, we did not observe significant thermal gradient(1 °C) in these circuits. To test our thermal simulator, we designed a synthetic benchmark circuit on which we can force high power

Table 4. Results on ISCAS circuits

Circuit	# of Cells	Area(um^2)	Total Power(mW)	Max $T_{rise}(K)$	$\triangle T(K)$
c432	210	27.2 × 28.6	0.069	4.49	0.00
c1355	313	40.0 × 41.6	0.456	15.2	0.02
c499	331	42.86 × 41.78	0.434	13.12	0.02
c1908	334	42.75 × 40.24	0.291	9.69	0.01
c880	353	40.0 × 39.0	0.089	2.96	0.00
c2670	529	47.0 × 49.4	0.212	6.44	0.01
c3540	969	62.0 × 62.4	0.372	5.20	0.01
c5315	1304	69.2 × 70.2	0.617	6.82	0.03
c7552	1443	75.43 × 73.45	0.793	7.86	0.02
c6288	2582	95.33 × 94.9	1.44	7.24	0.09

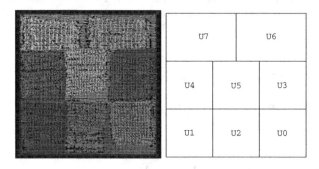

Fig. 2. Benchmark Circuit

Table 5. Results of synthetic benchmark

# of Act.Units	Active Units	Tot.Power(mW)	Max $T_{rise}(K)$	$\triangle T(K)$	ratio
8	All	48.2	11.79	0.33	
4	1,2,4,5	24.3	6.82	1.89	+60%
	0,1,3,4	24.1	6.38	1.18	
2	1,6	12.2	3.61	1.08	+30%
	2,5	12.2	3.42	0.83	
1	5	6.1	1.75	0.45	

consumption in some regions while maintain a low power profile in the other regions. In this way, we can intentionally create thermal gradients to explore the correlation between functional and spatial hotspots. The circuit is composed of 8 identical $16bit \times 16bit$ multipliers and is synthesized into 14000 standard cells with a size of $480um$ on each side. The circuit after placement and the positions of each multiplier unit is shown in Fig.2. Cells within each multiplier are placed close together since the tool performs a timing driven placement. Consequently, the functional hotspot coincides with the spatial hotspot.

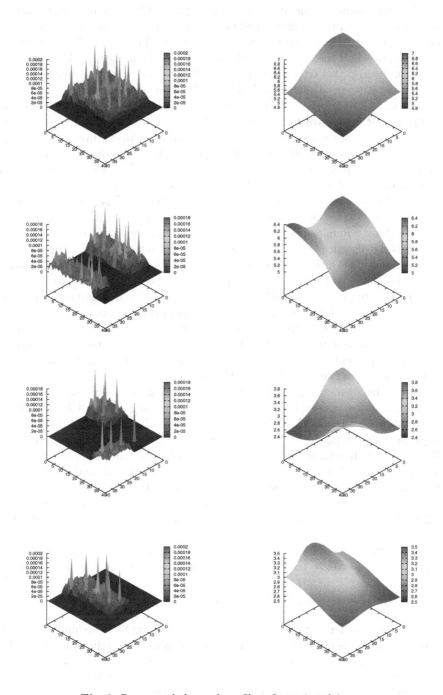

Fig. 3. Power and thermal profiles of test 2 and 3

The experiments are done by running a task of 800 multiplication operations using different multiplier units. Tests can be categorized into 4 groups as shown in Table 5. Fig.3 shows the power and thermal profiles of test 2 and 3. In test 1, we activated all the multipliers which results in the highest peak temperature since the total power consumption is the highest. The power profile is flat and the temperature gradient is small. In test 2, we used 4 multiplier units in two scenarios. In scenario 1, units 1,2,4 and 5 which are located in the same corner of the circuit are activated. In scenario 2, units 1,4,0 and 3 which are located in two separate sides are used. Both the maximum temperature and maximum temperature gradient in scenario 1 are higher than in scenario 2. This is because in scenario 1, all the hotspots are located close to each other and there's little room around to dissipate heat. While in scenario 2, the active units are surrounded by inactive units and thus more heat can be diffused into surrounding regions. In test 3, we used 2 multipliers with different configurations. In scenario 1, active units are multiplier 1 and 6, which are located in two corners in diagonal, thus the distance between the hotspots are the longest. In scenario 2, units 2 and 5 are active, which are located in the center. Results showed that scenario 1 has higher peak temperature and temperature gradient. The reason is that units 1 and 6 are in the corner and the thermal conductivity in the side are much smaller than that in the substrate. The thermal profile of scenario 2 also shows similar properties where the peak temperature appeared near the boundary of the circuit and not in the center. In test 4, we activated unit 5 only which is located in the center of the circuit. The hotspot is in the center but the peak temperature is the smallest in all test cases.

As can be seen, the maximum thermal gradient is much smaller than the maximum power gradient due to the short circuiting effect of heat diffusion in the substrate layer. The results also show that the thermal profile is highly dependent on the power profile and placement of high power consumption units. If we can place functional hotspots away from each other as illustrated by the two scenarios in test 2, we can reduce both the peak temperature and the maximum temperature gradient. On the other hand, the tests also show how the peak temperature can be reduced by using different scheduling policies on systems with redundant units. Test 1 and test 4 are two extreme cases where the task is performed either on all units or just one unit. If we activate all units, the execution time is short but the peak temperature is high. While if we use less units, it takes longer to finish the task but the temperature rise is much smaller.

6   Conclusion and Future Work

We have proposed a thermal modeling method based on SPICE simulation which can be easily integrated into thermal-aware placement or scheduling tools. Results of the experiment show how temperature variations correlate with power profile and placement. Taking into account the locations of hotspots, the placement or the scheduling tool can reduce the maximum temperature gradient by 50% on average. In the future, we will include analysis of self-heating in interconnects and the impact of many wires on heat redistribution between two regions.

We will also improve the thermal cell model which can allow us to model dynamic power profiles as well. Thermal analysis for dynamic power profiles is important in designs where aggressive power and thermal management techniques such as voltage and frequency scaling, clock gating and power gating.

References

1. Cheng, Y.K., Raha, P., Teng, C.C., Rosenbaum, E., Kang, S.M.: Thermal and power integrity based power/ground networks optimization. IEEE Transactions on Computer-Aided Design of Integrated Circuits and Systems 17(8), 668–681 (1998)
2. Wang, T.Y., Tsai, J.L., Chung-Ping Chen, C.: Thermal and power integrity based power/ground networks optimization, February 2004, vol. 2, pp. 830–835 (2004)
3. Chen, D., Li, E., Rosenbaum, E., Kang, S.M.: Interconnect thermal modeling for accurate simulation of circuit timing and reliability. IEEE Transactions on Computer-Aided Design of Integrated Circuits and Systems 19(2), 197–205 (2000)
4. Sabry, M.N., Bontemps, A., Aubert, V., Vahrmann, R.: Realistic and efficient simulation of electro-thermal effects in vlsi circuits. IEEE Transactions on Very Large Scale Integration (VLSI) Systems 5(3), 283–289 (1997)
5. Wunsche, S., Clauss, C., Schwarz, P., Winkler, F.: Electro-thermal circuit simulation using simulator coupling. IEEE Transactions on Very Large Scale Integration (VLSI) Systems 5(3), 277–282 (1997)
6. Cheng, Y.K., Kang, S.M.: An efficient method for hot-spot identification in ulsi circuits. In: ICCAD 1999: Proceedings of the 1999 IEEE/ACM international conference on Computer-aided design, Piscataway, NJ, USA, pp. 124–127. IEEE Press, Los Alamitos (1999)
7. Wang, B., Mazumder, P.: Fast thermal analysis for vlsi circuits via semi-analytical green's function in multi-layer materials, May 2004, vol. 2, pp. II–409–II412 (2004)
8. Zhan, Y., Sapatnekar, S.S.: A high efficiency full-chip thermal simulation algorithm. In: ICCAD 2005: Proceedings of the 2005 IEEE/ACM International conference on Computer-aided design, Washington, DC, USA, pp. 635–638. IEEE Computer Society, Los Alamitos (2005)
9. Tsai, C.H., Kang, S.M.: Cell-level placement for improving substrate thermal distribution. IEEE Transactions on Computer-Aided Design of Integrated Circuits and Systems 19(2), 253–266 (2000)
10. Chen, G., Sapatnekar, S.: Partition-driven standard cell thermal placement. In: ISPD 2003: Proceedings of the 2003 international symposium on Physical design, pp. 75–80. ACM, New York (2003)

Switching Noise Optimization in the Wake-Up Phase of Leakage-Aware Power Gating Structures

Javier Castro, Pilar Parra, and Antonio J. Acosta

Instituto de Microelectrónica de Sevilla-CNM-CSIC/Universidad de Sevilla
Avda. Americo Vespucio s/n, 41092-Sevilla, Spain
Tel.: +34-954466666; Fax: +34-954466600
{casram,parra,acojim}@imse.cnm.es

Abstract.[1] Leakage power dissipation has become a critical issue in advanced process technologies. The use of techniques to reduce leakage power consumption with negligible degradation in performances is needed for current and next technologies. Power gating is an effective technique to reduce leakage, taking advantage of the transistor stacking effect. However, the restoration from standby mode in power-gated circuits usually introduces a large amount of switching noise on the power supply and ground networks, that may affect the normal operation of circuits connected to the same polarizations. This paper analyzes the switching noise generated in the wake-up phase by several power-gating techniques, and their influence on the wake-up time. The best results are for the techniques that redistribute the amount of current flowing through the Vdd and Gnd nodes during the wake-up transition. Simulation results obtained on basic digital cells in a 90 nm technology show a variation of two in switching noise, while maintaining the same wake-up time and leakage saving.

1 Introduction

Power consumption and other power-related issues have become a first-order concern for most designs, because of the rising demand of portable systems [1-3]. Many techniques for low power design of VLSI circuits targeting both dynamic and leakage components of power dissipation in CMOS VLSI circuits have been recently presented -references in [2]. The primary method used to date for reducing power has been supply voltage (Vdd) reduction, although this technique reduces the switching speed of transistors. To compensate this performance loss, the transistor threshold voltages are decreased, which causes an exponential growth in the subthreshold leakage current, the dominant leakage component in the technology considered.

To mitigate the leakage problem, power gating techniques and a suited combination of Multi-Threshold CMOS devices (MTCMOS), among others, are widely used to reduce the leakage power in stand-by mode [2,3]. Sleep transistors (ST) are typically positioned between the circuit and the power supply rail or between the circuit

---

[1] This work has been sponsored by the Spanish MEC TEC2007-65105 TICOCO and the Junta de Andalucía P08-TIC-03674 Projects.

J. Monteiro and R. van Leuken (Eds.): PATMOS 2009, LNCS 5953, pp. 76–85, 2010.

and the ground rail. During active -normal- operation, the ST remains ON, supplying the current that the circuit needs to operate. During stand-by mode, turning OFF the ST disables the normal operation of the circuit, reducing the subthreshold leakage current flowing through the circuit. To optimize the leakage reduction, the ST is usually designed with high threshold voltage (high-Vth), if a MTCMOS technology is considered. With this approach, the circuit is designed with standard or low-Vth transistors to achieve delay specifications, while the STs use high-Vth.

The introduction of the STs has some side effects. During the normal operation of the circuit, the ST works as a resistor, and this resistance will cause a voltage drop across it. Therefore, the gate driving capability is reduced, degrading circuit performances. Furthermore, during the transitions between operation modes, especially from standby mode to active mode (namely power-on or wake-up), power gating schemes cause large in-rush current (switching noise) through the power supply and ground rails that greatly affects the reliability of the circuits nearby, especially in mixed-signal designs, causing functional errors [2,4-10]. So it is critical to limit in-rush current during power-on for such applications.

Many methods have been proposed for switching noise reduction during wake-up transition time [5-10]. Some of them are based on slowing down the power-on of the circuit, increasing the wake-up time [5,6], while the others achieve a reduction of switching noise by the inclusion of specific hardware. It would be desirable, on one hand, to develop low-cost techniques able to reduce the switching noise with negligible penalty in the wake-up time. On the other hand, the evaluation of power-gating techniques is needed, being this the aim of the paper. It will be demonstrated in this paper how to reduce switching noise in the wake-up phase by redistributing the amount of current passing through the power supply and ground rails.

The organization of the paper is as follows: Section 2 analyzes the power-gating technique related issues; Section 3 presents the techniques under evaluation and the experimental setup; Section 4 includes the simulation results. Finally, main conclusions are presented in Section 5.

2 Power Gating Overview

Power gating is a very useful technique for standby-mode leakage power reduction. In this technique, a high-threshold voltage (high-Vth) transistor is stacked, inserted in series between the power supply -or ground node, and the circuit [2]. This transistor, usually known as sleep transistor (ST), is also known as "footer", if gates the ground rail, or "header" if it gates the power supply rail. An example of power gating using a footer as ST is shown in figure 1. The transistors used in the logic circuit have low-Vth in order to switch as fast as possible.

The operating way of the circuit in figure 1 is as follows. During active mode of operation, the high-Vth transistor is turned ON, thereby facilitating normal operation of the circuit. During standby mode, this transistor is turned OFF creating a virtual ground rail because it cuts off the circuit from supply (the ST forces the circuit to go to "sleep"). Then, the output of the circuit has no path to ground, keeping a floating state and reaching a high value due to the connection to power supply, depending on the input pattern. All the internal capacitive nodes of the logic block and the virtual

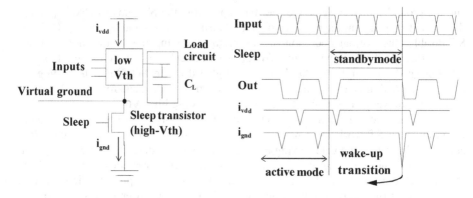

Fig. 1. Circuit (low-Vth) with footer ST (high-Vth)

ground node are charged to a steady-state value, normally near power supply voltage Vdd. When the circuit wakes up, parasitic capacitors are discharged through the footer ST, and a high amount of current is injected on the ground node. Thus, in the case of power gating with a footer ST, switching noise is generated on the ground rail in the wake-up transition, while the power supply node remains stable.

On the other side, if a header ST is used, when the circuit is in standby mode, there is not any connecting path from the floating output to the power supply node, reaching the output a low value depending on the input patterns. All the internal capacitive nodes of the logic block and virtual Vdd node will be discharged to a steady-state value near 0. When the circuit wakes up, parasitic capacitors are charged up and then a high amount of current is supplied from the power supply node, while the ground node remains stable. Now, switching noise is generated in the power supply node.

As a consequence, in any case there is a significant switching noise in the power or/ and ground rails during the wake-up time. This is a drawback of the power gating technique that must be minimized [2,4-10].

In a general way, the inclusion of STs reduces the leakage of the power gated block/ cell, but also the speed is reduced, and obviously, increasing the circuit area. A critical decision in power gating is how to manage the number, position and size of STs to switch power OFF. There are two main approaches: fine grain power gating and coarse grain power gating. In fine grain power gating the ST is locally placed inside each standard cell in the library. Since only one cell is gated, the ST size can be kept reduced. In coarse grain power gating, a block of gates has its power supply gated by a ST, with a size depending on the block size itself. A trade-off between leakage saving and performance degradation due to the inclusion of STs can be found, being this the aim of some previous work [2,3,11].

On the other hand, mechanisms conceived to reduce switching noise have been previously considered [5-10]. The work in [5-8] propose the reduction of ground bounce by turning the STs ON in a stepwise manner. Stepwise switching of the STs can be implemented either by dynamically controlling the gate-to-source voltage V_{GS} of the ST, by turning ON only a proportion of the STs at one time (as the scheme shown in figure 2), or by gradually releasing the trapped charge that causes the inductive noise. The work in [9,10] is mainly oriented toward the reduction of delay and energy consumed during mode transitions, based on the recycling charge between the virtual power and ground rails immediately after entering the standby mode and just before wake-up. This technique uses a transmission gate connecting virtual power and virtual ground, as it is shown in figure 3. The main restriction of this technique is the partition of the combinational logic into two sub-blocks, where the output of a sub block is used as input of the other one, as well as the inclusion of transmission gates and the generation of specific control signals.

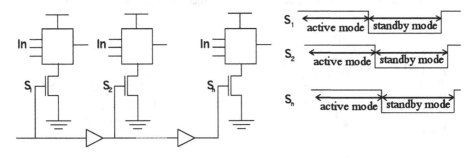

Fig. 2. Stepwise switching of the STs following the proposal in [5]

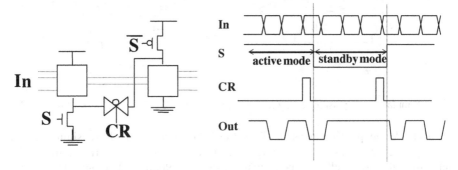

Fig. 3. Charge-recycling scheme proposed in [9,10]

3 Optimum Technique and Experimental Setup

The main way to reduce switching noise in a power-gated block is the redistribution of supply/ground current, to reduce its maximum value. This can be done considering a combination of both kind of STs, footer and header, as it is shown in figure 4. With this scheme (mixed STs), the whole circuit can be switched OFF by the activation of STs in footers and headers. Although it is not a novel idea itself, the main consequence of this partitioning is the redistribution of supply and ground current between the two rails in the wake-up transition, decreasing the value of the peak current, and hence, reducing switching noise. The clustering of blocks to optimize the subthreshold leakage is an important optimization step, outside the scope of the paper.

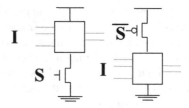

Fig. 4. Combination of footer and header STs (henceforth called mixed STs)

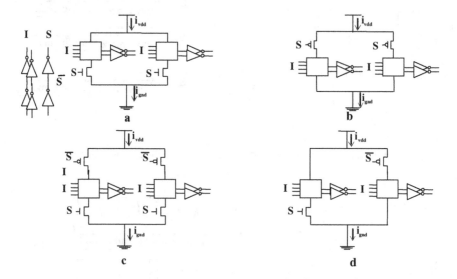

Fig. 5. Simulation setup using a) only footer ST, b) only header ST, c) dual STs, d) mixed STs

To check the performances of the different techniques we have simulated six power-gating structures, incorporating different circuit blocks (inverter, 2-in NAND and 28-t. full-adder cells) as benchmark, using ST 90nm technology. The circuit blocks are designed with low-Vth transistors and minimum dimensions (Wp=0.4μm, Wn=0.2 μm, L=0.1μm), while another inverters simulate the output load and generate a more realistic waveform at the inputs. A NMOS (PMOS) transistor with high-Vth (Wn=1μm, Wp=2μm, L=0.1μm) is used as footer ST (header ST). The inputs transition time is 100ps, Vdd=1v, and temperature is 27°C. Load and input inverters have different Vdd, to separately measure the current passing through the logic.

In figure 5a(b), logic blocks are gated only with footer (header) STs. The dual power-gating scheme using footer and header STs in every block is shown in figure 5c. Figure 5d illustrates the mixed STs method, combining footer ST in one logic block and header ST in the other one. In order to assess the different techniques, we measured the most relevant parameters related to the wake-up transition: the wake-up time (propagation delay of the circuit when the ST is switching ON) and the peak of current flowing through power supply (i_{vdd}) and ground (i_{gnd}) nodes at that time (as an indirect measurement of the noise generated). The standby leakage and active dynamic power consumptions have been also measured.

4   Simulation Results

The results have been obtained using SPECTRE simulations, considering the circuits in figure 5, and the equivalent circuits following the schemes of figure 2 [5] and figure 3 [9] for final comparison. As an illustrative analysis of results, figure 6 includes the waveform displays of the six structures, using inverters as logic blocks, under a 100 MHz pulse train as input.

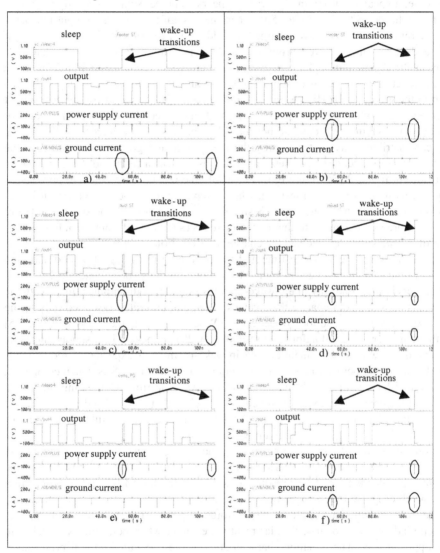

Fig. 6. Waveforms for the six cases when the logic block is an inverter and the input is a 100 MHz pulse train, using: a) footer ST, b) header ST, c) dual STs, d) combination mixed STs, e) stepwise/header [5] and f) charge-recycling [9] schemes. The signals represented in each case are the sleep signal (top), the output, power supply current, and ground current (bottom).

In the case of the footer ST (figure 5a), when the system is sleeping, the output reaches a "1" or remains floating, depending on the input, but there is no possibility of discharge to "0". When the system wakes up and one output switches to "0", a current is injected through the ground node, generating the maximum peak current in that node (figure 6a). If the system wakes up but there is no significant change in the outputs, it generates a peak current in the ground node lower than the previous one. In any case, no peak (or very small) current appears on power supply node (figure 6a).

In the header ST case (figure 5b), when the system is down, the output reaches a "0" or remains floating, never charged to Vdd, and if the output changes to a "1", it demands a maximum current from Vdd node, generating a peak current in that node (figure 6b). Again, although the outputs do not change in the wake-up transition, there is a peak current in the power supply node and in any case there is not any peak current in the ground node (figure 6b). If a dual power gating is used (figure 5c), we get high peaks in both power and ground rails, as it can be seen in figure 6c. In the case of using footer ST in one block and header ST in the other one (mixed STs, figure 5d), we can distribute this peak value by the two power and ground rails, and then the switching noise decreases on these rails, as it is shown in figure 6d. Contribution of structure in figure 2 [5] (figure 6e), is basically the reduction of peaks in power supply current in the wake-up transition, when comparing to the header ST circuit in figure 5a, because of the staggering in S signal. The contribution of the scheme in figure 3 [9] (figure 6f), is similar to that of the mixed STs (figure 6d), but including the effect of the transmission gate and the charge redistribution.

Table 1 shows the wake-up time and the peak current through the Vdd and Gnd nodes in the case of inverters as logic block. For simplicity, both logic blocks switch its outputs in the same way in the wake-up transition, i.e. both outputs remain with the previous value or both change their values. The peak current is observed only in the Gnd(Vdd) node using the footer(header) ST. When comparing the stepwise-header [5] with the header ST, a reduction of approximately 25% in peak power supply current is observed, but with an increment of 33% in wake-up time, as expected. A reduction of nearly two in the peak current values is obtained for the mixed STs, when comparing to the dual STs, with a slight increment of the wake-up time. Comparing the mixed STs and the charge recycling [9] schemes, it is clear that a strong reduction of about 33% in the peaks in both the Gnd and Vdd currents is achieved, although at the cost of about a 27% average degradation in wake-up time.

Comparing with the stepwise-header [5], the average reduction in peaks of supply current is a 25% for the mixed STs, even with a 40% of degradation of wake-up time for the stepwise-header. These results demonstrate that mixed STs is the best option for switching noise reduction in both Vdd and Gnd planes in the wake-up phase, because the symmetry in both logic blocks forces a perfect redistribution of peaks between Gnd and Vdd planes. Similar results are found when both blocks switches in the opposite way. The dynamic characteristics of these circuits, normal propagation delay and peak current on power rails when the system is active, are included in Table 2. Delay is similar in all the cases, with slight variations below 10% respecting to the fastest structures, the footer ST, the mixed ST and the charge-recycling one.

Table 1. Wake-up time and in-rush current on the power supply node (i_{pek_vdd}) and ground node (i_{peak_gnd}) in the wake-up transition for the case of inverters as logic blocks

	$t_{wake-up}$ (ps)		i_{peak_vdd} (μA)		i_{peak_gnd} (μA)	
Outputs	1->0	0->1	0->0	0->1	1->1	1->0
Footer ST	23.5	-	-	14.45	265.7	349
Header ST	-	35.1	356.8	363.1	-	
Dual STs	21.37	25.57	-	347.7	-	353.5
Mixed STs	23.45	37.61	174.7	174.7	127.7	176.8
Stepwise-Header [5]	-	52.23	198.7	285.5	-	
Charge Recycling [9]	14.68	30.37	262	258.6	189.6	257.3

Table 2. Propagation delay and power/ground rail peak currents in the active mode with inverters as logic blocks

	t_{delay} (ps)	i_{peak_vdd} (μA)	i_{peak_gnd} (μA)
Footer ST	21.78	207.4	217.1
Header ST	22.81	169.8	257.4
Dual STs	24.05	170.5	217.3
Mixed STs	21.78	187.5	237.5
Stepwise-header [5]	22.78	166.8	257.4
Charge recycling [9]	21.73	181.1	237.6

We assess the different techniques using 2-input NAND (Table 3) and standard 28-t. CMOS full-adder (Table 4) as logic blocks. As it can be seen in Table 3, a high peak current is obtained again in Gnd node with the footer ST (independently of the NAND inputs during wake-up), a high peak current on Vdd with the header ST, high peak currents in both rails using dual STs, while a significant reduction of these peak currents (up to 50%) are obtained using the mixed STs. The reduction in peak current when comparing the mixed STs to the stepwise-header and the charge-recycling scheme ranges between 10-30%. The wake-up times are quite similar in all cases, although the best cases are for the charge- recycling scheme, with an improvement ranging from 5-20%. The case of the full-adder in Table 4 is more complex, because it has internal nodes switching besides the output changes. Then, although one output changes to "0", some other internal nodes change to "1", contributing with a current through Gnd and Vdd nodes, respectively. The measurements show a good behavior of the charge-recycling technique with respect to switching noise and wake-up time.

The active power and standby leakage consumption results (Table 5) show that average power is similar for all the structures using the same block. The best case for leakage is the dual ST, since it uses both header and footer ST in each block, requiring double number of STs. The mixed STs gives leakage values between the footer and header STs, being lower than those of stepwise, but worse than charge-recycling.

Table 3. Average wake-up time and max/min in-rush current on the power supply (i $_{peak\_vdd}$) and ground (i$_{peak\_gnd}$) nodes in the case of 28-transistor full-adder as logic blocks

	i $_{peak\_vdd}$ (μA)		i $_{peak\_gnd}$ (μA)		t wake-up (ps)			
					Sum		Cout	
	max	min	max	min	1->0	0->1	1->0	0->1
Footer ST	290.9	97.29	675	580.5	64.91	-	42.22	-
Header ST	378.1	323.2	295.8	51.03	-	63.74	-	62.01
Dual STs	337.7	282.2	587.7	443.4	52.31	60.45	47.78	49.79
Mixed STs	277.3	214.6	381.1	305.4	64.75	67.75	42.28	66.12
Stepwise-header [5]	384.8	253.8	294.6	26.1	-	82.72	-	81.24
Charge recycling [9]	219.3	211.9	306.5	241.4	25.32	40.31	17.86	39.95

Table 4. Average wake-up time and max/min in-rush current on the power supply (i $_{peak\_vdd}$) and ground (i $_{peak\_gnd}$) nodes in the case of 28-transistor full-adder as logic blocks

	i $_{peak\_vdd}$ (μA)		i $_{peak\_gnd}$ (μA)		t wake-up (ps)			
					Sum		Cout	
	max	min	max	min	1->0	0->1	1->0	0->1
Footer ST	290.9	97.29	675	580.5	64.91	-	42.22	-
Header ST	378.1	323.2	295.8	51.03	-	63.74	-	62.01
Dual STs	337.7	282.2	587.7	443.4	52.31	60.45	47.78	49.79
Mixed STs	277.3	214.6	381.1	305.4	64.75	67.75	42.28	66.12
Stepwise-header [5]	384.8	253.8	294.6	26.1	-	82.72	-	81.24
Charge recycling [9]	219.3	211.9	306.5	241.4	25.32	40.31	17.86	39.95

Table 5. Power consumption for the different configurations

	INV (nA)		NAND (nA)		FA (μA)	
	Active	Standby	Active	Standby	Active	Standby
Footer ST	968.4	0.917	660.2	0.597	3193	1.614
Header ST	973	1.108	664.1	1.493	3288	2.014
Dual STs	975	0.351	667.8	0.325	3114	0.823
Mixed STs	970.7	1.026	661.8	1.045	3238	1.814
Stepwise-header [5]	972.4	1.135	658.8	1.493	3285	2.014
Charge recycling [9]	972.1	1.030	662.7	0.987	3243	0.966

5 Conclusions

This paper has presented a comparison of switching noise figures generated by different power-gating techniques during the wake-up transition, with emphasis in the solutions providing reduced degradation in the wake-up time. The solutions using only footer or header STs produce high peaks in one rail. The redistribution of the current through the opposite power rail in the wake-up transition, as it happens in the mixed STs and charge-recycling techniques, provides the best solutions, showing a good trade-off between leakage saving, wake-up time and hardware resource, especially for fine grain power gating, while the charge-recycling technique is the best for complex gates in coarse grain. Future work will be devoted to the optimum partitioning of combinational systems to achieve good switching noise figures in the wake-up phase.

References

1. Roy, K., Prasad, S.C.: Low-Power CMOS VLSI Circuit Design. Wiley-Interscience, Hoboken (2000)
2. Henzler, S.: Power Management Of Digital Circuits In Deep Sub-Micron CMOS Technologies. Springer Series in Advanced Microelectronics (2007)
3. Narendra, S.G., Chandrakasan, A.: Leakage in Nanometer CMOS Technologies. Springer, Heidelberg (2006)
4. Aragonès, X., González, J.L., Rubio, A.: Analysis and Solutions for Switching Noise Coupling in Mixed-Signal ICs. Kluwer Academic Publishers, Dordrecht (1999)
5. Kim, S., et al.: Reducing ground-bounce noise and stabilizing the data-retention voltage of power-gating structures. IEEE Trans. on Electron Devices 55(1), 197–205 (2008)
6. Kim, S., Kosonocky, S.V., Knebel, D.R.: Understanding and minimizing ground bounce during mode transition of power gating structures. In: Proc. of ISLPED, pp. 22–25 (2003)
7. Usami, K., et al.: Design and implementation of fine-grain power gating with ground bounce suppression. In: 22nd Conf. on VLSI Design, pp. 381–386 (2009)
8. Kim, S., et al.: Minimizing inductive noise in system-on-a-chip with multiple power gating structures. In: Proc. of the 29th ESSCIRC, pp. 635–638 (2003)
9. Pakbaznia, E., Fallah, F., Pedram, M.: Charge recycling in MTCMOS circuits: concept and analysis. In: Proc. of the 43rd DAC, pp. 97–102 (2006)
10. Pakbaznia, E., Fallah, F., Pedram, M.: Charge recycling in power-gated CMOS circuits. IEEE Trans. on CAD 27(10), 1798–1811 (2008)
11. Deepaksubramanyan, B.S., Núñez, A.: Analysis of subthreshold leakage reduction in CMOS digital circuits. In: Proc. of 50th MWSCAS, pp. 1400–1404 (2007)

Application-Specific Temperature Reduction Systematic Methodology for 2D and 3D Networks-on-Chip[*]

Iraklis Anagnostopoulos[1], Alexandros Bartzas[2], and Dimitrios Soudris[1]

[1] ECE School, National Technical University of Athens, 15780 Zografou, Greece
[2] ECE Department, Democritus University of Thrace, 67100 Xanthi, Greece

Abstract. Network-on-Chip (NoC), a new SoC paradigm, has been proposed as a solution to mitigate complex on-chip interconnection problems. NoC architectures are able to accommodate a large number of IP cores in the same chip implementing a set of complex applications. Power consumption is a critical issue in interconnection network in NoC design, driven by power-related design constraints, such as thermal and power delivery design. In this work, we introduce a systematic methodology for NoC temperature reduction consisting of novel techniques: i) application independent power-aware routing algorithms; and ii) application-specific platform optimizations, such as buffer sizing. The methodology achieves significant peak temperature reduction. The effectiveness of the proposed approach is evaluated both on 2D and 3D mesh topologies employing real DSP applications. A temperature reduction of $13°C$ and $22°C$ for 2D and 3D NoCs, respectively, on average, is achieved without any performance penalty.

1 Introduction

Future integrated systems will contain billion of transistors, composing tens to hundreds of IP cores. These IP cores, implementing emerging complex DSP, multimedia and network applications, should be able to deliver rich services. An efficient cooperation among these IP cores (e.g., efficient data transfers, high bandwidth) can be achieved through utilization of the available resources. An architecture able to accommodate such a high number of cores, satisfying the needs for communication and data transfers, is the Networks-on-Chip (NoCs) architecture.

Furthermore, the emerging three-dimensional (3D) integration and process technologies allow the design of multi-level Integrated Circuits. This creates new design opportunities in NoC field as illustrated in [1]. These advancements in technology exhibit, among others, higher performance and smaller energy consumption. 3D integration is a way to accommodate the demands of emerging systems for scaling, performance and functionality. For example, a considerable reduction can be achieved in the number and length of global interconnects using three-dimensional integration. On deciding whether to choose a 2D or 3D NoC as architecture it is shown in [2] that 3D NoCs are advantageous, providing better performance.

Temperature reduction and hotspot minimization is of extreme importance to modern systems because it affects the overall power consumption, performance and reliability

---

[*] This work is partially supported by the E.C. funded FP7-215244 MOSART Project, www.mosart-project.org

J. Monteiro and R. van Leuken (Eds.): PATMOS 2009, LNCS 5953, pp. 86–95, 2010.

of the device. For these reasons, the reduction of peak temperature is something that the designer should always take into consideration. In Figure 1(a) the steady temperature profile of an NoC is presented. It is evident that due to the application behaviour and the routing algorithm used, some hotspots are created (depicted red in this Figure). Especially, on an NoC system the designer can tweak the interconnection network in order to reduce the number of hotspots. So, the main goal in the design time is to minimize the numbers of hotspots and keep temperature in low levels. In Figure 1(b) the same NoC is presented having reduced the number of hotspots and the mean temperature without violating any performance constraints. The thermal problem is exacerbated in 3D architectures for two reasons: i) the vertically stacked layers cause a rapid increase of power density; and ii) the thermal conductivity of the dielectric inserted between device layers for insulation is very low compared to silicon and metal.

In this work we present a peak temperature reduction methodology for NoCs. First, the designer utilizes a power-aware routing scheme. This leads to redistribution of the traffic over the NoC, in such a way to redistribute the power consumption of the routers without any

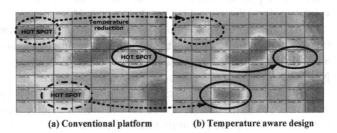

(a) Conventional platform   (b) Temperature aware design

Fig. 1. Temperature profile of an NoC platform

penalty in the system performance. Second, to have a greater impact on the reduction of power consumption, where most of the power consumption is spent, we propose the insertion of peer-to-peer connections between nodes that heavily communicate with each other. This has as an effect: i) the minimization of the required buffer space; and ii) heavy traffic between nodes bypass the network, leading to power dissipation only in the wires that connect the components and not on the routers.

The rest of the paper is organized as follows. An overview of the related work is presented in Section 2. The methodology is shown in Section 3, whereas the results of the evaluation using three applications are presented in Section 4. Finally, conclusions are drawn in Section 5.

2   Related Work

Real chip implementation issues of NoCs and their solutions along with a series of chip design examples are presented in [3]. A comparison of the NOC and Point-to-Point (P2P) communication architectures in terms of power, performance, and area is performed in [4]. In that work complete P2P and NoC-based implementations of a real multimedia application (MPEG-2 encoder) are compared. In [5] the authors compare the VOPD application on a mesh 2D NoC and a 2D Fat tree NoC.

Hu and Marculescu [6] proposed an energy-aware mapping algorithm which minimizes the total communication cost for a 2D mesh NoC architecture. Cong et al. [7] introduced a thermal-driven floorplanning algorithm for 3D ICs, whereas a thermal driven multilevel routing has been proposed in [8]. A method to calculate the temperature based on power estimation for standard cell placement was presented in [9]. In [10] the authors show that the network interconnection in NoCs has comparable thermal impact as the processing elements and contributing significantly to overall chip temperature. A power-aware routing algorithm, named PowerHerd was presented in [11], which is an architecture-level run-time power management scheme targeting network peak power. Chaparro et al. [12] present the organization of a distributed, thus temperature-aware, front end for clustered microarchitectures. Davis et al. show an implementation of an FFT in a 3D IC achieving 33% reduction in maximum wire length, proving that the move to 3D ICs is beneficial [13]. However, they highlight as limiting factors the heat dissipation and yield. Modern SoC designs, such as CMPs, can benefit from 3D integration as well. For example, by placing processing memory, such as DRAM or L2 caches, on top of the processing core in different layers, the bandwidth between them is increased and the critical path is shortened [14].

The main differentiators of this work, from previous ones, are actually the contributions of the current research. These contributions are: a) Methodology: Introduction of a systematic methodology for temperature reduction of the interconnection network in NoCs; b) Architecture: Introduction of buffer sizing and direct link techniques in order to reduce peak temperature; c) Routing: Introduction of a new power-aware routing algorithm which redistributes the power consumption of the routers and d) Implementation: Realization of DSP/Multimedia applications on 2D and 3D NoC topologies using temperature power-aware criteria.

3   Temperature Reduction Methodology Overview

The methodology flow for temperature reduction is presented in Figure 2. The starting point of the proposed methodology (STEP 1) is the bandwidth-constraint mapping algorithm [15]. The next step consists of two main categories (STEP 2). The first contains the selection of platform independent power-aware routing algorithms while the other contains application-specific platform optimizations for temperature reduction, based on the power and the temperature profile of a given application. The main goal of the proposed methodology is to devise a strategy that is able to reduce the peak and the average temperature of the interconnection network of an NoC. So, taking into consideration all the aforementioned techniques and utilizations, a strategy for temperature reduction is proposed. The proposed approach is the combination of the Power-Aware XY routing algorithm, the buffer sizing and the direct-link connection technique which includes the advantages of all the three above techniques. In the following Subsections details are given for each one of these techniques.

Selection of Power-Aware Routing Algorithms. In an NoC power is dissipated when flits traverse routers and links. When a packet is injected into an interconnection network, it is decomposed into flits, which travel through the network, invoking a stream of power consuming operations such as buffer reads and writes, crossbar switching, routing decisions, virtual channel allocation and link utilization. It is obvious that a power-aware routing algorithm is the first step of a temperature reduction methodology.

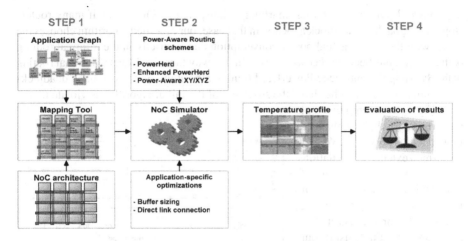

Fig. 2. The proposed temperature reduction methodology

By keeping power consumption steady and without many local peaks, our die has a uniform power dissipation behaviour and thermal profile. Here, three platform-independent power-aware routing algorithms are presented. First, we have implemented in our high-level NoC Simulator the PowerHerd routing protocol proposed in [11]. As a second step, we modified PowerHerd in order to avoid deadlocks and keep the average packet latency in low levels. Last, a new power-aware routing algorithm is presented. This new algorithm (called Power-Aware XY/XYZ) supports both 2D and 3D NoC architectures and is based on the XY routing algorithm.

PowerHerd Routing Algorithm. PowerHerd routing algorithm [11] is a distributed power-aware routing protocol for 2D NoCs where routing decisions are made dynamically based on the local power resources available in neighbouring routers. First, the designer defines a global power budget for the interconnection network which is divided evenly among routers and is stored in a specific register. In that way every router has a power limit that should not be exceeded. Neighbouring routers exchange power budget information and when a router is running close to its allocated power budget it is marked as a hotspot. If so, packets do not run through it and the routing logic finds alternative routing paths to redirect network traffic taking always into consideration the minimal routing path. As time passes, the hotspot router has enough breathing room between actual power consumption and its allocated power budget, and so it unmarked. Obviously, if a router is marked as hotspot its neighbours undertake its traffic and so their activity and their power consumption increases rapidly. So, if the allocated power budget is strict and low, neighbouring routers can be marked as hotspots while the first router is still a hotspot, thus leading to deadlock.

Enhanced PowerHerd Routing Algorithm. The enhanced PowerHerd algorithm uses the same power management technique for 2D NoCs as the original PowerHerd routing protocol [11]. The differentiation of the enhanced one is that is deadlock-free. As mentioned previously, when a router is marked as hotspot its neighbours serve the traffic that otherwise would go through it, and there is always a chance that they exceed their power limit leading to their marking as hotspots too. Obviously, if many routers stop serving packets, deadlock appears. In that case, our modified algorithm chooses the router with the lowest actual power consumption that is strictly in the minimal routing path even if it has been marked as hotspot. In that way there is always a minimal routing path. By using the enhanced PowerHerd routing algorithm, on the one hand deadlocks are avoided but on the other hand the strictness of the initial algorithm is violated.

In Figure 3, a comparison of the original and the enhanced PowerHerd is presented. We have performed extensive simulations of the temperature behaviour of three DSP applications (Section 4. In this subsection we present the results only for the VOPD application [15]. First, using our high-level NoC Simulator [16], we recorded the power consumption of each router for the given application. Then we calculated the mean value for all of them

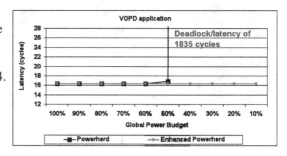

Fig. 3. Comparison of PowerHerd [11] and enhanced PowerHerd routing algorithms

and used various percentages of this value as a global power budget for the Power-Herd and the enhanced PowerHerd routing algorithms. The X-axis represents the global power budget as a percentage of the mean value of the power consumption for all routers in the NoC. The Y-axis presents the average packet latency in cycles for the interconnection network. As it can be seen, when the global power budget becomes 40% of the mean value, the latency of the PowerHerd algorithm increases dramatically while the enhanced one keeps it low. This happens because when the allocated power budget is strict and low, an increasing number of neighbouring routers are marked as hotspots, leading to deadlock.

Power-Aware XY/XYZ Routing Algorithm. The Power-Aware XY/XYZ Routing Algorithm is a deadlock-free routing algorithm based on the widely used XY routing algorithm. XY is a deadlock-free routing algorithm and ensures a minimal routing path in a mesh topology. Because of its simplicity, it can be used for 3D architectures too with minor changes. The generic Power-Aware XYZ routing algorithm is presented in Algorithm 1. When a packet arrives in a router, the router reads the packet's header information (line 1). The router checks its position in comparison with the destination (lines 2-4). If the destination is in the same direction, meaning that two coordinates of the router are the same with destinations coordinates, the router calculates the next hop using the conventional XYZ routing algorithm (lines 5-6). If not, the router, regarding its position, checks the power consumption of its neighbouring routers that are in the minimal routing path, and sends the packet to the one with the smallest power consumption (lines 7-15). In Figure 4(a), a peak temperature comparison between the enhanced PowerHerd, the power-aware XY, and the XY routing algorithm for the VOPD application is presented. The application was simulated for an 8×8 mesh NoC and the

---

Algorithm 1. Routing algorithm

```
1: function POWERAWAREXYZROUTING(x_src, y_src, z_src, x_dst, y_dst, z_dst)
2:      x_off = |x_dst − x_src|
3:      y_off = |y_dst − y_src|
4:      z_off = |z_dst − z_src|
5:      if (x_off = y_off = 0) OR (x_off = z_off = 0) OR (y_off = y_off = 0) then
6:          nextRouter = XYZ()
7:      else if x_off ! = 0 AND y_off ! = 0 AND z_off ! = 0 then
8:          nextRouter = min(powerX, powerY, powerZ)
9:      else
10:             if x_off = 0 then
11:                 nextRouter = min(powerY, powerZ)
12:             end if
13:             if y_off = 0 then
14:                 nextRouter = min(powerX, powerZ)
15:             end if
16:             if z_off = 0 then
17:                 nextRouter = min(powerY, powerY)
18:             end if
19:         end if
20:         RETURN nextRouter
21: end function
```

---

temperature was measured using the Hotspot tool [17]. The power-aware XY is better, having the lowest peak temperature without any performance penalty.

3.1 Application-Specific Platform Customizations

So far, the platform is considered dedicated and no hardware optimizations were used. This gives us the advantage of flexibility and simplicity but the effect in temperature reduction needs to be widened. In order to further reduce the steady temperature of the NoC, two platform optimization techniques are proposed: the buffer sizing and the direct-link connection. Both techniques are tailored to the needs of the application.

Buffer Sizing. The energy consumption is a very crucial metric in evaluating NoC architectures. As aforementioned, input buffers, crossbar switch and link circuits dominate network power consumption. Especially, input buffers have the biggest impact in network power consumption. The goal of this methodology step is to reduce, both in 2D and 3D NoCs, the energy consumption, keeping constant the applications average latency. The problem formulation is: 1) Given an application graph G and a network topology $T(r, ch)$, packet size and architecture-specific parameters such as the routing protocol $PR(r, Src, Dst)$ and total available buffering space B; 2) then find the buffer size $l(ch, r)$ for each channel ch, at each router r in the network; such that the average latency $L(Arch, G)$ remains the same and satisfies the constraints specified in $Const(Arch, G)$.

$$\sum_{\forall r} \sum_{\forall ch} l(ch, r) < B \qquad (1)$$

In order to achieve this, the designer needs to compute the appropriate-minimum buffer size of each router for the given application so as not to waste energy by maintaining empty buffer slots. At the beginning of the simulation, we set the size of every buffer to size B (e.g. 5). Then, every time there is a reference or a new flit arrives in a buffer, we examine how many flits are stored that moment by calculating the equation:

$$tmp[i]_t = size - empty\_slots[i]_t \tag{2}$$

where $i \in [0, n-1]$ indicates the nodes of the NoC, size is the buffer size in number of flits and $empty\_slots[i]$ is the number of buffer empty slots of i-th node. Finally, the maximum value of each node in an interval of length T is calculated and stored:

$$buf\_used[i]_{0 \le t < T} = max \{tmp[i]_0, \ldots, tmp[i]_t, \ldots, tmp[i]_{T-1}\} \tag{3}$$

because the periodic producer model [18] is used.

Direct-Link Connection. In order to keep average packet latency in low levels for the interconnection network, nodes that exchange data frequently are mapped into neighbouring positions. But even nodes that are in one hop distance inject their packets into the network and wait for the routing engine to find and route the packets. This action has great impact on average latency and total energy consumption. By using the direct-link connection technique, neighbouring (within one hop distance) Intellectual Properties (IP) that exchange data with the maximum rate, are connected with a peer-to-peer fashion. Their packets are not injected into the network and travel with no network latency. The energy they consume is only due to the consumption of the wires/link that connect them. In order to keep the NoC generality, the direct links must serve a specific and limited number of connections.

Evaluation is performed by comparing the energy cost of routing the stream through the network and by a point-to-point link. Adding a direct link, will add a static installation cost, which includes the static and leakage energy of network interfaces. To be more specific, the direct links that were implemented in an 8×8 mesh NoC, correspond to about 5% of the total wire connections and the number of nodes that connected with direct link, were 6 out of 64 in worst case. In this way, the homogeneity of the NoC is maintained and the floorplanning is not affected. In Figure 4(b), a peak temperature comparison between the buffer sizing technique with Power-Aware XY routing algorithm, the direct-link connection technique with Power-Aware XY routing algorithm and a "conventional" NoC platform with XY routing algorithm for the VOPD application is presented. The application was simulated on an 8×8 mesh NoC and the temperature was measured using the Hotspot tool [17]. The Power-Aware XY exhibits the lowest peak temperature without any performance penalty. As can be seen, with the direct-link technique the peak temperature is reduced by 6°C and with the buffer sizing technique by 10°C.

4   Experimental Results

Extensive simulations of the temperature behaviour of three data-intensive DSP applications (a) VOPD [15], (b) MPEG-4 and (c) MMS [19] in 2D and 3D NoCs were performed. However, due to lack of space we present the diagrams for only two of them. We assume mesh network topologies of 64 nodes formulated as an 8×8 2D NoC and

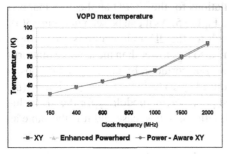
(a) Power-Aware Routing Algorithms

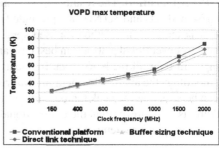
(b) Application-Specific Optimizations

Fig. 4. Comparison of routing algorithms and platform-dependent optimizations

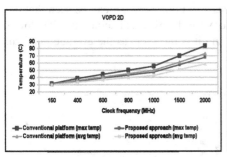
(a) Peak temperature of VOPD – 2D NoC

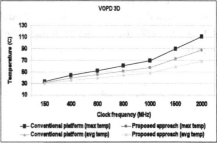
(b) Peak temperature of VOPD – 3D NoC

Fig. 5. Impact of temperature reduction strategy on VOPD application

as a $4 \times 4 \times 4$ 3D NoC. Each router has 3 virtual channels and 6 flit buffers, each 64 bits wide, per input port. The 3D router uses a 7×7 crossbar switch, whereas the 2D one uses a 5×5 crossbar switch. The applications and are mapped using the bandwidth-constraint mapping algorithm [15] and the size of the buffers in the routers is calculated using the periodic model [18].

The average and peak temperature of the NoC are the metrics we used to evaluate the proposed approach. As aforementioned, the methodology is the combination of the Power-Aware XY routing algorithm, the buffer sizing and the direct-link connection techniques. In other words, it is the combination with which greater temperature reduction can be achieved. The baseline for this experiment is the values of the simulations considering an NoC mesh topology. The traffic is served on Best Effort basis, whereas a XY routing scheme is followed with wormhole switching. For the baseline, all buffers have the same size and no direct-links are used. HotSpot [17] was used to measure the steady temperatures of functional units of the interconnection network. HotSpot is originally developed to model the temperature functional units by making use of the duality that exists between heat flow and electricity. HotSpot can also model the temperature of 3D stacked chips. For our experiments, we used a power passive layer with thickness 2×10^{-3} mm above each power dissipating layer and a HotFloorplan to generate thermal-aware floorplanning for our designs.

VOPD Application. The results of our simulations for the VOPD application mapped on a 64-node 2D and 3D NoC are presented in Figure 5. As it can be seen in Figure 5(a), the peak temperature of the proposed approach for the 2D architecture is 15°C lower than the conventional platform in best case and also it is lower than the average platform temperature for all the NoC clock frequencies. Furthermore, by utilizing the proposed methodology the average temperature was reduced by 15°C in best case. In Figure 5(b), it can be seen that the peak temperature of the proposed methodology for the 3D architecture, is 23°C lower than the conventional platform in best case and it is the same as the average platform temperature.

MPEG-4 Application. The simulation results for the MPEG-4 application are shown in Figure 6. As it can be seen in Figure 6(a), the peak steady temperature of the proposed approach for the 2D architecture is 16 °C lower than one of the conventional platform (in the highest clock frequency). Furthermore, with the proposed approach the average temperature, was reduced by 15°C in best case. In Figure 6(b), it can be seen that the peak temperature of the proposed methodology for the 3D architecture, is 33°C lower than the conventional platform in best case and it is the same as the average platform temperature.

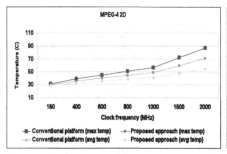   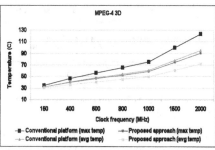

(a) Peak temperature of MPEG-4 – 2D NoC   (b) Peak temperature of MPEG-4 – 3D NoC

Fig. 6. Impact of temperature reduction strategy on MPEG-4 application

MMS Application. For the MMS application the peak temperature of the proposed methodology for the 2D architecture is 7°C lower than the conventional platform in best case. Also, with the proposed strategy the average temperature was reduced by 15°C in best case. For the 3D architecture, is 10°C lower than the conventional platform in best case and the average temperature, was reduced by 8°C in best case.

5   Conclusions

Nowadays, the problem of high temperature in the die arises and becomes more challenging than ever. Especially in 3D NoCs, temperature constrains and management is a necessity and one of the most crucial problems. In this paper an application specific temperature reduction strategy was presented that first redistributes the power consumption and then takes full advantage of the platform features in both 2D and 3D NoCs. Utilizing the proposed strategy we were able to achieve reduction of an average of 13°C for 2D NoCs and an average of 22°C in 3D NoCs in die peak steady temperature without any performance penalty.

References

1. Pavlidis, V.F., Friedman, E.G.: 3-D topologies for networks-on-chip. IEEE TVLSI 15(10), 1081–1090 (2007)
2. Feero, B., Pande, P.P.: Performance evaluation for three-dimensional networks-on-chip. In: Proc. of ISVLSI, pp. 305–310 (2007)
3. Kim, D., Kim, K., Kim, J.Y., Lee, S.J., Yoo, H.J.: Solutions for real chip implementation issues of noc and their application to memory-centric noc. In: Proc. of NOCS, pp. 30–39 (2007)
4. Lee, H.G., Ogras, U.Y., Marculescu, R., Chang, N.: Design space exploration and prototyping for on-chip multimedia applications. In: Proc. of DAC, pp. 137–142 (2006)
5. Nguyen, H., Ngo, V., Choi, H.: Realization of Video Object Plane Decoder on On-Chip Network Architecture (2005)
6. Hu, J., Ogras, U.Y., Marculescu, R.: System-level buffer allocation for application-specific networks-on-chip router design. IEEE TCAD 25(12), 2919–2933 (2006)
7. Cong, J., Wei, J., Zhang, Y.: A thermal-driven floorplanning algorithm for 3d ics. In: Proc. of ICCAD, pp. 306–313 (2004)
8. Cong, J., Zhang, Y.: Thermal via planning for 3-D ICs. In: Proc. of ICCAD, pp. 745–752 (2005)
9. Tsai, C.H., Kang, S.M.S.: Standard cell placement for even on-chip thermal distribution. In: Proc. of ISPD, pp. 179–184 (1999)
10. Shang, L., Peh, L.S., Kumar, A., Jha, N.K.: Thermal modeling, characterization and management of on-chip networks. In: Proc. of MICRO, pp. 67–78 (2004)
11. Shang, L., Peh, L.S., Jha, N.K.: Powerherd: dynamic satisfaction of peak power constraints in interconnection networks. In: Proc. of ICS, pp. 98–108 (2003)
12. Chaparro, P., Magklis, G., Gonzalez, J., Gonzalez, A.: Distributing the frontend for temperature reduction. In: Proc. of HPCA, pp. 61–70 (2005)
13. Davis, W.R., Wilson, J., Mick, S., Xu, J., Hua, H., Mineo, C., Sule, A.M., Steer, M., Franzon, P.D.: Demystifying 3D ICs: The pros and cons of going vertical. IEEE Des. Test 22(6), 498–510 (2005)
14. Li, F., Nicopoulos, C., Richardson, T., Xie, Y., Narayanan, V., Kandemir, M.: Design and management of 3D chip multiprocessors using network-in-memory. In: Proc. of ISCA, pp. 130–141 (2006)
15. Murali, S., Micheli, G.D.: Bandwidth-constrained mapping of cores onto NoC architectures. In: Proc. of DATE, p. 20896 (2004)
16. Bartzas, A., Skalis, N., Siozios, K., Soudris, D.: Exploration of alternative topologies for application-specific 3d networks-on-chip. In: Proc. of WASP (2007)
17. Huang, W., Stan, M.R., Skadron, K., Sankaranarayanan, K., Ghosh, S., Velusam, S.: Compact thermal modeling for temperature-aware design. In: Proc. of DAC, pp. 878–883 (2004)
18. Coenen, M., Murali, S., Ruadulescu, A., Goossens, K., De Micheli, G.: A buffer-sizing algorithm for networks on chip using tdma and credit-based end-to-end flow control. In: Proc. of CODES+ISSS, pp. 130–135 (2006)
19. Hu, J., Marculescu, R.: Energy- and performance-aware mapping for regular noc architectures. IEEE TCAD 24(4), 551–562 (2005)

Data-Driven Clock Gating for Digital Filters

Alberto Bonanno, Alberto Bocca, Alberto Macii, Enrico Macii, and Massimo Poncino

Politecnico di Torino, Corso Duca degli Abruzzi 24, Torino 10129, Italy

Abstract. Digital filters implement a continuos computation and therefore generally they do not exhibit any structural idleness. This can prevent the usage of classical low-power optimizations that exploit idleness, such as clock gating.

In this work, we propose a data-driven implementation of clock gating for digital filters, which relies on the observation that often times the dynamic range of the inputs uses only a small portion of the bidwith, resulting in most of the higher-order bits of the registers having very low switching activity. When this occurs, unused bits in each filter tap can be clock-gated; since all the gated flip-flops share the same idle condition (i.e., new and currently stored are identical) they can share a single clock gating cell. The number of flip-flops that can be gated with a single cell depends on the tradeoff between the power saved and the performance penalty.

This technique has been applied on a digital filter used within an ultra low-power industrial design; comparison with other standard and advanced automatic clock-gating methods highlights the effectiveness of the proposed technique.

1 Introduction

Digital filters are an essential building block of circuits and systems employed in application domains such as telecommunication (wired and wireless), image processing, speech recognition, biomedical, software radio, and cellphones. Many of these domains are typical of portable, battery-operated devices, for which power consumption is the foremost design criterion; designing power-aware digital filters would thus help in significantly reducing the total power budget of the system. For this reason, the low-power research community has put significant effort in the recent years in the search of solutions for the design and implementation of low-power digital filters ([1]–[6]).

There are essentially two classes of approaches for designing low-power filters: (i) optimization of the filter coefficients, and (ii) architectural transformations of the filter structure. The first class of approaches include the representation of coefficients using proper representations, such as signed-power-of-two (SPT) formats of which the canonical-sign-digit (CSD) format is most popular [1]. Another techniques represents coefficients using residue number systems (RNS), which result in smaller word-length, parallel, modular arithmetic calculations [2]. These schemes achieve power reduction indirectly by reducing the number of addition/subtraction operations.

Another popular scheme for coefficient representation is the use of differential coefficients for multiplication [3]. Since differential coefficients have shorter word-length, the resulting design and output can also use shorter word lengths, and thus can reduce power consumption. This idea can be improved by considering not just differential coefficients but also differential inputs [4]. Moreover, by observing that the magnitude of

J. Monteiro and R. van Leuken (Eds.): PATMOS 2009, LNCS 5953, pp. 96–105, 2010.

the difference between the absolute values of adjacent coefficients is typically bounded, it is possible to apply decorrelating transformations in order to reduce the number of bits required to represent the coefficients [5].

Concerning the class of solutions that use specialized filter structure, one popular architecture relies on common subexpression elimination (CSE) techniques [6]; these schemes consist of eliminating redundant computations in multiplier blocks using the most commonly occurring subexpressions (bit patterns) that exist in the (CSD) coefficients. By replacing all coefficient multiplications with a single multiplier block, the redundancy present in the CSD coefficients is then exploited to share some of the adders to further reduce the hardware complexity, thus reducing power consumption.

Most of the above techniques achieve power reduction as a by-product of complexity reduction by either reducing the effective bid-width or reducing the number of multipliers and/or adders. None of them, in any case, leverage traditional low-power solutions used for generic circuits based on extraction of idleness, such as clock gating, which has proven to be the most general, cheap, and effective strategy for dynamic power reduction ([8]–[11]). Since digital filters implement a sort of streaming computation, in which generally no *structural* idleness is present, it seems natural that clock gating has less opportunities for applications.

However, *functional* idleness can be extracted, depending on the statistics of the input data. This idea has been used in [7] to implement a clock-gated version of a FIR filter for image processing. By exploiting correlation of input data (i.e., consecutive pixels of an image), this work partitions the tap register into two sub-registers; the one that receives the highly correlated data is clock gated.

In this paper, we push this idea further without being constrained to a single application domain or making assumptions on the correlation of input data. Our approach relies on the observation that in many cases, during filter operations, not the whole dynamic range of the inputs is used, and unused or low-activity bits in each tap could then be clock-gated. Depending on the input dynamics, multiple flip-flops of a register can be gated using the same conditions, thus using a limited number of gating cells.

We applied our technique on a special filter architecture, namely a Cascaded Integrator-Comb (CIC) filter; CICs have emerged as a computationally efficient implementations of narrow-band low-pass filters and are often embedded in hardware implementations of decimation and interpolation in modern communications systems. CIC filters are a good benchmark for our technique for two reasons. First, they are intrinsically energy-efficient, since they do not require multipliers and use a limited amount of storage; thus, reducing their power consumption would be especially valuable for low-power design. Second, although CIC are effectively Finite-Impulse Response (FIR) filters, they are composed of a FIR section (the comb) and an IIR (Infinite Impulse Response) section (the integrator); this allows us to evaluate our optimization techniques on both types of filter architectures while using a single type of filter.

Results show that our clock gating strategy saves an extra 20% register power with respect to a conventional topological clock gating. This translates into about 10% total energy saving on the entire filter design. Furthermore, savings are much less insensitive to the input data: power savings range between 66% and 85%, as opposed to topological clock gating, which in some case yields savings as low as 6%.

2   Background and Previous Work

2.1   CIC Filters

CIC filters are a special class of linear-phase FIR filter. Their distinctive feature is that they do not require multipliers and use a limited amount of storage. Therefore, they are more efficient than conventional FIR filters, especially in fixed-point applications [12]. A CIC filter contains two basic building blocks: A comb element (a FIR configuration – Figure 1-(a)), and an integrator (an IIR configuration – Figure 1-(b)).

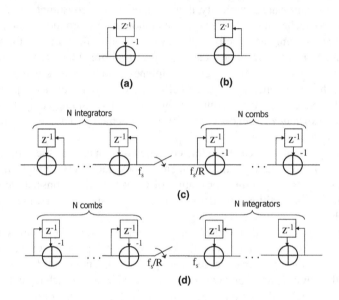

Fig. 1. CIC Filter Elements and Configurations: Comb (a), Integrator (b), a CIC Filter used for Decimation (c) and for Interpolation (d)

Figure 1-(c) and Figure 1-(d) show the two typical configurations of a CIC filter: a decimation CIC filter and an interpolation one, respectively. These block diagrams reflect the original architecture as proposed in the original paper [12]. Various optimized arrangements are possible [13].

2.2   Clock Gating

Clock gating is conceptually based on the idea of disabling (i.e., gating) the clock signal to a specific register that feeds a portion of combination logic that is not performing useful computations during some clock cycles [8,9]. A generic gated-clock architecture is shown in Figure 2; a signal called *activation function* (F_a) is defined in order to selectively stop (when $F_a = 1$) the clocking of the circuit when the latter does not result in a state or output transitions. The activation signal is filtered by a latch that is transparent when the global clock is low, so that potential glitches of the activation signal are filtered out.

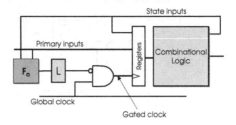

Fig. 2. Conceptual Clock-Gating Architecture

The activation function is a combinational logic block that extract idleness conditions from the knowledge of the primary inputs and the state inputs of the circuit. These conditions might be derived from a state-based description or from the netlist of the circuit and can be purely topological (as in commercial CAD tools, e.g., Synopsys' clock gating [10]) or include functional information ([11]).

The popularity of clock gating as a dynamic power optimization technique is also due to its relatively easy integration in a standard synthesis flow.

3   Data-Driven Clock Gating

In digital data processing systems, the number of bits (and thus the size of the register banks) are decided based on the data resolution and the dynamic range of the input signals. Although designers tend to fit the bit width to the data range as much as possible, this is done to match the maximum, worst-case dynamics of the inputs. The average dynamics, however, can be sensibly smaller than the worst-case one, thus resulting in situations in which only a fraction of the bit-width is utilized.

Apparently, this situation has no consequence on dynamic power consumption: unused register bits preserve their values and will not toggle, and should therefore consume no power. In practice, this is not true, however; the clock signal that switches at each cycle, thus causing internal power consumption in the flip-flop (FF). An analysis on the FFs of the library used in our experiment has shown that this clock-induced power is significant; even when the FF does not change state, it consumes about 45% of the power consumed by the FF when an input signal with 50% transition probability is applied (that is, the worst-case switching conditions on the data path of a FF). Gating the clock signal when the content of a FF is unchanged is the solution to this problem. This amounts to using the architecture proposed in [7], which is shown in Figure 3.

The enable signal 'EN' is generated by an XOR gate and thus it is at '1' only when the incoming data and the stored data are different. All the potential glitches are filtered by a latch-based clock-gating cell. When incoming and stored values differ, the clock signal is enabled and, as soon as it reaches the logic value '1', the FF can store the new data. This will be immediately reported at the input of the EXOR gate but the latch avoids any loop caused by the feedback. In the work of [7], this architecture is applied on individual bits in the context of image processing, using the spatial correlation property of consecutive pixels of bitmapped images.

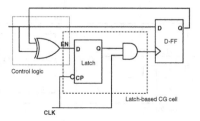

Fig. 3. Data-driven clock-gating architecture used in [7]

We apply their basic idea to our context, that is, by exploiting the under-utilization of the register width. Since multiple bits in a register will be idle, and their idleness condition (i.e., with reference to the scheme of Figure 2, the activation function) is identical, we *cluster* the unused FFs in such a way that the gating condition can be shared. We move thus from a bit-level scheme (as in [7], Figure 3) to a (partial) word-level scheme, as shown in Figure 4.

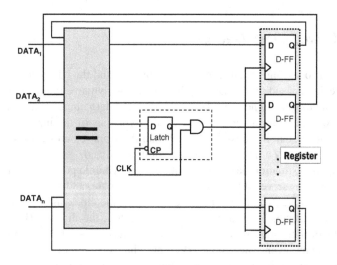

Fig. 4. Clustered Data-driven clock-gating architecture

The EXOR gate of Figure 3 is replaced by a comparator; the enable signal is asserted whenever one of the $(Data_i, Q_i)$ pairs differ.

It is clear that the benefits of the clustering should be traded off against the actual activity of the bits of a register. The enable signal is in fact asserted as soon as one of the $(Data_i, Q_i)$ pairs differ; when this occurs, all the FFs of the cluster will be enabled even if some of them do not toggle, thus consuming unnecessary power. Therefore, one essential step in the implementation of this clustered scheme consists of a profiling step, in which the activities of the bits of all the register are tracked. To this purpose, a cheap probabilistic simulation suffices, since only the switching activities are needed.

Based on this switching activity profile, several possible criteria can be used to determine the clusters for each register. In this work, we adopt a straightforward *threshold-based* selection mechanism. When the switching activity of a bit is below the threshold, it is included in the cluster. The threshold is chosen by comparing the cost of the gating cell of Figure 3 against the power saved by gating a single bit. Our experiments show that setting the threshold to 5% provides the best tradeoff. The threshold-based selection, besides being simple, can also work when some register bits are not truly unused (i.e., with zero switching probability), but simply have low activity due to the nature of the input signal.

Example 1. Figure 5 shows the switching profile for a 24-bit register of the filter design used in our experiments. One possible clustering would put bits 12 to 23, which have zero activity (because they are unused) into the cluster.

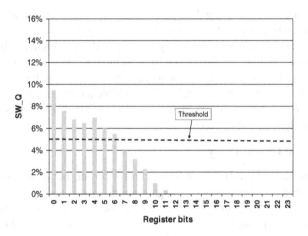

Fig. 5. Example of switching activity profile for a register of 24 bits

A clustering based on the above-mentioned 5% activity threshold, results in the addition of bits 7–11 in the cluster. The small percentage of clock cycles in which these bits toggle (thus causing bits 12 to 23 to be also enabled) is amortized by the savings obtained in the remaining fraction of the cycles in which they do not toggle.

3.1   Combining Enable-Based Clock Gating Conditions

Designers often explicitly add enable conditions to HDL code because this allows the synthesis tool the instantiation of topological clock gating [10]. Therefore, it is possible that the design already contains enable signals to be used as gating conditions. The proposed data-driven clock gating can exploit these enable-based conditions, which can be simply combined with the data-driven ones as shown in Figure 6-(a), where, for simplicity, the case of a 1-bit cluster is depicted.

The insertion of the multiplexer in the control logic cell avoids the comparison between the stored and incoming data if the register is not enabled (*reg_en* signal).

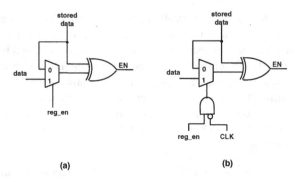

(a)   **(b)**

Fig. 6. Control logic structure with register enable signal: Combining with Data-Driven conditions (a), and Circuit Arrangement to Prevent Glitches (b)

In cases where the incoming data is the result of a complex operation, a significant amount of glitches could be propagated down to the latch. These glitches are not functionally relevant, but consume useless power; in order to eliminate this problem, we modify the basic architecture using the by AND-ing the enable signal with clock signal, as shown in Figure 6-(b). In this way, the output of control logic block is not used until the latch is not transparent and so the multiplexer can block the computation of the signal 'EN' when the clock is high or the *reg_en* is 0. The result is that all glitches are filtered for half period of clock.

3.2   Impact on Circuit Delay

Increasing the size of the cluster is beneficial for power, but it increases the delay on the FF data input. The increase in propagation time on this path is in the worst case the sum of the delay of the comparator plus the delay of the multiplexer, when the modified scheme of Figure 6 is used. The delay of the comparator is correlated to the number of bits in the cluster; therefore, for paths that are timing-critical we can control the size of the clusters for the register banks that belong to critical paths, by either preventing them to be added to clusters (if no increase in the critical path is tolerated), or by trading off power saving against delay increase.

The configuration of Figure 6-(b) implies an additional timing constraint to the design. In fact, the CLK signal masks the application of the *reg_en* condition in the second half of the cycle (CLK high). In the first half cycle, when the clock is low, the *data* signal propagates at the output of the multiplexer; the comparator must therefore generate the *EN* in this first half of the clock cycle, before the latch becomes non-transparent. This poses a limitation on the maximum size of a cluster.

4   Experimental Results

4.1   Experimental Setup

We have implemented the data-driven clock-gating in a commercial design flow based on Synopsys Design Compiler, using a 90nm industrial technology library. The benchmark used for the experiments is an optimized CIC filter with a customized low-power architecture. The data parallelism is 28 bits, whereas the order of the filter, the value of the decimation factor and the working frequency can be configured dynamically through external inputs. The design has been stimulated using 23 different testbenches that represent different working conditions of the application in which the filter is used. Simulations are done by using Cadence NCSIM at the gate-level, in order to capture activity for power estimation.

As already discussed in Section 3, our methodology does a preliminary profiling step on the filter (using probabilistic simulation) in order to extract the switching activity of each flip-flop. This is followed by the clustering phase, in which, for each register, the composition of each cluster is determined based on the switching activity threshold, and the data-driven clock gating cell (possibly combined with existing enable signals) are instantiated in the synthesized design.

4.2   Results on the CIC Filter

The configurable CIC filter used for our experiments contains 32 28-bit registers. The HDL description of the design contains enable signals for these registers, thus it is possible to apply separately the standard, topological clock gating [10] and the data-driven one in order to compare their results in term of power saving.

Table 1. Power saving on register banks for data processing

Testbench	Frequency [MHz]	Register Power Saving [%]		Total Power Saving [%]	
		Std CG	DD CG	Std CG	DD CG
1	12.5	72.21	78.83	56.75	59.80
2	12.5	84.76	82.98	67.05	66.18
3	12.5	86.74	84.02	68.15	66.82
4	12.5	61.94	75.71	47.04	52.46
5	1.0	56.95	73.79	49.09	50.73
6	12.5	74.85	79.06	58.43	60.38
7	12.5	59.87	74.77	48.08	54.54
8	12.5	56.08	77.33	43.90	52.44
9	12.5	32.96	73.45	31.45	45.66
10	10.0	45.16	74.37	38.89	50.64
11	12.5	21.22	70.32	26.33	44.50
12	12.5	6.28	66.37	19.84	41.19
13	12.5	28.78	71.50	30.19	46.34
14	12.5	70.04	78.47	53.53	57.26
15	12.5	86.78	84.94	72.99	72.03
16	12.5	22.73	71.43	27.50	45.30
17	12.5	22.06	71.44	27.17	45.17
18	12.5	68.65	79.78	53.54	58.51
19	12.5	57.29	73.03	43.73	49.78
20	12.5	60.93	74.04	45.81	50.96
21	8.3	68.61	80.46	53.35	57.96
22	5.0	58.99	77.96	48.44	54.05
23	5.0	48.16	74.93	43.30	51.04
Average		54.44	76.04	45.85	53.64

Table 1 summarizes the power savings achieved by application of the topological clock gating (Column *Std CG*) and the DDCG one (Column *DDCG*), on about one thousand flip-flops. We report both the power saved in the registers only (Columns *Register Power Savings*), and in the entire circuit (Columns *Total Power Savings*).

Starting with the observation of register power, we can notice two important advantages of the DDGC over a conventional CG. First, its savings are superior in all but three cases (2,3, and 15), where however the topological CG is only marginally better. The DD-CG saves on average about 76% power, whereas standard CG saves only 54%. Second, and more important, its effectiveness is roughly insensitive to the input workload and filter configuration. As a matter of fact, for some testbenches (e.g. *Test 12*) the standard CG is almost ineffective whereas the DD-CG technique consistently saves at least 66% power.

Results for the entire design are in agreement with those for registers. This is intuitive since the filter is dominated by sequential elements. Notice that power results for the entire filter design assumes that *all registers are clock gated*. In the *Std CG* case, all registers are gated using conventional CG. In the *DD CG* case, the FFs with low output switching (according to the analysis outlined in Section 4.1), are gated using the DD architecture; the remaining ones are gated with conventional CG.

The results show that even if the DDCG has been applied on part of circuit only, our approach saves about 8% more power in average. As before, however, the savings are consistent over the testbenches (minimum saving with DDCG is 41%, maximum 72%), unlike conventional CG (for which savings range from 19% to 68%).

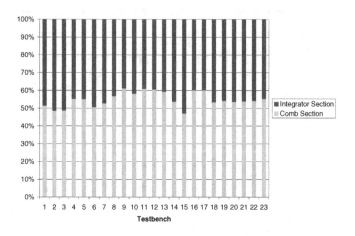

Fig. 7. Breakdown of power savings into comb and integrator section

Finally, Figure 7 shows the breakdown of the power saved in the two sections of the CIC filter, i.e., the integrator and comb. Since the latter represent two different filter structure (IIR for the integrator, FIR for the comb), this information is useful to see whether how the data-driven clock gating is effective on the two basic filter structures.

As the picture shows, the optimization is equally effective on the two sections, with a slight advantage of the comb (FIR) section (55% average saving) on the integrator (IIR) section (45% average saving).

5   Conclusions

We have proposed a clock gating scheme that is suitable for architectures such as digital filters, in which a functional "idleness" can be extracted from the circuit. Our scheme, called *data-driven clock gating* uses the fact that the parallelism of digital filters is determined based on the worst-case dynamic range of the inputs, which does not occur very frequently. A significant fraction of the register bits will therefore be often, or always unused; this allows to extract special gating conditions that cannot be observed using conventional tools.

Results on an industry-strength implementation of a CIC filter show that it is possible to save an additional 20% power, on average, with respect to a conventional clock gating scheme.

References

1. Hewlitt, R.M., Swartzlantler, E.: Canonical signed digit representation for FIR digital filters. In: 2000 IEEE Workshop on Signal Processing Systems, SiPS 2000., October 2000, pp. 416–426 (2000)
2. Freking, W.L., Parhi, K.K.: Low-power FIR digital filters using residue arithmetic. In: ASILOMAR 1997: Thirty-First Asilomar Conference on Signals, Systems & Computers, November 1997, vol. 1, pp. 739–743 (1997)
3. Sankarayya, N., Roy, K., Bhattacharya, D.: Algorithms for Low Power and high speed FIR filter realization using differential coefficients. IEEE Transactions on Circuits and Systems 44(6), 488–497 (1997)
4. Chang, T.S., Jen, C.W.: Low power FIR filter realizations with differential coefficients and inputs. In: ICASSP 2008: International Conference on Acoustics, Speech, and Signal Processing, pp. 3009–3012 (2008)
5. Ramprasad, S., Shanbhag, N.R., Hajj, I.N.: Decorrelating (DECOR) transformations for low-power adaptive filters. In: ISLPED 1998: International Symposium on Low-Power Electronics and Design, August 1998, pp. 250–255 (1998)
6. Yao, C., et al.: A Novel Common-Subexpression-Elimination Method for Synthesizing Fixed-Point FIR Filters. IEEE Transactions on Circuits and Systems I 51(11), 2215–2221 (2004)
7. Jung, J.M., Chong, J.-W.: A Low Power FIR Filter Design for Image Processing VLSI Design 12(3), 391–397 (2001)
8. Benini, L., De Micheli, G.: Transformation and Synthesis of FSMs for Low Power Gated Clock Implementation. IEEE Transactions on CAD 15(6), 630–643 (1996)
9. Benini, L., De Micheli, G., Macii, E., Poncino, M., Scarsi, R.: Symbolic Synthesis of Clock-Gating Logic for Power Optimization of Synchronous Controllers. ACM Transactions on Design Automation 4(4), 351–375 (1999)
10. Synopsys Inc., Power Compiler: Automatic Power Management within Galaxy Design Platform, www.synopsys.com/Tools/Implementation/RTLSynthesis/Documents/powercompilerds.pdf
11. Babighian, P., Benini, L., Macii, E.: A Scalable Algorithm for RTL Insertion of Gated Clocks based on Observability Don't Cares Computation. IEEE Transactions on CAD 24(1), 29–42 (2005)
12. Hogenauer, E.B.: An economical class of digital filters for decimation and interpolation. IEEE Transactions on Acoustics, Speech and Signal Processing 29(2), 155–162 (1981)
13. Losada, R.A., Lyons, R.: Reducing CIC Filter Complexity. IEEE Signal Processing Magazine 23(4), 124–126 (2006)

Power Management and Its Impact on Power Supply Noise

Howard Chen and Indira Nair

IBM Research Division, Thomas J. Watson Research Center,
1101 Kitchawan Road, Yorktown Heights, New York 10598-0218, U.S.A.
{haowei,indira}@us.ibm.com
http://www.research.ibm.com

Abstract. As device sizes continue to shrink and circuit complexity continues to grow, power has become the limiting factor in today's processor designs. This paper describes a hierarchical scalable power supply noise analysis methodology to simulate the switching events that arise from the ubiquitous use of clock gating, power gating, frequency scaling, and other power management techniques. By accurately extracting and modeling the electrical characteristics of both the package and chip design, our multi-core multi-voltage-domain transient noise analysis ensures the power and signal integrity of our design under different workloads and operating frequencies. A series of case studies will be presented to illustrate the effect of power management operations on transient noise and the design of a power management control unit to contain voltage droop.

Keywords: power gating, frequency scaling, supply noise.

1 Introduction

The advent of nanometer technology has not only increased the complexity of system-on-a-chip design, but also presented a significant challenge for power management. In our power-aware design methodology, clock gating is often used to save power in synchronous circuits. By pruning the clock tree and disabling portions of the circuits, we can effectively reduce the dynamic switching power. However, the sudden change of switching current may also introduce undesirable power supply noise, which must be contained. The power supply noise (ΔV) is caused by the impedance ($Z = R + j\omega L$) of the power supply network and the current (I) that flows through the power supply network. In order to accurately simulate the power supply noise, we need to consider not only the resistive IR drop, but also the inductive $L\Delta I/\Delta t$ noise. In traditional VLSI design, the resistive IR drop occurs mostly on the chip, and the inductive ΔI noise only occurs on the package. They are often analyzed separately and designed to be contained within their respective noise limits. Since the maximum ΔI noise occurs during switching when the current change ΔI is maximum, and the maximum IR drop occurs when the current I is at its peak, the worst-case ΔI noise and worst-case IR drop do not occur at the same time. Therefore, an integrated package-level

J. Monteiro and R. van Leuken (Eds.): PATMOS 2009, LNCS 5953, pp. 106–115, 2010.

and chip-level power bus model with detailed switching and timing information is needed to accurately analyze the V_{DD} variation over time, and properly calculate the total power supply noise $\Delta V = IR + L\Delta I/\Delta t$. If the power supply voltage drops more than 10% and lasts for an extended period of time, signals that are connected to this power supply may experience additional delay due to the voltage droop, and cause timing closure problems.

To prevent any potential chip failure due to the collapse of power rails, we have developed a hierarchical scalable power supply distribution model to analyze the resistive IR drop and the inductive $L\Delta I/\Delta t$ noise at both the unit level and chip level. The topology of our power distribution system includes not only the processor chip, but also second-level packaging such as the flip-chip plastic ball grid array (FCPBGA) package and FR4-dielectric printed wiring board. In order to reduce the complexity of a full-chip power supply noise analysis, a hierarchical approach is used to build the chip and package power distribution model. At the package level, a coarse-grid model is generated to represent the equivalent inductance between adjacent regions on a package. At the chip level, a C4-based fine-grid model is used to represent the back-end-of-line (BEOL) RLC power bus network.

To ensure the accuracy of a full-chip power supply noise analysis, we have developed a switching-circuit model to capture the dynamic effect of transient current. Based on the circuit simulation results of our common power analysis methodology, we model the switching activities of each functional unit with a piecewise linear current source that mimics the switching pattern and current signature of the real circuits. For example, if the circuits operate at a certain power level such as hold power, maximum average power, clock-gated hold power, or clock-gated maximum average power, within a given cycle, then the waveform that best represents the current switching condition in one of the several possible states will be selected. As the circuits switch from one state to another state, the composite waveform will change accordingly from cycle to cycle to facilitate a vector-based dynamic power supply noise analysis.

In this paper, we will first illustrate the effect of clock gating, power gating, and decoupling capacitance on power supply noise to underscore the importance of keeping power management activities away from the resonant frequency of power distribution system. Then we will describe a feedback mechanism in the power management control unit to limit voltage droop through dynamic frequency scaling.

2 Effect of Signal Gating on Power Supply Noise

Power management techniques such as data gating, clock gating, and power gating have been widely used to save power when circuits are not used. However, they also introduce undesirable transient noise, as shown in Fig. 1 and Fig. 2, which must be carefully controlled. For example, if the switching activity is gated in every other cycle, the transient peak-to-peak noise can reach 277 mV when the circuit switches from half-gated mode to non-gated mode (Fig. 1). On the other hand, when the circuit switches from non-gated mode back to half-gated mode, the transient peak-to-peak noise can reach 354 mV (Fig. 2). It is interesting to note that the average AC noise for circuits running in alternate cycles is actually higher than circuits that have switching activity in every cycle. This phenomenon is due to the LC resonant effect of package impedance. The closer the frequency of switching activity is to the resonant frequency, the higher the impedance and the greater the

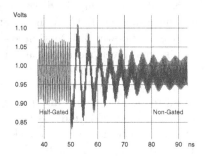

Fig. 1. Transient noise when the frequency of switching activity is doubled

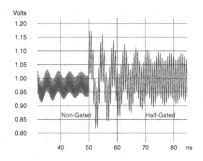

Fig. 2. Transient noise when the frequency of switching activity is halved

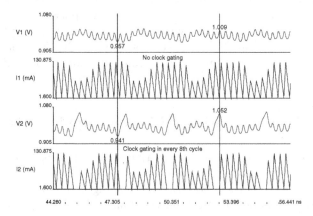

Fig. 3. Effect of 1/8 clock gating on power supply noise

noise. Since the resonant frequency of package impedance typically ranges from 100 to 300 MHz, the mid-frequency AC noise in this range is usually much higher than the high-frequency noise, because the high-frequency noise can be effectively suppressed by the on-chip decoupling capacitance.

Similarly, granular clock gating may have an adverse effect on power supply noise. For example, Fig. 3 compares the power supply voltage fluctuation for switching activity under non-gated mode and granularly-gated mode. When the clock is not gated, the power supply voltage of the circuit varies from 0.957 V to 1.009 V, with a peak-to-peak AC noise of 52 mV. However, when the clock is gated every 8th cycle, the power supply voltage of the circuit varies from 0.941 V to 1.052 V, which more than doubles the peak-to-peak AC noise to 111 mV. Therefore, although it may be advantageous to save 1/8 of the power by gating the clock in one of eight cycles, its potential impact on ΔI noise should also be considered.

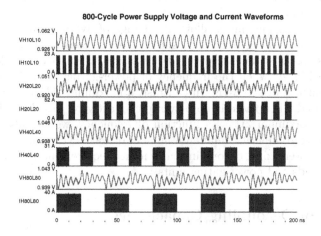

Fig. 4. The effect of repeated power gating on ΔI noise

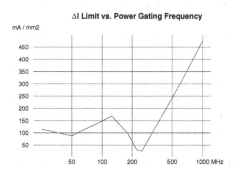

Fig. 5. Maximum allowable ΔI to limit peak-to-peak AC noise under 100 m V

3 ΔI Limit for Power Gating Activities

By disconnecting idle blocks from the power grid, power gating [1] can reduce not only the switching power, but also the leakage power. The scheduling of power gating activities, however, is important to prevent excessive transient noise. Given the average number of C4s and amount of decoupling capacitance per unit area, we have performed circuit simulation for 800 cycles of switching activity to analyze the AC noise under different power gating scenarios. The simulation results of 4 power gating operations (H10L10, H20L20, H40L40, and H80L80) are shown in Fig. 4. For example, VH10L10 and IH10L10 represent the power supply voltage and current waveforms when the circuits are gated every 20 cycles (10 cycles on and 10 cycles off). Similarly, VH80L80 and IH80L80 represent the power supply voltage and current waveforms when the circuits are gated every 160 cycles (80 cycles on and 80 cycles off). If IH80L80 is limited to a peak current of $40A$ and an average current of $20A$ during non-gated mode, then VH80L80 varies from 0.939V to 1.043V, which corresponds to a peak-to-peak AC noise of 104 mV.

Fig. 5 shows the maximum allowable change of average current (ΔI) as a function of power gating frequency, subject to the constraint of a maximum peak-to-peak AC noise under 100 mV. For example, the maximum allowable ΔI is only 26 mA/mm^2 when the frequency of power-gating activities is near the resonant frequency of 250 MHz. In contrast, a maximum ΔI of over 1 A/mm^2 can be tolerated when there is no power-gating activity. Based on this general guideline for maximum ΔI as a function of frequency, we can also determine the clock gating granularity, minimum number of wake cycles for regional power gating, wake footer sizing, decoupling capacitance requirement, and the partition of voltage islands and power gating units.

4   Effect of Decoupling Capacitance

To reduce the power supply fluctuation, decoupling capacitors are often used to support the large current transients generated by the simultaneous switching of on-chip circuits and off-chip drivers. In a simplified circuit model, the electric charge before switching can be represented by $C_D \times V_{DD}$, where C_D is the decoupling capacitance and V_{DD} is the nominal power supply voltage. The electric charge after switching can be represented by $(C_D + C_S) \times (V_{DD} + \Delta V)$, where C_S is the switching capacitance, and ΔV is the power supply noise. From the conservation of charge, where $C_D \times V_{DD} = (C_D + C_S) \times (V_{DD} + \Delta V)$, we can easily derive the upper bound on transient power supply voltage fluctuation $\Delta V = -V_{DD} \times C_S/(C_D + C_S)$. For today's multi-GHz microprocessor design, a significant amount of on-chip decoupling capacitance may be used to control the power-supply noise. For example, if the CMOS thick-oxide gate provides 10 $fF/\mu m^2$ [2], an area of 20 mm^2 will be needed to provide 200 nF of decoupling capacitance. Therefore, it is important to estimate and allocate the area needed for on-chip decoupling capacitors during the early design stage.

The proper amount of decoupling capacitance should also be carefully selected, so as not to generate a resonant frequency near the operating frequency, which will significantly increase the impedance and power supply noise. Fig. 6 shows the effect of on-chip decoupling capacitance on the magnitude of impedance and resonant frequency. Interestingly, the parasitic resistance that causes IR drop and latch-up problems can help to resolve the resonance problem by introducing a damping effect and reducing the resonance impedance $Z = L/(RC)$. Depending on the locations of the decoupling capacitors, on-chip decoupling capacitors are effective in reducing the high-frequency noise, while off-chip decoupling capacitors are effective in reducing the low-frequency noise.

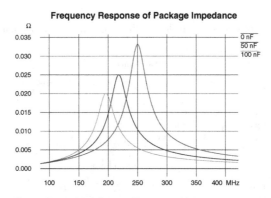

Fig. 6. The effect of on-chip decoupling capacitance on resonant frequency

Another important development in 45-nm technology is the integration of deep-trench capacitors [3] into logic circuits. The deep-trench decoupling capacitors could provide significantly more capacitance per unit area than traditional oxide capacitors [4]. Therefore, they are very effective in reducing the power supply noise. Fig. 7 compares the frequency response of package impedance for thick-oxide capacitors and deep-trench capacitors. Similarly, Fig. 8 shows the effect of deep-trench decoupling capacitors on containing power supply noise in the time domain. With the integration of deep-trench capacitors into logic circuits, it is conceivable that off-chip decoupling capacitors on the package can be completely eliminated in the future.

5   Dynamic Frequency Scaling and Voltage Droop Control

The package model for power supply noise analysis is implemented in our power management control unit (PMCU) to dynamically adjust the clock frequency and control voltage droop. Frequency scaling is a technique used in computer architecture to adjust a processor's frequency and achieve performance gain, as measured by the instruction throughput. However, as an application executes on a core, the increased switching activity also results in higher power consumption ($P = CV^2f$) and higher voltage droop, which may adversely affect

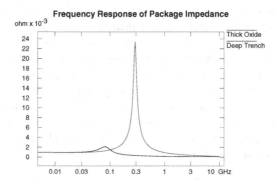

Fig. 7. The effect of deep-trench decoupling capacitance on package impedance

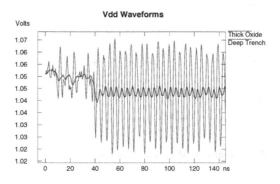

Fig. 8. The effect of deep-trench decoupling capacitance on power supply voltage

chip functionality. One approach to handling the voltage droop problem is to operate at conservatively low frequency, thereby delivering sub-optimal system performance. A more aggressive approach is through the use of dynamic frequency scaling along with a feedback control mechanism to deliver maximum performance while managing the voltage droop problem. In our system-level analysis tool for early exploration (SLATE) [5], the performance, power, thermal, and interconnect models are integrated into one complete analysis system. The feedback mechanism is evaluated by a proportional-integral-derivative (PID) controller to adjust the frequency and manage voltage droop while maximizing system performance.

Fig. 9 shows the model infrastructure for the power management control unit (PMCU) used in SLATE. The models in SLATE are implemented as cycle-accurate transaction-level models written in SystemC. The core model is a pipeline-accurate model based on the multicore Power4 processor [6] with a single-thread, out-of-order execution and in-order completion micro-architecture. Instruction traces corresponding to real applications are simulated in order to determine the performance as measured by the number of instructions completed

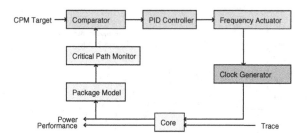

Fig. 9. Local PMCU control loop in SLATE

per time period, and the power dissipated by the core. The critical path monitor (CPM), comparator, PID controller and frequency actuator in the feedback mechanism are modeled as distinct modules with associated latencies, resulting in a delay of a few cycles between critical path monitoring and the resulting frequency change.

Power dissipation values computed by the core model on every clock cycle are used by the package model to generate voltage numbers. The voltage droops are then used to compute a CPM value corresponding to the number of inverters in an inverter chain that would switch, based on the current voltage and frequency. The error corresponding to the difference between the computed and target CPM values are fed to a PID controller which then determines the corrective action needed - in the form of a frequency scaling factor. The proportional value (P) determines the reaction to the current error, the integral value (I) determines the reaction based on the sum of recent errors, and the derivative value (D) determines the reaction based on the rate at which error has been changing. Tuning the PID controller to determine proportional, integral and derivative gain values is done by using several simulations on different workloads. Finally the frequency scaling factor provided by the PID controller is sent to the frequency actuator made of digital phase-locked loop (PLL) to adjust the frequency within a pre-specified range.

Fig. 10 shows the voltage droop profile for periods of activity corresponding to instructions being processed by the core and periods of inactivity following a cache miss, while the core idles and awaits cache data. The SLATE simulations were done for a system of four cores with L1 and L2 caches and a memory controller, all connected by a coherent bus. The same workload was applied to all the cores and the voltage droop was computed every cycle. The core's voltage droop profile was generated by simulating the workload for 10,000 cycles. Compared to the original voltage droop profile shown in dotted red curve, the solid blue curve in Fig. 10 shows the potential voltage droop reduction that can be achieved by a SLATE model with the PID controller. The CPM model computed a CPM value between 0 and $n - 1$, corresponding to a chain of n inverters and the model used several cycles of history in computing the Integral term for the PID control. It should be noted that due to the non-zero correction delay, the droop may not always be easy to control and we were not very aggressive in making fine-grained

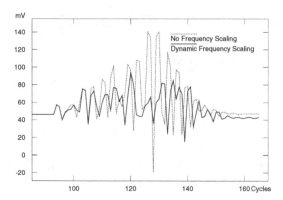

Fig. 10. Voltage droop correction profile

frequency adjustments. By limiting the operating frequency to within a narrow range of the base frequency, our goal was to achieve a maximum performance gain of 5%, which in itself was a difficult target at the microarchitectural level. We did not try to control the power dissipated by the system and our model did not include any other power management unit on the chip. The overall performance improvement that we observed from our simulations was in the 1-2% range, with some workload simulations showing almost no real performance gain. This was due to the fact that the higher frequencies were often being applied automatically by the feedback mechanism during inactive periods when the core was not processing any instructions and therefore did not benefit from the boost in frequency.

Making the feedback system stable requires careful tuning of the controller in order to make small corrections and thereby prevent the system from oscillating. Our simulations assumed a CPM value range between 0 and 15 which made our system quite sensitive to voltage droop changes. In the actual hardware implementation of a 16-inverter chain, however, it is unclear if this sensitivity would be easy to achieve.

6   Conclusions

As power becomes the limiting factor in today's processor design, the extensive use of power management techniques may introduce excessive power supply noise and impact system performance. In this paper, we describe a hierarchical methodology with a scalable power distribution model to analyze the noise at both the unit level and chip level. The scalable package model is implemented in our power management control unit to evaluate noise and provide a feedback mechanism for dynamic frequency scaling. A comprehensive case study is performed under different signal gating, power gating, and decoupling capacitance scenarios to underscore the importance of analyzing the frequency components of switching activity. By predicting and avoiding the resonant effect of power management activities, we can achieve power savings without compromising circuit performance.

References

1. Hu, Z., Buyuktosunoglu, A., Srinivasan, V., Zyuban, V., Jacobson, H., Bose, P.: Microarchitectural Techniques for Power Gating of Execution Units. In: International Symposium on Low Power Electronics and Design, pp. 32–37. ACM, New York (2004)
2. Popovich, M., Mezhiba, A., Friedman, E.: Power Distribution Networks with On-Chip Decoupling Capacitors. Springer, Heidelberg (2007)
3. Ho, H., Barth, J., Divakaruni, R., Ellis, W., Faltermeier, J., Anderson, B., Iyer, S., Kim, D., Mann, R., Parries, P.: Low-Cost Deep Trench Decoupling Capacitor Device and Process of Manufacture. U.S. Patent Number 7,193,262 (2007)
4. Knickerbocker, J., Andry, P., Dang, B., Horton, H., Interrante, M., Patel, C., Polastre, R., Sakuma, K., Sirdeshmukh, R., Sprogis, E., Sri-Jayantha, S., Stephens, A., Topol, A., Tsang, C., Webb, B., Wright, S.: Three-Dimension Silicon Integration. IBM Journal of Research and Development 52(6), 553–569 (2008)
5. Bergamaschi, R., Han, G., Buyuktosunoglu, A., Patel, H., Nair, I., Janssen, G., Dittman, G., Dhanwada, N., Hu, Z., Bose, P., Darringer, J.: Performance Modeling for Early Analysis of Multi-core System. In: The 5th International Conference on Hardware/Software Codesign and System Synthesis (CODES+ISSS 2007), pp. 209–214. ACM, New York (2007)
6. Warnock, J., Keaty, J., Petrovick, J., Clabes, J., Kircher, C., Krauter, B., Restle, P., Zoric, B., Anderson, C.: The Circuit and Physical Design of the POWER4 Microprocessor. IBM Journal of Research and Development 46(1), 27–51 (2002)

Assertive Dynamic Power Management (AsDPM) Strategy for Globally Scheduled RT Multiprocessor Systems*

Muhammad Khurram Bhatti, Muhammad Farooq, Cécile Belleudy,
Michel Auguin, and Ons Mbarek

LEAT, University of Nice-Sophia Antipolis-CNRS,
250-Rue Albert Einstein, Bâtiment-4, 06560-Valbonne, France
{bhatti,muhammad,belleudy,auguin,mbarek}@unice.fr

Abstract. Emerging trends in applications with the requirement of considerable computational performance and decreasing time-to-market have urged the need of multiprocessor systems. With the increase in number of processors, there is an increased demand to efficiently control the energy and power budget of such embedded systems. Dynamic Power Management (DPM) strategies attempt to control this budget by actively changing the power consumption profile of the system. This paper presents a novel DPM strategy for real time applications. It is based on the extraction of inherently present idleness in application's behavior to make appropriate decisions for state-transition of processors in a multiprocessor system. Experimental results show that conventional DPM approaches often yield suboptimal, if not incorrect, performance in the presence of real time constraints. Our strategy gives better energy consumption performance under the same constraints by 10.40%. Also, it reduces the number of overall state transitions by 74.85% and 59.76% for EDF and LLF scheduling policies respectively.

Keywords: Scheduling, real time multiprocessor systems, dynamic power management (DPM), energy.

1 Introduction

Energy efficiency in real time embedded systems is achieved by actively changing the power consumption profile of the system. This change in profile is performed in two ways: a) by Dynamic Power Management (DPM), i.e., putting system's components into low power/energy states while still meeting functional requirements b) by Dynamic Voltage and Frequency Scaling (DVFS), i.e., changing the operating frequency and supply voltage of active components. Relative to DPM strategies, DVFS is recent in embedded real time systems because of the evolution of processor technology permitting to have multiple operating frequencies. However, the evolved processor technology significantly increases the impact of static-power consumption as well but DVFS techniques work only with the dynamic component of power

---

* This work is supported by project PHERMA bearing reference ANR-06-ARFU06-003.

J. Monteiro and R. van Leuken (Eds.): PATMOS 2009, LNCS 5953, pp. 116–126, 2010.

consumption. Moreover, the number of frequency switching points supported by the modern-day processors is limited and frequency can not be reduced beyond a certain limit otherwise, the static power consumption significantly increases. Hence, the use of DPM strategies is still very interesting. This paper focuses on the DPM (dynamic power management) strategies. A DPM strategy exploits the inherently present idleness (if any) in the application's behavior which is a priori unknown or non-stationary. Whenever a DPM strategy (usually under the control of a scheduler) puts a component in an energy efficient state, bringing it back to the active state requires additional energy and/or latency to service an incoming task. The outcome of a DPM strategy is a decision whether to put a component (only processor in our case) into an energy efficient state or not? Since in an online schedule, the exact length of the idle interval is not known a priori therefore, there are several issues in coming to such decision intelligently based on this partial information. For instance, immediate shutdown—that is, shutdown as soon as an idle period is detected—may not save overall energy if the idle period is too short and the costs (temporal and energy) to recover a processor are greater than the gains in low power state. On the other hand, waiting too long to switch to low power state may not achieve the best possible energy reductions. Thus, there exists a need for effective (and efficient) decision making procedures to manage power consumption. [1, 2, 3, and 4]. We propose in this paper a novel DPM strategy called Assertive Dynamic Power Management (AsDPM), to make such intelligent decisions. AsDPM differs from the existing approaches in the way it exploits the inherent idleness in a schedule. It is important to note at this stage that AsDPM is not a scheduling algorithm itself. Rather it's an admission control technique for tasks to make an already schedulable task set more energy efficient. The remainder of this paper is organized as follows. In Section-II, we briefly describe some related research. In Section-III we provide our strategy in detail and discuss its efficiency. In Section-IV, we provide our experimental setup, simulation environment, and results. In Section-V, we conclude our paper.

2 Related Work

DPM strategies are well studied and the most implemented for long time. The studied techniques include predictive strategies [8], stochastic-modeling-based strategies [9], session clustering strategies [10], online strategies [11], and adaptive learning-based strategies [3]. Authors in [1, 2, and 7] classify DPM strategies into two main categories: a) *predictive schemes* and b) *stochastic optimum control schemes.* Predictive schemes attempt to predict the timing of future occurrences of idle interval in the system and schedule state-transition based on these predictions. The chief characteristic of stochastic approaches is the construction (and validation) of a mathematical model of the system that lends itself to a formulation of a stochastic optimization problem. Then strategies to guide the system power profile are devised. Most of the mentioned strategies are predictive in the sense that they use a sequence of past idle period lengths to predict the length of future idle interval. Also, they make assumptions on the application's characteristics and the probabilistic distribution of idle time intervals. While several useful and practical techniques have been developed using the predictive and stochastic optimum control schemes, it is difficult to develop bounds on the quality of the results without extensive simulations and/or model justification [1]. Our approach differs with the existing approaches in the sense that it is not predictive and it does not make any assumptions on the application's characteristics and the probabilistic distribution of idle intervals. It extracts the idleness in a deterministic way from the schedule and clusters it on some processors to better exploit by putting processors in energy-efficient states.

3 Assertive Dynamic Power Management (AsDPM) Strategy

3.1 System Model and Notations

Architecture and application model. A multiprocessor platform composed of m identical processors ($\pi = \{\pi_1,...,\pi_m\}$) is considered. Application is modeled as a finite set of n real time, asynchronous, independent, and recurring tasks ($\tau = \{\tau_1,...,\tau_n\}$). Each task is characterized by at least a quadruplet (r_i, C_i, d_i, T_i) where the parameters are; arrival or release time (r_i), worst-case execution requirement (C_i), relative deadline (d_i), and periodicity (T_i) of task respectively. The relative deadline of a task is considered equal to its period ($d_i=T_i$). All tasks are pre-emptive and support full migration. Moreover, a task may have runtime parameters such as best-case (B_i), worst-case (C_i) or actual-case (AET$_i$) execution times (Fig.1). Individual utilization u_i of a task is given by $u_i = C_i / T_i$ and the total utilization of task set is given by $u_{sum}(\tau) \overset{def}{=} \sum_{\tau_i \in \tau} u_i$.

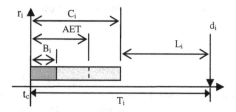

Fig. 1. Task's parameters

Energy model. Each processor support k-power states denoted by $\{S_1... S_k\}$. The power and time consumed in a particular state j is denoted by α_j and ψ_j respectively. States are ordered such that $\alpha_j > \alpha_k$ as long as $j < k$. Transition energy and time between two states j and k is given by γ_{j-k} and ψ_{j-k} respectively. Transitions are allowed only to active state from any state when powering up. The power consumed in transitioning from any state j to the *active* state (S_1) is denoted by β_j.

3.2 Strategy in Detail

We consider Earliest Deadline First (EDF) global scheduling policy to demonstrate how AsDPM works in conjunction with the scheduler.

EDF global. EDF uses, for execution at each instant in time, the jobs (of tasks) which have the smallest deadline. The utilization guarantees for a periodic task set with implicit deadlines under EDF or any other static-priority multiprocessor scheduling algorithm cannot be higher than (m+1)/2 for an m-processor platform [7, 8]. This definition is preserved except that a released job may be deferred (delayed) from execution unless its urgency level is critical.

Approach. AsDPM determines the minimum platform resources (number of active processors working at nominal frequency F_{ref}) needed to fulfill the execution requirement of released jobs at runtime. The deadline guarantees are provided for all ready tasks between any two Standard Scheduling Events (SSEs), i.e., release or termination event of tasks. AsDPM takes into account the anticipated laxities (explained in the following) of all released tasks to analyze, if the tasks are scheduled according to the given priority order (by scheduler) then is it possible to delay the execution of some low priority tasks in order to use the same number of processor(s) as long as possible? If so, then low priority tasks are deferred till the next SSE and remaining processors are either put in low power state (if they were already in active state) or at least no further processor is activated. Otherwise, if a task cannot be deferred then a processor is put into active state (S_1) to meet the execution requirement. AsDPM is an admission control technique which decides when a ready task enters in running tasks' queue of the scheduler. Without this admission control, all ready tasks are executed as soon as there are enough computing resources available in the system leading to poor possibilities of putting some processors in low power state. The decision related to state-transition is taken based on the WCET requirement of released tasks. However, we will demonstrate in later sections that AsDPM is optimist and takes full advantage in case where tasks execute with their AET. The admission of a ready task into running tasks' queue is controlled through a test called Laxity Bottom Test (LBT). Laxity is a run time parameter of a task showing its urgency to execution and anticipated laxity of a task is a measure of how long it can be delayed from execution in the presence of higher priority tasks (than itself) on a certain processor. AsDPM uses anticipated laxity to perform LBT. A negative value of anticipated laxity of a task is interpreted as if the scheduler continues to execute all released tasks with the same number of processors currently active then at least this job of task will miss its deadline in future and therefore, additional processor(s) must be activated to meet execution requirements. AsDPM uses different task queues. All task queues are sorted according to the scheduler's priority order. The global scheduler works with ReTQ and RuTQ only. AsDPM visualizes all task queues (fig. 2):

i. **Task Queue (TQ):** Contains all tasks at all time instances.
ii. **Released Task Queue (ReTQ):** Contains tasks which are released but not executing currently on any processor. When released, a task is immediately put in this queue.
iii. **Running Task Queue (RuTQ):** Contains tasks that are currently running on active processors (m_{act}). When a task is executing on a processor, it is represented as $\pi_j [\tau_i]$.

iv. Deferred Task Queue (DeTQ): Contains tasks that are released but deferred from execution. When a task is deferred, it is virtually assigned affinity to a currently active processor and represented as $\tau_i\left[\pi_j\right]$. All tasks in DeTQ are referred as a sub set called τ^d.

Working principle. Upon the arrival of an SSE, all released tasks are immediately put in ReTQ and scheduler is called. The scheduler sorts ReTQ according to EDF priority order (task with smaller deadline has higher priority). Algorithm-1 demonstrates that AsDPM works with this sorted ReTQ to control the admission of tasks into RuTQ through LBT. In the following we explain how LBT is performed.

The laxity (L_i) of task τ_i at time instance t_c is given by Eq.1.

$$L_i = d_i - \left(t_c + C_i^{rem}\right) \tag{1}$$

Here, C_i^{rem} refers to the remaining execution requirement of task τ_i. Since there may be multiple higher priority tasks currently executing on different processors and the remaining execution requirement (C_i^{rem}) of these tasks can be equal or less than their worst-case execution requirement (C_i) therefore, while computing anticipated laxity, the particular processor must be taken into account on which laxity is computed. Moreover, a higher priority task may not be currently executing but present in DeTQ. Thus, while computing the anticipated laxity of a task, all higher priority tasks (than itself) from RuTQ and DeTQ must be considered (Eq.2).

$$l_i^c = d_i - \left(t_c + C_c^{rem} + C_i^{rem} + \sum_{\tau_k \in \tau^d, \tau_k[\pi_j]} C_k^{rem}\right) \tag{2}$$

Here, C_c^{rem} refers to the remaining execution requirement of the higher priority task which is currently executing on a processor π_j and C_k^{rem} is the remaining execution requirement of a higher priority task which is already in DeTQ. When a task is deferred, it is virtually associated to a particular processor until next SSE. This virtual task-processor affinity helps in reducing the pessimism in computations. Eq.2 shows that the sum of the remaining execution requirement of only those tasks in τ^d shall be considered which have the same processor affinity. Hence, the contributing factor to anticipated laxity l_i^c of task τ_i on processor π_j is only the collective C_k^{rem} of those tasks which have the same processor affinity. LBT checks the value of l_i^c before admitting a task to either RuTQ or DeTQ as shown by Algorithm-1. The computation is of the linear complexity order $(g+1)$ where, g refers to the number of *activations* of processors being performed at an SSE. Example-1 helps in understanding AsDPM working principle.

Example 1. Let's consider three periodic independent and synchronous tasks (τ_1, τ_2, and τ_3) to be scheduled on two processors (π_1 and π_2). The quadruplet values for tasks are $(0,3,8,8)$, $(0,6,10,10)$ and $(0,4,16,16)$ respectively. Fig.3 (a) represents EDF global schedule which generates some random idle intervals (gray dashed area) because of the under-utilization present in the schedule. Fig.3 (b) shows the same schedule where AsDPM has extracted these idle intervals from processor π_1 and clustered them on processor π_2. These clustered idle intervals can be used to put π_2 in an energy efficient state for long time while π_1 continues to execute released jobs at the nominal frequency.

Algorithm 1. Working mechanism of AsDPM

@ Standard Scheduling Event (SSE) occurred @ t_c

- *Sort* ReTQ *by scheduler's priority order*
- *Move the highest priority task from* ReTQ *to* RuTQ
- *Perform LBT for all tasks remaining in* ReTQ
   *for (i=1; i≥ size (*ReTQ*); i++)*
    if $l_i^c \geq 0$ *then*

       Move τ_i *to* DeTQ

     else

       $m_{act} = m_{act}+1$
       Move back all tasks from DeTQ *to* ReTQ
       Move highest priority task from ReTQ *to* RuTQ
       break

    end if
- *Reiterate LBT until* ReTQ *becomes empty*
- *Execute tasks present in* RuTQ

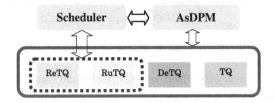

Fig. 2. Scheduler's view of task queues

Transition penalties. Transition costs in terms of energy consumed (γ_{j-k}) and time taken (ψ_{j-k}) for recovery from any state j to the *active* state (S_1) is not negligible in real time systems (eq.3). To model these penalties in AsDPM strategy, we consider that if $(j>k)$ then ($\gamma_{j-1} > \gamma_{k-1}$) and ($\psi_{j-1} > \psi_{k-1}$).

$$\text{Energy (per state)} = \alpha_j \times \psi_j + h * \gamma_{j-1} \tag{3}$$

Here, 'h' is the total number of transitions performed from state j to *active* state. Power consumed in transition from any state j to *active* state S_1 is given by Eq.4.

$$\beta_{j-1} = \gamma_{j-1} \Big/ \psi_{j-1} \tag{4}$$

Thanks to the anticipated laxity, AsDPM can know a priori that the number of processors currently in S_l state may not be sufficient to meet future deadlines for ready tasks and therefore, a processor should be immediately recovered to share the system's workload. However, a processor will take ψ_{j-1} time units to recover. Since, the anticipated laxity of a task does not represent its real urgency; a newly activated processor has time to recover before executing a ready task. In other words, the recovery time ψ_{j-1} of a processor can be masked with the remaining execution requirement C_c^{rem} of currently executing task(s). However, there may be some situation in which this time masking is not so evident such as case-1.

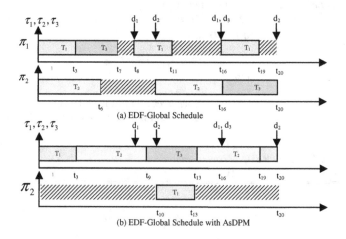

Fig. 3. Idle time extraction and clustering using AsDPM

Case 1. *Processor's recovery time from an energy-efficient state j is greater than the offered laxity of a task τ_i at its release ($\psi_{j-1} > L_i$).*

At an SSE, A task may get released such that its anticipated laxity goes negative while there is no intermediate priority task between itself and the currently running tasks, i.e. $\sum_{\tau_i \in \tau^d, \tau_i[\pi_j]} C_i^{rem} = 0$. In this case another processor must be immediately put in active state. But if $C_c^{rem} < \psi_{j-1}$ and $L_i < \psi_{j-1}$ are true then recovery time can not be masked with the currently executing task and the released task will miss its deadline in any case. To avoid such a case, the anticipated laxity must be computed while considering the maxima between C_c^{rem} and ψ_{j-1} (Eq.5).

$$C_c^{rem-max} = \max\left(C_c^{rem}, \psi_{i-1}\right) \qquad (5)$$

Hence, Eq.2 transforms into Eq.6.

$$l_i^c = d_i - \left(t_c + C_c^{rem-max} + C_i^{rem} + \sum_{\tau_k \in \tau^d, \tau_k[\pi_j]} C_k^{rem} \right) \tag{6}$$

Furthermore, we constraint task model such that ($L_i \geq \psi_{j-1}$) where j is the most energy efficient state. We'll discuss later how to remove this constraint.

Energy-efficient state transitions. AsDPM does not have a prior knowledge of the impact of upcoming SSE on the execution requirement. This uncertainty may cause potential over-optimism in the sense that AsDPM over-extract the idleness in the beginning and require more processors to meet deadlines later. This over-optimism may have two drawbacks: a) the next scheduling event is too close b) some processors remain too long in low-power state such that the deferred task(s) miss deadlines. Lemma-1 explains how to avoid this over-optimism.

Lemma 1. *AsDPM does not extract lossy idleness from the schedule and therefore, a state-transition is always energy-efficient.*

The proof is based on the knowledge of instances where the platform resource demand may augment. A release event (of a task) is different from a termination event (of a task) such that the termination of task never increases the execution requirement of system and consequently the platform resource requirement. However, a release event increases the execution requirement of system which may eventually increase the demand for platform resource. Therefore, knowledge of the occurrence of next release instance is helpful to determine the length of idle interval. AsDPM uses the information available in sorted TQ, ReTQ and RuTQ. Since $d_i = T_i$, i.e., next deadline of a task is also a reference to the release of its next job therefore, it is sufficient to compare the deadlines of top-most tasks in TQ, ReTQ, and RuTQ to determine next release instance (Eq.7).

$$r^{next} = \min\left(d_q, d_u, d_e\right) \tag{7}$$

r^{next} is the earliest release event. Based on the arrival pattern of r^{next}, a threshold on the minimum (non-lossy) length of idle interval is learned. On the termination of a task, AsDPM determines the next r^{next}, compares the length of time with learned threshold, and decides whether to transition a processor to energy-efficient state or not. Hence, AsDPM does not perform a transition which is not energy-efficient.

4   Experimental Setup, Results and Performance Analysis

All experiments are performed using a freeware tool STORM (Simulation TOol for Real-time Multiprocessor Scheduling) [12]. For the simulation results presented in this paper, we have used the hardware parameters of Intel's XScale® technology-based processor PXA270 (table-2) for embedded computing. All timing characteristics are given in milliseconds. Our example task set is composed of six periodic tasks ($n=6$) with the quadruplet values of Table-1. All results are provided while considering state-transitions between S_1 and S_4. The total utilization is given by $u_{sum}(\tau) = 2.20$. We simulate this task set on maximum three processors for simulation time equal to the hyper-period of tasks. The hyper-period of task set is 1200ms and all tasks execute with their WCET. We have observed various performance parameters to determine the impact of AsDPM on the schedules generated by EDF and LLF. Table-5 shows the percentage of time each processor is busy over the entire simulation time. Results show that AsDPM has extracted the idleness from π_1 and π_2 to cluster it on π_3 (Table-5). Another important amelioration in performance is that AsDPM reduces the number of state-transitions (Table-3) on all processors collectively by 74.85% and 59.76% for EDF and LLF respectively. Referring to Table-3 again, the example task set consumes 10.38% less average power and 10.40% less energy while scheduled under EDF-AsDPM. Similarly, it consumes 9.71% less average power and 9.70% less total energy while scheduled under LLF-AsDPM. We have provided real simulation traces of tasks on every processor. Fig.4 (a) presents a simulation trace showing the distribution of idleness of all tasks on three processors for simulation time 50ms under EDF and Fig.4 (b) shows the simulation traces generated with EDF-AsDPM. At runtime, it is often the case that tasks do not execute always with their WCET. We have simulated the same task set with AET of every task. Upon every new release of task, we randomly generate a value of AET which ranges between its WCET and not less than 60% of WCET. We notice that the gains on energy and average power for EDF increase up to 15.86% and 15.79% respectively and for LLF they increase up to 17.58% and 17.60% respectively (Table-4). Moreover, the number of state-transitions reduces by 74.53% 66.35% for EDF and LLF respectively.

Table 1. Task set

Task	r_i	C_i	d_i	T_i
T_1	0	6	16	16
T_2	0	8	20	20
T_3	10	8	24	24
T_4	10	8	30	30
T_5	16	16	40	40
T_6	20	20	50	50

Table 2. Parameters of XScale® PXA270 processor

State	α (mw)	ψ (ms)
S_1 (Running)	925	
S_2 (Idle)	260	0.001
S_3 (Standby)	1.70	11.28
S_4 (Sleep)	0.16	136

Table 3. System-level performance with WCET of tasks

Performance	EDF	EDF-AsDPM	LLF	LLF-AsDPM
Average power(W)	2.224	1.993	2.224	2.008
Total Energy(J)	2.671	2.393	2.671	2.412
No. of state-transitions	167	42	169	68

Table 4. System level performance with AET of tasks

Performance	EDF	EDF-AsDPM	LLF	LLF-AsDPM
Average power(W)	1.906	1.605	1.917	1.580
Total Energy(J)	2.289	1.926	2.303	1.898
No. of state-transitions	216	55	211	71

Table 5. Occupancy of processors with WCET of tasks

Processor occupancy (%)	EDF	EDF-AsDPM	LLF	LLF-AsDPM
P_1	86	99	83	99
P_2	73	94	75	90
P_3	56	20	58	26

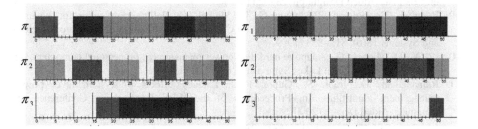

Fig. 4. Idle time distribution in EDF and EDF-AsDPM schedules

5 Conclusion

This paper presented a novel strategy for dynamic power management in real time multiprocessor systems called **As**sertive **D**ynamic **P**ower **M**anagement (AsDPM). AsDPM determines the minimum number of active processors needed to fulfill the execution requirement of released jobs at runtime. Experimental results show that using AsDPM in conjunction with EDF and LLF as global scheduling policies optimizes system's energy consumption by 10.40% and 9.70% respectively. In addition, AsDPM reduces the number of state-transitions by 74.85% and 59.76% while used in conjunction with EDF and LLF as global scheduling policies respectively. In near future work, we will be working to relax the constraint of $L_i \geq \psi_{j-1}$ discussed in section-IV.

References

1. Irani, S., Shukla, S., Gupta, R.: Online Strategies for Dynamic Power Management in Systems with Multiple Power-Saving States. ACM Transactions on Embedded Computing Systems 2(3), 325–346 (2003)
2. Benni, L., De Micheli, G.: Dynamic Power Management: Design Techniques and CAD Tools. Kluwer Dordrecht, Dordrecht (1998)
3. Chung, E.Y., Benni, L., Bogliolo, A., De Micheli, G.: Dynamic power management for non-stationary service requests. In: Proceedings of the Design Automation and Test Europe (1999)

4. Irani, S., Shulka, S., Gupta, R.: Competitive analysis of dynamic power management strategies for systems with multiple power saving states. In: Proceedings of the Design Automation and Test Europe Conference (2002)
5. Andersson, B., Baruah, S., Jonsson, J.: Static-priority scheduling on multiprocessors. In: Proc. 22nd IEEE Real-Time Systems Symposium, London, UK, December 2001, pp. 193–202 (2001)
6. Lopez, J.M., Diaz, J.L., Garcia, M., Garcia, D.F.: Worst-case utilization bound for EDF scheduling on real-time multiprocessor systems. In: Proc. 12th Euromicro Conf. Real-Time Systems, pp. 25–33 (2000)
7. Benni, L., Bogliolo, A., De Micheli, G.: A survey of design techniques for systemlevel dynamic power management. IEEE Transactions on Very Large Scale Integration (TVLSI) Systems 8(3), 299–316 (2000)
8. Hwang, C.-H., Allen, C., Wu, H.: A predictive system shutdown method for energy saving of event-driven computation. In: Proceedings of the IEEE/ACM International Conference on Computer Aided Design, pp. 28–32 (1996)
9. Benni, L., Bogliolo, A., Paleologo, G., De Micheli, G.: Policy optimization for dynamic power management. IEEE Transactions on Computer-Aided Design of Integrated Circuits and Systems 18(6), 813–833 (1999)
10. Lu, Y., De Micheli, G.: Adaptive hard disk power management on personal computers. In: Proceedings of the Great Lakes Symposium on VLSI (1999)
11. Ramanathan, D., Irani, S., Gupta, R.K.: Latency effects of system level power management algorithms. In: Proceedings of the IEEE International Conference on Computer-Aided Design (2000)
12. http://storm.rts-software.org

Design Optimization of Low-Power 90nm CMOS SOC Application Using 0.5V Bulk PMOS Dynamic-Threshold with Dual Threshold (MTCMOS): BP-DTMOS-DT Technique

Chih-Hsiang Lin and James B. Kuo

Dept of Electrical Engineering, BL-528
National Taiwan University
Taipei, Taiwan 10617
jbkuo@cc.ee.ntu.edu.tw

Abstract. This paper reports a 0.5V bulk PMOS dynamic-threshold technique enhanced with dual threshold (MTCMOS): BP-DTMOS-DT for design optimization of low-power SOC application using 90nm multi-threshold CMOS technology. Via the HVT/BP-DTMOS-DT-type logic cell technique generated by the special gate-level dual-threshold static power optimization methodology (GDSPOM) procedure, a 0.5V 16-bit multiplier circuit has been designed and optimized, consuming 22% less static leakage power at the operating frequency of 400MHz as compared to the HVT/LVT-type counterpart optimized by the GDSPOM reported before.

Keywords: System on a chip, design optimization, dynamic threshold, multi-threshold.

1 Introduction

For low-power SOC applications, multi-threshold CMOS (MTCMOS) circuit techniques have been adopted for their strength in optimization of low power and high speed performance [1]-[3]. Using 90nm MTCMOS technology, the gate-level dual-threshold static power optimization methodology (GDSPOM) procedure has been created [4]. Dynamic threshold CMOS (DTCMOS) circuit technique has been reported for enhancing the speed performance of an SOI CMOS digital circuit using a low power supply voltage [1][5]. In fact, DTMOS circuit techniques could also be used for PMOS devices in standard bulk CMOS technology to achieve low power and high speed performance [6][7]. In this paper, via the high-threshold (HVT)/BP-DTMOS-DT-type logic cell technique generated by the special GDSPOM procedure to achieve the MTCMOS goal, a test circuit of the 0.5V 16-bit multiplier has been designed. It will be shown that it consumes 22% less static leakage power at the operating frequency of 400MHz as compared to the HVT/LVT counterpart. In the following sections, the BP-DTMOS technique is described first, followed by the BP-DTMOS-DT GDSPOM procedure, performance and discussion.

J. Monteiro and R. van Leuken (Eds.): PATMOS 2009, LNCS 5953, pp. 127–135, 2010.

2 BP-DTMOS Technique

For a 90nm CMOS technology with the multi-threshold (MTCMOS) capability, high-threshold (HVT) and low-threshold (LVT) devices are available. HVT devices have low leakage current but the on current is small. LVT devices have a large on current, however, their leakage current when device is off, may not be acceptable for low-power applications. Based on 90nm bulk CMOS technology, the main PMOS device could be designed with an auxiliary PMOS device with its gate controlled by the gate of the main transistor and the source connected to the body such that the dynamic threshold (DTMOS) capability could be facilitated- BP-DTMOS technique [6][7]. In addition, as shown in Fig. 1, adopting the dual threshold (MTCMOS) technique with a small aspect ratio for the auxiliary LVT transistor and a large aspect ratio for the main HVT transistor, the bulk PMOS dynamic threshold (BP-DTMOS) device could be further enhanced with dual threshold (MTCMOS) technique (BP-DTMOS-DT). This BP-DTMOS-DT device combines the best of the high-threshold (HVT) and the low-threshold (LVT) devices- it has a low leakage current in the subthreshold region due to the dominance of the main HVT device since the leakage current of the auxiliary LVT device with a small aspect ratio could. In the strong inversion region its drain current is enhanced owing to the addition of the auxiliary LVT device for lowering the magnitude of threshold voltage dynamically. It is a new bulk DTMOS device enhanced with dual threshold (MTCMOS) built in- the BP-DTMOS enhanced with Dual Threshold (MTCMOS): BP-DTMOS-DT.

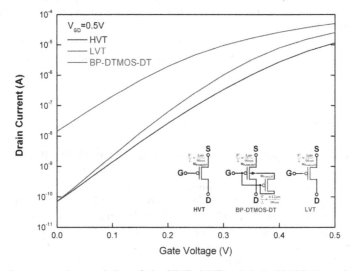

Fig. 1. Drain current characteristics of the HVT, LVT and bulk PMOS dynamic threshold PMOS with dual threshold (BP-DTMOS-DT) devices biased at VSD=0.5V, in 90nm CMOS technology with MTCMOS

Fig. 2 shows the 0.5V NAND logic gate circuit using the BP-DTMOS-DT technique in a 90nm CMOS technology with MTCMOS. Note that low-threshold (LVT) devices have been adopted for the NMOS. As shown in the figure, the dynamic control of the threshold voltage of the BP-DTMOS-DT device is carried out by the auxiliary PMOS device with a small aspect ratio to control the body voltage of the main transistor with a large aspect ratio. Fig. 3 shows the voltage and the current waveforms during the pull-up transient of this 0.5V NAND logic gate circuit using HVT, LVT and BPDTMOS-DT techniques, with an output capacitive load of 20fF. As shown in the figure, the propagation delay time of the circuit using the BP-DTMOS-DT technique is close to the LVT one while its consumed transient current is smaller.

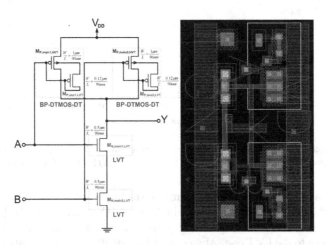

Fig. 2. 0.5V NAND logic gate circuit with its layout using the BP-DTMOS-DT technique in a 90nm CMOS technology with. Note that LVT has been used for NMOS devices.

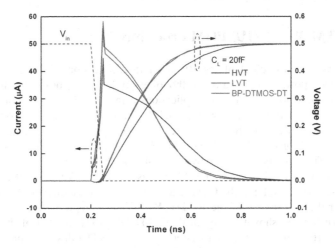

Fig. 3. Voltage and current waveforms during the pull-up transient of the 0.5V NAND logic circuit using HVT, LVT, and BP-DTMOS-DT techniques

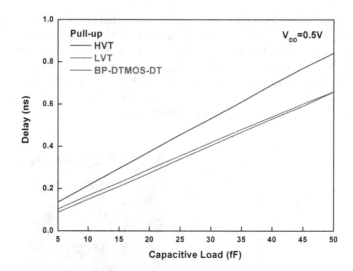

Fig. 4. Propagation delay time versus load capacitance during the pull-up transient of the 0.5V NAND logic gate circuit using the HVT, LVT, and the BP-DTMOS-DT techniques

Fig. 4 shows the propagation delay time versus load capacitance during the pull-up transient of the 0.5V NAND logic gate circuit using HVT, LVT, and BP-DTMOS-DT techniques. As shown in the figure, the propagation delay time of the BP-DTMOS-DT one is close to the LVT one. At an output load of 20fF, the propagation delay time of the BP-DTMOS-DT one is about 27% smaller as compared to the HVT one. Therefore, using the BP-DTMOS-DT technique, high speed and low power consumption could be obtained for the logic gate cell circuits.

3 BP-DTMOS-DT GDSPOM Procedure

Fig. 5 shows the flow chart of the BP-DTMOS-DT version of the gate-level dual-threshold static power optimization methodology (GDSPOM) procedure used for designing high-speed low-power SOC applications using MTCMOS techniques. In order to facilitate GDSPOM procedure with the BP-DTMOS-DT technique, two types of the basic logic gate cell circuits have been created. One type is the logic gate cell circuits realized by HVT for both NMOS and PMOS, which are called HVT-type logic gate cell circuits. The other type is made by the BP-DTMOS-DT for the PMOS devices and the LVT for the NMOS ones, which defined as the BP-DTMOS-DT-type logic gate cell circuits. In order to build the GDSPOM procedure, the timing and the power models used for the cell library of the BP-DTMOS-DT-type logic gate cell circuits have been constructed. As shown in Fig. 5, the BP-DTMOS-DT version of the GDSPOM procedure starts with the register transfer language (RTL) design, which is Synthesized into a gate level netlist of cells using CMOS devices with all HVT-type logic gate cells. Then, static timing analysis (STA) is performed to report a list of cells that are required to swap from the HVT-type to the BP-DTMOS-DT-type logic cells such that the specified timing constraints could be met. Finally, a cell-swapping script is executed to create the netlist built with the HVT-type and the BP-DTMOS-DT-type cells. This completes the BP-DTMOS-DT version of the GDSPOM procedure.

4 Performance

In order to evaluate the effectiveness of the BP-DTMOS-DT circuit technique used for BP-DTMOS version of the GDSPOM procedure for low-power SOC applications, three 16-bit multipliers with Wallace tree reduction architecture [8] using the BPDTMOS-DT technique have been designed. The designs are generated from the same RTL source except that one multiplier uses all HVT-type logic cells, another one has all BP-DTMOS-DT-type logic cells, and the other one contains both types of cellsHVT/BP-DTMOS-DT-type logic cells obtained after optimized by the

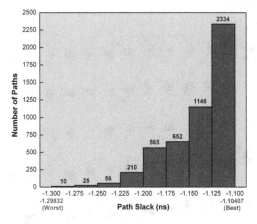

Fig. 6. Number of timing violated paths in the 0.5V 16-bit multiplier with all HV type logic gate cells

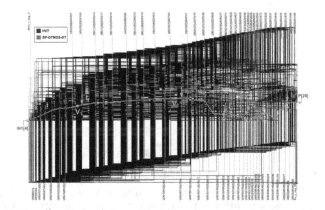

Fig. 7. Schematic view of the 0.5V 16-bit multiplier design optimized by the BP-DTMOS-DT version of the GDSPOM procedure with HVT/BP-DTMOS-DT type logic cells

BP-DTMOS-DT version of the GDSPOM procedure. The targeting frequency of this design is 400MHz. Cell library is developed for use in this study. In this 16-bit multiplier, it has over 7000 logic gate cells with a total of about 30,000 MOS devices.

Fig. 6 shows the number of the timing violated paths in this 0.5V 16-bit multiplier using all HVT-type logic gate cells. As shown in the figure, with the 400MHz clock frequency constraint, about five thousand paths do not pass the speed test. Ten paths have the longest delay time, which is the bottleneck in determining the operating speed of the 16-bit multiplier.

In this study, the BP-DTMOS-DT GDSPOM procedure reassigned 38% of the total cells from the HVT-type to the BP-DTMOS-DT type to meet the 400MHz speed constraint. Fig. 7 shows the schematic view of the 16-bit multiplier design optimized by the BP-DTMOS-DT version of the GDSPOM procedure to generate HVT-type (blue) and BP-DTMOS-DT-type (green) logic cells. Yellow lines indicate the originally timing violated paths.

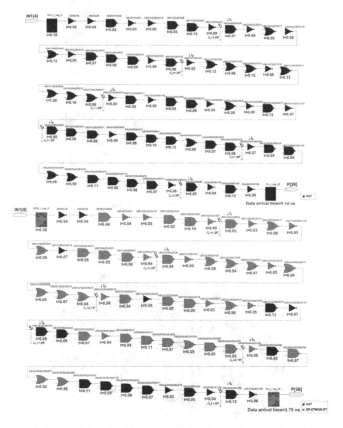

Fig. 8. Timing path from IN14 to P26 in the 0.5V 16-bit multiplier before (all HVT-type logic cells) and after (with the HVT/BP-DTMOS-DT-type logic cells) the BP-DTMOS-DT version of the GDSPOM procedure

Fig. 8 shows a path between input IN14 (the 4multiplicand bit) and output P26 (the 26product bit) with the individual delay time of the each logic gate listed before (all HVT-type logic cells) and after (with the HVT/BP-DTMOS-DT-type logic cells) the BPDTMOS-DT version of the GDSPOM procedure. This path is randomly selected to show how the swapping of the cell types for resolving the timing violation is accomplished. As shown in the figure, before the BP-DTMOS-DT GDSPOM procedure, this path is in all HVT-type, having an arrival time of 5.74ns- against the 400MHz operating frequency constraint. After the BP-DTMOS-DT procedure, many cells swapped into the BP-DTMOS-DT-type with the arrival time of 3.75, which is acceptable under the 400 MHz operating frequency constraint.

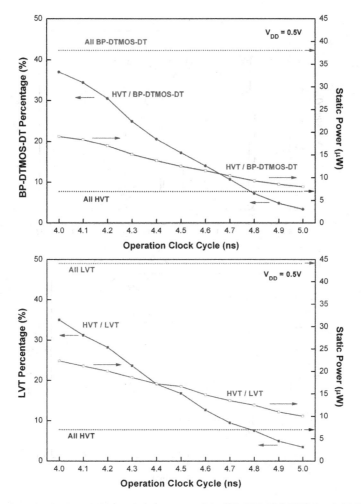

Fig. 9. Static power consumption and percentage of (a) BP-DTMOS-DT-type / (b) LVT-type logic cells in the 0.5V 16-bit multiplier design after (a) the BP-DTMOS-DT version and (b) the previous version of the GDSPOM procedure

The merits of the BP-DTMOS-DT GDSPOM could be understood by making comparison of the 0.5V 16-bit multiplier design optimized with the HVT/BP-DTMOS-DT logic cells with the HVT/LVT logic cells after the standard GDSPOM procedure reported before [4]. As shown in Fig. 9, with the HVT/BP-DTMOS-DT approach, the static leakage power consumption could be reduced substantially- from 22μW to 17μW at 400MHz and from 10μW to 7.5μW at 200MHz. In contrast, with all LVT-type cells, the static leakage power consumption is 44μW. Hence, with the HVT/BP-DTMOS-DT approach via the BP-DTMOS-DT GDSPOM procedure, a reduction in the static leakage power consumption of 61% at 400MHz and 81% at 200MHz has been obtained.

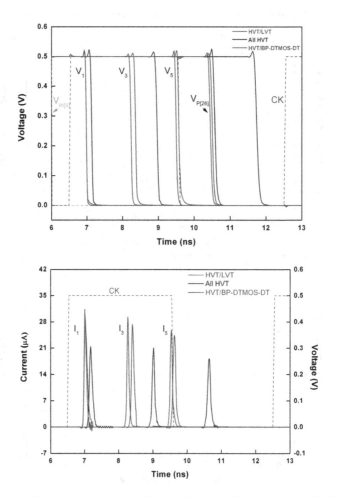

Fig. 10. Voltage and current transient waveform at the internal nodes in the critical path from IN14 to P26 of the 0.5V 16-bit multiplier based on all HVT-type, HVT/LVT-type and HVT/BP-DTMOS-DT-type logic cells

5 Discussion

The BP-DTMOS-DT technique presented in this paper for implementing the logic gate cells is not just useful for reducing the static leakage power consumption. It could also be advantageous for cutting the dynamic power consumption. Fig. 10 shows the voltage and the current transient waveforms at the internal nodes in the critical path from IN14 to P26 of the 0.5V 16-bit multiplier based on all HVT-type, HVT/LVT-type and HVT/BP-DTMOS-DT-type logic cells. As shown in the figure, along with the voltage waveforms during the transient, the current waveforms, which are correlated to the dynamic power consumption, are also dependent on the types of the logic cell circuits adopted. The multiplier using all HVT-type cells shows the smallest peaks in the transient current at the internal nodes.

The one using the HVT/LVT-type has the largest ones. The HVT/BP-DTMOS-DT-type is between the two. Therefore, the HVT/BP-DTMOS-DT-type approach is advantageous not just for enhancing the switching speed. It is also helpful for reducing both the static and the dynamic power consumptions.

Acknowledgments. This project is supported under a research grant from National Science Council.

References

1. Kuo, J.B.: Low-Voltage SOI CMOS Devices and Circuits. Wiley, New York (2004)
2. Usami, K., Kawabe, N., Koizuki, M., Seta, K., Furusawa, T.: Automated Selective Multi-Threshold Design for Ultra-Low Standby Applications. In: Low Power Electronics and Design Conf. Proc., pp. 202–206 (2002)
3. Kao, J., Narendra, S., Chandrakasan, A.: MTCNMOS Hierarchical Sizing Based on Mutual Exclusive Discharge Pattern. In: Design Automation Conf. Proc., pp. 495–500 (1998)
4. Chung, B., Kuo, J.B.: Gate-Level Dual-Threshold Static Power Optimization Methodology (GDSPOM) Using Path-Based Static Timing Analysis (STA) Technique for SOC Application. Integration, the VLSI J., 9–16 (2008)
5. Assaderaghi, F., Sinitsky, D., Parke, S.A., Boker, J., Ko, P.K., Hu, C.: Dynamic Threshold-Voltage MOSFET (DTMOS) for Ultra-Low Voltage VLSI. IEEE Trans. Elec. Dev., 414–422 (1997)
6. Shen, E., Kuo, J.B.: A Novel 0.8V BP-DTMOS Content Addressable Memory Cell Circuit Derived from SOI-DTMOS Techniques. In: IEEE Conf. Elec. Dev. and Solid State Ckts, pp. 243–245 (2003)
7. Shen, E., Kuo, J.B.: 0.8V CMOS CAM Cell Circuit with a Fast Tag-Compare Capability Using Bulk PMOS Dynamic-Threshold (BP-DTMOS) Technique Based on Standard CMOS Technology for Low-Voltage VLSI Systems. In: IEEE International Symp. Circuits and Systems Proc., vol. IV, pp. 583–586 (2002)
8. Wallace, C.S.: A Suggestion for a Fast Multiplier. IEEE Trans. Comput., 14–17 (1964)

Crosstalk in High-Performance Asynchronous Designs

Ritej Bachhawat[1], Pankaj Golani[2], and Peter A. Beerel[1,2]

[1] Department of Electronics and Electrical Communication Engineering
Indian Institute of Technology, Kharagpur, WB – 721302, India
[2] Department of Electrical Engineering – Systems,
University of Southern California, Los Angeles, CA – 90008, USA
iitkgp.ritej@gmail.com, {pabeerel,pgolani}@usc.edu

Abstract. This paper discusses the effect of crosstalk noise on high performance designs using the static single-track full-buffer template (SSTFB). We
identify the conditions where a crosstalk noise event can lead to functional failures and derive constraints on the maximum coupling capacitance to prevent
these failures. We conclude by discussing how these constraints can be integrated into advanced ASIC flows for high-performance asynchronous circuits.

Keywords: Crosstalk, dynamic logic, asynchronous, single-track.

1   Introduction

Driven by overwhelming design-time constraints, standard-cell based synchronous
design styles supported by mature CAD design tools and a largely automated flow
dominate the ASSP and ASIC market places. As device feature sizes shrink and process variability increases, however, the reliance on a global clock becomes increasingly
difficult, yielding far-from-optimal solutions. Because standard-cell designs use very
conservative circuit families and are often over-designed to accommodate worst-case
variations, the performance and power gap between full-custom and standard-cell
designs continuously widens [1]. Our prior research demonstrates that it is possible to
dramatically narrow this gap using asynchronous techniques by showing that conventional standard-cell techniques with an asynchronous cell library which uses dynamic
logic can produce very high-performance power-efficient circuits [2]. We also demonstrate the application of standard ASIC flow to estimate timing and power through
characterization of our asynchronous standard cell library [3], thus making asynchronous designs a more viable design alternative to synchronous designs.

With the minimum feature size of the semiconductor shrinking to nanometer range
and with the increase in clock frequencies, crosstalk noise has become a serious problem. As the process technology shrinks further the wires are becoming closer and
closer effectively increasing the coupling between two wires, thus possibly destroying
the signal integrity. The most accurate method to ensure signal integrity is SPICE
simulations, however due to size of the circuit this method is often time consuming
and impractical, which motivates the need of sophisticated and accurate models to
model noise for any arbitrary interconnect topology. Dynamic CMOS logic are
widely employed in high performance VLSI circuits, however due to there inherent

J. Monteiro and R. van Leuken (Eds.): PATMOS 2009, LNCS 5953, pp. 136–145, 2010.
© Springer-Verlag Berlin Heidelberg 2010

behavior they are less immune to crosstalk noise. Also the existing CAD tools are lacking in a proper ASIC flow to ensure the signal integrity in designs with dynamic logic.

The paper is organized as follows. Section 2 provides background on a high performance asynchronous template known as static single-track full buffer (SSTFB), background on a domino noise model which we will use to characterize the noise immunity of the dynamic gates used in SSTFB. In Section 3 we analyze how crosstalk noise can create an adverse effect on our circuits thus creating functional failures and in Section 4 we use the Vittal's metric [8] to estimate the crosstalk noise in a SSTFB design and we also derive constraints on the maximum coupling capacitance allowed to ensure no functional failures. In Section 5 we discuss how our analysis can be integrated into an ASIC flow and finally we conclude with future works to enhance the accuracy of our models in Section 6.

2 Background

In this section, we first give a brief introduction on template-based asynchronous designs and specifically the ultra high-performance SSTFB template. We also present the existing noise margin models that are used to compare the noise immunity of dynamic circuit families. Finally, we discuss the vital metric which is used to estimate the crosstalk noise amplitude and pulse widths.

2.1 Static Single-Track Asynchronous Templates

Among the numerous asynchronous design styles being developed template-based design styles have demonstrated very high performance capabilities. These template-based designs follow standard ASIC design flows which helps a designer in creating push-play designs thus reducing the design times. Template based design is similar to standard cell based design in synchronous world with the key advantage being that the set of gates used and timing constraints needed is well constrained and known apriori, simplifying the task of library design and constraint generation.

This paper focuses on a template that uses the 2-phase static single-track protocol [9] in which the sender initiates the handshake by driving the handshake wires (channel) high thus sending a request and then tristates the channel. The receiver then is responsible for holding the wire high until it acknowledges the input by driving the channel low and then tristating the channel. The sender is then responsible for holding the channel low until it drives it high again thus sending a new request. The transistor-level channel drivers are shown in Figure 1(a). For the sake of simplicity we may show a static single-track channel with its sender and receivers more abstractly using special gate-level symbols S_{UP} and S_{DOWN} shown in Figure 1(b).

An interesting application of the single-track protocol is the high-performance static single-track template SSTFB [4], illustrated in Figure 1(c), which has been designed for ultra-high speed fine-grained asynchronous pipelines. The cycle time of the SSTFB template can be as low as 6 transitions (~1.2GHz in 180nm technology [5]) with a forward latency of 2 transitions. The SSTFB template is very flexible and can be expended to different functionalities including logic gates (e.g., AND, OR, XOR)

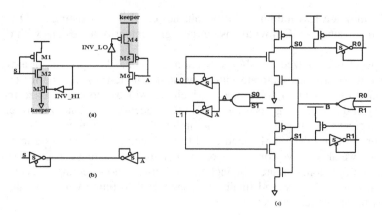

Fig. 1. Static Single Track interface and SSTFB transistor-level diagram

gates, functional elements (e.g., half and full-adders), and non-linear pipeline templates (e.g., forks, joins, splits and merges), making it a viable design template for both datapath and control.

2.2 Noise Margin for Domino Gates

Crosstalk noise occurs due to capacitive coupling between neighboring wires and can hurt a circuit in two ways, firstly causing a capacitive coupling glitch which if propagated will lead to functional failures, and secondly increasing signal propagation delay that in general can lead to timing failures for some types of circuits. Fortunately, due to adaptive nature of SSTFB designs, the increase in signal propagation delays does not affect the functional correctness of the design. Thus, our focus will be on the propagation of glitches.

Traditionally to analyze the effect of noise on a circuit we compare the peak value of the noise with the DC noise margin of the gates. However for dynamic gates this model is quite conservative as it doesn't capture the temporal property of the noise. In particular, a sharp noise spike can occur in with peak value of the noise greater then DC noise margin without causing any functional failure. To capture the temporal property of the noise event a domino noise model (DNM_{domino}) is proposed in [7] to compare noise immunities of different dynamic circuit families.

In this work we propose to use the DC noise margin model to characterize the noise robustness of the static gates in the SSTFB template and the domino noise model to characterize the robustness of our domino gates.

3 Effect of Noise on SSTFB Circuits

In this section we will analyze the effects of crosstalk noise on a channel driven by two single-track pipeline stages. Specifically we will analyze four cases which may lead to creation of a token or loss of a token due to noise leading to functional failures. We will then develop crosstalk noise constraints to prevent these failures using the models proposed in Section. 2.2.

3.1 Loss of a Valid Token Due to Noise on the Channel

In this particular case we analyze when due to crosstalk noise a valid token is lost on a channel, causing the circuit to deadlock. Consider a victim channel as shown in Figure 2 (a) with a valid token (value on the wire is 1). Here M4 and M5 are turned on while transistors M1, M3 and M6 are off. The combination of M4 and M5 acts as keeper and is responsible for holding the channel high. As the aggressor switches from $1 \rightarrow 0$, noise is introduced on the victim channel as shown in Figure 2(a).

Due to noise introduced on the victim channel, M3 will be turned weakly on allowing a weak discharge path to operate between the channel and the ground via M2 & M3. However due to M4 and M5 being strongly on, this weak discharge path is not strong enough to counter the effect of keeper and hence the token on the victim channel does not get lost and the aggressor has a $1 \rightarrow 0$ transition on it. However if this induced noise on the victim channel exceeds the DC noise margin of INV_HI then it may lead to a strong discharge path leading to loss of a token. Similarly, if the noise exceeds the DC noise margin of INV_LO then the keeper will be turned off and the channel will be driven to a tri-state. Once being driven to tri-state a successive noise even can more easily lead to the loss of token.

Hence to ensure the functional correctness we propose to make sure that the peak value of the induced noise at the node NS should not exceed the relevant DC noise margin of INV_HI and the peak value of the noise (V_P) should not exceed the relevant DC noise margin of INV_LO.

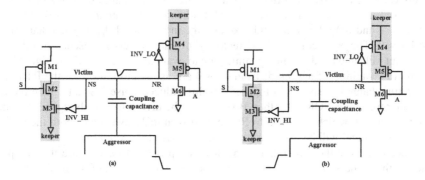

Fig. 2. Switching of aggressor leading to loss and creation of tokens

$$V_P \leq \min(NM_{INV\_LO}^{0->1}, NM_{INV\_HI}^{0->1}) \tag{1}$$

In fact, to be more accurate the peak noise voltage at node NR should be less than $NM_{INV\_HI}^{0->1}$ and peak noise voltage at node NS should be less than $NM_{INV\_LO}^{0->1}$.

3.2 Creation of a Token Due to Noise on the Channel

In this case we will analyze the scenario where a token is generated on the channels due to crosstalk noise possibly leading to deadlock and functional failure. Consider a victim channel as shown in Figure 2 (b) with the channel being in neutral state (value of the wire is 0). Here, M2 and M3 are turned on while transistors M1, M4 and M6 are off. The combination of M2 and M3 acts as keeper and are responsible for holding the channel low.

The scenario presented in this case is similar to one presented in Case 1 with the difference being here the aggressor switches from $0 \rightarrow 1$ instead from $1 \rightarrow 0$ and the consequence may be the incorrect creation of a token rather than a loss of a token. In particular, if the noise induced on the channel exceeds the DC noise margin of INV_LO, then M4 and M5 will be turned on leading to creation of a token. Similarly if the noise exceeds the DC noise margin of INV_HI then the keeper will be turned off and the channel will be driven to a tri-state which allows a successive noise event to more easily create a new token.

Hence we propose to make sure that the peak value of the induced noise at the node NS should not exceed the relevant DC noise margins of the INV_HI and INV_LO gates.

$$V_P \leq \min(NM_{INV\_LO}^{1->0}, NM_{INV\_HI}^{1->0}) \tag{2}$$

In fact, to be more accurate the peak noise voltage at node NR should be less than $NM_{INV\_HI}^{1->0}$ and peak noise voltage at node NS should be less than $NM_{INV\_LO}^{1->0}$.

3.3 Loss of a Valid Token Due to Domino Logic Violation

In this case we analyze the effect on one rail due to crosstalk noise induced on the second rail. In Figure 3 (a) we have a valid token on the output rails (R0, R1) such that R1 = 1 and R0 = 0 and a valid token on the input rails (L0, L1) such that L0 = 1 and L1 = 0. The right completion detector NOR gate detects a presence of token on the output rails and disables the dynamic gate to evaluate by driving the B signal low.

Due to switching of aggressor from $1 \rightarrow 0$ a noise is introduced on the R1 rail of the victim channel as shown in Figure 3. If this induced noise is greater then the DC noise margin of the NOR gate, then B signal will be driven to 1 enabling the dynamic gate to evaluate, which will lead to R0 being driven to 1. Eventually both the rails of the output channel will be driven high leading to loss of the valid token.

Hence to ensure the functional correctness we propose to make sure that the peak value of the induced noise does not exceed the DC noise margin of the NOR gate.

$$V_P \leq NM_{NOR}^{0->1} \tag{3}$$

where $NM_{NOR}^{0->1}$ is the DC noise margin of the NOR gate for a $0 \rightarrow 1$ transition. To be more accurate the peak noise voltage at node NS should be less than $NM_{NOR}^{0->1}$.

3.4 Creation of a Token Due to Domino Logic Violation

In this case we analyze the effect of crosstalk noise on input channels which may lead to creation of token on the output channel. In this case we have a null token on input channels (L0 = 0 and L1 = 0) and a null token on the output channels (R0 = 0 and R1 = 0), such that B signal is asserted which enables the dynamic gate in evaluation stage.

As the aggressor switches from $0 \rightarrow 1$ a noise is induced on the input channel L0 as shown in Figure 3 (b). As the dynamic gate is ready to evaluate, if this induced noise is greater then the threshold voltage of the NMOS transistor the dynamic gate will evaluate thus discharging the charge stored on the dynamic node S0. If the voltage deviation due to charge lost on S0 exceeds the DC noise margin of the S gate, a token will be created on the output channel R0 causing a functional failure.

In this case we are concerned about the charge lost on the dynamic node S0 which is not only the function of the peak value of the noise on input L0 but also the duration during which the noise on L0 is greater then the threshold voltage of the NMOS transistor. Hence for this case to ensure functional correctness we have to make sure that the crosstalk noise induced on channel L0 is less than the DNM of the domino gate.

$$DNM_{domino} = \int_T (V_{in}(t) - V_{th})\, dt = \frac{NM_{Sup}^{0->1}.C_d + |\frac{1}{2}.T.I_{kMAX}|}{g_m} \qquad (4)$$

where $NM_{S_{UP}}^{0->1}$ is the DC noise margin for the S_{UP} gate for $0 \rightarrow 1$ transition and I_{kMAX} is peak current flowing through M4 assuming the maximum voltage deviation at S0 node is $NM_{S_{UP}}^{0->1}$ and T is the pulse width of the noise. To be more accurate the crosstalk noise induced at node NR should be less than DNM_{domino}.

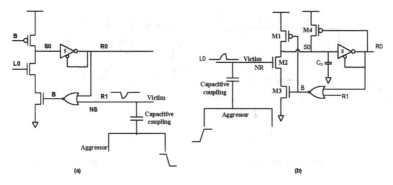

Fig. 3. Effect of noise causing domino logic to incorrectly evaluate

4   Estimation of Noise in Static Single-Track Circuits

This section derives constraints on maximum coupling capacitance that guarantees functional correctness. To do this, we consider Figure 4 that shows two single-track channels running parallel on the same metal layer. For the sake of simplicity we have chosen a very simple noise environment with only a single aggressor and the wires are modeled as lumped π models, however the analysis easily extends to more complex environments including multiple aggressors and different coupling locations. Also for simplicity, the wires are modeled as lumped π models and the effect of noise at the near and far end of the victim is considered to be the same. This section performs analysis of the crosstalk noise on the victim due to switching of the aggressor.

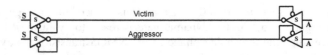

Fig. 4. Noise coupling in single-track channels to far and near-end coupling

From this estimation and the constraints derived in Section 3 we then derive the constraints on maximum coupling capacitance to prevent functional failures.

In Figure 5(a) we present an equivalent circuit model for the case when victim is held at logic level 1 through the keeper resistance $R_{keeperH}$ and $R_{keeperL}$ are the keeper resistance responsible for holding the victim high and low respectively and R_{PD} and R_{PU} are the aggressor driver resistance responsible for aggressor switching from $1 \rightarrow 0$ and $0 \rightarrow 1$ respectively. Cc denotes half the coupling capacitance. C1 is sum of half line capacitance and the intrinsic load of the driver of the aggressor while C2 is the sum of the half line capacitance and the load capacitance of the receiver. Similarly C3 is the sum of half line capacitance and the intrinsic load of the keeper while C4 is the sum of half line capacitance and the load capacitance provided by the receivers.

Using Vittal's metric [8] to solve the nodal equation for the node near receiver (NR) in Figure 5(a) we compute parameters K and b1 such that

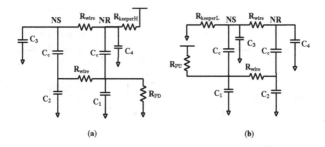

(a)   (b)

Fig. 5. Equivalent RC network for a quiet victim and aggressor switching

$$K = (2R_{keeperH} + R_{wire}).C_c \tag{5}$$

$$b_1 = R_{PD}(C_1 + C_2 + 2C_c) + R_{keeperH}(C_3 + C_4 + 2C_c) + R_{wire}(C_2 + C_4 + 2C_c) \tag{6}$$

Using (5) and (6) we can compute the peak noise at node NR as

$$V_{PNR} = \frac{(2R_{keeperH} + R_{wire}).C_c}{R_{PD}(C_1 + C_2 + 2C_c) + R_{keeperH}(C_3 + C_4 + 2C_c) + R_{wire}(C_2 + C_4 + 2C_c)} \tag{7}$$

Similarly for node NR in Figure 5 (b)

$$K = (2R_{keeperL} + R_{wire}).C_c \tag{8}$$

$$b_1 = R_{PD}(C_1 + C_2 + 2C_c) + R_{keeperH}(C_3 + C_4 + 2C_c) + R_{wire}(C_2 + C_4 + 2C_c) \tag{9}$$

and the peak noise at node NR as

$$V_{PNR} = \frac{(2R_{keeperL}+R_{wire}).C_c}{R_{PD}(C_1+C_2+2C_c)+R_{keeperL}(C_3+C_4+2C_c)+R_{wire}(C_2+C_4+2C_c)} \quad (10)$$

4.1 Maximum Coupling Capacitance

Using equations (11), (8), (9), and (10) as well as the constraints derived in Section 3 we can calculate the maximum coupling capacitance that can be tolerated before causing any functional failure.

For simplicity, we assume $R_{PD} = R_{PU} = R_{keeperH} = R_{keeperL} = R$ and $C_1 = C_2 = C_3 = C_4 = C$, $g_m = 1 / R$, $I_{kMAX} = \frac{NM_{SUP}^{0->1}}{R}$ and $NM_{INV\_HI} = NM_{INV\_LO} = NM_{SUP}$. Figure 6(a) shows the maximum capacitance allowed as a function the wire resistance, which is dependent upon the length of the victim wire.

In Figure 6(b) we try to validate our analysis by comparing the behavior of maximum coupling capacitance with spice simulations. These spice simulations are done on a typical single-track environment with a single-track gate driving another single-track gate with a varying interconnect length from 100 μm to 1200 μm. We assume that the victim net is quiescent with a single aggressor coupled with it, based on 65nm predictive technology models [10] [11] we plot the maximum coupling capacitance allowed so that no functional failures occur.

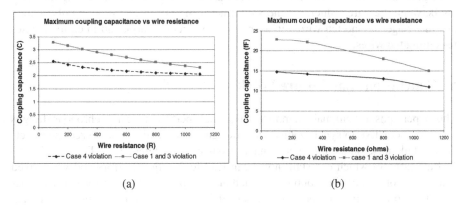

(a)   (b)

Fig. 6. Maximum coupling capacitance from analysis and spice simulations

The shapes of the curves seem to agree with our analysis fairly well giving some credence to our analysis. And, as one might expect, in both cases they show that violations of the domino logic (Case 4) is more sensitive to noise than inverters (Cases 1 and 3). Interestingly, these figures suggest that the maximum coupling capacitance of the staticized domino logic is about 20% lower than that of inverters for relatively short wires and more for longer wires. And, we also note that this difference may drop if we were to take into account the domino logic's footer transistor that is always present in SSTFB templates.

5 Integration into an ASIC Flow

With the advance of process technologies signal integrity in ASIC environment has become very challenging. There are many commercial CAD tools in the market which ensures the signal integrity in an ASIC which use sophisticated method to analyze the circuit and generate the list of victim nets which might be in danger. Traditionally in these tools signal integrity in an ASIC environment is measured in terms of the peak noise voltage that occurs on the victim due to switching of aggressor. If this peak noise voltage is greater then a characterized voltage of the receiver gate then that particular victim net is considered to be a violation. For designs involving domino gates like the template discussed in this paper where not only the peak noise voltage is critical but also the temporal property of the noise or "area under the curve".   For such gates noise immunity can be characterized as a noise rejection curve [12] that plots the allowable noise pulse height vs noise width so that no functional failures occur. Fortunately, noise rejection curves have been integrated in the latest state-of-the-art ASIC tools. Thus, to support single-track designs these advanced tools could either compute the noise rejection curve using an analysis similar to proposed in this paper or could compute and use the simpler proposed maximum coupling capacitance.

In case of a violation on a victim net the tools can try to fix the violating net through a variety of methods like inserting buffers on the victim, increasing the spacing between the wires, shielding the victim net using power and ground rails, adding pipeline stages to shorten wires (in asynchronous circuits only), and in extreme cases re-routing the wires.

6 Conclusions and Future Work

This paper aims to help make template-based high-performance asynchronous designs a viable alternative to synchronous ASIC design. Specifically we analyzed the effects of crosstalk noise on the high performance asynchronous template SSTFB. We identified all cases in which crosstalk noise can lead to functional errors and we derived constraints on maximum coupling capacitance to prevent these errors. These constraints help us in finding the violated nets and/or that can be fixed during optimization and/or in a post-routing ECO flow.

This paper uses a very simple interconnect model for the sake of simplicity. In order to be more accurate in nanometer technologies future works involved a more accurate interconnect model such as RC ladder model instead of simple π model and multiple aggressors to model crosstalk noise at near and far end of coupling. The future work also involves the use of this analysis to motivate library design choices including transistor sizing, keeper sizing to trade-off performance and noise immunity.

In this paper we have also limited the source of noise to crosstalk, however for future work we can extend this analysis to other sources of noise like IR drop, power and ground bounce and inductive coupling.

References

1. Chinnery, D.G., Keutzer, K.: Closing the Gap between ASIC and Custom: Tools and Techniques for High-Performance ASIC Design. Kluwer Academic Publishers, Dordrecht (2002)
2. Beerel, P.A.: Asynchronous Circuits: An Increasingly Practical Design Solution. In: ISQED 2002 (March 2002)
3. Prakash, M., Golani, P., Bandlish, A., Joshi, P., Rithe, R., Beerel, P.A.: Accurate timing and power characterization of Static Single-Track Full-Buffers. In: Semiconductors Research Corporation's (SRC) conference TechCon (2007)
4. Ferretti, M.: Single-track Asynchronous Pipeline Template, Ph.D. Thesis, University of Southern California (August 2004)
5. Golani, P., Dimou, G.D., Prakash, M., Beerel, P.A.: Design of a high speed asynchronous turbo decoder. In: Proc. International Symposium on Asynchronous Circuits and Systems, ASYNC (2007)
6. Choi, S.H.: Dynamic noise margin in Precharge-Evaluate Circuits. In: Proc. of 37th Design Automation Conference, DAC (2000)
7. Choi, S.H., Roy, K.: DOMINO noise model: A new crosstalk noise model for dynamic logic circuits. In: International SoC conference (2003)
8. Vittal, A., Chen, L.H., Marek-Sadowska, M., Wang, K.P., Yang, S.: Crosstalk in VLSI interconnections. IEEE Trans. Computer Aided Design (1999)
9. van Berkel, K., Brink, A.: Single-Track Handshake Signaling with Application to Micropipelines and Handshake Circuits. In: ASYNC 1996, pp. 122–133 (1996)
10. http://www.eas.asu.edu/~ptm/
11. Cao, Y., Sato, T., Sylvester, D., Orshansky, M., Hu, C.: New paradigm of predictive MOSFET and interconnect modeling for early circuit design. In: CICC, pp. 201–204 (2000)
12. Korshak, A.: Noise rejection model based on charge-transfer equation for digital CMOS circuits. IEEE Trans. Computer Aided Design (2004)

Modeling and Reducing EMI in GALS and Synchronous Systems

Tomasz Król, Milos Krstić, Xin Fan, and Eckhard Grass

IHP, Im Technologiepark 25, 15236 Frankfurt (Oder), Germany
{krol,krstic,fan,grass}@ihp-microelectronics.com

Abstract. In this paper, the possibilities of reducing EMI in GALS systems are investigated and presented. Based on the special software tool for EMI analysis, several different abstract models of GALS circuits have been designed in order to extract a realistic pausable clock behavior. Based on the clock behavior, we have been able to analyze using our tool the current profile of each modeled system, both in frequency and in time domain. The results have been compared with the synchronous counterparts including low-EMI solutions. As a result, a reduction up to 25 dB can be achieved when applying a low-EMI GALS methodology in comparison to the synchronous designs.

1 Introduction

Rapid and continuous development of the process technologies and device miniaturization imposes enormous challenges on designers and CAD tools. The classical synchronous paradigm became very difficult to achieve due to the problems in clock tree generation and timing closure. For mixed digital-analog designs, the challenges are even harder. Analog systems are very sensitive to the noise introduced by the digital components. Therefore, additional methods must be used for lowering of EMI (Electromagnetic Interference).

The GALS (Globally Asynchronous Locally Synchronous) methodology has been proposed as a solution for the system integration many years ago and mature solutions are already available [1]. There have been some proposals to use the GALS methodology also for EMI reduction [2]. It has been shown on several examples that asynchronous design can significantly reduce EMI in comparison to the classical synchronous design. The examples are the asynchronous designs of ARM processors [3, 4]. There are also some initial studies regarding the GALS approach for EMI reduction [2]. They have shown that the GALS systems can achieve EMI reduction up to 20 dB in comparison with a synchronous design. In time domain, the noise peaks can be lowered up to 40%. However, the real on-chip measurements [5] have shown smaller EMI reduction. Additionally, those activities were not systematic and have been focused only on specific design cases, not taking into consideration GALS as a general methodology for system integration. The technology advance and further device miniaturization increases a demand for deep investigation of EMI because of its detrimental influence on a whole system preformance.

Moreover, there are no dedicated tools to model EMI in GALS and synchronous circuits on a high abstract level. It is needed to have the possibility to predict at least

J. Monteiro and R. van Leuken (Eds.): PATMOS 2009, LNCS 5953, pp. 146–155, 2010.

approximate values of EMI in designed digital systems. In synchronous systems, which are much more evaluated because of their wide application, it is easier to estimate EMI. There are many investigations showing the possibility of reduction of EMI in synchronous systems by adding clock skew and phase modulation of the clock [6, 7]. However, adding a clock skew or a phase modulation of a clock to a synchronous chip demands additional work and sometimes is extremely difficult or even not possible.

The aim of this work is facilitating crossbenchmarking of EMI features for GALS and synchronous design style. It is important to make such EMI analysis, which would let system designers choose optimal solutions to their needs. A first step to make this is to a create software able to model and evaluate EMI in synchronous and GALS systems. In this paper, we would like to present a software tool able to simulate the EMI behavior caused by clock activity in GALS and synchronous systems on a very high abstract level. This tool is able to model additional features, such as introduced jitter, and phase shifting that can be embedded into GALS or synchronous systems in order to reduce EMI characteristic. This tool enables performing many simulations in order to investigate the best way to reduce EMI in GALS and synchronous circuits. Several GALS topologies have been evaluated and compared to their synchronous counterparts.

The paper is structured as follows: Section 2 describes EMI sources and the possibilities of its reduction in digital circuits. In Section 3, the accurate models of GALS systems are discussed, and the software to model EMI is presented. In Section 4, the results of simulations for different GALS topologies are presented and compared with synchronous designs. Finally, the last section sums up the work conclusions.

2 EMI in Digital Circuits

EMI in digital systems is caused by the simultaneous switching of logic components. Each active edge of a clock pulse, in a synchronous system, triggers all flip-flops that generate noise. This triggering is not exactly at a same moment because of the clock tree and its skew that spreads triggering of the flip-flops in time. EMI generated by the digital circuits can be analyzed in the easiest way by analyzing the supply current shape. Reduction of EMI is possible in several ways including improvement of physical elements. However, we have focused here only on a modification of a clock behavior by adding jitter or a fixed phase to each sub block.

Modeling the supply current shape. In order to build an exact model of any digital system, we need an accurate supply current shape profile. It is very difficult to define the supply current shape for each digital block and in each clock cycle, when the system is defined on a very abstract HDL level. The current profile varies significantly in each design. Moreover, it can change from cycle to cycle depending on activity and processing load. An important issue is to model the current profile in each particular clock cycle. In [6] it is shown that for digital systems triangular modeling of the current shape can be used. However, different clock cycles may have totally different current shapes depending on the logic activation in the digital block. In principle, the triangular model cannot always satisfy the real behavior of the system. For some complicated cases, we could model the current profile as a superposition of several triangular shapes.

In order to confirm this we have modeled realistic digital synchronous circuits consisting of complex sequential stage (512 flip-flops), combinational logic (813 basic combinational cells), reset and clock tree (369 buffers). We have modeled such system using 0.25 um CMOS library from IHP and simulated it in different scenarios in Cadence Spectre. Some results are shown in Fig.1. The current shape from 1a) can be modeled with the triangular shape but for 1b) a more appropriate model would be the superposition of two triangles.

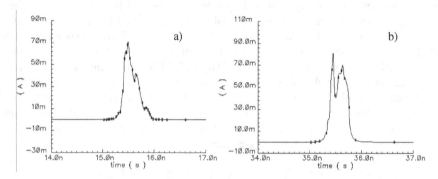

Fig. 1. Analog current profile simulation using 0.25 um CMOS process

Reducing EMI in digital circuits. Two techniques are mainly applicable to reduce EMI in synchronous systems, if we concentrate on modifying the clock behavior [2]. First we can add a clock phase shift to each LS block. Phase shift decreases the current peaks for a whole circuit, thus reducing EMI.

Additionally, we can add jitter to the clock source. Jitter introduces a phase modulation (rapid phase fluctuations) to a clock wave from cycle to cycle influencing EMR (Electromagnetic Radiation) [9]. It modifies slightly, up to a defined part of a period, the starting point of a rising edge, while the time of the high level stays constant. Hence, jitter can increase or decrease the clock period for a cycle but generally the average base frequency remains the same. To build a digital jitter generator, a Linear Feedback Shift Registers (LFSR) can be utilized as a Pseudo Noise Generator (PNG) [2]. In GALS systems with a pausable clock, we can only add jitter to a system. Integrating a phase shift would be a useless procedure. Variable phase shift is already present there by the nature of the GALS methodology.

3 Modeling EMI in Digital Systems

In order to evaluate EMI features of the digital systems caused by the digital clock behavior, we have generated a special software tool called "GalsEmilator". GalsEmilator is a program created in Matlab in order to investigate EMI in various types and topologies of GALS systems (including synchronous solutions). It contains many options to model, as precisely as possible, the parameters of each GALS/synchronous system. Hence, we are able to observe the noise behavior in frequency and time domain.

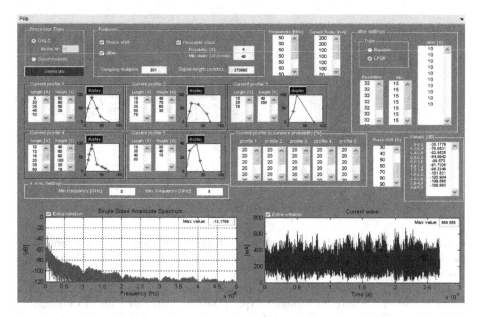

Fig. 2. GalsEmilator – software for modeling EMI in digital systems

In the developed tool, we were trying to enable modeling different supply current shapes for different clock cycles. The supply current profile is modeled as triangular shape (or superposition of different triangles) that appears periodically based on the clock behavior of the system. In software it possible to describe up to five different supply current profiles and specify the probability of their appearance in the system. For each block of the synchronous system, we can also set: a clock phase shift (in respect to the global clock frequency) and additional jitter. For GALS modules, we can model extra clock jitter and also model pausable clocking [1] as a dominant technique for low-EMI GALS circuits. Our model of GALS with pausable clocking allows us to simulate GALS wrappers that can pause the clock in order to perform a handshake operation. The behavior can be modeled by setting a probability of pause occurrence and a maximum delay of the pause. The delay is variable and, therefore, in our model it is randomized. Additionally, we have the possibility to automatically extract clock behavior directly from RTL simulation. All results, in timing and in frequency domain, as shown in Fig. 2, can be observed and analyzed both graphically and in a generated table. The complete software has its own user-friendly GUI.

Modeling GALS. We have utilized our software to model and evaluate EMI of different GALS and synchronous systems. For the GALS approach, we have concentrated on the pausable clocking scheme, that is very commonly used even in today's GALS NoC systems [1, 8]. In order to exactly model the clock behavior of the GALS system, all evaluated systems have been described in VHDL and simulated. The clock behavior is automatically extracted from the simulation using our software tool. Data is directly fed to the EMI analyzer and evaluated. Such extension of our tool was necessary in order to achieve one-to-one matching to the real system behavior of the

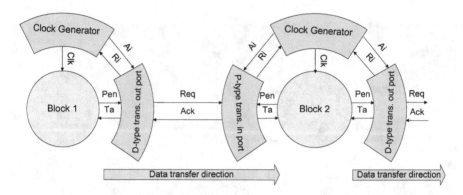

Fig. 3. Sample of connection between two adjacent LS blocks used in models

GALS interfaces. Especially, it was difficult to extract, without real simulation data, clock behavior during the data transfer process between the GALS blocks when clocks can be paused.

In our VHDL models, we have used D-type output and P-type input GALS ports [1] as shown in a Figure 3. 'Demand Type' (D-type) ports pause the clock immediately after receiving request from the Locally Synchronous (LS) block. For the input side, 'Poll Type' (P-type) ports have been used. The standard handshake operation between adjacent GALS modules was completely modeled in our simulation. The behavior of the clocking changes dramatically with the intensity of the data transfer since the clock pausing appears only during the data transfer process. Therefore, we have modeled three different scenarios of the system behavior:

    A. Low data transfer, where the data transfer is performed relatively rarely (once per 6 clocks in the example we were using)
    B. Medium-to-high data transfer, where half of the clock cycles are involved in data transfer
    C. Burst mode, where 80% of the clock cycles are data transfer related.

Topologies of the evaluated GALS systems. In our evaluation four different structures of GALS circuits have been analyzed as shown in Figure 4. We have analyzed different system topologies. Here, we have taken into consideration point-to-point (a), star (b) and mesh (c) topologies. In order to check if a granulation can influence the

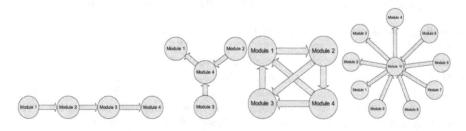

Fig. 4. Topologies of models: a) point-to-point b) star c) mesh d) large star

reduction of EMI, we have also examined the star with a large number of blocks (d). The goal was to evaluate different interconnect structures and to see their impact on EMI in GALS systems. The arrow in the Fig. 4 indicates a direction of handshake and data transfer.

System parameters of the model. For the system modeling, we have defined a base frequency which is a median for all other derived clock frequencies in the system. We needed such a frequency to be able to compare a synchronous system that normally has just a single clock domain with a GALS system that is usually triggered with different clocks. In our model, as an example, this base frequency was 50 MHz. GALS systems can be implemented very differently. Some systems may use very similar clock frequencies for local blocks (plesiochronous clocking). On the other hand other systems may have totally different LS clock frequencies. Generally, we have used three different frequency sets for modules in our GALS systems. The first set represents plesiochronous operation where the frequencies of each block are almost the same as the base frequency. In the second set, the difference is higher and in the third one, we have frequencies ranging up to a ratio of 1:3.

It can also make a difference which block has the slowest and which block the highest frequency. In particular, for the star topology, if the slowest block is in the centre, the complete system will be very slow and vice versa. We have tested, therefore, the star topology with both slow and fast setting.

In all cases, we have used 10 GHz sampling frequency. This sampling is quite sufficient for the systems we were modeling since the current profile with 50 MHz clock was represented as 200 points in simulation. In the model, we have used equal probability of occurrence for each of the five modeled supply current shapes. Also, we have used the same jitter settings for each simulation, with the LFSR length of 15 bits. The sum of the current peaks in all cases was the same in order to correctly compare results. In the 4-module systems we have defined that the peaks were 100 mA, 400 mA, 200 mA, and 300 mA. In 10-module systems the distribution was following: 2 X 200 mA, 4 X 100 mA, 4 X 50 mA.

4 Results

Synchronous system. In Figure 5, we can observe the EMI characteristic and its reduction in synchronous systems. In particular, we can see the EMI reduction in the synchronous system with a jitter applied. As we can notice, the jitter reduces only higher frequencies starting from 400 MHz. It has no significant influence to the lower spectral range. However, to achieve the reduction, the circuit should be able to be immune to 10% jitter, what is sometimes even not possible in a synchronous design, both for hold and setup time optimization. Moreover, Fig. 5 shows the effect of adding a phase shift to a system. We have modeled cases with 0%, 10%, 20%, 30% phase shift of a clock period. By introducing a phase shift to a circuit, we can alleviate EMI in a low frequency range, thus reducing current peaks. The high frequency spectrum remains not significantly changed compared to a basic synchronous approach. The tests were conducted also with a combination of jitter and phase shift. The results are promising because they incorporate advantages of both features. However, it would

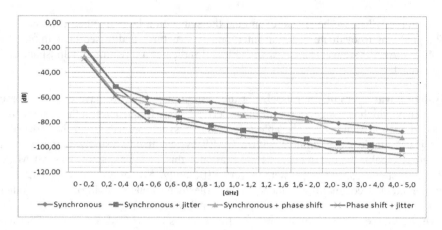

Fig. 5. EMI characteristic in the synchronous systems

be a real challenge to guarantee safe data transfer between the blocks in such synchronous system. For many applications, such as processor pipeline, introduction of such low-EMI techniques (jitter, phase shift) is not possible at all due to the difficulties in timing closure.

Evaluating GALS systems. Figure 6 represents results of comparing two sets of frequencies with medium data transfer and also showing the behavior for low granularity systems (4 GALS blocks) and high granularity systems (10 GALS blocks). We can observe that plesiochronous systems can achieve a significant EMI reduction in the high frequency range. However, it doesn't improve EMI for low frequency operation. On the other hand, the GALS system, with a larger difference of frequencies, reduces much better EMI of low frequencies in a spectrum, still preserving good parameters for higher frequencies. The test performed on various transfers rate with the same frequencies has shown very low differences in EMI reduction. The range of the result variations didn't exceed 5 dB. The clock behavior is automatically extracted from VHDL simulation at RTL level.

Figure 6 shows the EMI reduction in GALS systems with added jitter. We can observe that there is almost no impact of jitter at low frequencies. However, the higher frequency range is more attenuated giving a better reduction of EMI. Every set of frequencies has a similar spectrum starting from 400 MHz and we can observe reductions around 15 dB.

Comparing different topologies of 4-modules GALS systems: point-to-point, mesh and star, we have noticed a similar behavior. There is a very little influence of data rate transfer intensity on EMI reduction. The most important parameter is the frequency of LS blocks. The more frequency spread, the better EMI reduction in the lower spectrum. Moreover, in each case jitter has a positive effect on reduction of EMI. It significantly reduces higher frequencies in a spectrum. The average reduction of EMI for all 4-module topologies in comparison to a totally synchronous system is around 20 dB starting from 400 MHz.

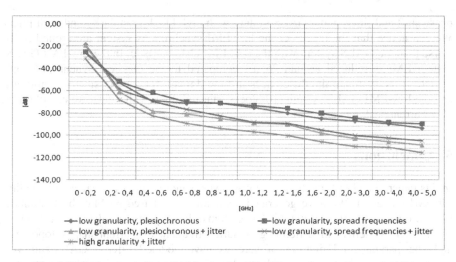

Fig. 6. EMI characteristic in GALS systems with different frequencies set and jitter

We can extract similar results from a star topology with more satellite blocks. However, we notice a greater difference in EMI reduction after adding jitter. The worst results are observable with the frequencies set, where the center block is the slowest one. The best results, in respect to EMI, are achieved when the center block is the fastest one. Hence, we can conclude that the most reasonable architecture from the point of view of the performance, with the fastest center block, is also the most appropriate approach for EMI reduction.

We have also compared the effect of block granularity to the final results. Comparing 4-module and 10-module GALS system, we can observe the better results for the more granular design. In Figure 6 this can be clearly observed. The gain reduction is around 5 dB. In general, it means that the finer the granularity of the GALS system the better reduction of EMI.

Finally, in Figure 7 combinations of both systems with the best results are presented. We have selected a standard synchronous system, synchronous system with

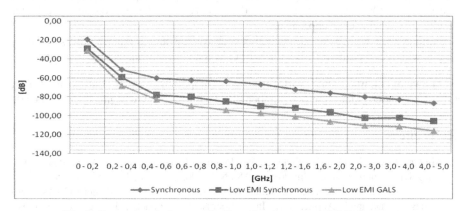

Fig. 7. Comparing the best results from Synchronous and GALS systems

phase shift and jitter, and a GALS system with high block granularity and with jitter. We can notice that the results of the low-EMI synchronous system are around 5 dB worse than the GALS system with the best EMI characteristic. In the low-EMI GALS system EMI is reduced around 25 dB compared to the classical synchronous approach. If we compare the differences in time domain for the classical synchronous and the low-EMI GALS system (10 blocks, star topology with jitter), we can observe 40% current peak reduction.

5 Conclusions

In this paper, the GALS methodology was investigated in order to evaluate the ability for EMI reduction. We have generated a software tool based on Matlab to simulate EMI properties of the digital GALS systems. It supports simulations of GALS/ synchronous systems with different granularity, frequencies, current shapes, topology, and other parameters. Using the software, we have modeled different GALS and synchronous systems in order to evaluate different topologies, architectures and EMI reduction techniques.

The results show that the reduction of high spectral components can be successfully achieved with jitter introduction. EMI at low frequencies can be reduced by a phase shift introduction for synchronous systems. However combining those two features would be hard in synchronous systems because of data transfer between blocks. In GALS systems, phase shift is already present by the nature of the GALS methodology. Local clock generators also naturally generate clocks with jitter, but this feature of ring oscillators was not deeply analyzed here. In this work, we have modeled explicit jitter introduction with the special jitter generators based on LFSR structures. By adding jitter in a GALS system, we can achieve a significant reduction over whole spectrum, not affecting the functionality of a system. The reduction of over 20 dB can be achievable, as illustrated in the results. Moreover, the current peaks in time domain can be reduced up to 40% in GALS systems. We have found that there is almost no correlation between EMI reduction and data transfer intensity (i.e. clock pausing rate) in GALS modules. The greatest impact has the used set of frequencies and the granularity of GALS partitioning. Finally, comparing synchronous solutions and GALS methods, we can conclude that low-EMI GALS approaches give better results than synchronous approaches.

Further work will focus on evaluating real systems and comparing the simulation results with real measured EMI values for GALS and synchronous implementations.

Acknowledgements. This work has been supported by the European Project GALAXY under grant reference number FP7-ICT-214364 (www.galaxy-project.org).

References

1. Muttersbach, J., Villiger, T., Fichtner, W.: Practical Design of Globall-Asynchronous Locally-Synchronous Systems. In: Proc. of ASYNC 2000, Eilat, Israel, pp. 52–59 (2000)
2. Grass, E., Winkler, F., Krstić, M., Julius, A.A., Stahl, C., Piz, M.: Enhanced GALS Techniques for Datapath Applications. In: Paliouras, V., Vounckx, J., Verkest, D. (eds.) PATMOS 2005. LNCS, vol. 3728, pp. 581–590. Springer, Heidelberg (2005)

3. Furber, S.B., et al.: AMULET2e: An Asynchronous Embedded Controller. Proceedings of the IEEE 87(2), 243–256 (1999)
4. Bink, A., York, R.: ARM996HS: The First Licensable, Clockless 32-Bit Processor Core. IEEE Micro 27(2), 58–68 (2007)
5. Krstić, M., Grass, E., Stahl, C.: Request-driven GALS Technique for Wireless Communication System. In: Proceedings of ASYNC 2005, NY, March 2005, pp. 76–85 (2005)
6. Blunno, I., Passerone, C., Narboni, G.A.: An automated methodology for low electromagnetic emissions digital circuits design. In: Proceedings of DSD, pp. 540–547 (2004)
7. Badaroglu, M., et al.: Clock-skew-optimization methodology for substrate-noise reduction with supply-current folding. IEEE Transactions on CAD/ICAS 25(6), 1146–1154 (2006)
8. Beigne, E., et al.: Dynamic voltage and frequency scaling architecture for units integration within a GALS NoC. In: Proc. Intl. Symp. on Networks-on-Chip, pp. 129–138 (2008)
9. Badaroglu, M., et al.: Digital Ground Bounce Reduction by Phase Modulation of the Clock. In: Proc. DATE 2004, vol. 1, p. 10088 (2004)

Low-Power Dual-Edge Triggered State Retention Scan Flip-Flop

Hossein Karimiyan[1], Sayed Masoud Sayedi[2], and Hossein Saidi[2]

ECE Departement, Isfahan University of Technology, Isfahan, Iran, 84154-83111
hkarimiyan@ec.iut.ac.ir, {m_sayedi,hsaidi}@cc.iut.ac.ir

Abstract. This work presents a low-power dual-edge triggered static scanable flip-flop that uses reduced swing-clock and -data to manage dynamic power. The circuit employs clock- and power-gating during idle mode to eliminate dynamic power and reduce static power, while retaining circuit's state. The static structure of the circuit makes it feasible to be employed in variable frequency power control designs. HSPICE post-layout simulation conducted for 90nm CMOS technology showed that in terms of power-delay product, device count, and leakage power the proposed design is comparable to other high performance static flip-flops.

Keywords: Low-power flip-flop, state retention, test.

1 Introduction

Continuous scaling in CMOS technology increases device density and enhances circuit performance in terms of computing power, which also increases power consumption. As more transistors are integrated with each new technology, leakage power is also going to dominate the dynamic power consumption [3]. In modern high performance microprocessors, more than 40% of total energy is consumed due to leakage currents. Furthermore, leakage is the only source of energy consumption for the circuit in its idle mode [1].

Flip-flops and latches are important circuit elements in synchronous VLSI chips [2]. The energy consumption of the clocking sub-system which is composed of clock distribution networks and clocked storage elements is about 30% to 50% of total dynamic energy consumption [13]. Since clock distribution network is closely related to flip-flops, any attempt to reduce power consumption of flip-flops has significant impact on the clock network and hence on reduction of total power consumption.

Although power-gating is the most effective method to reduce all consumed power coefficients of the circuit, it leads to state loss. For continuous system operation, the state of all storage elements in a design needs to be preserved during sleep mode. State retention techniques based on shadow latch is implemented with a provided path to move data to and from the shadow latch [8]. Another technique is to use leakage feedback flip-flop [9], which retains its state by conditionally maintaining an active path to voltage rails based on a feedback from the output.

J. Monteiro and R. van Leuken (Eds.): PATMOS 2009, LNCS 5953, pp. 156–164, 2010.

The main optimization target of flip-flops in the literature is higher performance and lower dynamic power, and static power is usually sacrificed [15][17]. In this work, in addition to issues related to the conventional low-power high-speed flip-flops, state retention, testability, and leakage power reduction are also addressed. Section 2 analytically reviews static and dynamic power consumption of both flip-flops and clock distribution network. Section 3 presents proposed flip-flopstructure. Simulation results and comparisons are presented in section 4. Finally, summary and conclusion remarks are provided in Section 5.

2 Power Dissipation Reduction in Clocking Circuits

Neglecting the impact of short circuit power, the average power consumption of clocking circuit can be expressed as [2]:

$$P_{av} = P_{av,clock} + P_{av,ff}$$
$$= \left(C_{clock} \cdot f \cdot V_{dd}^2 + I_{Leakage,clock} \cdot V_{dd} \right) + \sum_{FFs} \left(\alpha_{data} \cdot C_{ff} \cdot f \cdot V_{dd}^2 + I_{Leakage,ff} \cdot V_{dd} \right) \quad (1)$$

in which $P_{av,clock}$ and $P_{av,ff}$ are average dissipated power in clock distribution network and flip-flops, respectively, C_{ff} and C_{clock} are total capacitance of flip-flop and clock network, f is clock frequency, and V_{dd} is the supply voltage. Activity rate of the clock network is the highest $(=1)$, while data activity rate, α_{data}, depends on the input data pattern. Leakage current, $I_{Leakage}$, is combination of subthreshold and gate leakage currents.

For power reduction, capacitive load which originate from transistor's gate, diffusion, and interconnect wiring should be minimized. This is achieved by having optimal sized transistors and small interconnections.

Based on the quadratic relationship of power and supply voltage in eq. (1), lowering the supply voltage is an effective method to reduce power consumption, but it degrades timing. Multiple supply voltage technique helps to reduce power consumption without sacrificing performance, but with this scheme, interfacing low voltage region to high voltage region requires level conversion [16]. To reduce the area and power overhead, outputs from low voltage regions can be followed by level converting flip-flops [17]. In this configuration, those flip-flops perform data capturing and level conversion simultaneously.

With varying computational load, variable frequency is also effective method to avoid unnecessary power consumption. In this scheme circuit operates at minimum frequency which is sufficient to perform the task. Using dual edge triggering flip-flop (DETFF) is also helpful to reduce effective frequency. Using DETFFs can help to reduce the clock frequency and hence the dynamic power to half while maintaining the same data throughput [12]. This operating frequency reduction usually affects the clock distribution network, but for the flip-flops, it remains unchanged due to required activity on both edges.

The streamline approach to reduce runtime subthreshold leakage is to employ multi-V_{th} CMOS processes. In this approach, cells located in non-critical paths are assigned a high-V_{th} while cells in critical paths are assigned a low-V_{th} [10].

Another useful method to eliminate or reduce dynamic and leakage power of unnecessary sub-blocks during their idle mode is to make them inactive, which can be done through power-gating [4] or clock-gating [13]. By simultaneously using of these methods the idle circuits are separated from clock source and power supply.

Applying appropriate power reduction methods, the average power consumption of clocking subsystem in eq. (1) can be approximated by following equations for active and idle modes:

$$
\begin{aligned}
P_{av}^{active} &\approx P_{av,clock}^{active} + P_{av,ff}^{active} \\
&\approx \left(C_{clock} \cdot \frac{f}{2} \cdot \beta^2 \cdot V_{dd}^2 + I_{Leakage,clock}^{active} \cdot \beta \cdot V_{dd} \right) + \sum_{FFs} \left(\alpha_{data} \cdot C_{ff} \cdot f \cdot V_{dd}^2 + I_{Leakage,ff}^{active} \cdot V_{dd} \right)
\end{aligned}
\tag{2}
$$

$$
\begin{aligned}
P_{av}^{idle} &\approx P_{av,clock}^{active} + P_{av,ff}^{idle} \\
&\approx \left(C_{clock} \cdot \frac{f}{2} \cdot \beta^2 \cdot V_{dd}^2 + I_{Leakage,clock}^{active} \cdot \beta \cdot V_{dd} \right) + \sum_{FFs} \left(I_{Leakage,ff}^{idle} \cdot V_{dd} \right)
\end{aligned}
\tag{3}
$$

where P_{av}^{active} and P_{av}^{idle} are the average power in active and idle modes, and β is the power supply scaling factor. In active mode both flip-flop and clocking system are running, while in the idle mode flip-flops are disabled but clock system is still running. Considering parameter definition in Fig. 1, and using eq. (2) and (3), the overall average power can be approximated by:

$$
P_{av} \approx d \cdot P_{av}^{active} + (1-d) \cdot P_{av}^{idle} + 2P_{Switch}, \quad \left(d = \frac{t_{active}}{t_{active} + t_{idle}} \right)
\tag{4}
$$

where t_{active} and t_{idle} are the average interval times of active and idle modes, respectively, and d is the circuit's active time duty cycle. Switching between active and idle modes dissipates power which is accounted for by P_{Switch}, with assumption that dissipated power in both cases is the same.

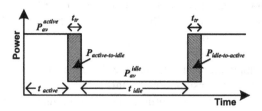

Fig. 1. Power consumption switching between two modes

Using DETFFs with state retention property makes it possible to switch between two modes smoothly. By choosing proper voltage scaling factor, and as long as possible idle time, substantial reduction in both static and dynamic power consumption is achievable.

3 Dual-Edge Triggered State-Retention Scan Flip-Flop

Fig. 2 shows the schematic of proposed flip-flop called Dual-Edge Triggered State-Retention Scan Flip-flop (DET_SRSFF). The circuit is a pulsed latch that incorporates the benefits of static topology and clock- and power-gating. It consists of two stages: pulse generator (Fig. 2(a)), static latch and leakage feedback buffer (Fig. 2(b)).

In Fig. 2(a) MN1-2 and MP1-2 construct clock-gating capability. Clock gating could be done with other circuitry at system level and a NOR gate is used here for sake of clarity. IV1, MN3-4 and MP3-4 construct a low-power XOR gate [14], and IV2-3 are chain of inverters to construct a delay line. In order to reduce dynamic power consumption, the pulse generator is able to use low-swing clock to generate the required narrow pulses without a need for an extra level-converting circuit.

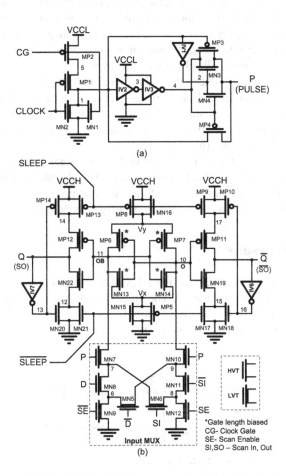

(a)

(b)

Fig. 2. The proposed DET_SRSFF, (a) Pulse Generator (b) Static Latch, Input MUX, and Leakage feedback buffer

The static latch implementation in Fig. 2(b) consists of input MUX, storage cell, and leakage feedback buffers. Depending on the operational mode (i.e., normal or test mode) input MUX selects the appropriate input [11]; and during narrow pulse time MN7 and MN10 turn on and the latch captures the input. The storage cell, composed of MN13-14 and MP6-7, is connected to the VCCH and GND by MP8-MN16 and MP5-MN15 pairs, respectively. In the active mode (SLEEP=0) MP8 and MN15 are on, providing nearly full supply voltage for the static latch. While in the idle mode (SLEEP=1) MP8 and MN15 are off and MN16 and MP5 are on, which limits the voltage of virtual supply nodes, Vx and Vy, to $|V_{tp}|$ and VCC-V_{tn}, respectively. This reduced supply of static latch, i.e. VCC-V_{tn}- $|V_{tp}|$, is sufficient to keep its state [5].

Since the output of pulse generator in idle mode is zero, MN7 and MN10 act like a cut-off sleep transistor, which helps to further reduce leakage current. Since D and SI inputs are only connected to NMOS devices, the proposed flip-flop also can be used as a level converting flip-flop without a need to an extra level converter circuit.

In idle mode, lower supply voltage of static latch can cause substantial leakage current if it connects directly to the next stage. In order to avoid leakage current and also buffer the outputs, leakage feedback buffer [9] is used.

The gate-length biasing reduces the leakage current by up to 38%, while incurred delay penalty is less than 10%. Thus, it is possible to increase gate-length marginally to take advantage of the exponential leakage reduction, while impairing performance only linearly [6]. The gate length biasing is applied selectively, and those transistors are indicated with "*" in Fig. 2(b).

In order to keep leakage currents further under control and at the same time retain the circuit's speed, low-V_{th} transistors are used in critical paths and high-V_{th} transistors in non-critical paths. In addition to aforementioned properties, the proposed flip-flop uses single power rail and so can be used easily in standard digital design flow.

4   Simulation Results

The simulation results are obtained using HSPICE and post-layout netlist in 90nm technology with 1.2V supply voltage. The circuit setup used in simulations is shown in Fig. 3. In order to have realistic test condition, the clock and data inputs are driven by input buffer fan out of 4 (FO4) and the outputs are loaded with FO7 [7].

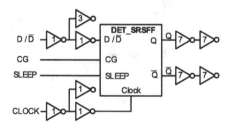

Fig. 3. Simulation Environment Setup

Fig. 4 shows pulse generator waveforms in both active and idle modes. The active mode is indicated by low logic value in CG signal. In this mode it generates narrow pulses on each transition of low swing clock signal. Entering sleep mode is initiated by clock disconnection, and then the sleep signal is applied to the circuit.

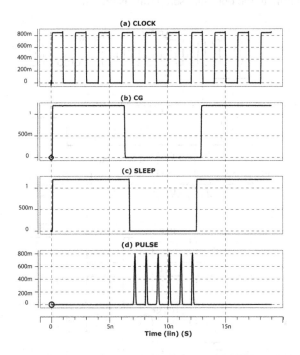

Fig. 4. Pulse generator signals, (a) Clock, (b) Clock Gate, (c) SLEEP, and (d) Narrow Pulses

The idle and active mode operations of DET_SRSFF are illustrated in Fig. 5. After a long time in the idle mode, latch supply lines reached the steady state reduced values, yet retaining the state. In this period, outputs are kept close to supply. When the SLEEP is set to low, latch supply recovers but since clock gating is still active, no change happens. At the second step clock gating is removed, and the flip-flop starts capturing D input at each clock edge.

Fig. 6 shows the power consumption of DET_SRSFF in single ended and differential output modes with various data rates. Fig. 7 compares idle mode power with power dissipation in, all 0's, all 1's, and a normal transition. Values indicate that using single ended mode and putting circuit in sleep mode is effective method for power reduction.

The DET_SRSFF is a pulsed flip-flop with soft clock edge property. The soft clock edge property allows time borrowing between adjacent stages which can be traded for skew absorption. Fig. 8 shows the negative setup time property. If data arrives close to the reference edge of the clock or even after the clock edge, it will be captured [7].

Specifications of proposed flip-flop in single-ended form and operating in normal mode are compared with other similar designs in Table 1. Circuits were' optimized for minimum power delay product, PDP. The D-to-Q delay is obtained by sweeping the data transition times with respect to the clock edge, and the minimum data to output delay corresponding to the optimum setup time is recorded.

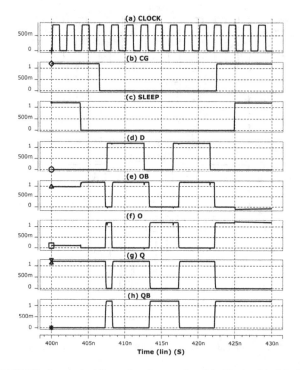

Fig. 5. The DET_SRFF signals in idle and active modes, (a) Clock, (b) CG (Clock Gate), (c) Sleep Signal, (d) Input Data, (e)-(f) Storage cell outputs, (g)-(h) Flip-flop outputs

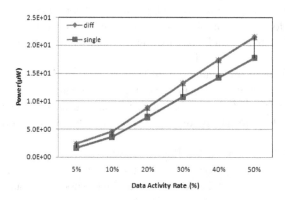

Fig. 6. Power dissipation versus data activity rate in single ended and differential output

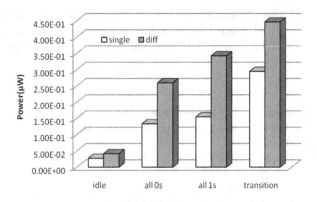

Fig. 7. Power consumption comparison in single ended and differential mode

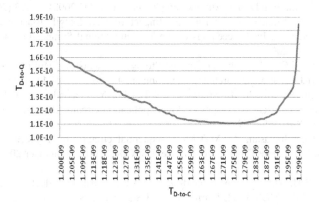

Fig. 8. Flip-flop Input-Output Delay

Table 1. Simulation and comparison results ($\alpha = 0.5$)

PDP (fJ)	P (μW)	Setup (ps)	T_{DQ} (ps)	State Reten.	Low Swing	Tr.#	FLIP-FLOPs
2.33	13	43.9	179	N	Y	23	CBS_ip[15]
2.25	14.5	-158	155	N	N	20	ep-DSFF[17]
2.66	16.4	35	162	N	N	30	SPGFF[18]
2.36	21.5	-270	110	Y	Y	32	DET_SRSFF

5   Conclusion

The power consumption in clock circuit and storage elements for active and idle modes is analyzed. A low-power state-retention flip-flop (DET_SRSFF) with a pulse generating circuit is developed. The DET_SRSFF helps to reduce static and dynamic power consumption in both the clock tree and flip-flops. For continuous operation between idle and active modes state retention is implemented and leakage-feedback buffer is added to avoid floating output nodes. The post-layout simulations in different corner cases of technology reveal circuit stability and correct operation.

References

1. Roy, K., Mukhopadhyay, S., Mahmoodi-Meimand, H.: Leakage current mechanisms and leakage reduction techniques in deep-submicrometer CMOS circuits. Proceedings of the IEEE 91(2), 305–327 (2003)
2. Weste, N., Harris, D.: CMOS VLSI Design, 3rd edn. Addison-Wesley, Reading (2004)
3. ITRS, http://public.itrs.net
4. Powell, M., Yang, S., Falsafi, B., Roy, K., Vijaykumar, T.N.: Gated-Vdd: A circuit technique to reduce leakage in deep-submicron cache memories. In: Proceedings of International Symposium on Low Power Electronics and Design, pp. 90–95 (2000)
5. Agarwal, A., Li, H., Roy, K.: DRG-Cache: A Data Retention Gated-Ground Cache for Low Power. In: 39th Design Automation Conference (DAC 2002), p. 473 (2002)
6. Kahng, A.B., Muddu, S., Sharma, P.: Impact of Gate-Length Biasing on Threshold-Voltage Selection. In: Proceedings of the 7th international Symposium on Quality Electronic Design (2006)
7. Oklobdzija, V.G.: Clocking and Clocked Storage Elements in a Multi-Gigahertz Environment. IBM Journal of Research and Development 47(5/6), 567–584 (2003)
8. Shigematsu, S., Mutoh, S., Matsuya, Y., Tanabe, Y., Yamada, J.: A 1-V high-speed MTCMOS circuit scheme for power-down application circuits. IEEE J. of Solid-State Circuits 32(6), 861–869 (1997)
9. Kao, J., Chandrakasan, A.: MTCMOS sequential circuits. In: Proceedings of the 27th European Solid-State Circuits Conference, ESSCIRC 2001, September 2001, pp. 317–320 (2001)
10. Calhoun, B.H., Honore, F.A., Chandrakasan, A.P.: A leakage reduction methodology for distributed MTCMOS. IEEE Journal of Solid-State Circuits 39(5), 818–826 (2004)
11. Vesterbacka, M.: A Robust Differential Scan Flip-Flop. In: Proc. IEEE Int. Symp. on Circuits and Systems, I, pp. 334–337 (1999)
12. Stojanovic, V., Oklobdzija, V.G.: Comparative analysis of master-slave latches and flip-flops for high-performance and low-power systems. IEEE Journal of Solid-State Circuits 34(4), 536–548 (1999)
13. Kursun, V., Friedman, E.G.: Multi-Voltage CMOS Circuit Design. John Wiley & Sons Ltd., Chichester (2006)
14. Goel, S., Elgamel, M.A., Bayoumi, M.A., Hanafy, Y.: Design methodologies for high-performance noise-tolerant XOR-XNOR circuits. IEEE Transactions on Circuits and Systems I: Regular Papers 53(4), 867–878 (2006)
15. Zhao, P., McNeely, J., Golconda, P., Bayoumi, M.A., Barcenas, R.A., Kuang, W.: Low-power clock branch sharing double-edge triggered flip-flop. IEEE Trans. Very Large Scale Integr. Syst. 15(3), 338–345 (2007)
16. Ishihara, F., Sheikh, F., Nikolić, B.: Level conversion for dual-supply systems. IEEE Trans. Very Large Scale Integr. Syst. 12(2), 185–195 (2004)
17. Tschanz, J., Narendra, S., Chen, Z., Borkar, S., Sachdev, M., De, V.: Comparative Delay and Energy of Single Edge-triggered and Dual Edge Triggered Pulsed Flip-flops for High-performance Microprocessors. In: Proc. ISPLED 2001, pp. 207–212 (2001)
18. Nedovic, N., Oklobdzija, V.G.: Dual-edge triggered storage elements and clocking strategy for low-power systems. IEEE Trans. Very Large Scale Integr. Syst. 13(5) (May 2005)

Multi-granularity NoC Simulation Framework for Early Phase Exploration of SDR Hardware Platforms

Nikolaos Zompakis[1], Martin Trautmann[2,3], Alexandros Bartzas[1], Stylianos Mamagkakis[2], Dimitrios Soudris[1], Liesbet Van der Perre[2], and Francky Catthoor[2,3]

[1] ECE School, National Technical Univ. of Athens, 15780 Zografou, Greece
[2] IMEC vzw, Kapeldreef 75, 3001 Heverlee, Belgium
[3] Katholieke Universiteit, 3000 Leuven, Belgium
{nzompaki,alexis,dsoudris}@microlab.ntua.gr
{trautman,mamagka,vdperre,catthoor}@imec.be

Abstract. Software-defined radio (SDR) terminals are critical to enable concrete and consecutive inter-working between fourth generation wireless access systems or communication modes. The next generation of SDR terminals is intended to have heavy hardware resource requirements and switching between them will introduce dynamism in respect with timing and size of resource requests. This paper presents a system-level framework which combines a cycle-accurate NoC (Network-on-Chip) simulation environment with a pre-existing SDR simulator, thus enabling a cycle accurate simulation and exploration of such complex, dynamic hardware/software SDR designs. The platform specifications are represented as a virtual architecture by a coarse-grain simulator described in SystemC that includes a set of configuration parameters. The key of our approach is that our simulator environment provides automatic wrapper tools able to explore the SDR platform parameters and simultaneously transmit the interconnection traffic in a cycle-accurate NoC simulator giving the opportunity to examine the impact of different topologies at the system bandwidth at execution time. Our simulation results have shown that we can achieve remarkable improvement at the final performance (65-40%) choosing at the early design phase specific platform configurations.

Keywords: SDR, MIMO, NoC, Multi-granularity, Platforms.

1 Introduction

Today, nearly all processor chips use multiple cores in an attempt to deliver more system performance within their power-constrained environment. The related trend at the embedded system design industry is the appearance of an increasing number of hardware components on a single chip pressured by rising performance requirements of embedded applications and manufacturing cost. The combination of this trend and the power consumption issues led to the rise of the Multi-Processor System-on-Chip (MPSoC) paradigm where multiple Processing Elements (PEs) are linked via a Network on Chip (NoC), which manages the on-chip data communication between the PEs and the memories in the memory hierarchy. Moreover, it is widely acknowledged

J. Monteiro and R. van Leuken (Eds.): PATMOS 2009, LNCS 5953, pp. 165–174, 2010.

that early design decisions have the most significant impact on the final system performance and power consumption [1].

Furthermore, new applications such as Software Defined Radio (SDR) make usage of the additional resources offered by these MPSoC platforms. The traditional approach to design and develop SDR and their successor Cognitive Radio platforms is based on the worst-case scenario of the dynamic software requirements in order to determine the hardware resources characteristics. The SDR system can dynamically switch between the available operation modes to get the optimal quality of the communication service [5] and [6]. The increased demands on performance combined with an increase in user control and interactivity with the environment have a significant impact on the resource requests. The latter is becoming more dynamic and event driven because different wireless protocols (with different symbol rate and performance requirements) must be switched at unknown timing moments.

On the other hand, it has been proved that run-time resource management optimizations can reduce resource requests without affecting significantly the Quality of Service (QoS) and the interaction between user and application [2]. The key for the software developers who design dynamic wireless applications is to incorporate such run-time mechanisms without over-provisioning the resources. The real challenge is to estimate the performance characteristics of the software including the impact of run time mechanisms, at a time when no source code exists. Thus, it is clear that in a design process of a dynamic application a hardware-software co-design simulation framework should be available, capable of dealing with a combination of hardware, software and run-time models in order to take into account the various dependencies between hardware and software development and their refinement efforts. Especially it should be possible to create this in a very early phase of the development process, when decisions have the most impact on the system design.

In this paper, we propose a novel simulation framework designed for SDR terminals in an early development phase. This simulation framework can be configured according to different inputs (i.e., above the Data Link OSI layer), different wireless protocols (i.e, Data Link and Physical OSI layers), different run-time resource management policies (i.e., for scheduling, memory management and on-chip communication) and finally for different hardware component configurations[7].

The major contributions of this work are the extensions to the run-time resource management simulator and the hardware component simulator. More specifically, they include: 1) the implementation of a scheduling technique as well as extraction of the bandwidth requirements at execution time; and 2) the development of two automatic wrappers offering automation of the whole simulation and evaluation process of different SDR platforms for cycle accurate NoC simulation (a generic version of the simulation framework without these features and respective measurements can be seen in [18]. The first wrapper encapsulates the coarse grain simulation and automates the exploration of platform parameters design space. The second wrapper establishes an interface layer between the HL (High-Level) SDR coarse grain platform and LL (Low-Level) cycle-accurate NoC simulation layer. In addition, the second wrapper encapsulates the NoC simulation (supporting functions such as the automatic NoC topology exploration) and also implements the automatic transfer, split and mapping of the interconnection traffic dimensioning produced at the higher layer. Finally, the main advantage of the work presented in this paper is to allow a cycle accurate design flexibility.

The rest of the paper is organized as follows. The related work is outlined in Section 2. An overview of the application characteristics is given in Section 3. The simulation flow is presented in Section 4, whereas simulation environment is explained in detail in Section 5. The simulation results are presented in Section 6 and finally, the conclusions are drawn is Section 7.

2 Related Work

The successful handling of the embedded systems design complexity presupposes concurrent component-based methodologies. Today, many tools have been developed, which put together the hardware and software components. Examples are the CoCentric System Studio [8], Matlab/Simulink, Metropolis [9], and Chinook [13] is a hardware-software co-synthesis CAD tool for control dominated, reactive embedded systems, with emphasis on IP integration. The POLIS project [12] provides a hardware-software co-synthesis tool for design and synthesis of embedded micro-controllers. Additionally, the Unified Modeling Language (UML) [14] has emerged in recent years as the de-facto standard for software systems modeling. Furthermore, specific UML profiles have been developed, such as MARTE for real time embedded systems [15].

Our proposal aims at modeling embedded systems of the SDR application domain for the early design phase dimensioning of the system components. Thus, the aforementioned environments provide us with useful models and extensions, which are viable for the integration of our tools but can not provide a simulation for the SDR functionality, which play a key role in measuring the SDR run-time resource management requirements which in turn define the SDR hardware platform requirements.

A characteristic on-chip interconnect simulation environment that focuses on communication aspects is WormSim [10]. Another example, which is included as component in our framework, is Nostrum [16] and can be used as reliable cycle accurate model. In the context of this work, we aim to achieve a fast design flow by performing early-phase exploration, coarse-grain dimensioning of the on-chip interconnect and accurate estimation of the performance transferring this dimensioning at a NoC simulation platform.

3 Application Characteristics

This paper focuses on a particular set of applications, which is used in SDR and Cognitive Radio systems. Both SDR and Cognitive Radio systems reuse available hardware components for handling multiple wireless communication protocols. Therefore they need reconfigurable or reprogrammable hardware, which is capable of processing large amounts of data with high-energy efficiency. Creating a flexible and energy efficient solution is a challenging task, however, the benefits of SDR systems compared to hard wired radio solutions are higher volume hardware manufacturing and faster time to market for new features. In addition to these cost saving factors of SDR, Cognitive Radio systems use the increased flexibility to approach the goal of high bandwidth connectivity anytime everywhere under spectrum scarcity. The characteristics of the applications targeted in the context of this work are:

a) Protocols. Both SDR and Cognitive Radio systems target a wide range of wireless communication protocols such as GPRS, UMTS (3GPP), WiMAX (802.16e), 802.11a/g/n,etc. However, this work focuses on those protocols, which firstly use OFDM as technique to deal with multipath interference and secondly use space division multiplexing to increase throughput with multiple sender and receiver antennas (MIMO). An Example for such a protocol is 802.11n.

b) Varying Load. The experiments presented in this paper use a model of wireless baseband processing as application. Baseband processing is characterized on the one hand by compute intensities, which cannot be efficiently handled by general-purpose processors and on the other hand by algorithms, which exhibit variability in their resource utilization. One source of variability of baseband processing algorithms is the user of an SDR or Cognitive Radio system who can request the use of multiple communication protocols as well as a handover from one protocol to another. A second source of variability is the communication channel, which introduces a varying amount of noise, which in turn can enable algorithms to trade-off accuracy for computation complexity without a noticeable noise increase.

4 Simulation Flow

The levels that compose our simulation flow are shown in Figure 1.The basic implementation is separated in two abstract layers (High-Level and Low-Level) that represent the two wrappers, which are responsible for the automatic and continuous execution of our simulation flow and the storing of our simulation results.

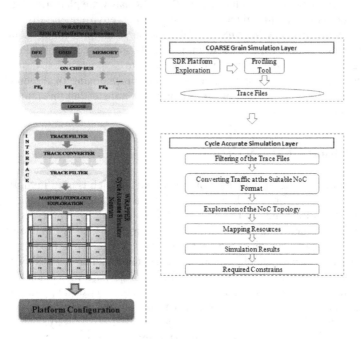

Fig. 1. Simulation Flow

The functionality of each layer is shown clearly in Figure 1. High-level wrapper implements the automatic exploration of the platform parameters and the automatic run. The coarse grain SDR platform permits us to configure totally seven parameters (the number and the frequency of the processing elements, the frequency of the communication bus, the number of antennas, the packet size, the symbol rate of the communication protocol 802.11a and the kind of the signal modulation).These parameters create a large exploration space that requests huge effort for the designer to do it manually. For every combination of parameters in exploration space the SDR wrapper is responsible, in cooperation with a profiling tool, to trace the interconnect traffic and transfer it at run-time at the cycle accurate layer.

At the cycle-accurate simulation (which in our case is performed employing the Nostrum NoC Simulation Environment [16]) a second wrapper is accountable to analyze the traffic dimensioning (Figure 1) at execution time, synthesize the resources (based on the SDR platform parameters of the specific exploration) and mapping them on the NoC. The mapping is performed using a bandwidth constrained algorithm to meet the platform constraints In addition the low level wrapper is responsible to configure the topology of the NoC and extract the simulation results.

5   Simulation Environment

5.1   Coarse Grain Simulator

The simulation framework presented in the next sections of the paper is a coarse grain simulator environment, which has been developed for SDR platform exploration at an early design phase. The included software modeling for driving the platform exploration allows taking run-time resource management solutions into account by providing realistic input data during the simulation.

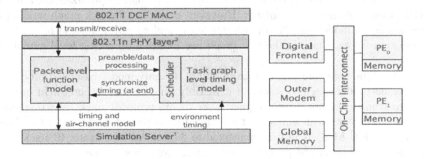

Fig. 2. Coarse grain simulator model and hardware platform template [7]

5.1.1   Early Phase SDR Platform Exploration
At an early design phase it is enough to use models, which are less than cycle-accurate, such as task graph based software modeling and transaction level hardware modeling, because neither the hardware platform instance is selected nor the software source code is refined to its final form. Such coarse-grain models represent resource

requirements and performance characteristics independent from the instructions that describe the functionality. Furthermore, some resource requirements are assigned by means of resource budgets or targets that have to be achieved by optimization efforts, later, during the refinement process. For the SDR platform exploration we focus on baseband processing software of OFDM receivers such as defined by the 802.11n standard – physical layer. The software is modeled as task graphs where tasks are annotated with execution times for prospective target processors. The execution times are extrapolated from profiling results of a current SDR system that implements the 802.11a standard. Task graph granularity timing modeling has also been used by previous research like [3].

5.1.2 WRAPPER for the SDR RT Platform Exploration

The main role of the high-level wrapper is to be the arbiter of the SDR coarse-grain simulator environment. The implementation of the SDR wrapper includes a user interface in which the designer can define the exploration space of the SDR platform parameter. Except for the dynamic parameter changes, the wrapper is responsible to (i) open and close the receiver's and transmitter's terminals, (ii) regulate the communication between them and them with the central wireless server, (iii) monitor the data transfers among the components of the SDR platform capturing the interconnection traffic at an output CSV file extracted at a fixed repository. This repository implements the interface layer through which the two simulation levels (low and high) exchange information. The wrapper has the ability to filter only the necessary information and merge all the simulation traffic in a unique file. Thus, there is one file, which has the whole traffic, for every simulation test. After the completion of every combination (fixed exploration space) SDR wrapper calls the low-level simulation wrapper.

5.1.3 Functionality Simulation for Providing Realistic Inputs

In order to provide realistic input data for run-time resource optimizations, a timing model of the software is not enough. However, extending the task graph model to a fully functional model greatly complicates the modeling effort. Instead of modeling the function for each task in the task graph, we model it on packet level granularity only.

For the SDR hardware platform exploration, we only model baseband processing software detailed enough to schedule it flexibly on platform resources. In order to generate realistic inputs from a higher layer of the protocol stack, we co-simulate baseband processing with a model of the time critical part of the 802.11 MAC layer. The time critical MAC is in turn connected to the bottom of a Linux IP stack to retrieve a realistic stream of packets. Furthermore, we can simulate multiple protocol stacks in parallel with the task graphs of the baseband processing being mapped to a single platform model.

5.2 Cycle Accurate NoC Simulation – Nostrum

The Nostrum NoC [16] simulator is a tool for fully simulating a network-on-chip system. It provides the cycle-accurate communications on a NoC which support a number of topologies and uses deflective routing mechanism. The Nostrum NoC simulator is a layered network simulator. In order to communicate over the network, resources in the simulator are equipped with a Network Interface (NI) and Resource Network Interface (RNI). The NI provides a standard set of services that can be utilized by the RNI. The role of the RNI is to act as an adaptor between the resource's internal communication infrastructure and the standard set of services of the NI. The Nostrum Simulator can be used for both best effort traffic using single-message passing between resources where switching decisions are made locally in the switches for every data routed through the network, as well as for guaranteed bandwidth traffic using virtual circuit. In addition the Nostrum simulator is compliant with AMBA AXI [4], which is an interface protocol between the applications and RNI.

5.2.1 WRAPPER for the NoC Cycle Accurate Simulator

The low level wrapper is responsible to receive the traffic files from the high level simulator and convert them in a suitable input format for the selected cycle accurate NoC simulator which in our case is Nostrum. So the wrapper analyzes the information of every transfer and splits the traffic for every different SDR component (for example for every different processor element) in a separate trace file. The produced trace files have the suitable format and can be used as input at the Nostrum simulator. In addition, the wrapper extracts information in relation with the platform dimensioning (for example the frequency of the buses and the processor elements) and the NoC topology (Torus, Mesh, ...) making the corresponding changes at the NoC platform. Also, the wrapper is engaged to implement specific mapping methodology. In more details, the wrapper analyzes the trace files of every resource and calculates the best resource allocation based on a bandwidth constrained algorithm [11]. Finally, the wrapper captures the results of every simulation run and prunes them, thus providing only the most interesting design configuration combinations.

6 Simulation Results

The main contribution of our approach is the accurate estimation of the final performance of the SDR wireless application at the very early design phase exploring specific platform configurations. To evaluate our simulation framework, we use a wireless SDR application modeled as task graph at the coarse grain layer of the SDR simulator (for more details see Subsections 5.1.3 and 5.1.1) and we explore a series of parameters of the SDR platform. The purpose of our exploration is to present the influence grade of every dynamic SDR parameter at the final application performance. These parameters as well as their values are presented in Table 1, constituting an exploration space of 288 combinations (288 = 4 #PEs x 2 #Antennas x 3 PE_Fr x 4 Bus_Fr x 3 Sign. Mod.). Also, they are separated in static and dynamic according with the capabilities of the SDR resource manager to switch dynamically their values. The dynamic resources in which we focus on our research are the frequency of the processor elements, the frequency of the interconnection bus, and the kind of the transmitted signal modulation. The static parameters (packet size and symbol rate) are fixed and are included at the standards of the 802.11n communication protocol. Also, we explore cases that we have multiple antennas and multiple processor elements. Furthermore, at the cycle accurate layer, we use two basic NoC topologies (mesh and 2D torus) of 16 nodes each.

Table 1. SDR Exploration Space

Static SDR Platform Parameters				Dynamic SDR Platform Parameters		
#PEs	#Antennas	Protocol 802.11n Symbol rate (ns/ OFDM_Symbol)	Protocol 802.11n Packet_Size (Bytes)	PE_Fr (MHz)	Bus_Fr (MHz)	Signal Modulation
2, 4, 6, 8	2, 4	2000	2000	400, 600,800	200, 400, 600, 800	QAM16, QPSK,BPSK

The simulation time of the coarse grain simulation stage, for the 288 SDR platform combinations, was about 19 hours. While the cycle accurate simulation stage, for every NoC topology, was holding about 34 hours (for the two NoC topologies totally we have 2x 288=576 combinations). At the next figures, we perform some indicative results (due to limited space) which elevate the impact of every dynamic resource at the final performance. In more detail, in figure 3 we present the best performance results for different values of the three dynamic resources. The SDR platform employing an interconnection scheme of a 2D torus NoC which contains four processor elements while the results are estimated for four and two antennas. From the analysis of our simulation results (fig. 3 (a)) we conclude that the bandwidth improvement achieved by the increase of the processor elements frequency is not so remarkable compared with this which is achieved by bus frequency (fig. 3 (b)). More particularly, for an increase step of 200 MHz at Pe_fr we have an improvement at the final bandwidth about 25-23% when with the same step at the Bus_fr we have a corresponding gain about 46-25%. If we take into account that the interconnection power consumption represents only the 4% of the total platform consumption this is an interesting inference which can help at the attainment high performance with limited rise of the total power consumption. Another interesting point at our analysis is that 4 antennas have a considerable impact at the final bandwidth unless the bus frequency is 400 MHz or higher. Finally, it is clear that the QAM16 modulation (fig3 (c)) have a clear advantage compared with others two modulation (65% and 41% higher bandwidth compared with BPSK and QPSK).

PE_fr (MHz)	Bandw. (Gbps)	Ant.	Bandw. (Gbps)	Ant.
400	1,394	4	1,203	2
600	1,723	4	1,393	2
800	2,158	4	1,503	2

Bus_fr (MHz)	Bandw. (Gbps)	Ant	Bandw. (Gbps)	Ant.
200	0,924	4	0,889	2
400	1,354	4	1,108	2
600	1,682	4	1,25	2
800	2,158	4	1,503	2

Signal Modes	Bandw. (Gbps)	Ant	Bandw. (Gbps)	Ant.
QAM16	2,158	4	1,503	2
QPSK	1,528	4	1,218	2
BPSK	1,303	4	0,953	2

Fig. 3. Simulation results of SDR platform parameters exploration on a 2D -Torus 4x4 NoC with 4 #PEs

In figure 4 the simulation results of the SDR platform employing an interconnection scheme of a Mesh NoC are presented. The differentiation from the previous example, except from the interconnection topology, is that now we have six processor elements. The previous conclusions are verified and here with the only exceptions to be the threshold up of which the usage of four antennas is remarkable and in our case is 600MHz (instead of 400MHz). In addition, the general bandwidth increase with six processor elements instead of four are about (45-20)%. In conclusion, from the overall simulation results and compared the results from similar platform configurations, we conclude that the usage of the 2D torus topology provide an improvement at the final bandwidth in approximately 13-11% in relation with Mesh.

PE_fr (MHz)	Bandw. (Gbps)	Ant.	Bandw. (Gbps)	Ant.	Bus_fr (MHz)	Bandw. (Gbps)	Ant	Bandw. (Gbps)	Ant	Signal Modes	Bandw. (Gbps)	Ant	Bandw. (Gbps)	Ant.
400	1,243	4	0,912	2	200	0,858	4	0,833	2	QAM16	1,811	4	1,291	2
600	1,401	4	0,977	2	400	1,017	4	0,997	2	QPSK	1,403	4	1,199	2
800	1,811	4	1,291	2	600	1,341	4	1,121	2	BPSK	1,0999	4	0,883	2
					800	1,811	4	1,291	2					

Fig. 4. Simulation results of SDR platform parameters exploration on a 2D-Mesh 4x4 NoC with 6 #PEs

7 Conclusion

In this paper, we present a simulation framework that can be used at the early phase of the SDR hardware platform design. In order to provide the requested accuracy we combine a coarse grain with a cycle accurate simulator. The advantage is that most of the exploration space can be explored very fast with the coarse grain simulator and only the most promising solutions can be further explored with the fine grain simulator. The automatic exploration of the SDR platform and the interface between the two layers succeed through two wrappers, which ensure the automatic execution of our framework, and thus the automatic exploration of different SDR hardware platform configurations. In this way a set of trade-offs are extracted at early design stages and presented to the designer, which is the responsible for choosing the SDR parameters and NoC topology that meets best the design constraints. The whole SDR design space exploration, NoC simulation and result visualization are completely automated through the usage of the developed wrappers thus significantly alleviating the manual effort of the designer.

Acknowledgements

This work is partially supported by E.C. funded program MOSART IST-215244 (http://www.mosart-project.org). In addition, this work has been funded in part by the Artist Design Network of Excellence (http://www.artist-embedded.org).

References

[1] Catthoor, F., et al.: Custom Memory Management Methodology: Exploration of Memory Organization for Embedded Multimedia System Design. Kluwer Academic Pub., Dordrecht (1998)
[2] Bougard, B., et al.: Cross-layer power management in wireless networks and consequences on system-level architecture. Signal Processing 86(8), 1792–1803 (2006)

[3] Mahadevan, S., Storgaard, M., Madsen, J., Virk, K.: ARTS: A System-Level Framework for Modeling MPSoC Components and Analysis of their Causality. In: Proc. MASCOTS 2005, pp. 480–483 (2005)

[4] I AMBA AXI Protocol v1.0 Specification. 2003-2004 ARM Limited

[5] David, L., Tennen house, D.L., Bose, V.G.: The Spectrum ware Approach to Wireless Signal Processing. Wireless Network Journal (1996)

[6] Laurent, P.A.: Exact and approximate construction of digital phase modulations by superposition of amplitude modulated pulses (amp). IEEE Trans. Commun. (February 1986)

[7] Trautmann, M., Mamagkakis, S., Bougard, B., Declerck, J., Umans, E., Dejonghe, A., Van der Perre, L., Catthoor, F.: Simulation framework for early phase exploration of SDR platforms: a case study of platform dimensioning. In: DATE 2009 (2009)

[8] http://www.synopsys.com/products/cocentric_studio/cocentric_studio.html (2003)

[9] Balarin, F., Lavagno, L., Passerone, C., Sangiovanni-Vincentelli, A., Watanabe, Y., Yang, G.: Concurrent execution semantics and sequential simulation algorithms for the metropolis meta-model. In: Proc. CODES 2002 (2002)

[10] Hu, J.: Design methodologies for application specific networks-on-chip. Ph.D. dissertation, Carnegie Mellon Univ. (2005)

[11] Murali, S., Micheli, G.D.: Bandwidth-constrained mapping of cores onto NoC architectures. In: Proc. of DATE. IEEE Computer Society, Los Alamitos (2004)

[12] Balarin, F., et al.: Hardware-Software Co-Design of Embedded Systems: The POLIS Approach. Kluwer Academic Publisher, Massachusetts (1997)

[13] Chou, P., et al.: IPCHINOOK: An Integrated IP-based Design Framework for Distributed Embedded Systems. In: Design Automation Conference (June 1999)

[14] The Object Management Group: Unified Modeling Language: Superstructure. OMG ad/2003-04-01 (2003)

[15] Object Management Group, UML Profile for Modeling and Analysis of Real-Time and Embedded systems (MARTE), Request for proposals. OMG document: realtime/05-02-06 (2005), http://www.omg.org/cgibin/doc?realtime/05-02-06

[16] Jantsch, A.: Models of computation for networks on chip. In: Proc. ACSD 2006, pp. 165–178 (2006)

Dynamic Data Type Optimization and Memory Assignment Methodologies*

Alexandros Bartzas[1], Christos Baloukas[1], Dimitrios Soudris[2],
Konstantinos Potamianos[3], Fragkiskos Ieromnimon[3], and Nikolaos S. Voros[3,4]

[1] ECE Department, Democritus University of Thrace, 67100 Xanthi, Greece
[2] ECE School, National Technical University of Athens, 15780 Zografou, Greece
[3] Intracom Telecom Solutions S.A., Paeania 19002, Athens, Greece
[4] Dept. of Telecommunication Systems & Networks, T.E.I. of Mesolonghi, Greece

Abstract. It is evident that most new computing platforms are becoming more and more complex encapsulating multiple cores and reconfigurable elements. This offers the designers a multitude of resources. It is their responsibility to exploit the available resources in such a way to efficiently implement their applications. Furthermore, the complexity of the applications that run on such platforms is increasing as well. Applications running on such platforms need to cope with dynamic events and have their resource requirements vary during the execution time. In order to cope with this dynamism applications rely in the usage of dynamic data. Applications use containers such as dynamic data types in order to store and retrieve these dynamic data. In this work a set of methodologies that is able to optimize the containers holding the dynamic data and efficiently assign them on the available memory resources is presented. The proposed approach is evaluated in a scheduler for an IEEE802.16-based broadband wireless telecom system and a 3D game application, achieving reductions in the memory energy consumption of 32% and 51% respectively.

1 Introduction

Modern computing platforms are becoming more and more complex encapsulating multiple cores and reconfigurable elements. This makes the design, implementation and mapping of applications into them a challenging task. It is the responsibility of the designers to cope with increased complexity, shorten the design productivity gap, decide which parts of the applications will be in software, which parts will be executed in reconfigurable units and exploit the RTOS services and the multitude of hardware resources offered [1].

Additionally, the complexity of the applications running on such systems is increasing, together with the dynamism of such applications. There are many factors that contribute to the dynamism of modern telecom and network applications. As far as these applications are concerned, the varying size and timing of the packets, that run the network, create an unknown set of requests in data storage and data access. Until recently

---

* This work is partially supported by E.C. funded MORPHEUS IST-4-02734 Project, www.morpheus-ist.org

J. Monteiro and R. van Leuken (Eds.): PATMOS 2009, LNCS 5953, pp. 175–185, 2010.

the problem of storing and transferring data to the physical memories was limited to the management of stack and global data statically allocated at design time [2]. Nowadays, increased user control and interaction with the environment have increased the unpredictability of the data management needs of each software application. Moreover, in the future this unpredictability will increase due to the ever-increasing functionality and complexity of telecom systems. This is a turning point for the data management of these applications since the optimal allocation and de-allocation of dynamic data needs to be performed at run-time (through the usage of heap data in addition to stack and global data) [3].

Dynamically allocated data structures, such as linked lists, which are present in telecom and multimedia applications, allocate and access their stored elements in quantities and at time intervals, which can not be known at design-time and become manifest only at run-time. In modern dynamic applications, data are stored in entities called data structures, dynamic data types (DDTs from now on) or simply containers, like arrays, lists or trees, which can adapt dynamically to the amount of memory used by each application. These containers are realized at the software architecture level and are responsible for keeping and organizing the data in the memory and also servicing the applications requests at run-time. Therefore, a systematic exploration is needed, helping the designer to select the optimal data structure implementation for each application. The cost factors that are taken under consideration are the number of memory accesses and the required memory footprint needed by the applications.

In order to optimize the usage of dynamic memory, the designer must choose an efficient implementation for each existing DDT in the application from a design space of possible implementations [4, 5] (examples are dynamic arrays, linked lists, etc.). According to the specific constraints of typical embedded system design metrics, such as performance, memory footprint and energy consumption, the designer should explore the DDT design space and then to choose the DDT implementation that performs the best and does not violate the system constraints. This task is typically performed using a pseudo-exhaustive evaluation of the design space of DDT implementations (i.e., multiple executions) for the application to attain the Pareto front, which would try to cover all the optimal implementation points for the aforementioned required design metrics [6]. The construction of this Pareto front is a very time-consuming process, sometimes even unaffordable without proper DDT optimization and exploration methods.

Another equally important aspect of the implementation phase involves the assignment of the application data, both static and dynamic. It is the responsibility of the designer to derive an efficient data assignment on the available resources of the computing platform. In the context of this work the assignment problem is formulated as a knapsack one. Modern platforms offer scratchpad memories apart from caches. These memories are directly addressable and the designer has the full responsibility on placing and removing data from there. Usually scratchpad memories are used to store static data. In this paper a more holistic approach is taken, in contrast to previous works, considering the placement of dynamic data into such memories. This can be achieved by the explicit placement of dynamic memory pools in the address space of the scratchpad memory. We formulate such a problem as a multi-objective knapsack problem. In order to evaluate the proposed approach we use a scheduler for an IEEE802.16-based broadband wireless telecom system and 3D game.

The rest of the paper is organized as follows. An overview of the related work is presented in Section 2. The methodologies for dynamic data type optimization and memory assignment are presented in Section 3. The evaluation of the proposed methodologies is presented in Section 4 and finally the conclusions are drawn in Section 5.

2   Related Work

Regarding DDT optimization, in general-purpose software and algorithms design [4,5], primitive data structures are commonly implemented as mapping tables. They are used to achieve software implementations with high performance or with low memory footprint. Additionally, the Standard Template C++ Library (STL) provides many basic data structures to help designers to develop new algorithms without being worried about complex DDT implementation issues. These libraries usually provide interfaces to simple DDT implementations and the construction of complex ones is a responsibility of the developer. A previous approach in DDT optimization was presented in [7], where a systematic methodology for generating performance-energy trade-offs by implementing dynamic data types, targeting network applications was proposed. The library of DDTs used in that work had several limitations that the authors of [8] addressed and overcame.

An important aspect of assigning data on computing systems is how to perform the partitioning of the data (decide which data structure goes where, evaluate possible trade-offs etc.) [9]. Ideally, data should be allocated so that simultaneous accesses are possible without having to resort to duplicating data. In [10] a dynamic method is proposed for allocating portions of the heap to the scratchpad memory. These portions are called "bins" and are moved between the main memory and the scratchpad, when the data they hold is known not to be accessed in the running phase of the application. For each dynamic data type, a bin is created and only the first instances of it will reside into the bin (and so into the scratchpad), while the rest will be kept into a different pool permanently mapped into the main memory. It is important to place the most frequently accessed data in the closest memories to the processor.

Most of the previous approaches focus on the problem of mapping static data (stack and global variables). This is highlighted in [11,12,13,14] where various techniques are presented that map static structures into scratchpad memories. Moreover, [15,16] are good overviews of the available techniques to improve memory footprint and decrease energy consumption in statically allocated data. However, all these approaches focus only at optimizations of global and stack data, which are allocated at compile-time. In this work, we propose optimizations of heap data, which are allocated at run-time. Furthermore, we combine the data assignment step with a first step that is able to optimize the dynamic data type implementations. The aforementioned approaches are compatible with the proposed one and can be combined in order to optimize data of embedded applications, which are allocated both at compile-time and at run-time.

3 Methodology Overview

The overview of the methodology is presented in Figure 1. The application source code is instrumented (insertion of profiling directives and interface to the DDT Library) keeping the functionality intact.

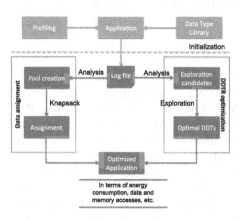

Fig. 1. Methodology Overview

All DDTs are replaced by customized implementations that incorporate a profiling library to log all accesses made within the DDT mechanisms. This insertion is manually executed but a well-defined interface (STL compliant) alleviates the effort of the designer. This is the only manual step of this flow. Afterwards, using typical inputs a platform independent exploration based on the aforementioned cost factors can be performed. In particular, the log file is analyzed by two different modules targeting the optimization of the DDT implementations and the assignment of the memory accesses to suitable memory pools.

The exploration phase is fully automated. Finally the results are integrated into the now optimized application.

3.1 Dynamic Data Type Optimization

Choosing an improper DDT implementation can deteriorate the performance of the dynamic memory subsystem of the computing system. On the one hand, inefficient data access and storage operations cause performance issues, due to the added computational overhead of the internal DDT mechanisms. On the other hand, each access of the DDTs to the physical memory (where the data is stored) consumes energy and unnecessary accesses can comprise a very significant portion of the overall power of the system.

A dynamic application consists of various functions and concurrent tasks. Each function (or task) accesses and processes its own set of data in different ways and patterns, leading to a complex overall dynamic behaviour. Each set of data is assigned to specific DDT. The final decision about the optimal combination of the different DDTs that should be implemented in the application is influenced of this complex algorithmic-based dynamic behaviour. Therefore, no general, domain-specific, optimal solution
exists but only custom, application-specific ones. Thus, the decision should be in accordance to both the application's algorithmic-based dynamic behaviour and the dynamic behaviour influenced by the network configuration. Finally, the system design restrictions also have to be met. This decision requires a very complex exploration task.

A modified version of the DDT Library [8] has been used to implement variations of the dynamic data structures used in the test cases. Differentiated by their access pattern, two types of DDTs, namely a queue and an unsorted linked list, are used in the applications under test. A queue can be implemented either as an array (QAR), or as a singly linked list (QLL); while a linked list in general can have countless implementation variations. Using the componentized architecture of the DDT Library the designer can easily set up nine implementations of a linked list that can be regarded as the most representative ones (see Table 1).

Table 1. Implementations used in the exploration

DDT Implementations	Description
AR	a simple dynamic array modeling the STL Vector DDT
SLL	a singly linked list
DLL	a doubly linked list
SLLO	a singly linked list with roving pointer
DLLO	a doubly linked list with roving pointer
SLL(AR)	a singly linked list of arrays
DLL(AR)	a doubly linked list of arrays
SLL(ARO)	a singly linked list of arrays with roving pointer
DLL(ARO)	a doubly linked list of arrays with roving pointer

The exploration phase of the dynamic data type optimization module involves testing each different DDT implementation and logging related accesses and memory footprint. For each DDT, all available implementations are separately tested. In the end, the implementations that perform best are chosen for each DDT (forming a Pareto solution space). The final combination of implementations for all DDTs is simulated and tested against the original implementations to calculate improvements (see Section 4).

3.2 Dynamic Data Type Assignment

The step that follows the optimization of the DDTs is the data assignment one. In this step the decision on where the data should be placed is taken. The DDTs that were optimized in the previous step serve as a container for the dynamic data handled by the application. So the number of accesses and requested footprint is the one corresponding to these DDT implementations. At this stage the results from the profiling performed at the DDTs of the applications allow the ranking of these data types, according to their size, number of accesses, access pattern, allocation/de-allocation pattern and lifetime, for each cost function relevant to the system. These DDTs are placed into pools which in turn are managed by the system's memory allocators. The main focus is on the internal (on-chip/scratchpad) memory, but data can be allocated, according to the configuration of the memory manager, to the main memory as well (off-chip memory, usually SDRAM). The data assignment provides guidelines about which pools reside in which level of the memory hierarchy.

Taking into consideration all these criteria the assignment problem is modelled as a multi-choice knapsack problem. In order the problem to be solved the knapsack algorithm is fed with the list of data types and with the characteristics of the memory hierarchy (levels of hierarchy, number of modules etc). The solution of this problem is the assignment decisions need to be taken by the system, organizing the data types into pools.

One last important issue remains whether it is convenient or not to split pools across several memory modules. If pools are split over different memory modules, then the assignment problem becomes equivalent to the fractional multiple knap-sack problem and can be solved with a greedy algorithm in polynomial time. The problem with this approach is that it is not possible to know a priori the access pattern to each of the parts of the pools, so it is not easy to quantify the overall impact on cost of the assignment decisions. On the contrary, if pools are not split, the assignment problem is a binary (0/1) multiple knap-sack problem. This problem is much harder to solve as no polynomial-time algorithm can be employed to solve it [17]. Therefore, it is important to keep the size of the input as small as possible. Also, if a problem can be modelled as a fractional knap-sack one, then a better solution can usually be found with this method. However, as pools are not spread over different memory resources at all, it is much easier to quantify the number of accesses that are mapped into the corresponding one.

If pools cannot be split over different memory resources then we define an assignment function $f(i, j)$ that for a given pool P_i and memory resource M_j returns 1 if and only if P_i should be contained into M_j. Then it is possible to formalize the assignment process as a binary multiple knapsack problem. C_j is the cost of the memory module M_j (it can be energy per access, cycles per access etc.), A_i and $Size_i$ are the number of accesses and the size the pool P_i respectively, whereas S_i is the size of the memory module M_j. The target that must be minimized can be characterized according to the following formula:

$$\min \left(\sum_{i=1}^{n} \sum_{j=1}^{m} f(i, j) \times C_j \times A_i \right) \tag{1}$$

The solution must comply with the two following constraints:

1. The total size of all the pools assigned to a given memory resource cannot exceed its capacity

$$\left(\sum_{i=1}^{n} f(i, j) \times Size_i \right) \le S_j, \qquad j = 1...m \tag{2}$$

2. Each pool is assigned exactly once to a memory resource

$$\sum_{j=1}^{m} f(i, j) = 1, \qquad i = 1...n \tag{3}$$

4   Experimental Results

The first application used to evaluate the proposed methodologies is the scheduler of an IEEE802.16-based system terminal and is responsible for establishing connections and then servicing them by inserting and removing cells while supporting interrupts in the scheduling procedure. The number of connections can reach up to 16. Furthermore, the requirements for each connection can be different since several bitrates are supported as well as Quality-of-Service requirements. The designer can set up connections with the desired characteristics and then employ a simulator to check their performance. The application provides detailed information about the current situation of the network for each scheduling cycle. So we can monitor the cell delay, the length of the queues, etc. In this application two are the dynamic data types of interest and these ones are handling data regarding the list of connections and the queues of traffic cells. The connections are being hold in a list, while the traffic cells are being placed in queues. Even though the number of DDT basic building blocks is limited, developers tend to write custom

DDTs for each application. Therefore, the number of alternatives is limited to the developer's skill and the available time to implement each one of them. Ten different DDT implementations were developed and used in the exploration and final refinement. In general the factors that influence the overall performance of the memory system are the amount of memory accesses, the optional auxiliary mechanisms to access the data (e.g., pointers, roving pointers) and the access pattern based on the implemented algorithm and its configuration.

In Figure 2 the exploration results are depicted when the queue is implemented as an array (QAR) and when the queue is implemented as linked list (QLL). For the queue we evaluate two implementations and for the list we evaluate the 9 implementations presented in Table 1. In both figures the values for the requested memory footprint and data accesses are normalized to the values of the list data type implemented as array (that is the list holding the connection is implemented as an array). As we can see in both figures the DDTs implemented as linked list exhibit the best behaviour in terms of data accesses and memory footprint. Compared to the performance of the array the single linked list (SLL) implementations exhibit 5% reduced data accesses and using a memory model from MICRON we can see the same implementation can achieve a 6% improvement on energy consumption. Having as goal the combined reduction in data accesses and memory footprint, the SLL implementation is the designers choice.

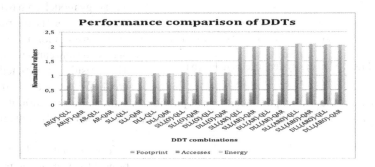

Fig. 2. Comparison of the performance of various implementations for two DDTs

The next step in the flow is the assignment of the dynamic data. The information needed to perform this step is: a) the size of the dynamic data type; the numbers of objects alive during the execution, and c) the number of reads and writes to these data. A tool has been developed to process the profiling information and produce a report of the behaviour of the data types. The elements that reside in the connection list and in the queue of traffic cells are of certain size that is not changing during the execution time. The designer chooses the creation of pools that are capable of handling requests of a specific, predefined size. So the size of each allocation is fixed at the moment the pool is created. The big advantage of using such a pool is the lack of fragmentation, which is a significant degrading factor in the dynamic memory management. Assuming that the system has a 4kB scratchpad and an SDRAM memory we conclude that not all dynamic data can fit into the scratchpad memory, since we have to reserve the space for some scalar variables and static data structures that are more frequently accessed. In this work it was chosen to profile not only the dynamic data types but the static data structures contributing to the resource usage of the application. These structures hold information about the scheduling, the contention, the QoS, etc. Using the extracted information the problem is formulated as a knapsack one and solved using an ILP approach. The outcome of this step provides to the designer a list of static data structures and pools, which can be accommodated into the scratchpad memory and the DRAM.

The case when all the dynamic data are allocated in the SDRAM (solution1) is used as a baseline. As a second solution we place explicitly at the scratchpad memory only the pool that can fit there (the only holding the connections) (solution2). The final solution (solution3) is the one proposed by the mapping algorithm placing dynamic and static data at the scratchpad memory. The reduction in the cycles consumed to access the data is shown in Figure 3.

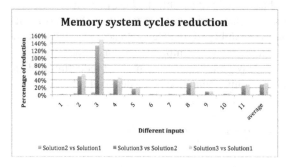

Fig. 3. Memory system cycles reduction

We can see that even a simple pool allocation at the scratchpad memory can achieve gains of 2% on average. The more elaborate solution proposed by the methodology achieves a reduction of 32% on average. Using an energy model from MICRON the improvements in term of energy consumption in the memory subsystem can be calculated. These results are depicted in Figure 4. We can see that the pool assignment in the scratchpad memory can provide us with a 3% reduction in energy consumption and when we test the combined approach we reach a 30% reduction (on average).

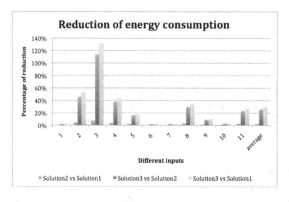

Fig. 4. Reduction of the energy consumption in the memory system

The second application employed to evaluate the proposed approach is from the multimedia domain. It is a 3D game called Vdrift [18]. Vdrift is an open source racing simulator that uses STL Vector to handle its dynamic behaviour. The application uses very realistic physics to simulate the car's behaviour and also includes a full 3D environment for interaction. Vdrift uses 37 dynamic DDTs to hold its dynamic data that are all sequences. The objects put inside the containers vary from wheel objects to float numbers required by the game's physics. During the game, some containers get accessed sequentially, while others exhibit a random access pattern. This means that the applications requests regard objects, which are not successive in the list structure, increasing the complexity of the access pattern. All DDTs were originally implemented using the STL Vector data structure. Vector is a dynamic array, offering fast random access, but also requiring large amounts of memory. The alternative to vector is a list. Using our framework, we explored the behaviour of Vdrift's DDTs testing 9 different implementations as presented in table 1. Vdrift utilizes various access patterns from sequential access of a container to pure random access pattern. Each container can have a different dominant access pattern, a property that renders it difficult for the designers to choose the right data structure for it. The solution usually followed is the implementation of all the DDTs using a single implementation, like the STL vector. However, as it is shown in Figure 5, choosing different implementations for each container individually can have a major positive impact on the number of memory accesses needed (which is also linked to performance) and the total memory footprint. The proposed solution is a combination of different implementations for each DDT.

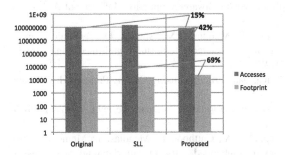

Fig. 5. Reduction in memory accesses and memory footprint comparing to the original implementation

In Figure 5 the proposed solution is compared to the original implementation (an exact model of vector), as well as a singly linked list, as this would be a decent choice for keeping the memory footprint in low levels. A 15% reduction in memory accesses and 69% reduction in memory footprint can be achieved compared to the original application. If all DDTs were implemented as singly linked lists instead of vectors, we could achieve even further reduction in memory footprint, but with a significant loss in performance. Our proposed combination of DDT implementations is 42% lower in memory accesses than the singly linked list implementation. For this case study the solution of the assignment problem is compared to the baseline solution (all heap data to be allocated at the SDRAM memory of the system). Out of the 37 DDTs 7 are to be placed in the scratchpad memory. This assignment manages to reduce the energy consumption to the memory subsystem by 51% and the mean latency per access by 50%.

5   Conclusions

It is evident that most new computing platforms are becoming more and more complex encapsulating multiple cores and reconfigurable elements. This offers the designers a multitude of resources. But not only is the complexity of the platform increasing. The same happens with the applications as they need to cope with dynamic events and have their resource requirements vary during the execution time. In order to cope with this dynamism applications rely in the usage of dynamic data. In this work an exploration framework and methodology is presented that searches the available design space of dynamic data type implementations and offers the designer a number of solutions and the potential trade-offs among them. Furthermore, decisions are taken on placing these DDTs on the available on-chip memory resoures. The proposed approach has been evaluated using two applications. The first one is the scheduler part of an IEEE 802.16-based terminal broadband telecom system, achieving reduction of the energy consumption of 32%, whereas the second application is a 3D game, achieving reduction of the energy consumption of 51%.

References

1. Thoma, F., Kuhnle, M., Bonnot, P., Panainte, E., Bertels, K., Goller, S., Schneider, A., Guyetant, S., Schuler, E., Muller-Glaser, K., Becker, J.: Morpheus: Heterogeneous reconfigurable computing. In: Proc. of FPL, August 2007, pp. 409–414 (2007)
2. Marwedel, P., Wehmeyer, L., Verma, M., Steinke, S., Helmig, U.: Fast, predictable and low energy memory references through architecture-aware compilation. In: Proc. of ASP-DAC, pp. 4–11 (2004)
3. Atienza, D., Mamagkakis, S., Catthoor, F., Mendias, J.M., Soudris, D.: Dynamic memory management design methodology for reduced memory footprint in multimedia and wireless network applications. In: Proc. of DATE (2004)
4. Antonakos, J., Mansfield, K.: Practical data structures using C/C++. Prentice-Hall, Englewood Cliffs (1999)
5. Wood, D.: Data structures, algorithms, and performance. Addison-Wesley Longman Publishing Co., Inc., Amsterdam (1993)
6. Daylight, E., Atienza, D., Vandecappelle, A., Catthoor, F., Mendias, J.: Memory-access-aware data structure transformations for embedded software with dynamic data accesses. IEEE TVLSI 12(3), 269–280 (2004)
7. Bartzas, A., Mamagkakis, S., Pouiklis, G., Atienza, D., Catthoor, F., Soudris, D., Thanailakis, A.: Dynamic data type refinement methodology for systematic performance-energy design exploration of network applications. In: Proc. of DATE (March 2006)
8. Papadopoulos, L., Baloukas, C., Zompakis, N., Soudris, D.: Systematic data structure exploration of multimedia and network applications realized embedded systems. In: Proc. of IC-SAMOS 2007, July 2007, pp. 58–65 (2007)
9. Palermo, D.J., Banerjee, P.: Automatic selection of dynamic data partitioning schemes for distributed-memory multicomputers. In: Sehr, D., Banerjee, U., Gelernter, D., Nicolau, A., Padua, D.A. (eds.) LCPC 1996. LNCS, vol. 1239, pp. 392–406. Springer, Heidelberg (1997)
10. Dominguez, A., Udayakumaran, S., Barua, R.: Heap Data Allocation to Scratch-Pad Memory in Embedded Systems. Journal of Embedded Computing (2005)
11. Kandemir, M., Kadayif, I., Choudhary, A., Ramanujam, J., Kolcu, I.: Compiler-directed scratch pad memory optimization for embedded multiprocessors. IEEE TVLSI 12, 281–287 (2004)
12. Verma, M., Steinke, S., Marwedel, P.: Data partitioning for maximal scratchpad usage. In: Proc. of ASP-DAC, pp. 77–83. ACM Press, New York (2003)
13. Verma, M., Wehmeyer, L., Marwedel, P.: Cache-aware scratchpad allocation algorithm. In: Proc. of DATE (2004)
14. Udayakumaran, S., Dominguez, A., Barua, R.: Dynamic allocation for scratch-pad memory using compile-time decisions. Trans. on Embedded Computing Sys. 5(2), 472–511 (2006)

15. Panda, P.R., Dutt, N.D., Nicolau, A.: On-chip vs. off-chip memory: the data partitioning problem in embedded processor-based systems. ACM Trans. Des. Autom. Electron. Syst. 5(3), 682–704 (2000)
16. Benini, L., de Micheli, G.: System-level power optimization: techniques and tools. ACM Trans. Des. Autom. Electron. Syst. 5(2), 115–192 (2000)
17. Khuri, S., Bäck, T., Heitkötter, J.: The zero/one multiple knapsack problem and genetic algorithms. In: Proc. of SAC, pp. 188–193. ACM, New York (1994)
18. Vdrift, http://vdrift.net/

Accelerating Embedded Software Power Profiling Using Run-Time Power Emulation

Christian Bachmann[1], Andreas Genser[1],
Christian Steger[1], Reinhold Weiß[1], and Josef Haid[2]

[1] Institute for Technical Informatics, Graz University of Technology, Austria
[2] Infineon Technologies Austria AG, Design Center Graz, Austria

Abstract. Power-aware software development of complex applications is frequently rendered infeasible by the extensive simulation times required for the power estimation process. In this paper, we propose a methodology for rapidly estimating the power profile of a given system based on high-level power emulation. By augmenting the HDL implementation of the system with a high-level power model, a power profile is generated during run-time. We evaluate our approach on a deep-submicron 80251-based smart-card microcontroller-system. The additional hardware effort for introducing the power emulation functionality is only 1.5% while the average estimation error is below 10% as compared to gate-level simulations.

1 Introduction

Power consumption has emerged as the most important design metric for embedded systems, influencing operating time as well as system stability. Therefore, power estimation has become an essential part of today's embedded system design process. In this process, increasingly complex designs have to be handled. Systems-on-chip (SoC) contain large numbers of components, each contributing to the overall power consumption. For these systems, the power consumption is increasingly dependent on software applications determining the utilization of components as well as controlling available power management features.

Currently available simulation tools are usually operating on low levels of abstraction and fail to deliver power estimates in admissible time. Higher levels of abstraction are favourable in order to speed up the estimation process. Furthermore, the greatest power reduction potential can be identified on high levels, e.g., the application layer [1]. However, for estimating the power consumption of elaborate program sequences such as the booting sequence of an operating system (OS), software simulators require extensive runtimes. This curtails the usability of these tools for power-aware software development of complex applications.

Hardware-accelerated methods employing existing hardware counters [2,3], dedicated power estimation co-processors [4,5,6,7] and emulation-based approaches [8,9,10] have therefore been explored. While low-level emulation-based approaches suffer from high hardware overhead (on average 3x increased area requirements)

J. Monteiro and R. van Leuken (Eds.): PATMOS 2009, LNCS 5953, pp. 186–195, 2010.

[8], high-level event counter-based methods often require additional software processing overhead for evaluating the counters and converting their values to power estimates [10].

We propose a solution to the problem of software power profiling by using an estimation approach based on high-level power models implemented alongside the original system design on a hardware emulation platform.[1] Power consumption estimates are generated during run-time by special power estimation hardware added to the functionally emulated system. By analyzing these estimates, a truly power aware software design methodology can be enabled.

This paper is structured as follows. In Section 2 we discuss related work on software power estimation. Section 3 introduces our contributions to the area, whereas Section 4 evaluates experimental results. Conclusions drawn from our current work are presented in Section 5.

2   Related Work

Previous work on software power estimation can be grouped in two distinct categories: (i) simulation-based and (ii) hardware-accelerated (run-time) estimators.

Simulation-based software power estimation methods determine activity and state data through simulated program execution on a model of the system-under-test. Different levels of abstraction used in describing these models yield different estimation accuracies and variably long simulation times.

Many commercial power estimation tools, e.g., [11], operate on low levels of abstraction such as gate or register transfer level (RTL). These low levels of abstraction allow for very high estimation accuracies but slow down the estimation process. At higher levels, instruction-level power models have been explored. Models consisting of base costs per instruction as well as overhead costs for switching between different instructions have been defined [12]. By considering microarchitectural effects in a pipeline-aware model, the estimation accuracy has been improved [13]. At the system level, a transaction-based framework for complex SoCs has been introduced in [14].

Hardware-accelerated power estimation methods leverage existing or specially added hardware blocks. Using existing hardware event counters, the thread-specific power consumption of operating systems can be determined [15]. Using a similar approach, run-time power estimation in high performance microprocessors using hardware counters is shown in [2] and [3]. Dedicated power estimation co-processors are utilized in [4,5,6,7].

By using a standard FPGA platform and a HDL model of a given system that has been augmented with power estimation hardware, *power emulation* and functional emulation can be performed concurrently. RTL [8,9], high-level event counter-based [10] as well as hybrid methods using simulation and emulation have been explored [16]. In [17] we have introduced a system-level power

---

[1] The PowerHouse project is funded by the Austrian Federal Ministry for Transport, Innovation, and Technology under the FIT-IT contract FFG 815193. Project partners are Infineon Technologies Austria AG, Austria Card GmbH and TU Graz.

profiling unit based on the emulation principle. It allows for generating run-time power estimates and forms the basis of our accelerated software power estimation methodology as first outlined in [18].

3 Embedded Software Power Profiling Using High-Level Power Emulation

Our embedded software power profiling method is based on the *power emulation principle* as initially introduced in [8]. A *high-level power model*, created by an adaptable *characterization procedure*, is utilized to estimate the current power consumption as a function of the overall system state.

This model is implemented in hardware as a *power emulation unit* monitoring the states of system components and generating according power estimates during run-time [17]. Out of the power estimates a power trace is recorded and stored on the emulation platform alongside the standard functional trace. These traces are transferred to a host computer running an *integrated software development and debugging environment* (IDE) that is used for visualizing and analyzing the recorded traces.

3.1 Principle of High-Level Power Emulation

Hardware emulation on prototyping platforms, typically on FPGA boards, has become a widespread technique for functional verification. The principle of power emulation is to augment the emulated circuit with special power estimation hardware [8]. By doing so, power consumption estimates can be generated as a by-product of functional emulation.

Emulation-based power estimation offers a number of advantages as compared to power profiling using physical measurements or software simulators. In contrast to physical measurements that are often very coarse-grained and limited to the entire system due to packaging, the emulator allows for calculating cycle-accurate estimates for the whole chip as well as for system subcomponents. Simulation-based estimators offer a high degree of accuracy. However, this accuracy comes at the cost of large simulation times. Due to the calculation of power models in hardware, this simulation time is reduced vastly by the power emulation technique.

Unlike RTL power emulation [8], we employ a high-level model that, due to its high level of abstraction, significantly decreases the complexity of the estimation hardware and therefore reduces its implementation effort. Thus, long combinational paths in the power emulation unit are avoided, enabling the system-under-test to be emulated in or near the targeted clocking frequency of the system's physical implementation. In contrast to high-level event counter-based power emulation approaches, e.g. [10], no further post-processing of counter values in software is required to obtain the power estimates. Our power model is outlined in the following section.

3.2 Power Model

High-level power models, such as system- or component-level power models, often derive power consumption estimates from the state of the system and its components respectively. For a system-level state-based power model this is shown, e.g., in [19]. In our high-level model, the power consumption estimate $\hat{P}_{total}$ of the system takes the form of

$$\hat{P}_{total}(t) = \hat{P}_{idle} + \sum_{i=1}^{N} \hat{P}_i(\tilde{S}_i(t)) = \sum_{i=0}^{N} \hat{P}_i(S_i(t)) \tag{1}$$

where $\hat{P}_i$ denotes the sets of power estimates for a number of N different system components (e.g., CPU, coprocessors, peripherals) for their respective time-dependent states $S_i(t)$. The idle power coefficient $\hat{P}_{idle}$ comprises system components with a constant, i.e., not state-dependent, power consumption such as certain analog components or non-clock-gated parts of the system. We can include the idle term into our power model as a power estimate set containing only one constant power value.

Hence, the state parameters $S_i(t)$ given as

$$S_i(t) = \begin{cases} S_{idle}, & i = 0 \\ \tilde{S}_i(t) = f_i(\mathbf{x_i}(t)), & 0 < i \leq N \end{cases} \tag{2}$$

represents the state of each component including the idle power component. It is a function of the time-dependent component state signal vector $\mathbf{x_i}(t) = [x_{i,0}(t) \ldots x_{i,K_i-1}(t)]$, containing the K_i binary control signals x_i that contribute to the state information of the individual module. The mapping function f_i maps the binary control signals x_i to a state value that is used to select the power estimate in the set $\hat{P}_i$. Note that the mapping functions f_i differ for each component, based on the number of control signals and the meaning of each individual signal in terms of state information.

We establish the power model for a given system-under-test by applying our characterization methodology (see Section 3.4) to the HDL model of the system. In the characterization process the granularity of the model is determined by varying the number of included components and the number of states considered, influencing the model's accuracy and its complexity.

3.3 Power Emulation Unit Architecture

Our estimation architecture, as introduced in a previous publication [17], resembles the implementation of the power model in hardware and generates power consumption estimates that are transmitted to and evaluated by a host computer. It is composed of a number of sub-modules as depicted in Figure 1. Power sensors are used to observe the activity and the state of all system components (CPU, coprocessors, memories, peripherals, etc.). Each power sensor monitors the K_i control signals of the according system component and maps the observed

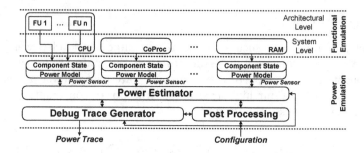

Fig. 1. Architecture of the power emulation unit [17]

state vector $\mathbf{x}_i$ to a corresponding state value S_i by means of the mapping function f_i. The component's state information is then translated to a corresponding power value using a table-lookup approach based on a set of power tables P_i. The power estimator accumulates the outputs generated by the power sensors. The result of a sequence of additions constitutes the instantaneous, cycle-accurate power estimate $\hat{P}_{total}$ for the overall system as pointed out in Equation 1. It is worth noting that the power tables can also be reconfigured during program run-time in order to adapt to, e.g., operating frequency or voltage changes and to allow for the tracking of single components or certain groups of components.

3.4   Characterization Methodology

The straightforward adaptability of the power model and the power emulation architecture to a given system-under-test is one of the key goals of our accelerated power estimation approach. We use a comprehensive characterization methodology for determining a system's power consumption and mapping these results to our power model and the power emulation unit. The basic structure of the characterization process is outlined in Figure 2.

The starting point for this process is a HDL model of the system to be power-emulated. This HDL model is fed to a standard synthesis and place & route design flow, yielding a model of the physical implementation of the system. Based on the physical model, state-of-the-art power estimation tools, in our case *Magma Blastfusion* 5.2.2, can be used to generate power profiles of the system.

A power modelling process derives model coefficients from a set of benchmarking applications covering all system components that contribute significantly to the overall power consumption. Our methodology automatically extracts a list of state signals based on user-defined name patterns, e.g., *busy*, *ready*, *action*, etc. from the HDL model of the system. By analyzing the switching activity data for each signal across all benchmarks, highly correlated (i.e., redundant) and nonrelevant signals are removed. Using regression analysis, power consumption weights are assigned to the remaining control signals. For each system component, all occurring control signal combinations are determined and uniquely mapped to states.

The information obtained in the power modelling step is used in a threefold manner: First, the architecture of the power estimation unit is adapted to suit the requirements of the power model. Therefore, the number of available modules and number of states within each module is adjusted. Second, the original HDL model of the system is adapted in order to allow the power estimation unit to track the internal state of every significant component. This means that signals that can be used to monitor various power states of a component are routed to the power estimation unit. Third, configuration information is generated that is used to setup the power coefficients table inside the power estimation unit according to the system's power model.

The modified HDL model of the system-under-test, augmented with the power emulation functionality, and the set of configuration data obtained in the characterization process can then be used to enable power emulation in a standard software development process.

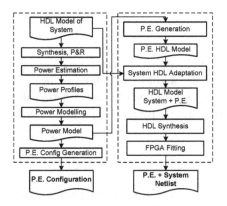

Fig. 2. Characterization methodology for high-level power emulation [18]

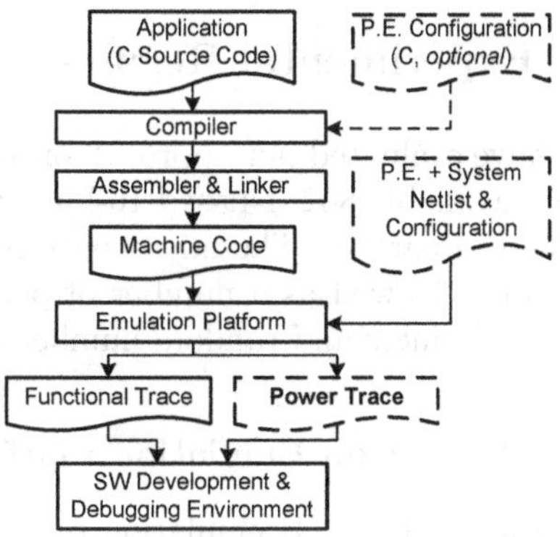

Fig. 3. Software development flow utilizing power emulation

3.5   Power-Aware Software Development Flow

We use a standard software development flow augmented with the power emulation methodology as depicted by Figure 3 to enable power-aware software development.

A software application in C is processed using a C compiler, assembler and linker tool-chain. The resulting machine code is then loaded onto and executed on the power-emulated system. Note that this process of loading and executing an application is not affected by the use of the power emulation methodology. Optionally, the behaviour of the power estimation unit can also be changed by modifying the power configuration tables during normal program execution using routines implemented in C.

The only required change as compared to the standard development flow is the use of a modified netlist for the emulation platform. A netlist resembling the FPGA implementation of the system including the power estimation unit is loaded onto the emulation platform instead of the standard netlist. While executing the machine code on the emulated system a functional trace as well as a power trace are being generated. These traces are stored within an on-board trace memory until they are transferred to the host computer. The software development and debugging environment on the host computer controls the program execution on the emulator (e.g., breakpoint insertion) and evaluates the trace messages received from the emulator.

The power traces can then be plotted alongside the functional trace within the IDE. We use the functional trace to derive the program counter (PC) status as well as the operation code (Opcode) of the current instruction. The functional trace could also be used to correlate the estimated power profile to higher-level debugging information, e.g., for displaying the profile alongside C source code.

4   Experimental Results

We have evaluated our approach on software applications written for a commercially available 80251-based 16-bit microcontroller architecture supplied by our industrial partner. The microcontroller is composed of volatile and non-volatile memories as well as a number of peripherals, e.g., cryptographic coprocessors, UARTs, timers and random number generators.

4.1   Impact on Emulation Platform

An Altera Stratix II emulation platform was used for implementing the microcontroller as well as the power estimation hardware. The microcontroller itself, as it can be used for purely functional emulation, employs approximately 66% of the platform's available adaptive look-up tables (ALUTs). After augmenting the system with the power estimation hardware, roughly 67.5% of the ALUTs are required. Hence, with the additional 1.5% ALUTs we consider the impact of the power emulation hardware on the emulation platform as minor. Note that our approach is generic and could also be implemented on another emulation platform as we do not employ any platform-specific processing elements (e.g., DSP blocks).

4.2   Speed Up

Due to the fact that our estimation unit has only minor impact on the total system and no additional critical paths are introduced, we are able to operate the emulated microprocessor and the estimation unit at the targeted clocking frequency of 33 MHz. Therefore, cycle-accurate power estimates can be generated during run-time. Note that the current implementation of the power estimation unit only employs single-cycle arithmetic operators due to the relatively low

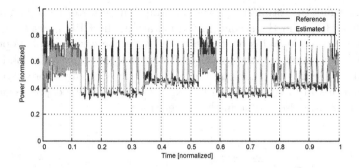

Fig. 4. Comparison of gate-level simulation and power emulation results

clocking frequency of the system-under-test. For higher frequencies, pipelined multi-cycle operators could be introduced to reduce the critical path.

Compared to the extensive runtime of gate- and RTL simulations the run-time estimation represents a major speed-up. The significant timely difference can be illustrated on a test-run of the Dhrystone benchmark: While a gate-level power simulation on a state-of-the-art server system takes 18.1 hours, the emulation is finished within 139 μs. This vast reduction of simulation time, of course, comes with losses in accuracy which are discussed below.

4.3   Comparison of Accuracy

Figure 4 depicts a comparison between the reference gate-level simulations and the emulated power estimates for a benchmarking application.[1] The magnitude of the average estimation error for the whole application is below 10%. The given results were achieved using a power model taking 5 system modules into account: Two 16 state modules (CPU, cache+memories) and four peripheral modules consisting of two states each. This represents a rather small overall model that could be further extended to include more modules and states, hence improving the estimates. Note that, as pointed out in Section 4.1, considerable FPGA ressources are still available for increasing the accuracy of the model.

4.4   Power-Aware Application Examples

We illustrate the usability of our high-level power emulation approach on two prototypical examples.[1] In these examples the system's power consumption while executing an authentication application exceeds a given maximum power limit. These power-critical events are easily detected by our power emulation methodology and, hence, can be avoided.

The first example, as depicted in Figure 5, shows the invocation of a cryptographic coprocessor for an encryption operation. While waiting for the cryptographic operation to finish, the CPU polls a status register of the coprocessor.

---

[1] Data normalized due to existing NDA.

During this time, the estimated power consumption indicates that the limit will be exceeded. Hence, in the second implementation, the CPU is set to a special low-power sleep mode and is only reactivated after the cryptographic operation has finished. By emulating the power profile of the power-aware, second implementation we clearly see that the limit is not exceeded any more. Note that slight variations in program execution exist due to different coprocessor setup algorithms and are also visible in the power trace.

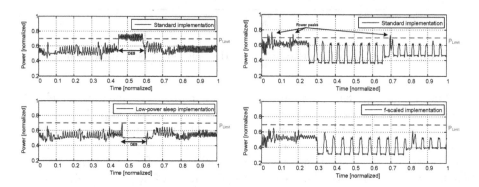

Fig. 5. Profiling of an application utilizing a component's low-power mode

Fig. 6. Profiling of an application utilizing frequency scaling

In the second example (see Figure 6), the cryptographic results from the example above are further processed. In this phase, additional power peaks above the limit are identified with the help of power emulation. In the power-optimized implementation, these peaks can be diminished by scaling the clock frequency from 33 MHz to 29 MHz. The power emulation result of the modified implementation indicates an acceptable execution time increase while observing the permissible power limit.

5   Conclusions

Power-aware software development is often hindered by the lack of quick power profiling methods. The rapid high-level power emulation approach presented in this paper circumvents this limitation by exploiting hardware acceleration techniques. By combining the functional emulation of a system's HDL model with power estimation hardware, run-time power estimates can be generated on a standard FPGA emulation platform.

We have evaluated our approach on an 80251-based microcontroller system, yielding cycle-accurate power estimates with an average estimation error below 10% in magnitude. These numbers were reported for a high-level power model requiring only 1.5% of the available FPGA ressources. We believe that by marrying these estimates with a standard software development environment truly power-aware software engineering is enabled.

References

1. Macii, E., Poncino, M.: Power macro-models for high-level power estimation. In: Piguet, C. (ed.) Low-Power Electronics Design. CRC Press, Boca Raton (2005)
2. Joseph, R., Martonosi, M.: Run-time power estimation in high performance micro-processors. In: Proc. of the ISLPED, pp. 135–140 (2001)
3. Contreras, G., Martonosi, M.: Power prediction for intel xscale processors using performance monitoring unit events. In: Proc. of the ISLPED 2005, pp. 221–226. ACM, New York (2005)
4. Haid, J., Kaefer, G., Steger, C., Weiss, R.: A co-processor for real-time energy estimation of system-on-a-chip. In: Proc. 45th MWSCAS, pp. II–99–II–102 (2002)
5. Haid, J., Kaefer, G., Steger, C., Weiss, R.: Run-time energy estimation in system-on-a-chip designs. In: Proc. of the ASP-DAC 2003, pp. 595–599 (2003)
6. Peddersen, J., Parameswaran, S.: Clipper: Counter-based low impact processor power estimation at run-time. In: Proc. of the ASP-DAC 2007, pp. 890–895 (2007)
7. Peddersen, J., Parameswaran, S.: Low-impact processor for dynamic runtime power management. IEEE Design & Test of Computers 25(1), 52–62 (2008)
8. Coburn, J., Ravi, S., Raghunathan, A.: Power emulation: a new paradigm for power estimation. In: Proc. 42nd DAC 2005, pp. 700–705 (2005)
9. Coburn, J., Ravi, S., Raghunathan, A.: Hardware accelerated power estimation. In: Proc. DATE 2005, vol. 1, pp. 528–529 (2005)
10. Bhattacharjee, A., Contreras, G., Martonosi, M.: Full-system chip multiprocessor power evaluations using fpga-based emulation. In: Proc. of the ISLPED 2008 (2008)
11. Flynn, J., Waldo, B.: Power management in complex soc design. Technical report, Synopsys Inc. White Paper (2005)
12. Tiwari, V., Malik, S., Wolfe, A.: Power analysis of embedded software: A first step towards software power minimization. In: Proc. IEEE/ACM International Conference on Computer-Aided Design, pp. 384–390 (1994)
13. Sami, M., Sciuto, D., Silvano, C., Zaccaria, V.: An instruction-level energy model for embedded vliw architectures. IEEE (J-CAD) 21(9), 998–1010 (2002)
14. Lee, I., Kim, H., Yang, P., Yoo, S., Chung, E.Y., Choi, K.M., Kong, J.T., Eo, S.K.: Powervip: Soc power estimation framework at transaction level. In: Proc. of the ASP-DAC 2006 (2006)
15. Bellosa, F.: The benefits of event: driven energy accounting in power-sensitive systems. In: EW 9: Proceedings of the 9th workshop on ACM SIGOPS European workshop, pp. 37–42. ACM, New York (2000)
16. Ghodrat, M., Lahiri, K., Raghunathan, A.: Accelerating system-on-chip power analysis using hybrid power estimation. In: Proc. DAC 2007, pp. 883–886 (2007)
17. Genser, A., Bachmann, C., Haid, J., Steger, C., Weiss, R.: An emulation-based real-time power profiling unit for embedded software. In: Proc. SAMOS 2009, pp. 67–73 (2009)
18. Bachmann, C., Genser, A., Haid, J., Steger, C., Weiss, R.: Rapid system-level power estimation for power-aware embedded software design. In: Proc. DSD Work In Progress Session (2009)
19. Benini, L., Hodgson, R., Siegel, P.: System-level power estimation and optimization. In: Proc. of the ISLPED 1998, pp. 173–178 (1998)

Write Invalidation Analysis in Chip Multiprocessors

Newsha Ardalani[1,2] and Amirali Baniasadi[3,*]

[1] School of Computer Science, IPM, Tehran, Iran
[2] CE Department, Sharif University of Technology, Tehran, Iran
[3] ECE Department, University of Victoria, Victoria, B. C., Canada
ardalani@ce.sharif.edu, amirali@ece.uvic.ca

Abstract. Chip multiprocessors (CMPs) issue write invalidations (WIs) to assure program correctness. In conventional snoop-based protocols, writers broadcast invalidations to all nodes as soon as possible. In this work we show that this approach, while protecting correctness, is inefficient due to two reasons. First, many of the invalidated blocks are not accessed after invalidation making the invalidation unnecessary. Second, among the invalidated blocks many are not accessed anytime soon, making immediate invalidation unnecessary. While invalidating the first group could be avoided altogether, the second group's invalidation could be delayed without any performance or correctness cost. Accordingly, we show that there exists an ample opportunity to eliminate and/or delay many WIs without harming performance or correctness. Moreover we investigate invalidation necessity and urgency and show that a large share of WIs could be delayed without impacting program outcome. Our study shows that WIs often repeats their behavior from both the necessity and urgency point of view. Finally we study how eliminating unnecessary WIs could potentially reduce bus occupancy.

Keywords: Cache coherency; Chip multiprocessors; Write Invalidation.

1 Introduction

A key challenge in CMP design is maintaining coherency among many cores. Two strategies currently exist for maintaining coherency: snooping protocols and directory protocols. These protocols, despite their obvious differences, treat invalidations similarly in a rather aggressive manner: they send invalidation messages to the superset of nodes that they guess may contain the memory block and as soon as possible. This aggressive approach assures program correctness but is inefficient from both bandwidth and energy point of view.

Necessary WIs (i.e., those WIs whose presence is essential to assure program correctness) account for a small share of all WIs. The rest of the WIs could be avoided without compromising correctness. We explore if such WIs show a repeatable (and hence predictable) behavior. We find out that unnecessary WIs are highly predictable.

---

* The author was spending his sabbatical leave at the school of computer science of IPM when this work was done.

J. Monteiro and R. van Leuken (Eds.): PATMOS 2009, LNCS 5953, pp. 196–205, 2010.

In this paper, we also show that not all WIs are highly urgent. Recognizing the slack associated with write invalidations, gives us the opportunity to postpone invalidation to an appropriate point in time, when interconnect is less busy.

The rest of the paper is structured as follows. In Section 2, we discuss methodology. In Section 3, we study WI behavior from different points of view. In Section 4, we investigate WI behavior predictability. In Section 5, we go over the impact of eliminating unnecessary WIs on bus occupancy. In Section 6, we summarize the related work on coherence prediction and discuss our contributions comparing to previous studies. Finally, in Section 7, we offer concluding remarks.

2 Methodology

In this study we used and modified the SESC simulator [1] to simulate invalidation behavior in this study. The experiments are carried out using a subset of the SPLASH-2 benchmark suite [2]. Since a large portion of this study focuses on the share of cold misses, we fast-forwarded the first 500M instructions so cold misses occurring prior to the steady phase do not impact results. We run each benchmarks for 500M instructions after skipping the first 500M. We simulated systems with two, four, eight, 16, 32 and 64 processors connected together via a shared bus. The configuration of our system is shown in Table 1. We used all SPLASH-2 applications in our simulation, but for the sake of brevity, we only show a subset of benchmarks. Table 2 shows the input parameters used for each benchmark.

Table 1. System Configuration Parameters

Processor
Frequency/Issue Width/Window Size:1 GHZ/4/80
Memory System
I-L1: 32KB/2 way/ WT/32-byte block
D-L1: 32KB/4 way/ WB/32-byte block
L2: 1MB/8 way
L1/L2/Memory latency: 2/11/469 ns
Interconnect
Instruction bus between L1 and L2:
Bandwidth/Link latency/Port occupancy:256b/1cycle/1ns
Data and address bus between L1 and L2:
Bandwidth/Link latency/Port occupancy:256b/1cycle/1ns

Table 2. Benchmarks Input Parameter

Benchmark	Input Parameters
Barnes	16K particles
Cholesky	tk29.O
FFT	1G complex data points
FMM	16K particles
Ocean(contig)	258×258 grid
Radiosity	-batch -room -ae 5000.0 -en 0.050 -bf 0.10
Radix	1G keys
Raytrace	balls4.env

3 Invalidation Behavior

Each benchmark has different WI characteristics compared to others. We study WI behavior using three different metrics: Invalidation distribution, Invalidation necessity and Invalidation urgency. In the following sections we first introduce each metric and then study the WI behavior of the selected SPLASH-2 benchmarks.

3.1 Invalidation Distribution

WI messages are initiated when a write occurs and the invalidated block is either not in the cache (referred to as cold write-miss) or is in one of two known coherency states: shared (referred to as shared write-miss) or already invalid (referred to as invalid write-miss).

Our investigation shows most of invalidation messages initiated, are cold write-misses. Shared and invalid write-misses account for a small share of all invalidation messages initiated. Based upon these observations, we categorize applications into three different groups:

1. Cold-Dominated: More than 98% of all WIs are cold write-misses regardless of the number of cores.
2. Cold-Decreasing: More than half of the WIs are cold write-misses but this share decreases as the number of cores increases.
3. Cold-Independent: More than half of the WIs are cold write-misses but this share does not follow the core number in any monotonic way.

3.2 Invalidation Necessity

We refer to a write-invalidation as necessary if at least one of the sharers (other than the writer) makes an attempt to read the invalidated block. A WI, whose invalidated block is no longer required by any other node, is deemed as an unnecessary WI. Intuitively, if no other node needs the invalidated data, the WI could have been avoided without any cost.

We also define necessity degree as the average number of readers that make an attempt to access an invalid block. We show in Section 3.4 that necessity degree of cold write-misses(referred to as cold necessity degree) is considerably less than the necessity degree for shared and invalid write-misses (also referred to as shared and invalid necessity degree) indicating a small group of static necessary WIs (with high necessity degrees), are responsible for the majority of dynamic WIs.

3.3 Invalidation Urgency

Typical multi-core systems take an aggressive approach, invalidating written blocks as soon as possible. This aggressive approach is not necessary as (a) not all WIs are necessary and (b) not all necessary WIs are urgent. An urgent WI is one whose invalidated block is required by another core "shortly" after the WI is issued. In other words, invalidation urgency depends on how soon the invalidated data will be needed. Our study shows that only a small group of the invalidated WIs is highly urgent. The rest can be further postponed to a later point in time and as late as the moment before the first read occurs.

We define invalidation slack and invalidation urgency for necessary WIs as follows: invalidation slack is the period between a write access and a read access to the same block by any node other than writer. Invalidation urgency is its reverse.

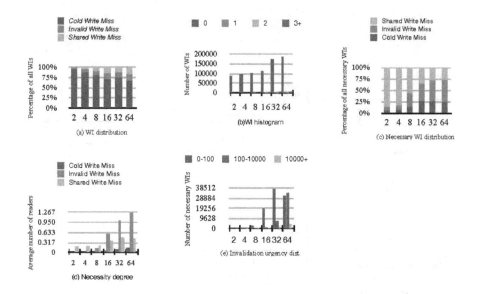

Fig. 1. Barnes:(a) The relative share of cold, invalid and shared write-miss among all WIs. (b) The portion of WIs followed by zero, one, two and more than two read accesses. (c) The relative share of cold, invalid and shared write-misses among necessary WIs. (d) The necessity degree for each category.(e) The portion of high, medium and low urgent WIs.

We categorize WIs into three groups based on their invalidation slack. We use the following classification to cover a wide range of possible slacks.

1. High-Urgency: Invalidation slack period is less than 100 cycles.
2. Medium-Urgency: Invalidation slack period is between 100 to 10,000 cycles.
3. Low-Urgency: Invalidation slack period is more than 10,000 cycles.

3.4   Applications Behavior Analysis

In this section we characterize a subset of SPLASH-2 benchmarks using the metrics discussed above and using a series of graphs presented in different parts of Figures 1 and 2. Part (a) represents the relative share of cold, invalid and shared write-misses among all WIs for different number of cores. Part (b) shows what portion of WIs are followed by zero, one, two and more than two read accesses. The zero-access bar presents the number of unnecessary WIs. Part (c) is similar to part (a) but reports invalidation distribution among necessary WIs. Part (d) shows necessity degree for each category and part (e) reports what portion of necessary WIs are low-urgency, medium-urgency or high-urgency.

As we present in Figure 1(a), Barnes is a cold-independent application where the majority of write-misses initiated are in the cold state. This share, however, does not follow the core number in any monotonic way. Figure 1(b) shows that large share of WIs are unnecessary. This share is 93% for 64 cores and grows up to 99% for a quad-core

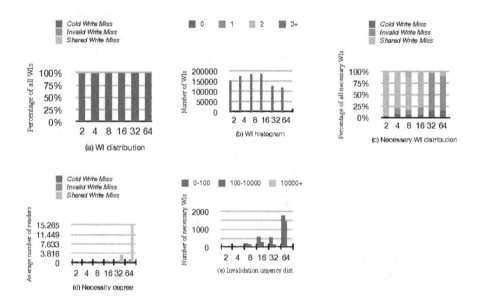

Fig. 2. FMM: (a) The relative share of cold, invalid and shared write-miss among all WIs. (b) The portion of WIs followed by zero, one, two and more than two read accesses. (c) The relative share of cold, invalid and shared write-misses among necessary WIs. (d) The necessity degree for each category. (e) The portion of high, medium and low urgent WIs.

system. A closer look at the share of invalid and shared write-misses presented in Figure 1(a) and 1(c) shows that the vast majority of necessary WIs are initiated by a small number of static WIs. For four cores, for example, 94% of necessary WIs are initiated by shared and invalid write-misses, which account for only 13% of all WIs. Figure 1(d) reports that cold necessity degree is lower than 0.1 which indicates a large number of WIs are unnecessary. Meantime, invalid necessity degree reaches 1.2 as the number of processors increases. Moreover, shared necessity degree (i.e., necessity degree of shared write-misses), while increasing from 0.18 to 0.44, remains below one. Invalid necessity degree (i.e., necessity degree of invalid write-misses) grows faster than shared necessity degree. Figure 1(e) demonstrates that large share of necessary WIs are high-urgency.

As we present in Figure 2(a), FMM is a cold-dominated application where more than 99% of WIs are cold write-misses regardless of the number of cores. As reported in Figure 2(b) the majority of WIs are unnecessary. Figure 2(d) reports a necessity degree of 3.2 and 15.2 for 32 and 64 cores respectively. This high necessity degree results in a high bus read miss traffic. Figure 2(c) shows that the vast majority of necessary WIs are initiated by shared and invalid write-misses which account a small share of static WIs. As presented in Figure 2(e), and similar to Barnes, a large share of necessary WIs are high-urgency.

4 Invalidation Behavior Predictability

From the writer point of view, we are interested to know if a write can speculate if a WI is necessary or unnecessary. For example, if a write knows in advance the (old) copy of the invalidated data sitting in other caches will not be read anymore, it can avoid sending the invalidation signal. In Section 4.1, we show that while invalidation necessity does not show a predictable behavior, invalidation unnecessity does.

From the readers point of view, we are interested to know if the next read access can speculate if it will be accessing an invalid data. Intuitively, if a read instruction can identify invalid data independently, then sending invalidation signals would not be necessary. We study invalid read predictability in Section 4.2. We also study invalidation urgency predictability. We investigate the possibility of speculating invalidation urgency based on past behavior and report our findings in 4.3.

4.1 Necessity and Unnecessity Predictability

(Un)Necessity predictability indicates how often a WI which has been (un)necessary before, will be (un)necessary next time encountered. A WI can be tagged using the written block address or the PC of the writing instruction. Our prediction estimation works as follows: if a WI, on its first occurrence, has been (un)necessary, we check how often it will be (un)necessary on its next occurrences. The (un)necessity predictability is defined as the ratio of the number of WIs which we expect to be (un)necessary and are actually (un)necessary to all WIs. Figures 3 and 4 report the necessity and unnecessity predictability, respectively using both PC and the block address. In most of the benchmarks presented in Figure 4, using block address results in higher accuracy in detecting unnecessary WIs compared to the case when we use instruction PC. Comparing figures 3 and 4 shows that unnecessary WIs are highly predictable, compared to necessary ones. Unnecessity predictability indicates that if an invalid block left untouched between two writes, there is high chance that the same block will not be read between the next two write instructions too.

4.2 Invalid Read Predictability

Invalid read predictability indicates how often a block which has been invalid last time read, will be invalid next time being read. An invalid read can also be identified using block address or the PC of the reading instruction. Figure 5 compares the invalid read predictability for both PC and block address. The first bar reports predictability using PC and the second bar reports the results assuming block address is used. Since all mispredictions are not equally costly, we categorize them into two groups: soft mispredcitions and hard mispredictions. If a valid block is mispredicted as an invalid one, it will result in an excessive read request on the bus, but does not threaten system safety. We refer to this type of misprediction as a soft one. On the other hand, if an invalid block is mispredcited as a valid one, system safety will be threatened. We refer to this type as a hard mispredcition. Note that hard mispredictions are very infrequent, i.e., in range of E-5%.

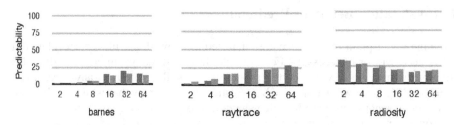

Fig. 3. WI necessity predictability using (1) PC (2) Block address

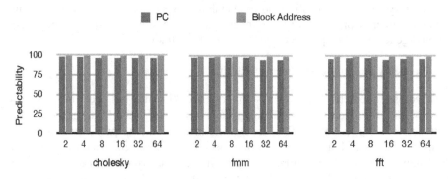

Fig. 4. WI unnecessity predictability using (1) PC (2) Block address

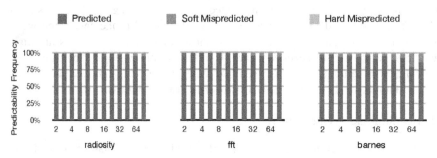

Fig. 5. Invalid read predictability using (1) PC (2) Block address. Hard mispredictions are too infrequent and therefore are not visible

4.3 Invalidation Urgency Predictability

Invalidation urgency predictability indicates how often the invalidation urgency of a WI belongs to the same category it belonged last time. The categories are low, medium and high urgency. As mentioned before, a WI can be tagged using the written block address or the PC of the writing instruction. Figure 6 shows the likelihood that a write-invalidated block address belonging to one of the urgency classes will belong to the same class next time encountered. Figure 7 shows the likelihood of belonging a

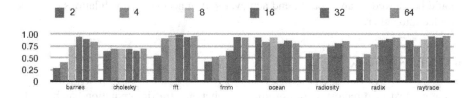

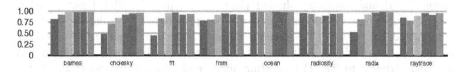

Fig. 6. Invalidation urgency predictability using block address for different core numbers

Fig. 7. Invalidation urgency predictability using PC for different core numbers

PC to the same urgency class it belonged last time. Comparing these two figures indicates that (1) instruction PC provides more accurate urgency class predictions compared to using the block address (2) although urgency class predictability increases with the number of cores for both PC and block address, PC is less sensitive to the number of cores making PC is a better choice in predicting next urgency class.

5   Bus Occupancy Reduction

In this section we show that eliminating unnecessary write invalidations reduces bus occupancy without compromising performance.

Bus occupancy reduction impacts static power; the less the requests stay in the buffer, the less static power they dissipate. Figure 8 shows the average time a request has to spend waiting before accessing the bus with or without sending unnecessary invalidations. While the former represents a conventional bus system, the latter is a theoretical simulation with the purpose of providing additional insight. These results

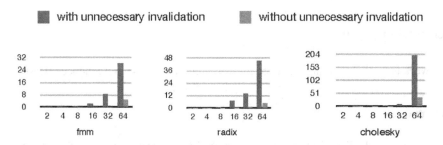

Fig. 8. Average bus occupancy with and without broadcasting unnecessary invalidations

should be viewed as an upper bound achievable if unnecessary invalidations could be avoided altogether.

6 Related Work

In the context of directory-based protocols, coherence traffic prediction has been the focus of many studies. Early works on reducing coherency traffic studied static sharing patterns observed in the directory, including read-modify-write [3], producer-consumer [4] and migratory sharing [5,6]. Mukherji and Hill [7] introduced the general pattern-based predictor which was designed based upon the two-level PAp branch predictor scheme [8]. Recent studies have focused specifically on reducing the invalidation overhead, taking the responsibility of invalidating sharers from directory and giving it to the (1) requesting node or (2) sharers. Acacio et al. [9] have assigned invalidating responsibility to the requesting node. They have focused on invalidations initiated in shared state, the so-called upgrade misses. Lebeck and Wood [10] suggested triggering invalidation of shared blocks at critical section boundaries. Lai and Falsafi [11] proposed the last touch predictor which associates each invalidation event with a sequence of PCs prior to invalidations. Our study is different from the above in three ways: First, we propose a detailed classification of invalidation traffic. Second, while previous studies focus on necessary WIs, we study unnecessary WIs. Third, most previous studies attempt to accelerate directory coherence protocols we study the opportunity to delay WIs to save power and reduce bus contention.

7 Conclusion

In this work, we studied WI behavior from different perspectives. We classified WIs into three classes: cold-dominated, cold-decreasing and cold-independent. We also studied invalidation necessity and showed that the majority of WIs are not necessary. We also investigated invalidation urgency and classified WIs. Urgency also shows a predictable behavior as often a WI belonging to one class of urgency continues to stay in the same class. We showed that eliminating unnecessary WIs could reduce bus occupancy.

Acknowledgment

This work is funded by Iran's Institute for Research in Fundamental Sciences (IPM).

References

1. Renau, J., et al.: SESC Simulator (January 2005), http://sesc.sourceforge.net
2. Woo, S.C., et al.: The SPLASH-2 programs: characterization and methodological considerations. In: Proc. of 22nd ISCA (June 1995)

3. Laudon, J., Lenoski, D.: The SGI Origin: A cc-Numma Highly Scalabale Server. In: Proc. of 24th ISCA (1997)
4. Cheng, L., Carter, J., Dai, D.: An adaptive cache coherence protocol optimized for producer-consumer sharing. In: 13th HPCA (2007)
5. Cox, A.L., Fowler, J.: Adaptive Cache Coherency for Detecting Migratory Shared Data. In: Proc. of the 20th ISCA (1993)
6. Stenstrom, P., Brosson, M., Sandberg, L.: Adaptive Cache Coherence Protocol Optimized for Migratory Sharing. In: Proc. of the 20th ISCA (1993)
7. Mukherji, S.S., Hill, M.D.: Using Prediction to Accelerate Coherence Protocols. In: Proc. of the 25th ISCA (1998)
8. Yeh, T.Y., Patt, Y.: Alternative Implementation of two-level adaptive branch prediction. In: Proc. of the 19th ISCA (1992)
9. Acacio, M.E., et al.: The Use of Prediction for Accelerating Upgrade Misses in cc-NUMA Mutiprocessors. In: Proc. ICPACT (2002)
10. Lebeck, A.R., Wood, D.A.: Dynamic Self-Invalidation: Reducing Coherence Overhead in Shared-Memory Multiprocessors. In: Proc. of the 22nd ISCA (1995)
11. Lai, A.C., Falsafi, B.: Selective, accurate, and timely self-invalidation using last-touch prediction. In: Proc. of the 27th ISCA (2000)

Practical Design Space Exploration of an H264 Decoder for Handheld Devices Using a Virtual Platform

Marius Gligor[1], Nicolas Fournel[1], Frédéric Pétrot[1], Fabien Colas-Bigey[2], Anne-Marie Fouilliart[2], Philippe Teninge[3], and Marcello Coppola[3]

[1] TIMA Laboratory, CNRS/INP Grenoble/UJF
[2] Thales Communications
[3] STMicroelectronics

Abstract. H264 is a promising standard for mobile appliances since it allows to play on the tradeoff between data transmission rates and processing needs. This tradeoff is a common issue in mobile appliance design as it leaves space for power savings. We propose here a virtual platform based global approach, *i.e.* investigating hardware solutions, software solutions and both, to define a set of energy-optimized degraded operating modes for a H264 decoder software. Results of this exploration show that reasonable energy savings for degraded modes can be achieved without loosing too much image quality.

1 Introduction

Limited bandwidth of communication channels and increased video sizes drive the need for efficient video compression techniques. These techniques have become essential to reduce the amount of data to store and to transmit and among the standard developed deal with these new constraints. Flexibility in coding, organization of data, high compression rates and error resilience features make of H264 a promising standard for embedded devices.

As many embedded appliances are battery-powered, it is necessary, on top of saving energy by transmitting less data, to pay attention to the energy required to process these data, *i.e.* decode video.

For critical applications, *e.g.* an operator on field, we have to ensure that communication (and video) must last long enough so that complete instructions can be transmitted. If the battery is low and cannot provide energy till the expected end of transmission, it is required to reduce the quality of the transmission (more precisely video) to run in a less energy consuming, degraded, mode.

We are proposing, in this paper, to apply a global, hardware plus software, approach to define a set of degraded operating modes for a video decoding application based on the H264 standard.

The rest of this article is organized as follows. Section 2 gives an overview of related works. Section 3 presents the target hardware, the H264 standards overview and the optimization possibilities. Section 4 describes the virtual platform used to perform this design space exploration. Section 5 gives the results of the exploration and describes the adaptation made to the system. Finally Section 6 summarizes the results.

J. Monteiro and R. van Leuken (Eds.): PATMOS 2009, LNCS 5953, pp. 206–215, 2010.

2   State of the Art

As of now many works have addressed the implementation and/or optimization of H264 decoder. These works investigated a large amount of solutions ranging from the pure software solution [1] to the full hardware one [13].

Some works interested in optimizing pure software versions of the H264 decoder, mainly by working on the parallelized version of the H264 decoder more precisely on balancing the slices workload [10].

The hardware solutions range from simple block implementation [7] to highly integrated chips [9]. Li *et al.* [7] proposes a hardware accelerator handling only a part of the complete H264 decoding task: the deblocking filter. Some other works propose more integrated chip [9], where hardware components are responsible of a large part of the decoding. Replacing the corresponding software by highly specialized hardware logic.

Stitt *et al.* in [11] proposes hardware software partitioning solution based on a different granularity functions of the software implementation of the H264 decoder. This approach replaces some of the functions by hardware versions based on its binary code.

Among these works, only few works on H264 optimization in an energy point of view. In [1], Baker *et al.* proposes a scheme to minimize energy consumption of a pure software implementation by working on priority of slice groups. On the other hand previous works on MPEG2 video decoded investigated the complete system optimization in a hardware software partionning scheme.

As far as we know, none of these works have based the design space exploration on a virtual platform, furthermore in an energy optimization perspective.

3   Application Architecture

3.1   Overview of the Specifications

Images Format. The version of the H264 decoder implemented here follows the 4:2:0 image format in which the image is decomposed into one luminance and two chrominance components. The video coding algorithms require a lot of temporary structures to be stored in memory: prediction modes, residuals, transform coefficients, predicted pixels, and others. As a consequence, images are subdivided into smaller more manageable pieces of data called macroblocks (16x16 pixels). Offering the possibility to reduce memory footprint and to offer new parallelization or pipelining possibilities.

Predictions. The compression efficiency of the H264 standard relies on predictions. At the encoder side, the value of each macroblock is predicted, then the difference, also called residual, between the predicted and the original macroblock is encoded and transmitted to the decoder. Using the same prediction algorithm, the decoder reconstructs the predicted macroblock, adds the transmitted errors and recovers the original macroblock. The value of a macroblock can therefore be predicted using the values of its surrounding macroblocks (intra coded macroblock) or the values of previous images (inter coded macroblock).

Dependencies. Since the H264 standard relies on predictions, the decoding of a macroblock requires the values of some previously decoded macroblocks, which can either belong to the current frame or to previous ones. Macroblocks therefore have to be decoded in a pre-defined order, which reduces parallelization options. Two series of predictions can be distinguished on the decoder side: prediction of prediction modes and prediction of macroblock values. In a first step, the decoder predicts the information that will be used to decode the macroblock: prediction mode, motion vectors values, and others. In a second step, using prediction information, the decoder predicts the value of the macroblock pixels and add residuals to reconstruct the original macroblock. All these predictions require data issued from surrounding macroblocks (Figure 1).

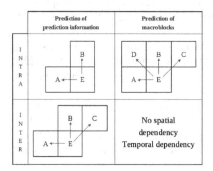

Fig. 1. Spatial dependencies for intra and inter predictions

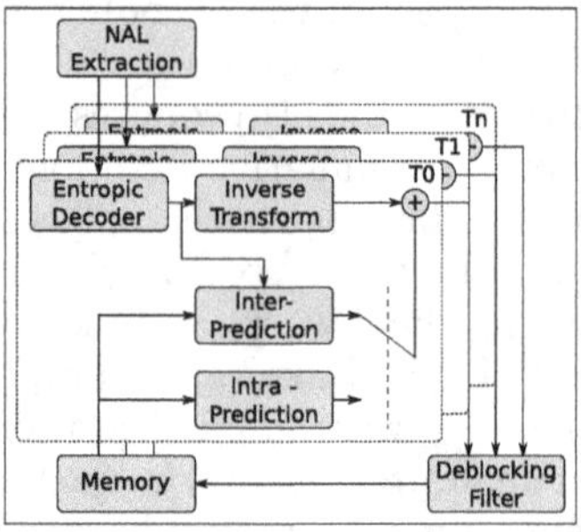

Fig. 2. Software architecture of the H264 decoder

The architecture of the decoder has to take macroblock dependencies into account. Macroblock E can only be decoded if macroblocks A, B, C and D have already been decoded. Moreover, if the macroblock is inter coded, previous frames also have to be decoded. These data dependencies have of course an impact on the parallelizing and pipelining options.

Constraints and Needs. Because of its complex set of prediction algorithms, H264 decoders require significant hardware resources. However, several profiles have been defined to adapt the structure of the decoder to the platform resources and user needs. In our case, the implementation of the decoder follows the baseline profile, which targets video-conferencing and mobile applications.

3.2   Possible Hardware/Software Choices

Mobile Appliances. We aim at defining a set of energy optimized operating modes for a H264 decoder in mobile appliances. The targeted devices are multi-purpose, *i.e.* video conferencing is only a feature among others of the appliance.

To allow several operating modes, the implementation of the decoder has to be largely reconfigurable. In case of a full hardware implementation of the decoder, supporting many profiles would make hardware more complex and costly.

The availability of energy efficient multi-processors systems makes software implementations of the decoder probably viable. This is the solution we investigate here.

Software Solutions. The parallelization of the decoding process can rely on several techniques: instruction level parallelism, task level parallelism, data parallelism, and others. The introduction of parallelism has to take advantage of dependencies, and of the hardware architecture.

A common solution consists of parallelizing the decoding process on macroblocks. Dependencies are then managed by a synchronization process that ensures the reliability of the referenced macroblocks. This parallelization option leads to good performances but targets high quality decoders and many-core architectures. For embedded devices, the implementation cost of such a solution is rather high because the number of processors is limited.

Another solution consists of applying the same concept at a higher hierarchical level by considering slices instead of macroblocks. Slices represent groups of macroblocks having common prediction characteristics. Because slices are independent, the management of dependencies is reduced to dependencies between frames. The implementation cost of this solution is rather low in the sense that the majority of algorithms can be applied in parallel to large image chunks.

The decoding process can also be pipelined by assigning parts of the decoding process to different tasks. However, this solution is not adapted to SMP architectures and better exploits streaming platform architectures. As a consequence, the solution selected is a parallelization based on slices division.

The decoding algorithm is divided into the following steps. First, the decoder reads the input stream and extracts slices. Each slice is sent to a task that handles part of the decoding process.

The block called entropic decoder first decodes the slice header, which contains decoding parameters. The process then iterates on all the macroblocks of the slice. For each macroblock, the process decodes prediction information and residuals. Prediction parameters are then sent to the intra and inter prediction blocks that reconstruct the predicted macroblock. The residuals are sent to the inverse transform block that reconstructs original residuals. Residuals and the predicted macroblock are then added in order to reconstruct the original macroblock: this process is called rendering. The reconstructed macroblock is then sent to the deblocking filter process. The software architecture of the application is depicted on Figure 2, where each T_n is a task.

Interconnect Solutions. The Spidergon STNoC [3] is a flexible and scalable packet-based on-chip micro-network designed according to a layered packet-based communication protocol. It is based on a pseudo-regular topology, called Spidergon which is essentially based on a bidirectional ring with cross connections. Thanks to of its short wires, and its support for Quality of Service through virtual channels, the Spidergon STNoC provides a power efficient way of interconnecting IPs.

3.3 Platform Preview

To summarize, the internal hardware platform architecture defined for H264 software implementation is a NoC based MPSoC. This architecture is depicted in Figure 3(a).

This MPSoC is based on an ARM11MPCore. This core is a Symmetric Multi-Processor system (SMP) embedding 4 ARM11MP ARMv6k ISA based

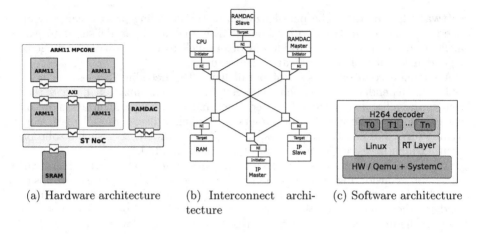

(a) Hardware architecture   (b) Interconnect architecture   (c) Software architecture

Fig. 3. Platform architecture

processors linked with an AXI AMBA bus. Interconnection between the ARM11MPCore and other devices is fulfilled thanks to the Network-on-Chip.

Through this interconnect, CPUs can access to an SRAM, which can be used for frame buffering for example, a RAMDAC, used to display freshly decoded video frames. As it can be seen on Figure 3(b), The interconnect allows each initiator to communicate with every targets in a one hop dedicated link. This ensures efficient and low contention communications on the platform.

In terms of software, Figure 3(c) gives an overview of the architecture of the system. The main characteristic of this software system is the use of a full featured operating system (*i.e.* Linux flavor) to manage a multi threaded version of a H264 decoder.

4   Virtual Platform

The simulation platform aims at giving accurate estimations of the performances of the complete system, hardware and software, in terms of timings and energy consumption. It will favour decision-making during the optimization process.

Simulation has a great importance in System on Chip (SoC) design. It allows early intervening in the SoC development in order to perform the exploration of multiprocessor SoC architectures, to test and debug hardware and software systems. Classical multiprocessor Systems on Chip (MPSoC) simulation techniques are based on Instruction set simulators (ISS).These approaches can achieve cycle accurate simulation models of the target architecture but at the price of a limited simulation speed. This speed is so reduced that the simulation of a complete system like the one investigated here is made hardly possible even with optimized simulators [5].

To allow fast simulation, our virtual platform takes advantage of the event driven simulation technology used in SystemC [12] at a TLM level of abstraction. Since processors architecture is not part of our exploration work and instruction interpretation is an important part of simulation time, we decided to use binary translation based simulation technology.

This technology consists of translating the target (i.e. ARM) instructions in micro-operations corresponding to an internal intermediate instruction set. This binary translation can either be followed by an interpretation step where each micro-instruction is decoded and executed, this is the case in Bochs [8], or be followed by a code generation step where each micro-instruction is translated in host (i.e. x86) instruction, this is the case in the open source processor emulator QEMU [2]. The complete simulation architecture that uses SystemC and wrapped QEMU CPUs is depicted on Figure 4. More details about this integration are available in [4].

To ease software debugging and optimization, the simulation tool offers common outputs (standard I/O) allowing to verify functional correctness and output quality (video). On top of that, the tool has been instrumented to give a power consumption feed back based on a simple state-based power consumption, i.e. operating modes of every platform devices are used to estimate the power consumption of the complete system. Calibration data are obtained from synthesis information. These outputs allow to accomplish a fast design space exploration to optimize the energy consumption of the H264 decoder operating modes.

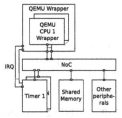

Fig. 4.   Simulation architecture

5   Design Space Exploration

5.1   Influence of Parallelism on H264 Performances

The objectives of this experimentation is to study the influence of the level of parallelism of the H264 decoder software on our NoC based hardware platform. For that purpose the system (hardware and software) presented in Section 3.3 was experimented on the virtual platform described in Section 4.

We investigate in the same experiment set the influence of image size and frame rate to study the influence of video quality in order to define the different degraded modes of the system. The studied configuration are CIF and QCIF image sizes (i.e. 352x288 pixels for CIF and 176x144 pixels for QCIF) and 10 and 25 frame per second as frame rates. Configuration were studied under four different levels of parallelism (form 1 to 4) adapted to the hardware platform architecture. It was not possible to experiment QCIF parallelism 2 and 4 because we did not have an encoding software producing it.

All experiments results are reported in Table 1, which shows average processors usage and average energy consumption for the different video quality configuration against the different parallelism levels.

These results are mean utilization rate and mean power consumption for each configuration. The mean utilization rate is obtained by averaging over 50 frames the ratio between the time needed to decode the frame and its deadline. For example, for a 10 frame per second video, a 50% utilization means that the average time to decode image is 50 ms. The mean power figures represents the average power consumed by the complete platform.

As it can be seen from these figures, the platform is not able to keep the pace of a 25 CIF frames per second video, which is demonstrated by utilization rate over 100%.

Table 1. Performances of the H264 decoder against number of threads

	1 thread		2 threads		3 threads		4 threads	
	Util.	Power	Util.	Power	Util.	Power	Util.	Power
cif@25	441.46	697	229.03	910	168.88	1060	121.81	1261
cif@10	176.59	697	91.56	841	64.53	832	63.90	821
qcif@25	108.43	686	x	x	69.48	658	x	x
qcif@10	43.36	555	x	x	28.12	549	x	x

These results however validate the fact that parallelizing this decoder is a valuable operation, since when the number of threads grows, the mean utilization and mean power decrease. These decreases are due to the fact that frames are decoded faster, so processors go to idle for a longer time.

5.2   DBF Function

[6] indicates that the DBF function is one of the most computation hungry of the H264 decoder and based on the fact that it is hardly efficiently parallelized, we will have a closer look at the behavior of this function in this section.

Although it is very valuable from an image quality point of view, the DBF consumes a great part of the decoding process. For example, with the mono-threaded version on a CIF image, the decoding time of a frame is about 160 ms with the DBF algorithm whereas it is only 70 ms without. This means that DBF algorithm represents about 55% of the results presented in 5.1.

In order to limit the processor workload of H264 decoding software, we investigate the solution of implementing the deblocking filter as an hardware accelerator accessible through the NoC. The overview of this hardware module is given on Figure 5(a). This hardware component has both initiator and target interfaces. Both interfaces are connected to the interconnect, as presented on Figure 5(b). The filter can be configured to inform the software when the process is finished by sending interruptions. As a consequence, the hardware deblocking filter reduces decoding time, and reduces the platform power consumption. It is well known that dedicated hardware is much more power efficient than software, and thanks

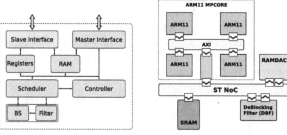

(a) Block diagram of the DBF

(b) Hardware architecture

Fig. 5. Deblocking filter and system architectures

Table 2. Performances of the H264 decoder with hardware DBF

	1 thread		2 threads		3 threads		4 threads	
	Util.	Power	Util.	Power	Util.	Power	Util.	Power
cif@25	285.18	693	182.09	844	141.32	980	163.07	927
cif@10	114.08	680	72.77	716	57.68	727	48.62	740
qcif@25	98.46	637	x	x	98.56	702	x	x
qcif@10	39.39	529	x	x	39.42	555	x	x

to the mapping of the components on the topology, no contention is added to the network. The hardware implementation can process up to four slices in parallel in CIF and QCIF images.

We reproduced the experiments of Section 5.1 but with the version of the decoder virtual platform which now integrates the hardware deblocking filter. This integration was obtained by adding a device driver for the filter in the linux kernel, and a SystemC TLM module of the DBF on the virtual platform. As far as timings and energy consumption are concerned, calibration were made thanks to fine grained approximation based on internal processing of the component and synthesis results. Results of this new run are given in Table 2. It clearly shows that the use of this hardware accelerator allowed to optimize the system usage and the energy consumption since CPUs are more often in idle mode. For example, for a 4 threads version of the decoder with a 10 CIF frames per second video, the utilization rate drops from 64% to 48% (a 25% reduction) and mean power decreases from 821 mW to 740 mW (a 10% reduction).

5.3 DVFS Capabilities

As can be viewed from figure 6, implementing the deblocking filter in hardware frees some processor time. The 4 threads version depicted in this figure is run in a software DBF flavor (6(a)) and in a hardware DBF flavor (6(b)). The workload difference can be mainly observed on the fifth curve representing the overall CPU usage. The goal is now to take advantage of the DVFS capabilities available on the ARM11 MPCore by using a simple scheduling policy.

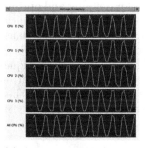 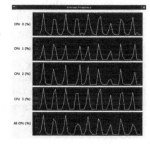

(a) Average CPU frequency with software deblocking filter

(b) Average CPU frequency with hardware deblocking filter

Fig. 6. Benefit of Hardware deblocking filter on a 4 threaded version

Chosen Policy. The DVFS algorithm aims at reducing processors lazy times by spreading the application tasks workload over the complete period (given by the frame rate). This allows to lower the voltage since maximum frequency is lower, allowing to gain energy.

In this work, the frequency is chosen by the application according to the previous deadlines (frames) and the previous decoding times. Technically, Linux returns the execution times to the application and sets its frequency.

Influence of DVFS Policy on H264 Decoder Performances. We applied the same experiment setup to the DVFS aware version of the system. Results are shown in Table 3. As can be seen in these figures, reducing frequency on lazy times makes average processors usage increasing, but effectively allows energy consumption reductions. The 10 CIF frames per second video running on the 4 threads version decoder now generates a 73% utilization rate with a 509 mW mean power. Compared to the 64% (respectively 49%) utilization rate and 821 mW (respectively 740 mW) mean power consumption of the original software version (respectively the hardware DBF version), this DVFS policy allows to achieve a power saving of 40% (respectively 31%). Using these experiments made easily feasible by the virtual platform fllexibility, we built a summary table that gives all the acceptable operating modes along with their power consumption. A system integrator can choose the modes required by its specific application.

Table 3. Performances of the H264 decoder with DVFS policy

	1 thread		2 threads		3 threads		4 threads	
	Util.	Power	Util.	Power	Util.	Power	Util.	Power
cif@25	285.19	693	185.30	838	145.93	966	127.72	1035
cif@10	114.08	681	80.22	628	73.17	507	72.62	509
qcif@25	98.46	637	x	x	98.54	703	x	x
qcif@10	64.39	316	x	x	59.17	334	x	x

6 Conclusion

In this paper, we presented a global approach for defining and optimizing a set of degraded mode for a H264 decoder software by reducing video quality, taking into account both hardware and software during the optimization phase. This was done using a virtual platform approach that has been shown to be efficient and adaptable for this purpose. We have investigated different techniques for timing and power performance optimization: parallelism of the application, hardware accelerator and DVFS policy. The interest of these techniques has been exploited experimentally and actually covers a wide range of usage.

References

1. Baker, M.A., Parameswaran, V., Chatha, K.S., Li, B.: Power reduction via macroblock prioritization for power aware h.264 video applications. In: CODES/ISSS 2008: Proceedings of the 6th IEEE/ACM/IFIP international conference on Hardware/Software codesign and system synthesis, pp. 261–266. ACM, New York (2008)

2. Bellard, F.: QEMU, a Fast and Portable Dynamic Translator. In: USENIX 2005 Annual Technical Conference, FREENIX Track, pp. 41–46 (2005)
3. Coppola, M., Grammatikakis, M., Locatelli, R., Maruccia, G., Pieralisi, L., Mafie, F.: System-on-chip design and technologies. In: Design of Cost-Efficient Interconnect Processing Units: Spidergon STNoC, p. 288. CRC Press, Boca Raton (2008)
4. Gligor, M., Fournel, N., Pétrot, F.: Using binary translation in event driven simulation for fast and flexible mpsoc simulation. In: 7th IEEE/ACM International Conference on Hardware/Software-Co-Design and System Synthesis, Grenoble, France, October 2009, pp. 71–80 (2009)
5. Hommais, D., Pétrot, F.: Efficient combinational loops handling for cycle precise simulation of system on a chip. In: Proceedings of the 24th Euromicro Conference, Vesteras, Sweden, vol. 1, pp. 51–54 (1998)
6. Horowitz, M., Joch, A., Kossentini, F., Hallapuro, A.: H.264/avc baseline profile decoder complexity analysis. IEEE Transactions on Circuits and Systems for Video Technology 13(7), 704–716 (2003)
7. Li, L., Goto, S., Ikenaga, T.: An efficient deblocking filter architecture with 2-dimensional parallel memory for h.264/avc. In: ASP-DAC 2005: Proceedings of the 2005 conference on Asia South Pacific design automation, pp. 623–626. ACM, New York (2005)
8. Mihocka, D., Shwartsman, S.: Virtualization without direct execution - designing a portable vm. In: 1st Workshop on Architectural and Microarchitectural Support for Binary Translation, ISCA35 (2008)
9. Peng, H.-K., Lee, C.-H., Chen, J.-W., Lo, T.-J., Chang, Y.-H., Hsu, S.-T., Lin, Y.-C., Chao, P., Hung, W.-C., Jan, K.-Y.: A highly integrated 8mw h.264/avc main profile real-time cif video decoder on a 16mhz soc platform. In: ASP-DAC 2007: Proceedings of the 2007 conference on Asia South Pacific design automation, Washington, DC, USA, pp. 112–113. IEEE Computer Society, Los Alamitos (2007)
10. Roitzsch, M.: Slice-balancing h.264 video encoding for improved scalability of multicore decoding. In: EMSOFT 2007: Proceedings of the 7th ACM & IEEE international conference on Embedded software, pp. 269–278. ACM, New York (2007)
11. Stitt, G., Vahid, F., McGregor, G., Einloth, B.: Hardware/software partitioning of software binaries: a case study of h.264 decode. In: CODES+ISSS 2005: Proceedings of the 3rd IEEE/ACM/IFIP international conference on Hardware/software codesign and system synthesis, pp. 285–290. ACM, New York (2005)
12. SystemC, http://www.systemc.org/
13. Xu, K., Choy, C.S.: Low-power h.264/avc baseline decoder for portable applications. In: ISLPED 2007: Proceedings of the 2007 international symposium on Low power electronics and design, pp. 256–261. ACM, New York (2007)

BSAA: A Switching Activity Analysis and Visualisation Tool for SoC Power Optimisation

Tom English[1], Ka Lok Man[2], and Emanuel Popovici[1]

[1] Dept of Microelectronic Engineering /
[2] Centre for Efficiency-Oriented Languages
University College Cork, Ireland

Abstract. We present Bus Switching Activity Analyser (*BSAA*), a switching activity analysis and visualisation tool for SoC power optimisation. *BSAA* reads switching metrics from RTL simulation, reporting the most active buses and hierarchies. Buses with typical address and data bus traffic are identified automatically. The tool can process multiple simulation runs simultaneously, analysing how switching varies with input data or software code. *BSAA* complements commercial tools, helping the designer find opportunities to apply power-saving techniques. To illustrate *BSAA*'s powerful features, we analyse switching in an MP3 decoder design using several audio inputs and in a microcontroller running a suite of software tasks. We demonstrate the tool's usefulness by applying it in the power optimisation of a small MPSoC, obtaining on average a 60% reduction in dynamic power across five software tasks and identifying opportunities to reduce static power.

1 Introduction

Total power (P_{tot}) dissipated in a CMOS System-on-Chip is made up of Static Power (P_{stat}) and Dynamic Power (P_{dyn}) components. Static Power is independent of switching activity and is a result of leakage currents, which vary with temperature, supply voltage V_{dd} and transistor threshold voltage V_T. Reductions in V_{dd} with each CMOS technology shift have increased P_{stat} such that it routinely accounts for close to 50% of P_{tot} in typical 65nm processes [1,2].

Dynamic power is the sum of two sub-components. P_{net_sw} represents power spent charging and discharging interconnect load capacitance, while P_{cell_int} represents the power cost of internal currents which flow as the cells switch. For any given cell, P_{net_sw} can be modelled using the expression:

$$P_{net\_sw} \approx \alpha\, C_{sw}\, V_{dd}^2\, f_{clk} \tag{1}$$

In Equation 1, α represents the output's switching probability ($0 \leq \alpha \leq 1$), C_{sw} the interconnect load capacitance, V_{dd} the supply voltage and f_{clk} the clock frequency. In deep sub-micron CMOS, global interconnect capacitance dwarfs individual gate capacitances. The ITRS [3] claims that P_{net_sw} accounts for approximately 50% of P_{dyn} in a 0.13μm microprocessor, with a projected rise

J. Monteiro and R. van Leuken (Eds.): PATMOS 2009, LNCS 5953, pp. 216–226, 2010.

towards 80% on smaller geometries. Accordingly, interconnect power and asso-ciated delay and reliability issues have become key concerns in SoC design [4].

SoCs are complex hardware systems co-ordinated by software. There are often many operating modes and input data profiles with differing resource usage. (These will be referred to as "scenarios".) To minimise power consumption, both P_{dyn} and P_{stat} must be considered for every scenario. We note that knowledge of switching activity across many scenarios helps to guide power optimisation:

- Opportunities for P_{net_sw} reduction techniques [1,2] such as operand isola-tion, low-power memory partitioning and switching-minimal bus encodings are easier to find when the switching activity in the circuit is known
- P_{cell_int} can be reduced by gating the clock to idle registers; switching activity suggests which registers might see a net power reduction from the technique
- comparing switching activity across scenarios identifies rarely-used resources to which leakage control techniques [1] can be applied, reducing P_{stat}

We report here on *BSAA* - Bus Switching Activity Analyser. The tool reads switching activity from RTL simulation, calculating activity statistics for each bus in the design. Buses are filtered and sorted, placing the "busiest" first. The tool produces plots called Switching Activity Profiles (*"SAPs"*). Certain com-mon types of bus traffic (such as incremental address words and random data) have characteristic SAPs that are automatically categorised. The tool's reports and plots help identify appropriate power-saving measures (such as encodings) on buses identified by the implementation tools as heavily-loaded.

Major improvements have been made to the tool since the last release [5]. A new C++ pre-processor now allows the analysis to cover the entire design or be limited only to "branches" or "leaves" of the hierarchy. (Previously only "flat" circuits could be processed.) In addition, *BSAA* can now simultaneously analyse multiple SAIFs (corresponding to several SoC scenarios). The tool performs a comparative analysis, producing plots and reports, including:

- a list of scenarios ranked according to total switching activity in each;
- a list of the most active buses and hierarchies in each scenario;
- an analysis of switching activity correlation & variation across scenarios.

These reports make *BSAA* a powerful tool for analysis of mode- or data depen-dency in circuit activity. They help identify opportunites to reduce both P_{dyn} and P_{stat} and make results from the power analysis flow easier to interpret.

To the best of the authors' knowledge, *BSAA*'s features have not yet ap-peared in commercial tools nor been reported in the literature. Landman and Rabaey [6] discuss their *Dual Bit Type* (DBT) methodology and *SPA* tool for dynamic power prediction from RTL simulation. The tool combines capacitances from a characterisation stage with switching activity statistics from simulation to estimate dynamic power. Fugger [7] describes a tool for the ModelSim *For-eign Language Interface* which records the word- and bit-level switching activity statistics required by the DBT methodology. Menon and Shankar [8] describe their *COMPASS* tool for code compression analysis in embedded processors. The tool can read simulation traces and takes account of bus toggles and cache misses to select optimal code compression strategies for particular applications.

2   Tool Architecture and Application

BSAA reads switching activity information from simulation via SAIF [9]. Along with the simulation timescale and duration, SAIF records switching activity metrics for each design node in a compact text format suitable for power and reliability analysis tools. It can be generated by popular commercial simulators or converted from VCD, facilitating analysis of any HDL with any simulator.

2.1   Extracting Switching Activity Profiles from SAIF

SAIF files begin with a header followed by a hierarchical data structure containing a set of activity metrics for each circuit node:

- *T0*, *T1* and *TX* - total time spent at logic 0, 1 and X, respectively
- *TC* - total number of logic transitions ($0 \rightarrow 1$, $1 \rightarrow 0$)
- *IG* - total number of glitch transitions (via X or Z)

BSAA reads the SAIF file, extracting three key components:

- *DUR* - the SAIF header "DURATION" field
- *TS* - the SAIF header "TIMESCALE" field
- *TCS* - all data structure *TC* and *IG* metrics

The simulation duration is calculated as:

$$duration = (TS \times DUR) \ sec \tag{2}$$

Switching activity $SA(i)$ is calculated for each bit $i \in \{0..(n-1)\}$ of each n-bit bus according to:

$$SA(i) = \left(\frac{TC(i) + IG(i)}{duration} \right) \ toggles/sec \tag{3}$$

We define a *Switching Activity Profile* (SAP) for any n-bit bus simply as the shape of the function $SA(i)$ over the domain $i \in \{0..(n-1)\}$. Certain types of bus traffic (such as binary counts and random data sequences) have distinctive SAPs. Examples of these two types are shown for a three-bit bus in Fig. 1. (The sequences are glitch-free with a duration of 1 second, giving $SA(i) = TC(i)$).

In Fig. 1(a), a 3-bit count sequence is transmitted over the bus. $SA(i)$ is decaying by a factor of two with each subsequent bit such that $SA(i) \approx \frac{1}{2}SA(i-1)$: $i \in \{1..(n-1)\}$. Because this SAP looks linear on a logarithmic scale, we refer to it as a "$\log_2$" SAP. For the random sequence in Fig. 1(b), the number of

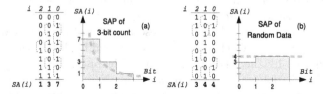

Fig. 1. SAPs for a 3-bit count and 3-bit random sequence

toggles on each bus bit is roughly constant. We refer to this as a "flat" SAP, because $SA(i) \approx SA(i-1) : i \in \{1..(n-1)\}$.

In addition to obtaining the SAP for each bus, *BSAA* calculates four useful statistics. Summing $SA(i)$ over all bus bits yields *ISA*, the Integral Switching Activity for a bus. *ISA* can be used to rank buses according to their overall activity cost (activity $\times$ # bits).

$$ISA = \frac{\sum_{i=0}^{n-1} (TC(i) + IG(i))}{duration} = \sum_{i=0}^{n-1} SA(i) \; toggles/sec \tag{4}$$

MSA and *SDV* represent the mean and standard deviation of switching activity $SA(i)$, respectively:

$$MSA = \mu = \frac{1}{n} \sum_{i=0}^{n-1} SA(i) = \frac{1}{n} ISA \; toggles/sec \tag{5}$$

$$SDV = \sigma = \sqrt{\frac{1}{n} \sum_{i=0}^{n-1} (SA(i) - MSA)^2} \; toggles/sec \tag{6}$$

Finally, *PSA* records peak switching activity over all bus bits:

$$PSA = max\left(SA(i) : i \in \{0..(n-1)\}\right) \; toggles/sec \tag{7}$$

2.2 Architecture

BSAA is implemented in MATLAB [10]. The tool's architecture is illustrated in Fig. 2. A pre-processor (written in C++) acts as a fast SAIF parser and supports three operation modes, exemplified by Fig. 3. In the *fullchip* mode, switching is analysed throughout the entire design. *Branch* mode isolates a hierarchy level or *scope* for analysis including all child levels, while *leaf* mode excludes both parent and child levels. The pre-processor passes *DUR*, *TS* and *TCS* data to Matlab. Simulation *duration* can then be obtained using Equation 2.

In the *Bus Extract* stage, hierarchy levels, buses and bus widths (n) are identified and scalar signals removed. $SA(i)$ is calculated for each bit $i \in \{0..(n-1)\}$ of each bus according to Equation 3. The *ISA*, *MSA*, *SDV* and *PSA* statistics are extracted according to Equations 4-7, respectively.

The *Rule Filter* thins out the bus list according to user-defined rules. The numerical values of n, *ISA*, *MSA*, *SDV* and *PSA* for each bus are compared against upper and lower bounds. Those with out-of-bounds statistics are excluded. The rule filter can also exclude buses whose names contain an *exclude tag* or omit an *include tag*. Rules responsible for every exclusion are listed in a report.

The *Analyse Hierarchy* stage integrates the *ISA*, *MSA*, *SDV* and *PSA* statistics of each hierarchy level's buses. The hierarchy levels are arranged according to user-specified criteria, placing levels with many wide and busy buses first by default. The "Most Active Hierarchies" report lists the hierarchy levels along with their switching statistics, identifying the busiest parts of the design hierarchy.

RTL buses which are logically distinct but electrically equivalent appear as "duplicates" in the analysis. An optional *Uniquify* stage compares all buses, reporting groups in which SAP, bus width n and statistics are all identical. The tool combines all group members into a single bus, excluding duplicates.

The *Sort* stage sorts the filtered bus list according to user-specified criteria. By default, buses are arranged in descending order by *ISA*, with wide, busy buses first. The "Most Active Buses" report lists bus names, widths n and statistics, identifying the design's busiest buses. The *Shape Filter* then categorises buses according to their SAPs. The common SAPs illustrated in Fig. 1 are identified. Having categorised the bus SAPs as either "$\log_2$", "flat" or "other", the tool produces reports listing all buses in each category, along with their statistics.

When multiple scenarios are analysed, *comparison reports* are generated. Scenarios are ranked according to total *ISA* in a "Most Active Scenario" report, identifying the scenario with the most switching. "Scenario Similarities" are analysed by ranking buses and hierarchy levels according to their overall activity in all scenarios. (Consistently-busy buses and hierarchy levels appear first, consistently-idle ones last.) "Scenario Differences" are highlighted by a histogram tracking how often each bus appears "active" across all scenarios.

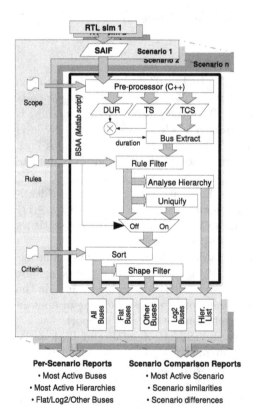

Fig. 2. BSAA architecture

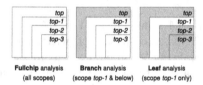

Fig. 3. BSAA Analysis Modes

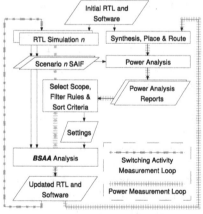

Fig. 4. BSAA Design Flow

2.3   Application

A design flow incorporating *BSAA* is shown in Fig. 4. The initial RTL is syn-thesised, placed and routed. A suite of scenario simulations is run, covering the SoC's various input data profiles and operation modes. Simulation SAIF is an-notated onto the netlist during power analysis. Power-hungry cross-chip bus nets in the design should be identified in the analysis reports at this stage.

BSAA analyses SAIF from scenario simulation(s), producing reports and plots. Scope selection, filtering and sort rules allow signals, functional blocks or hierarchies to be isolated for focused analysis. Buses are categorised by SAP, identifying classic "address" and "data" traffic suitable for traditional low-power bus coding. Comparison reports identify underused or idle resources suitable for leakage reduction measures and highlight code- or data dependencies in circuit switching. Operand isolation and clock gating opportunities can be identified by careful analysis of the "Most Active Buses" report.

Guided by SAPs and statistics, designers make changes to the RTL or soft-ware, iterating through the *Switching Activity Measurement Loop* until switching is reduced or re-distributed as required. Power analysis in the *Power Measure-ment Loop* is essential to ensure that a net reduction in power has been achieved.

3   Application Results

We present application results in two sub-sections. Section 3.1 illustrates the use of the tool for analysis of designs exhibiting code- and data-dependent switching. Section 3.2 presents a power optimisation case study guided by *BSAA*.

3.1   Switching Analysis Examples

McMaster University MP3 Decoder

RTL for an open-source MP3 decoder was obtained from McMaster University [11]. Four MP3s - "silence", "880Hz tone", "rock" and "pop" - were prepared in both mono and stereo versions, creating a total of eight input data scenarios. While they share the same duration, sample rate and wordlength, the power spectral densities of the clips vary considerably, as shown in Fig. 5.

We analysed the "Pop" (stereo) scenario using the tool's *leaf* mode, selecting the MP3 decoder's top-level scope. This scope includes top-level buses carrying compressed MP3 traffic, intermediate data and fully-decoded stereo PCM audio. The tool identifies sixteen flat SAPs and eleven $\log_2$ SAPs; we illustrate the top five from each category in Figures 6 and 7. The "Most Active Buses" report lists all top-level buses, starting with widest, busiest buses and finishing with the least active. The tool has immediately identified the busiest buses in the design and classified the traffic they carry, making it easier to select appropriate low-power coding measures for heavily-loaded interconnect.

To investigate the impact of differing audio inputs on switching, we anal-ysed all scenarios together in *fullchip* mode. (No filter rules were used.) Scenario comparisons highlight the data dependency in the design. Fig. 8 displays total *ISA* for each scenario, showing how both the number of channels and the spectral complexities of the input MP3s influence overall switching. The most data-sensitive hierarchies are candidates for P_{dyn} optimisation, while the most idle regions should be examined further in simulation to determine their suitability for power gating. Long, continous idle periods are preferred.

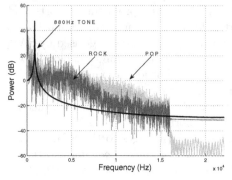

Fig. 5. MP3 Input Spectra

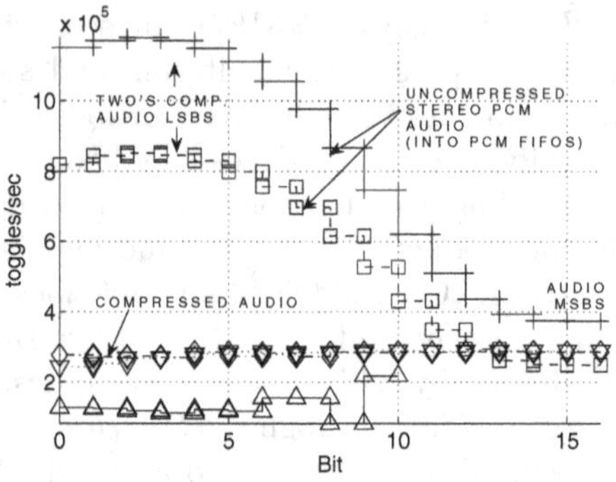

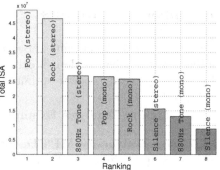

Fig. 6. "Pop" (stereo) Top 5 Flat SAPs

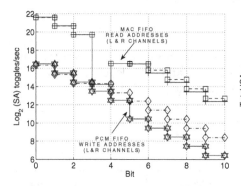

Fig. 7. "Pop" (stereo) Top 5 Log$_2$ SAPs

Fig. 8. MP3 Scenarios ranked by *ISA*

OpenCores OC8051 8-Bit Microcontroller

The OC8051 is an 8051-compatible 8-bit microcontroller developed by Open-Cores [12]. A wide variety of test programs is included with the design's RTL testbench. To investigate the variation in switching activity across different software tasks, we created a code scenario for each test program. All scenarios were analysed in *BSAA* using *fullchip* mode. (No filter rules were used.)

The "Most Active Scenario" plot (Fig. 9) identifies *mx_test* as the scenario with most switching overall. In the "Most Active Hierarchies" report, *oc8051_memory_interface1* and *oc8051_alu1* are identified (among others) as consistently busy. Within these hierarchies are some of the "Most Active Buses" in the design.

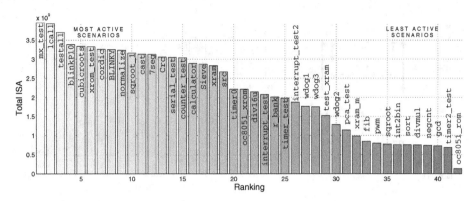

Fig. 9. OC8051 Code Scenarios ranked by Total ISA

By setting appropriate filter rules and re-analysing, the *Bus Activity Histogram* can be used to find idle buses - for example *p3_in*, an input bus exercised in only one of the 42 scenarios. This information identifies inactive parts of the design but could also be used for the measurement of functional coverage in SoC test suites. It is obtained in seconds from *BSAA* but is difficult to extract from simulation or power analysis.

Other Switching Analysis Applications

We have applied the tool experimentally to gate-level switching analysis as well as to SystemC RTL simulations. Initial results are promising but to develop robust methodologies for these types of application remains future work.

3.2   Power Optimisation Case Study

WishBone SoC

We designed a hardware-software system called *wb_soc* for experimentation with WishBone [12] interconnect. This was re-used as a *BSAA* power optimisation case study. The system, shown in Fig. 10, features two custom processing elements (*pe0* & *pe1*), two 32-bit general purpose IO blocks (*gpio0* & *gpio1*) and a FIFO (*fifo0*). We created five code scenarios for the platform by programming simple tasks such as "repeating" data words received via *gpio0* out to *gpio1*:

- *pe0_pe1_inactive* - *pe0* & *pe1* idle; no system activity
- *pe0_active_only* - interrupt-driven IO via *gpio0* and *gpio1* handled by *pe0*
- *pe1_active_only* - interrupt-driven IO via *gpio0* and *gpio1* handled by *pe1*
- *buffered_io* - interrupt-driven IO using *fifo0* handled by *pe0* and *pe1*
- *fifomgr* - polling-driven FIFO test performed by *pe0* and *pe1*

Our aim was to optimise P_{net_sw}, P_{cell_int} and P_{stat} according to the flow in Fig. 4, using *BSAA* for switching analysis. The RTL was simulated using Synopsys VCS and synthesised to TSMC 65nm GP CMOS in Synopsys DC-T. The design had a single, 50MHz primary clock (*wb_clk*) and roughly 30,000 gates. We used

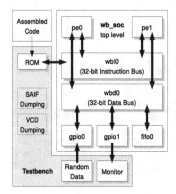

Fig. 10. *wb_soc* simulation

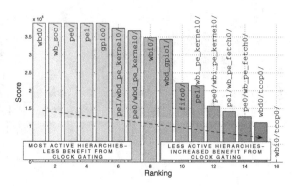

Fig. 11. The "Most Active Hierarchies" report can help identify clock gating opportunities

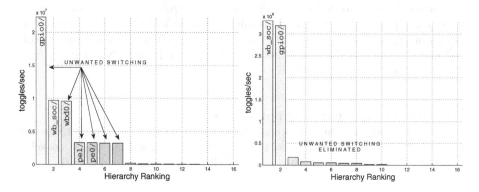

Fig. 12. Active Hierarchies before isolation **Fig. 13.** Active Hierarchies after isolation

delay-annotated gate-level VCD for power analysis in Synopsys PrimeTime-PX. (For this initial work, pre-placement netlists were analysed.)

Registers which switch least often benefit most from clock gating. To identify these, we analysed all scenarios of *wb_soc* simultaneously. In the scenario comparison reports, less-active buses and hierarchies appear towards the end, as shown in Fig. 11. Note for example that *wbi0/tcop0* (the instruction bus arbiter) switches very little in any scenario, making it ideal for clock gating. Guided by the tool, we applied clock gating to most of the registers in the processing elements, *gpios* and *fifo*. The clock gating measures reduced P_{cell_int} by 59% on average across all scenarios and by 81% for the *pe0_pe1_inactive* scenario.

In an analysis of the *pe0_pe1_inactive* scenario (in which very little switching should occur), the "Most Active Hierarchies" plot (Fig. 12) identified unexpected switching in *gpio0*, *wbd0*, *pe0* and *pe1*. The "Most Active Buses" report revealed that testbench input stimulus was propagating all the way to the processing elements, leading to unwanted switching. We modified the *gpio*, introducing an *input_en* register which allowed external inputs to be isolated from the rest of the design. Analysing updated RTL simulations in *BSAA* showed that the isolation measure was effective (Fig. 13). Updated power analysis results showed a reduction of 74% in P_{net_sw} for this scenario and 57% on average for all scenarios.

To reveal only the dormant buses in each scenario, we performed a multi-scenario *fullchip* analysis with the upper *ISA* threshold set to 1. The "bus activity histogram" identified buses never active in any scenario, including several 32-bit registers in *pe0* and *pe1*. Because this is a hardware/software system, this redundancy was not visible during synthesis, resulting in wasted area and power. The "Common Active Hierarchies" report showed that *wbi0*, *wbi0/tcop0* and *fifo0* had low activity across all scenarios. Due to the time-averaged nature of SAIF statistics, further simulation would be the only way to determine whether these blocks are continuously idle for long enough to justify power gating.

Fig. 14 plots P_{tot} for each scenario before and after optimisation.

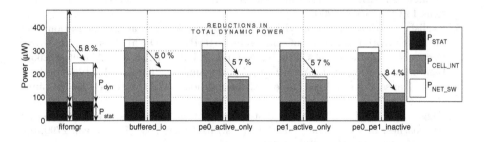

Fig. 14. *wb_soc* Total Power

4   Concluding Remarks

BSAA reports activity statistics of on-chip buses and presents their Switching Activity Profiles graphically. It identifies common types of bus traffic, exposes code- and data dependency and highlights active and idle regions in the design. Reports and plots uncover opportunities to apply power-saving techniques and help to explain power analysis results in complex hardware/software systems. *BSAA* complements commercial CAD tools. It supports all common HDLs and simulators and - even for large designs - has runtimes measured in minutes.

Case studies of an MP3 decoder and a microcontroller were presented, illustrating the tool's powerful analysis and visualisation features. In an MPSoC power optimisation using *BSAA*, an average reduction in P_{dyn} of over 60% across five software scenarios was achieved. In addition, idle buses and blocks were identified using the tool's versatile scenario comparison plots and reports.

Currently, *BSAA* supports VCD indirectly via translation to SAIF. For future work, we plan to enable the pre-processor to read VCD directly. The time-domain switching activity recorded in VCD will enable a number of additional analysis features not currently possible using only the time-averaged statistics in SAIF.

Acknowledgement

We are very grateful to IDA Ireland and Synopsys, Inc. for funding this research.

References

1. Keating, M., Flynn, D., Aitken, R., Gibbons, A., Shi, K.: Low Power Methodology Manual For System-on-Chip Design. Springer, Heidelberg (2007)
2. Macii, E., Zafalon, R.: Low-power EDA technologies: State-of-the-art and beyond. In: Advanced Signal Processing, Circuits, and System Design Techniques for Communications, May 2006, pp. 3–43 (2006)
3. International Technology Roadmap for Semiconductors (ITRS): 2007 edition. Technical report, Interconnect, page 44 (2007)
4. Sridhara, S., Shanbhag, N.: Coding for System-on-Chip Networks: A Unified Framework. IEEE Transactions on Very Large Scale Integration (VLSI) Systems 13(6), 655–667 (2005)
5. English, T., Man, K.L., Popovici, E.: A Switching Analysis and Visualisation Tool for Power Optimisation of SoC Buses. In: PRIME - 2009 PhD Research in Microelectronics and Electronics, Proceedings, pp. 264–267. IEEE, Los Alamitos (2009)
6. Landman, P., Rabaey, J.: Architectural power analysis: The dual bit type method. IEEE Transactions on Very Large Scale Integration (VLSI) Systems, 173–187 (June 1995)
7. Fugger, P.: RTL-Based Signal Statistics Calculation Facilitates Low Power Design Approaches. In: Chico, J.J., Macii, E. (eds.) PATMOS 2003. LNCS, vol. 2799, pp. 559–568. Springer, Heidelberg (2003)
8. Menon, S., Shankar, P.: COMPASS - A tool for evaluation of compression strategies for embedded processors. Journal of Systems Architecture 54(12), 995–1003 (2008)
9. Synopsys: Switching Activity Interchange Format, http://www.synopsys.com/.
10. The Mathworks: MATLAB, http://www.mathworks.com/products/matlab/
11. Kinsman, A., Nicolici, N., Ko, H.: MAC-MP3 decoder (2009), http://www.ece.mcmaster.ca/~nicola/mpeg.html
12. OpenCores: opencores.org, http://www.opencores.org/

Reducing Timing Overhead in Simultaneously Clock-Gated and Power-Gated Designs by Placement-Aware Clustering

Gaurang Upasani, Andrea Calimera,
Alberto Macii, Enrico Macii, and Massimo Poncino

Politecnico di Torino, Torino 10129, Italy

Abstract. Clock-gating and power-gating have proven to be two of the most effective techniques for reducing dynamic and leakage power, respectively, in VLSI CMOS circuits. Most commercial synthesis tools do support such techniques individually, but their combined implementation is not available, since some open issues in terms of power/timing overhead associated to the control logic required for the integration are not yet solved.

Moving from some recent work targeting clock-gating/power-gating integration, in this paper we present a solution for reducing the timing overhead that may occur when the integration is performed. In particular, we introduce a new, multilevel partitioning heuristic that increases the efficiency of the clustering phase, one of the key steps of our methodology. The results demonstrate the effectiveness of our solution; in fact, power-delay product and timing overhead of the circuits synthesized using the new clustering algorithm improve by 33% and 24%, respectively.

1 Introduction

Technology trends show that, in every circuit generation, delay and supply voltage have scaled down by around 30%, performance and transistor density have doubled every two years and transistors threshold voltage has reduced by almost 15% [1]. In this scenario, power consumption becomes one of the most important concerns in modern electronic systems, since the battery power increases by about 15% per year and the chip power requirements by about 35% [2].

For CMOS technologies downto $130nm$, dynamic power was considered the dominating component of the total power consumption. Analyzing the behavior of a circuit, one can see that not all the logic blocks perform computations in a clock period. Identifying these idle conditions and stopping the clock signal that feeds such blocks is known as clock-gating (CG) [3]. Clock-gating is considered as one of the most effective techniques to reduce dynamic power.

With the technology scaling to $65nm$ and below, leakage power is becoming a dominant component of the total power dissipation. The leakage power can be reduced using power-gating (PG) techniques, based on the insertion of a power switch with high-V_{th} and thick T_{ox} between the logic and the ground, in order to electrically isolate the circuit in the standby mode [4].

J. Monteiro and R. van Leuken (Eds.): PATMOS 2009, LNCS 5953, pp. 227–236, 2010.

Both clock-gating and power-gating are supported by several commercial EDA tools, but are used separately (i.e., the logic that controls the clock-gating mechanism is not the same that controls the power-gating).

Several attempts to merge the clock-gating and power-gating techniques, using the clock-gating conditions for power-gating the circuit, have been made. In [6], the authors described the possibility of integrating clock-gating and power-gating and presented an analysis tool which is able to provide a suitable evaluation of an RTL design in order to determine whether CG/PG integration is convenient or not.

In [7], the authors present a layout-oriented synthesis flow which integrates the two techniques and that relies on leading-edge, commercial EDA tools. Starting from a gated-clock netlist, the circuit is partitioned in a number of clusters that are implicitly determined by the groups of cells that are clock-gated by the same register. The main limitation of this approach is that the cost function that drives the clustering phase does not include placement information. In this way, the clustering is performed without such an information and the timing overhead that may result from the integration of the clock-gating and the power-gating techniques may grow too large.

In this paper, we introduce the concept of *placement-aware clustering*. The basic idea is to reduce the timing overhead seen in the model of [7]. To identify the potential bottlenecks of a such model, an exhaustive design space exploration of the cost-function is carried out. In this way, it is possible to understand the relationship that may exist between the selected variables as a function of the energy-delay product. Based on the results of the exploration, a novel concept of critical-interconnects is introduced and exploited for reducing the timing overhead of the CG/PG designs.

The remainder of the paper is organized as follows. Section 2 describes the concurrent clock-gating and power-gating flow, including a discussion of the feasibility issues, the proposed solution and the limitations. Section 3 details how the problem is translated into a mathematical model, it introduces the concept of critical interconnects and it explains the implemented partitioning heuristics. A detailed discussion of the design space exploration of the cost-function, as well as the experimental results are reported in Section 4. Finally, Section 5 closes the paper with some remarks and directions for future work.

2   Concurrent Clock- and Power-Gating

In a broader sense, clock-gating and power-gating are the techniques to selectively turn-off portions of a digital circuit based on suitable idle situations. However, the idleness is characterized differently for the two techniques. In particular, in clock-gating the idle conditions determine when the clock signal has to be stopped; on the other hand, in power-gating the occurrence of the idle situations drives the activation of an external signal (i.e., the sleep signal) for turning off the sleep transistor.

Integrating clock-gating and power-gating, in practice, entails the use of the idle conditions available for clock-gating also to control the power-gating mechanism. Such a combined exploitation of conceptually different idle situations poses some challenges, which we discuss in the sequel.

2.1 Feasibility Issues

In combining clock-gating and power-gating, there are some challenges related to the behavior of the circuit and the implementation of the CG/PG control circuitry.

Mutually Inclusive Nature of the Clusters

While applying the clock-gating conditions on a circuit, the netlist is divided into clusters based on the idle conditions. Clock-gated registers are inserted to all of these clusters according to the real-time switching activities. However, the intersection of the clusters in terms of idleness is not null. Hence, the clusters are not mutually exclusive. This intersected part must be treated carefully while power-gating, because electrically isolating such clusters may create traumatic behavior of the circuit. The solution is to generate new clusters which consist of the cells belonging to these overlapped regions of clusters. In other words, a new cluster is to be generated who's idle condition is the logical AND of the idle conditions of two or more intersected clusters.

Timing Granularity

This is a crucial design issue while integrating CG and PG. Time granularity for clock-gating can be defined in terms of number of clock-cycles; moreover, in PG the transition to reactivation has zero cost. On the contrary, power-gating can be applied only when the duration of the sleep mode is sufficiently longer than the reactivation time. For PG, a good practice is to determine the amount of power savings by sleep mode compared to the reactivation costs. This implies that, for optimum savings, designers can omit to power-gate some clusters.

Sleep-Transistor Insertion

In power-gating, a sleep-transistor is inserted between the cluster of logic and the corresponding ground rail. All the clusters who qualified to be power-gated should be assigned an independent sleep-transistor, whose size and virtual ground voltage are determined by the amount of current drawn by the respective cluster. This makes it necessary that all the cells belonging to the same cluster are to be placed in a close physical proximity during layout. Violating this constraint will result in scattering of the cells of a cluster all over the layout area; this will make the connections to the sleep-transistors impractical. In principle, it is also possible to dedicate a sleep-transistor per cluster, but this solution will force the placement-tool to allocate independent regions for each cluster, with the consequence of causing an higher performance penalty, because of an increased interconnect delay among them.

In this work, a row-based sleep-transistor insertion methodology is adopted. In this methodology, the regions are the rows of the layout, which will be further referred as "bounds" in the rest of the paper. Each bound will be allocated its own sleep-transistor and the corresponding virtual ground rail.

2.2 CG/PG Flow

To handle the issues discussed in the previous section, the CG/PG flow of [7] operates in two phases: An analysis phase and a clustering phase.

Analysis Phase

During analysis phase the information of the synthesized RTL (with clock-gating feature enabled) with the constraints, the place and route information (.def), the parasitics (.spef) and the net-lists, along with the real-time activities on each net of the design (.vcd), the OpenAccess database of the design and the standard cell library are provided as the inputs and it identifies the clock-tree and generates the information of the activation function for each clock-gating register. The analysis phase also generates the power-gated clusters and categorizes them as "clock-gated clusters" and "clock-gated intersection clusters".

Clock-gated clusters consist of the cells belonging to only a single cluster; in other words, they are the cells whose idleness is characterized by only one clock-gating register; let us call these clusters as "pure-clusters". Clock-gated intersection clusters consist of the cells which belong to two or more clusters; in other words, they are the cells whose idleness is determined by more than one clock-gating register; let us call such clusters as "hybrid-clusters". The flow also takes care of estimating the area required, leakage power, parasitic capacitance and total idle period for every power-gated cluster.

Clustering Phase

During clustering phase, the information of the activation function and the information of pure and hybrid clusters generated by the analysis phase are given as inputs and, based on this information, a cost-function is evaluated to generate a matrix. Such a matrix is partitioned to form the bounds, which are to be placed. A detailed discussion about the selection of cost-function with its design space exploration is provided in the next section.

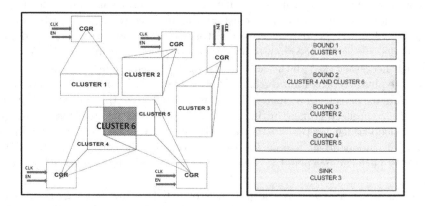

Fig. 1. Cluster Generation and Bound Formation

Figure 1 (left) shows the conceptual distribution of the cells in clusters after the analysis phase. As it can be seen, clusters 1, 2, 3, 4 and cluster 5 are the pure clusters, while cluster 6 is a hybrid cluster. Cluster 6 can be turned off only when both cluster 4 and cluster 5 are turned off. We have a total 6 clusters and now we want to partition them into only 3 bounds. The defined cost-function should be intelligent enough to decide what cluster will map to which bound. Figure 1 (right) shows how the clusters are mapped to the bounds after the clustering phase. The clusters that are non power-gated will be allocated to a special bound called "null bound". In this example, cluster 3 is non power-gated. It is noticeable here that, according to this approach, power-gating is applied only to clock-gated clusters.

3   Placement-Aware Clustering

Based on the discussion of Section 2, the problem can be described as the mapping of each of the n clusters to one of the suitable k bounds. The cost-function is described as the function of two characteristics for any pair of clusters:

- *Idleness.* This feature characterizes the amount of overlapping among the clusters. If the two clusters are significantly overlapped, then they should be merged together at the loss of some power savings. And if the clusters are leaky enough and the overlapping between them is smaller, then they should not be merged together.
- *Degree of Coupling.* Although all the *pure clusters* are completely disjoint among themselves, they share signal dependencies with the corresponding *hybrid clusters*, and vice versa. The clusters with maximum amount of coupling should be kept together. This will help reducing the timing overhead.

3.1   Mathematical Modeling

The problem can be described easily by traditional graph theory. The set of n clusters can be modeled as an undirected graph $G(V, E, w)$, where $V = \{v_1, ..., v_n\}$ are the vertexes representing n clusters, E represents the edges, forming a one-to-one relation among the clusters, w is a real number representing the weight of the edge. Edge weights can be defined as:

$$w_{i,j} = \alpha \cdot e_{i,j}^{\gamma} + \beta \left[\frac{I_{i,j} + I_{j,i}}{I_{tot_{i,j}}} \right] \tag{1}$$

where:

- $e_{i,j}$ is the overlapping of the activation functions e_i and e_j of clusters i and j, respectively. $e_{i,j} \in [0, 1]$. The $\gamma \in [1, 2]$ is a smoothing factor which reduces the importance of the lower values of $e_{i,j}$.
- $I_{i,j}$ is the total number of signals going from cluster i to cluster j, and vice versa for $I_{j,i}$. $I_{tot_{i,j}}$ is the total signals coming out from clusters i and j.
- α and $\beta = 1 - \alpha$ are values between 0 and 1.

3.2   Introduction to Critical Interconnects

Based on the observation of the timing overhead seen in the results obtained with only common idle conditions in Equation 1, one more characteristic of the clusters, called *criticality factor*, has been introduced in Equation 1. In the subsequent discussion, it is made clear that in Equation 1 the *degree of coupling* is a necessary, but not a sufficient characteristic to overcome the timing overhead.

Criticality Factor: This characteristic takes the possibility of the shared critical paths between two clusters into consideration. For any given net, the *criticality factor* $cf_{i,j}$ between two clusters i and j can be defined as:

$$cf_{i,j} = \left[\frac{WCCpath_{net}}{WCCpath_{circ}} \right] \tag{2}$$

where, $WCCpath_{net}$ is the worst-case critical path through the net, $WCCpath_{circ}$ is the worst-case critical path of the whole circuit and $cf_{i,j} \in [0,1]$.

For a better visualization of the model, consider Figure 2. In the example, we have a total of 3 clusters. Cluster 1 and cluster 2 share 3 signals; cluster 1 and cluster 3 share only one connection, which lies on the critical path. In general cases, with the equation 1 more weight will be given to the edge between cluster 1 and cluster 2, regardless of the critical path. But with the *criticality factor*, more weight will be given to the edge between cluster 1 and cluster 3. This also clears the argument of insertion of the *criticality factor* along with *degree of coupling*.

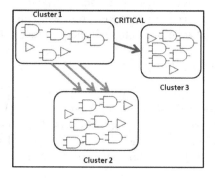

Fig. 2. Conceptualization of Critical Interconnect

Hence, including Equation 2 into Equation 1, as shown in Equation 3 below means giving priority to the critical interconnects between two clusters:

$$w_{i,j} = \alpha \cdot e_{i,j}^{\gamma} + \beta \left[\frac{I_{i,j} + I_{j,i}}{I_{tot_{i,j}}} \right] + cf_{i,j} \tag{3}$$

It is important to note here that for the graph G, all the clusters must be power-gated. To include non power-gated clusters, a unique node, *i.e.*, a "sink", is added to the graph and the attraction of the rest of the nodes to the *sink* is defined. So, the graph is modified to $G'(V', E', w')$, where $V' = V \bigcup \{v_0\}$, v_0 represents the *sink*, E' defines the edges and the edge weight $w'_{i,j} : E' \mapsto \mathbb{R}^+$.

$$w'_{i,j} = \begin{cases} w_{i,j}, \forall i \neq 0. \\ (\delta(1 - s_i)^\rho + \eta(1 - e_i) + \lambda(1 - l_i)), \forall i = 0. \end{cases} \quad (4)$$

where:

- s_i is the size of the cluster i. A significantly smaller value will force to put cluster i to the *sink*. A sufficiently larger exponent ρ (*i.e.*, $\rho > 5$) will make sure of this merging.
- e_i is the idleness of cluster i.
- l_i is the normalized value of leakage for cluster i. Which can be obtained by dividing the leakage of any cluster to the total leakage of all the clusters.

It is worth noticing that, since the edges model the attraction to the sink, the weight consists of waste of space $(1 - s_i)$, activity $(1 - e_i)$, no leakage $(1 - l_i)$ and $\delta + \eta + \lambda \equiv 1$.

3.3   Graph Partitioning Heuristics

As the model described above formulates a graph $G(V, E, w)$, the next task is to partition the graph into the desired number of sub-sets no larger than the computed size. This is an NP-complete problem. The partitioning heuristic, explained in [7], is a *uniform cost search* algorithm, which is a special case of A^* (pronounced *A star*) algorithm. The major limitation of this heuristic is that, for a significantly large graph, it spends a lot of time in the computation of redundant steps. This paper discusses a new, multilevel partitioning heuristic based on the *Kernighan and Lin algorithm* [8].

The pseudo-code of the proposed algorithm is the following:

Clustering(G,k)
> *Step 1* : Do until the graph is small enough.
>> graph = coarsen(graph);
> *Step 2* : Partition the graph.
> *Step 3* : Until graph = original graph.
>> graph = uncoarsen(graph);
>> partition = uncoarsen(partition);
>> Refinement using K-L algorithm.

This algorithm is based upon the iterative removal of the edges. But, as it will work by partitioning the larger graph into a number of smaller graphs, it is faster and it can be parallelized.

The coarsening phase (*step*−1) reduces the actual size of the graph by merging adjacent vertexes. The resulting vertex, which retains edges to the union of the neighbors of the merged vertexes, is characterized by weight equal to the sum of the weights of its constituent vertexes. The partitioning heuristic of [7] is now applied to the coarsen graph ($step - 2$), which shows a reduced number of vertexes thus assuring a faster execution of the algorithm. Finally, in the third phase ($step - 3$), the graph is expanded to its original size by adopting the uncoarsening procedure iteratively. To improve the optimality of this process, an iterative refinement method is implemented and adopted. The latter is based on the K-L algorithm presented in [8].

The cost of the worst-case operation is $O((B - 1) \cdot n + E)$, where $B \in [2, 7]$ is the number of bounds, n is the number of clusters and E is the number of edges. Considering a one-to-one relationship among the clusters, E can be written as $E = 1/2 \cdot n(n - 1)$.

4   Experimental Results

4.1   Experimental Set-Up

The entire flow is tested on the RTL description of a real-life circuit used in typical network-on-chip architectures (a *NoC switch*). The functionality of the module is to analyze the incoming packets, identify the source and the destination addresses and route the packets. The design consists of more than 8K logic gates. The RTL of the design was synthesized using Synopsys PhysicalCompiler and mapped onto a $65nm$ CMOS standard-cell library provided by STMicroelectronics. To measure the real-time switching activities at each and every net in the design, an output file (.vcd file) was generated by the simulation of the standard test-benches in Mentor Graphics Modelsim. A parser was developed to read the .vcd file and calculate the static probabilities and the switching for the internal nets. These values were provided to Synopsys PrimeTime for the power estimation phase. More accurate timing and power estimations were evaluated using the physical information provided with the standard-cell library. An OpenAccess database of the synthesized design was created. As mentioned in Section 2.2, the analysis phase identifies the original clusters, measures the distribution of the idle periods of each cluster, and determines the feasibility of CG/PG integration. Once this is done, the clustering phase uses this information to generate the necessary bounds for the final placement.

The information regarding the bounds is provided to the standard placement tool, which uses an interconnect-delay dominating cost-function. With such placement strategy, there is a chance that a bound containing a set of clusters will also contain the cells belonging to other clusters. This can result in multiple interconnects for each bound and, hence, a larger area penalty. The final step is to insert the sleep-transistors. A row-based power-gating strategy [5] is used.

The experiments were performed within the following design-space parameters ranges: $\alpha = \{0.1, 0.3, 0.5, 0.7, 0.9\}$, $B = \{3, 4, 5, 6, 7\}$. The main reason of limiting the number of bounds to 7 is that these bounds represents the number of virtual ground rails. Increasing the number of bounds further will make power-gating physical unfeasible.

4.2   Experimental Data

To measure the quality of results a term *Energy Delay Product* is defined. The EDP, calculated as the product of total consumed energy and propagation delay, is a representative sample of the ratio between savings (i.e., leakage energy) and overheads (i.e., circuit delay).

Figure 3 shows the plot of the *energy-delay product - EDP* for different values of α for the optimal number of bounds (i.e., $B = 7$). We note that, irrespective of the values of α, the EDP is smaller in the case where the criticality model is adopted. This result supports the arguments of Section 3. After the introduction of the criticality factor, an improvement upto 33% is achieved in the EDP. The difference is larger in the case of lower values of α, since less preference will be given to overlapped clusters during the partitioning process. And if such clusters are not merged, it could result in longer interconnects among the overlapped clusters. For sufficiently larger values of α this problem does not occur.

The design space exploration of the EDP also indicates that an optimal value of α (and β) does not exist. Instead we noticed that the selection of α is highly dependent on the design.

Figures 4-a and 4-b show the variations in propagation delay for different values of α and variations in dynamic power for different values of α, with and

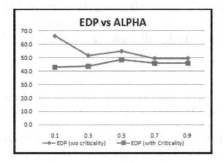

Fig. 3. Energy-Delay Product for Different Values of α

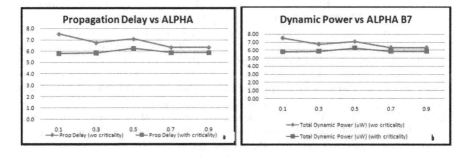

Fig. 4. Propagation Delay and Dynamic Power for Different Values of α

without the criticality factor considered. The results indicate a significant improvement of 24% in the total timing overhead and a noticeable reduction of 15% in the total dynamic power after the insertion of the criticality factor for the value of $\alpha=0.1$.

5   Conclusions and Future Work

Although promising from the point of view of the achievable results, the combination of clock-gating and power-gating is not mature enough to be applicable to real-life circuits. In particular, several aspects related to the support of integrated CG/PG in EDA frameworks are still open.

In this paper, we have proposed a new synthesis methodology to reduce the timing overhead due to the integration of clock-gating and power-gating. The key element we introduced in the methodology is the concept of interconnect criticality, which is exploited in the clustering phase of our synthesis flow. The tool which implements the methodology is flexible enough to work seamlessly with commercially available EDA tools. The results we have obtained show significant improvements in terms of both the power-delay product and the timing overhead with respect to circuits in which CG and PG are integrated without considering interconnect criticality information during clustering.

We believe that automatic CG/PG integration requires more investigation. Currently, our main focus is on parallelizing the partitioning process based upon the heuristic of multilevel partitioning. This will help in reducing the total runtime and memory usage, which will make the flow applicable to larger circuits.

References

1. Roy, K., Mukhopadhyay, S., Mahmoodi Meimand, H.: Leakage Current Mechanisms and Leakage Reduction Techniques in Deep-Submicrometer CMOS Circuits. Proceedings of the IEEE 91(2), 305–327 (2003)
2. Benini, L., De Micheli, G., Macii, E.: Designing Low-Power Circuits: Practical Recipes. IEEE Circuits and Systems Magazine 1(1), 6–25 (2001)
3. Benini, L., Siegel, P., De Micheli, G.: Automatic Synthesis of Gated Clocks for Power Reduction in Sequential Circuits. IEEE Design and Test of Computers 11(4), 32–40 (1994)
4. Anis, M., Areibi, S., Elmasry, M.: Design and Optimization of Multi-Threshold CMOS Circuits. IEEE Tran. on CAD 22(10), 1324–1342 (2003)
5. Sathanur, A., Pullini, A., Benini, L., Macii, A., Macii, E., Poncino, M.: Timing-Driven Row-Based Power Gating. In: ISLPED 2007: ACM/IEEE Intl. Symp. on Low Power Electronics and Design, Portland, OR, pp. 104–109 (2007)
6. Bolzani, L., Calimera, A., Macii, A., Macii, E., Poncino, M.: Enabling Concurrent Clock and Power Gating in an Industrial Design Flow. In: DATE 2009: IEEE Design Automation and Test in Europe, Nice, pp. 334–339 (2009)
7. Bolzani, L., Calimera, A., Macii, A., Macii, E., Poncino, M.: Placement-aware clustering for integrated clock and power gating. In: ISCAS 2009: IEEE Intl. Symp. on Circuits and Systems, Taipei, pp. 1723–1726 (2009)
8. Kernighan, W.B., Lin, S.: Efficient Heuristic Procedure for Partitioning Graphs. Bell System Tech. Journal 49, 291–307 (1970)

Low Energy Voltage Dithering in Dual V_{DD} Circuits

Thomas Schweizer, Julio Oliveira, Tommy Kuhn, and Wolfgang Rosenstiel

University of Tübingen, Wilhelm Schickard Institute,
Department of Computer Engineering,
Sand 13, 72076 Tübingen, Germany
{tschweiz,oliveira,kuhn,rosenstiel}@informatik.uni-tuebingen.de
http://www.ti.uni-tuebingen.de

Abstract. Voltage dithering is a voltage scaling technique for reducing the dynamic energy consumption. This technique enables to switch between two power supplies dynamically. However, switching consumes a considerable amount of additional energy. In this paper, we propose a new charge recycling circuit to reduce the energy overhead of voltage switching. The innovation of this circuit is that some charge is recycled by redirecting this charge from one power supply line to another before the voltage is switched. This charge transfer decreases the current driven from the power supply during voltage switching, thereby reducing the energy overhead. Applying the charge recycling technique to two carry-ripple adders reduces the dynamic energy overhead of voltage switching by 43.2%.

Keywords: charge recycling, voltage scaling, dual voltage.

1 Introduction

A reduction of the supply voltage leads to quadratic savings on energy consumption at the cost of longer execution delays. This fact is often used to convert non-performance critical tasks into energy gain on general-purpose and embedded processors. The most common approach for scaling the voltage of the entire chip is called dynamic voltage scaling (*DVS*). *DVS* can be realized on-chip or off-chip using *DC-DC* converters. The problem with *DVS* is that *DC-DC* converters require large inductors and capacitors resulting in significant power and area overhead. Another drawback is the transition latency due to voltage conversion and regulation circuitry.

Calhoun [1] proposes an alternative voltage scaling technique, called voltage dithering. Compared to *DVS*, voltage dithering allows to control individual parts of the chip and to switch faster between discrete voltage levels. In [2] a design was implemented using voltage dithering on an *AsAP* (Asynchronous Array of simple Processors) many-core chip. Such architectures are the target of our charge recycling approach, as we can assume that frequent voltage switching is applied to individual blocks of the chip and therefore one part of these blocks operates with low supply voltage and the other part with high supply voltage.

J. Monteiro and R. van Leuken (Eds.): PATMOS 2009, LNCS 5953, pp. 237–246, 2010.
© Springer-Verlag Berlin Heidelberg 2010

Voltage dithering circuits consist of a dual supply network (high supply voltage V_{DDH} and low supply voltage V_{DDL}) controlled by voltage switching elements as shown in Fig. 1. The voltage switching element consists of two p-channel *MOSFETs*, called power switches. Configuration bits are used to control the power switches so that an appropriate supply voltage can be chosen for the logic block. The chosen voltage is transferred to a virtual power supply line. Another component of the circuit is the level converter. The level converter has to prevent static currents that occur by the change from the lower voltage level to the higher voltage level.

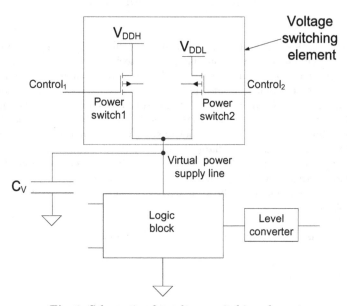

Fig. 1. Schematic of a voltage switching element

Voltage transitions consume a considerable amount of additional energy. The sources for energy consumption are the control circuits and the parasitic capacitances. The control circuits that drive the power switches consume energy every time they select a new voltage for the logic block. Each transition causes a charge or discharge of capacitances on the virtual power supply lines and on the power switches. The virtual power supply lines have high capacitance due to wire parasitics, a large number of transistors sharing a common power switch, and decoupling capacitors. In Fig. 1 these parasitic capacitances are illustrated by a single lumped capacitance, denoted as virtual capacitance C_v.

In this paper, we propose a new charge recycling circuit to reduce the energy overhead of voltage switching. The innovation of this circuit is that some charge is redirected from one virtual power supply line to another before the voltage is switched. This charge transfer decreases the current driven from the power supply during voltage switching, thereby reducing the energy overhead.

The paper is organized as follows. In the next section we describe the related work. The energy overhead of voltage switching is discussed in Section 3. The charge recycling technique and the charge recycling circuit are described in Section 4. Experimental results are presented in Section 5. Conclusions are drawn in Section 6.

2 Related Work

There exist a few charge recycling methods. Hahm [3] proposed a method for improving the power efficiency of conventional $CMOS$ through charge storage and reuse. In [5] a design for a charge recovery databus is presented. In this design charge is transferred from the falling bit-lines to pre-charge the rising bit-lines so that the additional energy required to fully charge the rising bit-lines is reduced. In [6] a power gating solution that minimizes the energy consumed during mode transitions in $MTCMOS$ circuits is presented.

3 Voltage Switching

In this section we estimate the energy overhead to control and execute a full cycle of voltage transitions $(V_{DDL} \rightarrow V_{DDH} \rightarrow V_{DDL})$ in a power switch based dual supply voltage circuit.

The energy drawn from the power supply to charge C_v from an initial voltage V_{DDL} to a final voltage V_{DDH} is

$$E_{V_{DDL} \rightarrow V_{DDH}} = C_v V_{DDH}(V_{DDH} - V_{DDL}) \tag{1}$$

The energy stored in the virtual capacitance after this transition is calculated as explained in [4]

$$E_{C_v} = \frac{1}{2}C_v(V_{DDH}^2 - V_{DDL}^2) \tag{2}$$

The remaining energy is dissipated in the parasitic resistance of the V_{DDH} power switch and is calculated as

$$E_{diss(V_{DDL} \rightarrow V_{DDH})} = \frac{1}{2}C_v(V_{DDL} - V_{DDH})^2 \tag{3}$$

During a V_{DDH} to V_{DDL} transition, the energy previously stored in the virtual capacitance is dissipated in the parasitic resistances, particularly in the resistance of the V_{DDL} power switch. The energy dissipated during discharging is

$$E_{diss(V_{DDH} \rightarrow V_{DDL})} = E_{C_v} = \frac{1}{2}C_v(V_{DDH}^2 - V_{DDL}^2) \tag{4}$$

In addition to the energy dissipation due to charging and discharging the virtual capacitance, the control circuit also dissipates energy $E_{control}$ for charging and discharging the gate-oxide capacitance of the power switches. For controlling a full cycle of voltage transitions $(V_{DDL} \rightarrow V_{DDH} \rightarrow V_{DDL})$ the gate-oxide capacitance of the two power switches must be charged and discharged once. Thus, under the assumption that the power switches are equally sized, the total energy overhead can be estimated by

$$E_{overhead} = E_{V_{DDL} \to V_{DDH}} + E_{control}$$
$$= \frac{1}{2} C_v (V_{DDL} - V_{DDH})^2$$
$$+ \frac{1}{2} C_v (V_{DDH}^2 - V_{DDL}^2)$$
$$+ 2 * C_{C_{ox} powerswitch} V_{DDH}^2 \qquad (5)$$

4   Charge Recycling Technique

In this section we discuss how to reduce $E_{V_{DDL} \to V_{DDH}}$, and therefore the total energy overhead. We propose implementing a new low energy voltage switching circuit. Then we determine the conditions under which the maximum energy saving can be achieved by this circuit.

4.1   Implementation

Every time a voltage switching circuit undergoes a V_{DDH} to V_{DDL} voltage transition, charge stored in the virtual capacitance is dumped and wasted. Similarly, charge is reapplied to the virtual capacitance during a V_{DDL} to V_{DDH} voltage transition. The concept of our proposed charge recycling technique is to bypass some of this charge to another virtual capacitance to save this amount of charge during the next V_{DDL} to V_{DDH} voltage transition. To enable the redirection of the charge, we use a *PMOS* pass transistor as a switch between two distinct virtual power supply lines.

The proposed charge recovering circuit has three modes of operation: a logical, a voltage switching and a charge recycling mode (see Fig. 2). In the logical mode the circuit works as a conventional dual supply circuit based on power switches. Signal changes are accomplished with the adjusted voltage and there is no path between the virtual power supply lines. The voltage switching mode is divided by the recycling mode into two phases. In the first phase the power switches are switched off. In the following recycling mode the virtual power supply lines are short-circuited and charge can be transferred between them. In the second phase the voltage transition takes place.

We illustrate the concept and the implementation of the charge recycling technique in details in Fig. 3. We consider two logic blocks A and B, each controlled by a power switching element. We assume that logic block A operates in V_{DDH} and will change to V_{DDL}. For logic block B we assume the opposite. During the logical mode power switches $P1_H$ and $P2_L$ are turned on. Power switches $P1_L$, $P2_H$ and the *PMOS* pass transistor are cut-off. The voltage of C_{v_A} is V_{DDH}. The voltage of the C_{v_B} is V_{DDL}. In the first phase of the voltage switching mode the power switches $P1_H$ and $P2_L$ are switched-off. When the circuit enters the recycling mode all power switches are in cut-off and the *PMOS* pass transistor

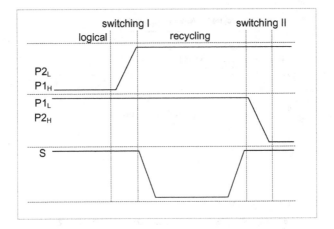

Fig. 2. Signal waveforms representing the modes and the control sequence of voltage switching with charge recycling

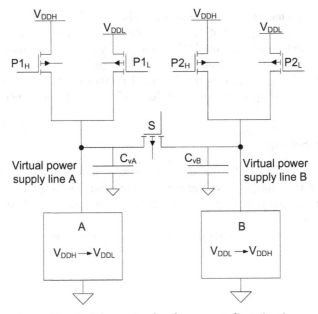

Fig. 3. Schematic of a charge recycling circuit

S is turned on. Charge is transferred from C_{v_A} to C_{v_B}. The charge recycling process stops when the voltages of the virtual power supply lines are equalized. After the charge recycling mode is completed the value of the common voltage of the virtual capacitances is

$$V_{common} = \frac{C_{v_A}V_{DDH} + C_{v_B}V_{DDL}}{C_{v_A} + C_{v_B}} \tag{6}$$

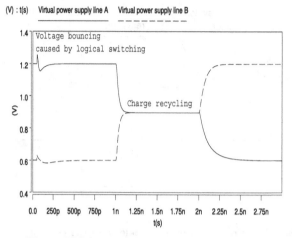

Fig. 4. Voltage switching and charge recycling

At this point, the charge recycling mode is finished and the pass transistor S is turned off. In the second phase of the voltage switching mode the power switches $P1_L$ and $P2_H$ are turned on. The discharging process of C_{v_A} continues until the voltage level V_{DDL} is reached, respectively the charging of C_{v_B} continues until the voltage level V_{DDH} is reached. Fig. 4 illustrates the voltage waveform on the virtual power supply lines in dependence of the control sequence explained previously.

4.2 Energy Saving

Now, we determine the conditions under which the maximum energy saving can be achieved by the charge recycling circuit. For that, we compare the energy dissipation for charging/discharging the virtual capacitances with and without charge recycling.

The energy dissipation for charging the virtual capacitance C_{v_B} from V_{common} to V_{DDH} is

$$E_{diss(V_{common} \rightarrow V_{DDH})} = \frac{1}{2} C_{v_B} (V_{common} - V_{DDH})^2 \tag{7}$$

The energy dissipation for discharging the virtual capacitance C_{v_A} from V_{common} to V_{DDL} is

$$E_{diss(V_{common} \rightarrow V_{DDL})} = \frac{1}{2} C_{v_A} (V_{common}^2 - V_{DDL}^2) \tag{8}$$

The corresponding energy saving due to charge recycling can then be calculated as

$$E_{saved} = E_{NO\_RECYCLING} - E_{RECYCLING} \tag{9}$$

$$= E_{V_{DDL} \rightarrow V_{DDH}} - E_{V_{common} \rightarrow V_{DDH}} \tag{10}$$

$$= \frac{1}{2}C_{vB}(V_{DDL} - V_{DDH})^2$$

$$+ \frac{1}{2}C_{vA}(V_{DDH}^2 - V_{DDL}^2)$$

$$- \frac{1}{2}C_{vB}(V_{common} - V_{DDH})^2$$

$$- \frac{1}{2}C_{vA}(V_{common}^2 - V_{DDL}^2)$$

$$= \frac{C_{vA}C_{vB}(V_{DDL}^2 - 4V_{DDH}V_{DDL} + 3V_{DDH}^2)}{2C_{vB} + 2C_{vA}} \tag{11}$$

We will show that the maximal energy saving is achieved, when C_{vA} is equal to C_{vB}.

Theorem 1. $max(E_{saved}) \Rightarrow C_{vA} = C_{vB}$

Proof. We cut E_{saved} with a plane $C_{vA} + C_{vB} = \alpha$. Therefore we can write

$$E_{saved}(C_{vA}, \alpha) = \frac{C_{vA}(-C_{vA} + \alpha)V_{DDL}^2}{2(-C_{vA} + \alpha) + 2C_{vA}} \tag{12}$$

$$- \frac{4C_{vA}(-C_{vA} + \alpha)V_{DDH}V_{DDL}}{2(-C_{vA} + \alpha) + 2C_{vA}}$$

$$+ \frac{3C_{vA}(-C_{vA} + \alpha)V_{DDH}^2}{2(-C_{vA} + \alpha) + 2C_{vA}}$$

$E_{saved}(C_{vA}, \alpha)$ describes the energy saving function in the plane $C_{vA} + C_{vB} = \alpha$. To find the maximum in $E_{saved}(C_{vA}, \alpha)$ we calculate

$$\frac{\partial E_{saved}(C_{vA}, \alpha)}{\partial C_{vA}} = 0 \tag{13}$$

$$\Rightarrow C_{vA} = \frac{1}{2}\alpha \tag{14}$$

$$C_{vB} = -C_{vA} + \alpha \tag{15}$$

$$\Rightarrow C_{vB} = \frac{1}{2}\alpha \tag{16}$$

$$\Rightarrow \forall \alpha : max(E_{saved}) \Rightarrow C_{vA} = C_{vB}$$

After determining the conditions under which the maximum energy saving can be achieved we define the energy saving ratio (*ESR*):

$$ESR(C_{vA} = C_{vB}) = \frac{E_{NO\_RECYCLING} - E_{RECYCLING}}{E_{NO\_RECYCLING}} \tag{17}$$

So far we neglect the energy consumption for turning off and on the charge recycling pass transistor. If we take into account this additional energy cost,

ESR is decreased by the energy $E_{control-pass-transistor}$ for controlling the pass transistor.

$$ESR_{pass}(C_{v_A} = C_{v_B}) = \frac{E_{NO\_RECYCLING} - E_{RECYCLING}}{E_{NO\_RECYCLING}}$$
$$+ \frac{E_{control-pass-transistor}}{E_{NO\_RECYCLING}} \qquad (18)$$

5   Experimental Results

We carried out three experiments. In the first experiment we determined the energy saving when the capacitances of the logical block are balanced. Then we computed the energy saving when the capacitances are unbalanced, that means in the case of $C_{v_A} \neq C_{v_B}$. In the second experiment we simulated the energy saving in dependence of various ratios of V_{DDL} to V_{DDH}. In the third experiment we determined the charge recycling duration in dependence of the width of the pass transistor switch.

For each experiment the following two simulations were done. We started the simulations in the logical mode. During the logical mode the parasitic capacitances are charged. Then in the first simulation the voltage switching mode occured and we determined the value of $E_{NO\_RECYCLING}$. In the second simulation we incorporated the pass transistor switch in the circuit. After the logical mode we turned off the power switches. Then the charge recycling mode started. Then the voltage switching mode is continued so that we could determine the value of $E_{RECYCLING} + E_{control-pass-transistor}$. With these simulation results we calculated $ESR_{pass}(C_{v_A} = C_{v_B})$.

We generated our experimental results on basis of two 16-bit carry-ripple adders (CRA). This circuit is similar to the circuit explained in Fig. 3. The difference is that we used two pass transistors for connecting the two $CRAs$. Each adder had one voltage switching element. For an accurate estimation of dynamic energy saving we carried out the simulations with $SPICE$ using the Berkeley Predictive Technology Models ($BPTM$) in a 65 nm $CMOS$ technology.

In the first experiment the width of the power switches were set to 8.6 μm and the width of the pass transistor switch was set to 4.3 μm. $SPICE$ simulations were done at $V_{DDH} = 1.2\ V$ and $V_{DDL} = 0.6\ V$. As a simulation result we can save 43.2% of the dynamic energy wasted during voltage switching with the parameter settings specified earlier. In the general case the virtual capacitance of logic blocks differs ($C_{v_A} \neq C_{v_B}$). In Fig. 5 we computed the energy saving in dependence of the virtual capacitances C_{v_A} and C_{v_B}.

In the second experiment, we altered V_{DDL} and determined the value of $ESR_{pass}(C_{v_A} = C_{v_B})$. In Table 1 we compare the energy saving achieved by various ratios of V_{DDL} to V_{DDH}. The results of this experiment show that the smaller the ratio of V_{DDL} to V_{DDH} the greater the energy saving.

The energy consumption for (de)activating the pass transistor switch increases with its size. However it is still a good trend because the duration of the charge recycling decreases much faster with increasing pass transistor size. Increasing

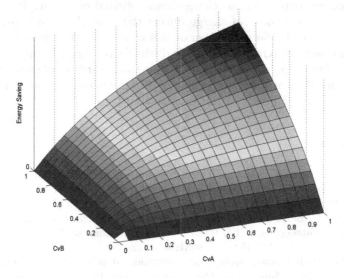

Fig. 5. Energy saving in dependence of the virtual capacitances

Table 1. Energy saving in dependence of the ratio of V_{DDL} to V_{DDH}

V_{DDL} Voltage[V]	V_{DDH} Voltage[V]	Energy saving %
1.1	1.2	3.0
1.0	1.2	17.5
0.9	1.2	28.8
0.8	1.2	36.2
0.7	1.2	41.0
0.6	1.2	43.2

the transistor width from 4.3 μm to 17.2 μm reduces ESR_{pass} from 43.2% to 40.7%, but the duration of charge recycling is decreased from 4.8 ns to 1 ns.

6   Conclusions

Voltage dithering is an alternative voltage scaling technique for reducing the dynamic energy consumption. Compared to DVS, voltage dithering allows to control individual parts of the chip and to switch faster between discrete voltage levels. However, switching between supply voltages consumes additional energy. This additional energy consumption must be amortized during running on low supply voltage. Therefore, a goal is to develop circuit techniques for reducing the energy overhead of voltage transitions, because this improves the chance that a voltage transition is worthwhile.

In this paper we presented a new charge recycling circuit for reducing the energy overhead of voltage switching in dual supply voltage circuits. The proposed circuit bypasses some charge from a virtual power supply line to another to save this amount of charge during the next V_{DDL} to V_{DDH} voltage transition. To enable the redirection of this charge a *PMOS* pass transistor is utilized for charge recycling between two distinct virtual power supply lines. Applying this charge recycling technique to two 16-bit carry-ripple adders reduces the energy overhead of voltage switching by 40.7%, which comes at an additional delay of 1 *ns* for a full cycle of voltage transitions.

References

1. Calhoun, B., Chandrakasan, A.: Ultra-dynamic voltage scaling (UDVS) using sub-threshold operation and local voltage dithering. IEEE Journal of Solid State Circuits 41(1), 238–245 (2006)
2. Cheng, W.H., Baas, B.M.: Dynamic voltage and frequency scaling circuits with two supply voltages. In: IEEE International Symposium on Circuits and Systems (ISCAS), pp. 1236–1239. IEEE, Los Alamitos (2008)
3. Hahm, M.: Modest power savings for applications dominated by switching of large capacitive loads. In: International Symposium on Low Power Electronics and Design (ISLPED), pp. 60–61. IEEE, Los Alamitos (1995)
4. Kursun, V., Friedman, E.: Multi-voltage CMOS Circuit Design. John Wiley and Sons, New York (2006)
5. Lyuboslavsky, V., Bishop, B., Narayanan, V., Irwin, M.: Design of databus charge recovery mechanism. In: ASIC/SOC Conference, pp. 283–287. IEEE, Los Alamitos (2000)
6. Pakbaznia, E., Fallah, F., Pedram, M.: Charge recycling in MTCMOS circuits: concept and analysis. In: Proceedings of the 43rd Design Automation Conference (DAC), pp. 97–102. ACM, New York (2006)

Product On-Chip Process Compensation for Low Power and Yield Enhancement

Nabila Moubdi[1, 2], Philippe Maurine[2], Robin Wilson[1], Nadine Azemard[2],
Vincent Dumettier[1], Abhishek Bansal[1], Sebastien Barasinski[1], Alain Tournier[1],
Guy Durieu[1], David Meyer[1], Pierre Busson[1], Sarah Verhaeren[1], and Sylvain Engels[1]

[1] STMicroelectronics Central CAD & Design Solutions,
850 rue Jean Monnet, 38921, Crolles, France
[2] LIRMM, Laboratory of Informatics, Robotics and Microelectronics of Montpellier,
UMR CNRS, 161 rue Ada, 34392, Montpellier, France
nabila.moubdi@st.com

Abstract. This paper aims at introducing a reliable on-chip process compensation flow for industrial integrated systems. Among the integrated process compensation techniques, the main one aims at reducing the supply voltage of fast circuits in order to reduce their power consumption while maintaining the specified operating frequency. The proposed design flow includes efficient methodologies to gather/sort on-chip process data but also post-silicon tuning strategies and validation methods at both design and test steps. Concrete results are introduced in this paper to demonstrate the added value of such a methodology. More precisely, it is shown that its application leads to an overall energy reduction ranging from 10% to 20% on fast chips.

Keywords: Variability, voltage scaling, sensors, process compensation.

1 Introduction

Energy consumption, not only the one of integrated systems, has become one of the most widely discussed topics in recent years because of the global warming effects. Since semiconductor electronic devices are increasingly used, designing products with the environmental impacts in mind through their entire life cycle becomes a necessity and technology development is now not only driven by a desire to improve circuit density and speed.

More precisely, the management of the power consumption of IC and its associated variability while warranting their functionality is now one of the major challenges in integrated system design.

Within this context, the process induced variability, which is a matter of a few atoms or less, appears as an important additional issue that cannot be neglected.

Indeed, leakage power varies now exponentially with key process parameters such as gate length, oxide thickness, threshold voltage[1], in addition to the variability related to local transistor environment and wires including circuit layout, pattern dependency and density[2].

J. Monteiro and R. van Leuken (Eds.): PATMOS 2009, LNCS 5953, pp. 247–255, 2010.

Up to now, this increasing variability has led designers to introduce additional design margins which increases pessimism and thus reduces both timing and power performances. To overcome the variability issue, a close cooperation between system design and technology development teams is required for the future technology nodes as technological solutions can no longer compensate for all the effects of scaling.

As a result, good process control techniques combined with on-chip performance monitoring and compensation techniques appears as an interesting solution for reducing both power and spread power consumption, maintaining a reasonable margins and maximizing the number of chips that will meet power and delay constraints.

If several Process Voltage Temperature (PVT) sensors have been proposed in the literature for variability compensation [3, 4 ,5, 6], no work related to the design and test flow of circuits integrating process compensation technique has been published up to now and to the best of our knowledge. This paper addresses this point.

The remainder of the paper is organized as follows. Section II describes some on-chip sensors used to gather and sort on-chip process data. Section III gives an overall view of the proposed process compensation flow and associated techniques related to design, manufacturing, test, speed binning, fuse coding, and the post-silicon tuning. Concrete results related to energy savings obtained using process compensation are given before to draw a conclusion in section V.

2 On Chip Performance Monitors

To allow on-chip performance monitoring, a set of specific oscillators were designed to monitor individually the performances of NMOS and PMOS in terms of speed and leakage current.

Each sensor is made of three specific oscillating structures called respectively 'Speedometer NMOS', 'Speedometer PMOS' and 'Leakometer'. Note these structures were designed to be as representative as possible of real circuits especially in terms of density and metal layers. The signals delivered by these structures are periodic square signals and it is the period of these signals that provides insights on the quality of the design in terms of speed and leakage.

These monitors were developed and validated on different successive technology nodes for all available process options to address a large product portfolio needs. The validation of these sensors was done through a large silicon campaign characterization to prove their efficiency in tracking process skews including process corners deviations but also within-wafer and within die variations.

As an illustration of this silicon validation campaign, figure 1 gives the measured frequencies at the output of the 'Speedometer NMOS' and 'Speedometer PMOS'. These measures represent five corner lots intentionally processed to obtain as N/P transistors SLOW, TYPICAL or FAST.

As shown and expected, the measured frequencies for the corner lots FAST/FAST, TYPICAL/TYPICAL, SLOW/SLOW nearly pile up on the first bisecting line validating the sensors. Moreover, for cross corner lots (FAST/SLOW and SLOW/FAST) the measured obtained respectively below and above the bisecting line. This result was expected from specifications and simulation results.

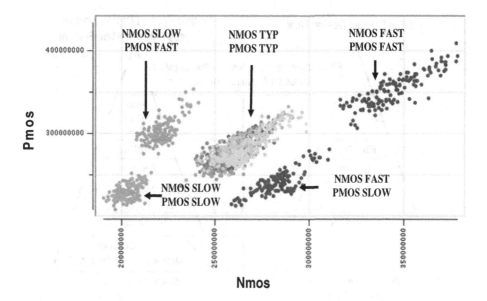

Fig. 1. Speedometer NMOS frequency vs Speedometer PMOS frequency for different corner lots (normalized).

3 Efficiency of Voltage Scaling as a Static Process Compensation Technique

If post silicon tuning techniques are now recognized as mandatory for the design of low power and/or high speed circuits in advanced technologies, their use requires the definition and the qualification of safe post silicon design and test flows. These flows, to be efficient, must target the best trade-off between delay, dynamic/static power consumption, reliability, tuning flexibility and design overhead in addition to exhaustive validation methods at each step of the flow.

In this section, we present the benefits and robustness of the developed process compensation flow. As illustrated in figure 2, this flow requires three additional steps compared to a standard design flow. In a first step, on-chip ring oscillators (sensors) and their control circuitry are integrated to the circuit at the design stage. In a second step, on-chip sensor's data are read at test level to enable part grading and on-chip fuse code is used to identify fast and standard parts. In a third step, post silicon tuning techniques such as static voltage scaling are performed to compensate and optimize fast parts speed and power performances.

This flow, shown figure 2, was established with close cooperation between system design teams and technology development teams.

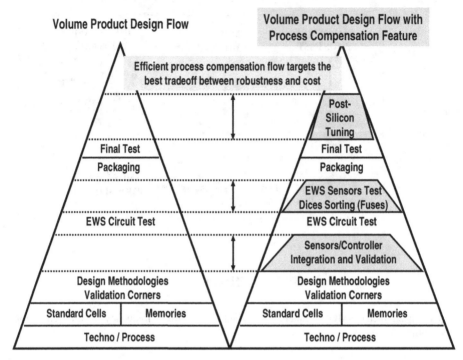

Fig. 2. Standard design and test flow vs advanced design and test flow with process compensation features

-a- Design approach

The first additional step resumes to the integration of the on-chip ring oscillators (sensors). To be compliant with a large product portfolio, the standard interface JTAG (Joint Test Action Group) is adopted to access the on-chip sensors data. This choice eases both the integration into circuits and the test in a production environment (see figure 3).

-b- Validation approach

As any product, integrated circuits designed accordingly to this methodology have to be validated. At design stage, it must be proved that a circuit may maintain its performances under reduced supply conditions.

To ensure the correct functionality of the design, exhaustive timing verifications are performed using multi-corners Timing Analysis (TA) including additional timing corners wrt to usual TA. This of course implies the characterization of all standard cell libraries and their post silicon characterization and validation.

-c- Test approach

To obtain accurate process data from the sensor and therefore choose the right fuse coding, the measurements of sensor outputs through the JTAG interface must be done at EWS test step (Electrical Wafer Sorting) in a controlled environment (see figure 3). This environment control must warrant a constant room temperature and a nominal supply voltage for the Device Under Test (DUT). Note that during this sensor data collecting phase, the reproducibility and repeatability of the measurements was checked.

Based on the results of measurement, each sensor output is compared against the corresponding reference value. If Speedometer NMOS (PMOS) output is above the corresponding reference value the NMOS (PMOS) transistors of the DUT are classified as FAST and inversely.

Manufactured fast parts are fused with a code to indicate to the final system that they can run at a reduced supply voltage, while standard parts operate at the nominal supply voltage. This policy results in an overall worst case power consumption reduction as illustrated figure 4.

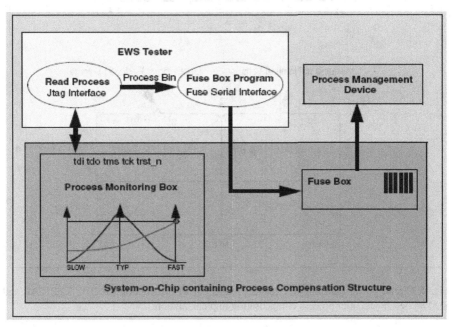

Fig. 3. Overview of the additional EWS test step to be applied to process compensated systems

-d- Process Compensation Implementation

According to the ITRS (International Technology Roadmap for Semiconductors), three types of products are identified: High Performance (HP), Low Operating Power (LOP), and Low Standby Power (LSTP) devices integrating different circuit level power optimization techniques such as multi-Vt [1], multi-Tox [1] and multi-Vdd [1]. This roadmap also suggests some additional power optimization techniques to be applied at architecture, and operating systems levels but also software level.

Among these techniques, voltage scaling technique was chosen since it reduces simultaneously both static and dynamic power consumption and this during all the product lifecycle. If this power optimization technique may be applied at different granularity, it was decided to apply it at the chip level. Several reasons explain this policy choice. First, the necessity of a generic- process compensation methodology which avoids the integration of level shifters and isolation cells, and results in a

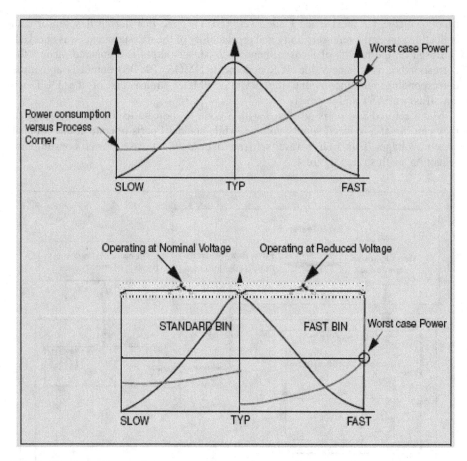

Fig. 4. Circuit power consumption versus process corner distribution (SLOW, TYPICAL and SLOW) before and after process compensation implementation

minimal area overhead. Second, it eases the design and offers a reasonable trade-off between design time, robustness and power savings.

Indeed, figure 4 shows the decrease of the worst case power consumption when the post-silicon process compensation is implemented on fast parts.

-e- Experimental results

This process compensation flow has been applied to several products. Within this section we present some concrete results related to a circuit designed in a 65 nm CMOSLPGP mix technology. This 1GHz Digital Channel Multiplexer for Satellite Outdoor Unit has a silicon area of 12.75 mm² and a digital total power of 950mW for standard parts at 1V supply voltage as described in reference [7].

The static voltage scaling policy was to supply slow dices with a nominal digital supply voltage of 1 V and to supply fast and leaky circuits with a voltage value reduced by 80mV.

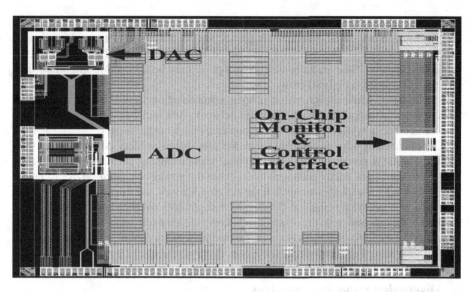

Fig. 5. 1GHz Digital Channel Multiplexer for Satellite Outdoor Unit in a 65 nm CMOSLPGP mix technology with embedded on-chip monitors (sensors)

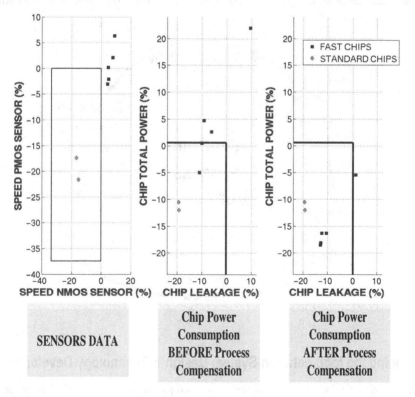

Fig. 6. Normalized Circuit performances before and after process compensation

As presented on figure 6, without applying any static voltage scaling policy, fast circuits may work at a maximal frequency up to 8% greater than the nominal maximum frequency. This is mainly explained by the quality of NMOS and PMOS devices. However their static power consumption may be 23% more important than the one of standard (nominal) chips.

As expected, when the proposed process compensation flow is implemented, the total power consumption reduction ranges between 10% and 20% and the circuit still operates correctly while maintaining the nominal operating frequency.

The obtained results demonstrate that the introduced process compensation flow reduces the total power of fast chips without compromising performances and may also avoid the use of costly packages to dissipate the power consumption of fast parts.

These results also demonstrate that the on-chip sensors and their associated control interface give accurate results at the cost of a slight area overhead of 0.04mm² and a moderate design and test time increase. However, this test-time increase must be compared to the 20% energy savings on fast circuits, energy savings that remains over the full lifecycle of the product.

4   Discussions and Perspectives

In addition to a significant power reduction on fast circuits, the integration of on-chip sensors may enhance the production quality. Indeed, the integration of sensors allows

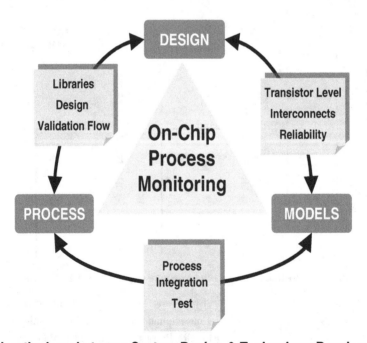

Fig. 7. Closing the loop between the design, test and process teams involved in the production of volume circuits

giving chips a unique ID with process centering data. As a result, it allows tracking on-chip process variability over fab-to-fab, wafer-to-wafer and die to die, and eases the implementation of diagnosis methodologies and yield learning [8].

In a second phase, the sensors may be used to check the process maturity evolution during the ramp up of a technology. This last point resumes in closing the loop between the design, test and process teams involved in the volume production circuits as illustrated figure 7.

Finally, a last advantage offered by the integration of on-chip sensors is the ability of monitoring hot spot zones identified during simulation at design level. Among the hot spot zones that can be monitored one can found circuit areas subjected to dynamic IR drops, temperature variations due to localized high activity rate.

5 Conclusion

The main contribution of this paper is to introduce a simple and robust process compensation flow for high volume circuit production. Some concrete results related to the power savings obtained by the application of this flow on a 12.75 mm² chip have been introduced. This savings may reach 20% of the total power consumption without impacting circuit functionality and operating frequency.

References

[1] Roy, K., Mukhopadhyay, S., Mahmoodi, H.: Leakage Current Mechanisms and Leakage Reduction Techniques in Deep-Submicrometer CMOS Circuits. Proceeding of the IEEE 91(2) (February 2003)
[2] Granneman, E., Pages, X., Rosseel, E.: Pattern-Dependent Heating of 3d Structures. IEEE, Los Alamitos (2007)
[3] Mukhopadhyay, S., Kim, K., Mahmoodi, H., Roy, K.: Design of a Process Variation Tolerant Self-Repairing SRAM for Yield Enhancement in Nanoscaled CMOS. IEEE Journal of Solid-State Circuits 42(6) (June 2007)
[4] Kanno, Y., Kondoh, Y., Irita, T., Hirose, K., Mori, R., Yasu, Y., Komatsu, S., Mizuno, H.: In-Situ Measurement of Supply-Noise Maps With Millivolt Accuracy and Nanosecond-Order Time Resolution. IEEE Journal of Solid-State Circuits 42(4) (April 2007)
[5] Nourani, M., Radhakrishnan, A.: Testing On-Die Process Variation in Nanometer VLSI. IEEE Design & Test of Computers (2006)
[6] Bhunia, S., Mukhopadhyay, S., Roy, K.: Process Variations and Process-Tolerant Design. In: 20th International Conference on VLSI Design (2007)
[7] Busson, P., Chawla, N., Bach, J., Le Tual, S., Singh, H., Gupta, V., Urard, P.: For anonymous review A 1GHz Digital Channel Multiplexer for Satellite Outdoor Unit Based on a 65nm CMOS Transceiver. In: IEEE International Solid-State Circuits Conference (2009)
[8] Epinat, A., Wilson, R.: Yield Enhancement Methodology for CMOS Standard Cells. In: Proceeding of the 7th International Symposium on Quality Electronic Design, ISQED 2006 (2006)

Low-Power Soft Error Hardened Latch

Hossein Karimiyan Alidash[1] and Vojin G. Oklobdzija[2]

[1] ECE Department, Isfahan University of Technology, Isfahan 74155, Iran
[2] University of Texas at Dallas, Richardson, TX 75080, USA
Hkarimiyan@ec.iut.ac.ir, Vojin@utdallas.edu

Abstract. This paper presents a low-power soft error-hardened latch suitable for reliable circuit operation. The proposed circuit uses redundant feedback loop to protect latch against soft error on the internal nodes, and transmission gate and Schmitt-trigger circuit to filter out transient resulting from particle hit on combinational logic. The proposed circuit has low power consumption with negative setup time and low timing overhead. The HSPICE post-layout simulation in 90nm CMOS technology reveals that circuit is able to recover from almost any single particle strike on internal nodes and tolerates input SETs up to 130ps of duration.

Keywords: soft-error, static latch, hardened latch, reliability.

1 Introduction

Continuous advances of microelectronic technology are leading to an aggressive shrinkage of device dimensions. The consequent node capacitance reduction along with the power supply voltage reduction [20], the amount of stored charge on each circuit node is becoming smaller. That smaller stored charge and higher operating frequency now make circuits more vulnerable to soft errors caused by charge deposited directly by alpha particle or indirectly by cosmic ray neutrons [1]. As a result soft errors which were traditionally regarded as reliability issue for space applications are going to be a terrestrial issue.

A study on radiation flux noted that particles with lower energy occur far more frequently than particles with higher energy [1]. So as CMOS device sizes decrease, it becomes more possible to be affected by lower energy particles, potentially leading to higher soft error rate.

Although package and process engineering may reduce alpha particle problem, there is no physical obstacle to cosmic neutrons. Thus improved circuit designs to reduce soft error vulnerability are becoming mainstream approach for high reliability systems.

Latches and flip-flops are also becoming more susceptible to particle strike on external logic and their own internal nodes, hence more hardening and soft error protection is required. Most common protective methods at circuit level are based on redundancy, namely temporal and spatial redundancy. Those methods, as well as scan based soft error resilient latch [16] and even transient detection of RAZOR I & II

J. Monteiro and R. van Leuken (Eds.): PATMOS 2009, LNCS 5953, pp. 256–265, 2010.
© Springer-Verlag Berlin Heidelberg 2010

flip-flop [14] cannot tolerate soft error due to particle hit in combinational logic. The temporal redundancy based latches as well as those based on Schmitt-trigger [11] and transmission gate [13] filtering effects has extended setup time problem. The idea in this work is to reduce single event upset (SEU) and single event transient (SET) susceptibility with less timing overhead.

The rest of this paper is organized as follows. In section 2, the previous works will be reviewed quickly. Section 3 proposes the SER-tolerant latch. Section 4 gives simulation results and section 5 concludes the paper.

2 Latch-Hardening Methods

In this section, starting with some basic definitions recent publication and latch hardening methods will be reviewed. An energetic particle may hit logic gates, storage elements, or clock network of a digital circuit. When it hits the logic gates, it causes a glitch in the output voltage of the gate which is called single event transient (SET) [1][2]. When a particle directly hits an internal node of a latch or flip-flop, it may change stored data and cause single event upset (SEU). Also SET may generate and propagate through the combinational part and captured by storage element which turns into an SEU [3]. If a particle hits a control signal, such as the clock signal, it generates a false control signal which can results in an unwanted data latch or timing violation [4]. The rate at which soft errors occur is referred to as soft error rate (SER).

Traditionally memories are protected by Error Correction Codes (ECC). Storage elements, i.e. latches and flip-flops, have also received more attention to make them more robust to soft errors [11]. However, recent studies indicate that logic also will be more vulnerable to soft error [2][5]. Gate sizing to mitigate SET effect at logic level [15] as well as guard ring effect [18], and negative feedback effect are studied extensively [17]. The objectives of those studies are to design and size gates in a way that they attenuate transient voltages caused by particle strike.

During the process of transient voltage propagation in logic circuits, a SET could be masked by logical, electrical, or latching-window masking [5][20]. These three mechanisms prevent some SETs from being latched and alleviate the soft error rate in digital systems. However, due to continuous scaling trends, increased frequency and wide spectrum of particle energy, the probability that transient voltage reaches storage elements in capturing window and getting latched is increasing, and so does the soft error rate. Thus circuit level hardening techniques are required.

The simplest form of hardening technique for latches and flip-flops is to increase stored node charge by adding resistance or capacitance [8] which degrade circuit speed and increase power consumption.

While error-correcting codes and latch-hardening designs can be used to reduce the effect of SEUs, complete protection against SETs is much more difficult and involves either spatial or temporal redundancy. The spatial redundancy uses multiple copies of a given circuit with majority voting to determine correct outputs. One effective way to overcome SEU effects is to triplicate each latch of the system and use Triple Module Redundancy (TMR-latch). Although TMR-latches are highly reliable and widely used [6], this technique suffers from high area and energy consumption overhead.

The temporal redundancy technique uses delayed sample of data, and is more acceptable for conventional designs due to its lower power consumption. This technique can eliminate all SET pulses which are smaller than a certain threshold value. The major drawback of this method is its delay penalty. Moreover it cannot guarantee fault-free operation.

The dual interlock storage element (DICE) is another SER-hardened topology based on spatial redundancy. It has been introduced [9] and applied to a standard 6T memory cell [10] and used in pulsed latch [10][19]. The hardened feedback of DICE circuit has the potential to improve SEU robustness of latch circuits without degrading its speed too much; however it comes with area and power penalty [19].

Redundant feedback loop is another soft error hardening method used in basic latch. According to analyses in [3], soft error of the internal nodes in feedback loop, i.e. node B and C in Fig. 1, has the major contribution to the total SER. If a particle strike causes an unexpected voltage drop or rise inside the loop during the holding mode, the stored value in the latch may change depending on the amount of deposited charge. Our study also shows that node B is much more sensitive than node C.

The SIN-LC latch [3] is proposed to solve the SER issue of basic latch; Fig. 2(a) shows the detailed schematic of this latch. It consists of duplicating feedback loop and C-element making the latch output change only when both duplicated nodes have the same logic value. Besides to sizing issue, the SIN-LC suffers from contention

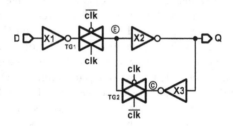

Fig. 1. Positive Level Sensitive Latch

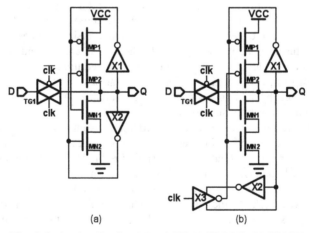

(a)   (b)

Fig. 2. Redundant Feedback Latch [3] (a) SIN-LC, (b) SIN-HR

drawback that occurs when the latch is in the transparent mode. The SIN-HR [3] of Fig. 2(b) is proposed to solve those problems, but the main problem still exists. The FERST [7] is another latch which is also based on duplicated feedback loop idea and tries to solve contention problem, but it comes up with large area, timing and power overhead.

Those methods, as well as scan based SER resilient latch [16] and even transient detection of RAZOR II flip-flop [14] cannot tolerate soft error due to capturing SET which resulted from particle hit in combinational logic. The transient filtering effect of Schmitt-trigger is studied and a latch based on its property is proposed [11]. The transmission gate [13], negative feedback [17], and circuit layout effect [18] on soft error are also reported separately.

3 Proposed Soft Error Hardened Latch

This section proposes a new soft error hardened latch which is based on temporal redundancy, dual feedback loop and incorporates extra glitch filtering. The detailed schematic of proposed latch is shown in Fig. 3. It employs C-element and controlled feedback loops to achieve low-power and filter out particle strike effect. Data redundancy and glitch filtering is used to reduce SET coming from combinational logic. Filtering is done in two steps. First the transmission gate based filter with hysteresis effect attenuates SETs and also adds delay to create temporal redundancy. At the second step, a C-element is used to filter out more SETs and reduce SEUs.

The proposed circuit is a pulsed latch and operates as follows in transparent and hold modes. A general purpose pulse generator circuit is used to generate tiny pulses on each clock edges. During the small period of tiny pulses the latch is transparent and feedback loops composed by X3-TG3 and X4-TG4 pairs are open. The data path is divided into two paths, normal and filtered. The pass transistors in the data paths, i.e. TG1 and TG2, are conducting and works as a low-pass filter [13]. The hysteresis

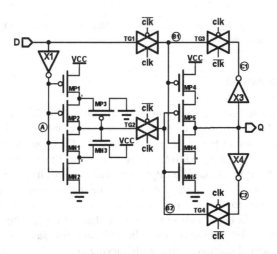

Fig. 3. The Soft Error Hardened Latch

effect is achieved using MP3 and MN3. During transparent time input data and its delayed/filtered version are applied to the C-element composed by MP4, MP5, MN4, and MN5. If both versions are the same and it is not a glitch, the output will change accordingly, unless the previous value is preserved. In other words, the data will be latched on the condition that it is not a single transient.

After tiny transparent pulse, the latch switches to hold state. In this period data paths are blocked and feedback loops are closed. The sensitive nodes in the proposed circuit are B1, C1, B2, and C2. If particle hit one of those nodes, it generates voltage spikes but dual feedback connection and C-element will remove its effect.

The temporal redundancy is implemented by adding a delay to the data path. The required delay value in the data path should be longer than the duration of the possible longest SET in order to effectively filter it out. The timing diagram in Fig. 4(a) shows the positive setup time of an ordinary clocked storage element. Applying temporal redundancy increases setup time (Fig. 4(b)) resulting in performance penalty. As a result, window of vulnerability (WOV) [3] to particle hit is also increases. The proposed topology uses the resulted negative setup time [21] of pulsed latches to mitigate setup time penalty. Applying the temporal redundancy to the pulsed latch (Fig. 4(c)) adds the positive delay value to the negative setup time, thus the setup time of hardened pulsed latch in Fig. 4(d) is still smaller than ordinary latch.

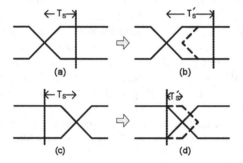

Fig. 4. Setup time (a) and (b) ordinary clocking, (c) and (d) pulsed clocking, (b) and (d) after applying hardening methods

5 Simulation Result

The proposed latch has been implemented using 90nm CMOS technology with 1.2V power supply voltage. In order to have realistic waveforms and rise/fall times the simulation setup, shown in Fig. 5, is used for all cases [21]. Due to inverted output of proposed circuit, inverter is added to the inputs whenever that it was needed.

Regardless of the type of particle (alpha particle or neutron), when it hits the drain of the MOSFET and loses energy, electron-hole pairs with a very high carrier concentration are generated. The resulting charges can be rapidly collected by the electric field to create a large transient current at that node [1]. The whole process of charge deposit and distribution is complicated, but for sake of simplicity, it is modeled by exponential current source with varying current levels and time constants to emulate particles with different energy level [3][7].

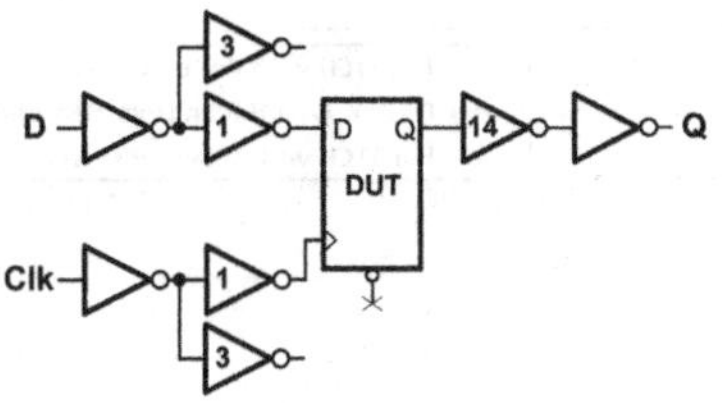

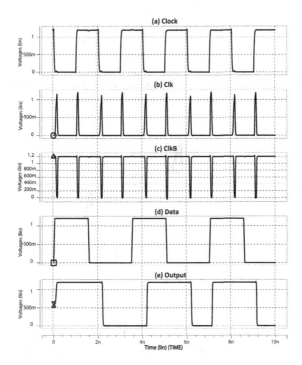

Fig. 5. Simulation Setup

Fig. 6. Latch normal operation (a) System Clock, tiny pulses (b) "CLK" and (c) "CLKB", (d) Data Input "D", and (d) Output "Q"

The performance of the proposed latch has been verified in the normal and particle affected mode. The particle affected mode is also divided in two modes. The first is SEU verification on internal nodes, which verifies robustness of the circuit against particles which hit on internal sensitive nodes. The second verifies filtering effect and circuit robustness against the particle hit on combinational part and the resulted SET, which reaches the latch on the sampling window.

Fig. 6 shows circuit's normal operation and Fig. 7 indicates its basic data to output delay (t_{DQ}) and setup time variation. This figure also gives the setup time and delay for ordinary latch of Fig. 1 in inverted mode, and proposed circuit in level sensitive mode for comparison. The flat region on the data-to-output delay and negative setup time of proposed latch reveals that if data arrive close to clock edge or even 40ps after clock edge, the latch is still able to capture it correctly [12]. While same circuit in

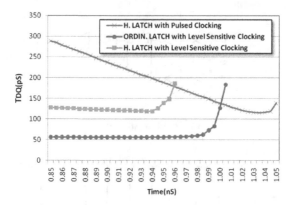

Fig. 7. Data to output delay variation and setup time of hardened latch with pulsed clocking, ordinary latch and hardened latch with level sensitive clocking

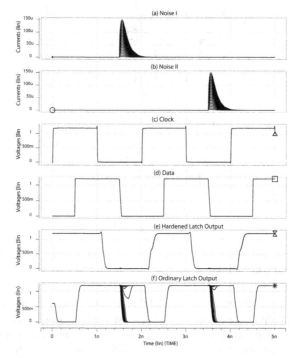

Fig. 8. Latch operation under particle affected mode, (a) Injected charge at 1.5ns, (b) Injected charge at 3.5ns, (c) Clock, (d) Data, and (e) Hardened latch output is still stable after particle hit on node B1 and C1 in Fig. 3, and (f) Ordinary latch output of Fig. 1 is unstable after 12.6fC and 19.8fC charge injection to nodes B and C, respectively.

level sensitive mode and with almost same output delay comes with large positive setup time. The extra negative setup time could be invested in input path by adding extra delay, to filter out more SETs.

The single particle hit on sensitive nodes is modeled by current injection to those nodes. Different current level is used to model particles with different energy levels. Charges are injected at 1.5ns and 2.5ns, to the nodes B1 and C1 in Fig. 3, and nodes B and C in Fig. 1. Fig. 8 shows the results and indicates that the ordinary latch output is unstable after 12.6fC and 19.8fC charge injection to nodes B and C, respectively. While the dual feedback structure of proposed circuit is able to recover from almost any single particle hit and resulting charge deposit.

The particle hit on combinational logic deposits charge which causes voltage glitch at gate's output. After passing levels of logics, those glitches convert to voltage pulses which may reaches to the latch "on-time" and gets captured. This phenomenon is modeled by voltage pulses with different width on the data line to represent various

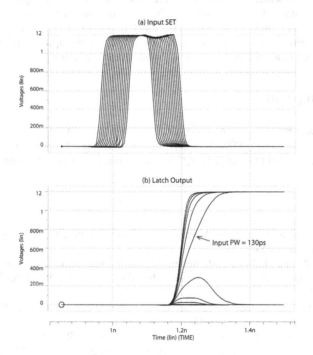

Fig. 9. SET filtering, (a) input, (b) latch output

Table 1. Different latches' setup time, delay, power consumption and power-delay-product comparison (* - TMR Specification is estimated)

Latch Type	Setup Time	Delay	Power	PDP
Basic latch (Fig. 1)	20ps	55ps	8.0μW	0.44fJ
Fig. 3 in level sensitive	60ps	120ps	23.3μW	2.8fJ
Fig. 3 in pulsed mode	-35ps	120ps	21.2μW	2.5fJ
TMR Latch*	60ps	120ps	24 μW	2.88fJ

particle energy levels. Fig. 9 shows the results and indicates that the proposed latch is able to filter out SETs with up to 130ps pulse width. Table 1 compare the specifications of basic latch and proposed circuit with TMR latch as a representative of hardened latches.

5 Conclusion

In this work, an SER-Hardened pulsed latch is proposed. The latch is able to tolerate particle strike on internal nodes as well as SET occurring in combinational logic. The HSPICE simulation on 90nm CMOS technology is conducted to precisely evaluate the proposed circuit in normal and under particle strike mode. The circuit operates as edge triggered flip-flop which is resilient to SET from combinational logic as well as SEU resulting from internal nodes. Extra reliability enhancement is achievable by careful layout design. In comparison with the TMR-Latch as a representative for SER-hardened designs, proposed circuit has less power consumption and lower timing overhead, which make it suitable for low-power reliable applications.

Acknowledgment

This work was performed at the Univ. of Texas at Dallas and supported in part by the SRC, under Grant No. 2008-HJ-1799. The authors would like to appreciate Dr. Mustafa AKTAN and Dursun BARAN for their review and valuable comments.

References

1. Baumann, R.: Soft Errors in Advanced Computer Systems. IEEE Design and Test of Computers 22(3), 258–266 (2005)
2. Mitra, S., Zhang, M., Mak, T.M., Seifert, N., Zia, V., Kim, K.S.: Logic soft errors: a major barrier to robust platform design. In: Proc. Int. Test Conference, November 2005, pp. 687–696 (2005)
3. Omana, M., Rossi, D., Metra, C.: Latch susceptibility to transient faults and new hardening approach. IEEE Trans. Comput. 56(9), 1255–1268 (2007)
4. Seifert, N., Shipleg, P., Pant, M.D., Ambrose, V., Gil, B.: Radiation induced clock jitter and race. In: Int. Physics Reliability Symposium, April 2005, pp. 215–22 (2005)
5. Shivakumar, P., Kistler, M., Keckler, S.W., Burger, D., Alvisi, L.: Modeling the effect of technology trends on the soft error rate of combinational logic. In: Proc. Int'l Conference on Dependable Systems and Networks (DSN), June 2002, pp. 389–399 (2002)
6. Kastensmidt, F., Sterpone, L., Sonza Reorda, M., Carrro, L.: On the optimal design of triple modular redundancy logic for SRAM-based FPGAs. In: Proc. IEEE Design, Automation and Test in Europe, pp. 1290–1295 (2005)
7. Fazeli, M., Miremadi, S.G., Ejlali, A., Patooghy, A.: Low energy single event upset/single event transient-tolerant latch for deep subMicron technologies. IET Computers & Digital Techniques 3(3), 289–303 (2009)
8. Karnik, T., Vangal, S., Veeramachaneni, V., Hazucha, P., Erraguntla, V., Borkar, S.: Selective node engineering for chip-level soft error rate improvement. In: IEEE Symp. VLSI Circuits, June 2002, pp. 204–205 (2002)

9. Calin, T., Nicolaidis, M., Velazco, R.: Upset hardened memory design for submicron CMOS technology. IEEE Trans. Nucl. Sci. 43, 2874–2878 (1996)
10. Hazucha, P., Karnik, T., Walstra, S., Bloechel, B.A., Tschanz, J.W., Maiz, J., Soumyanath, K., Dermer, G.E., Narendra, S., De, V., Borkar, S.: Measurements and analysis of SER-tolerant latch in a 90-nm dual-VT CMOS process. IEEE Journal of Solid-State Circuits 39(9), 1536–1543 (2004)
11. Sasaki, Y., Namba, K., Ito, H.: Circuit and Latch Capable of Masking Soft Errors with Schmitt Trigger. J. Electron. Test., 11–19 (June 2008)
12. Oklobdzija, V.G.: Clocking and Clocked Storage Elements in a Multi-Gigahertz Environment. IBM J. of Research and Development 47(5/6), 567–584 (2003)
13. Kumar, J., Tahoori, M.B.: Use of pass transistor logic to minimize the impact of soft errors in combinational circuits. In: Workshop on System Effects of Logic Soft Errors (2005)
14. Das, S., Tokunaga, C., Pant, S., Ma, W.-H., Kalaiselvan, S., Lai, K., Bull, D.M., Blaauw, D.T.: RazorII: In Situ Error Detection and Correction for PVT and SER Tolerance. IEEE J. of Solid-State Circuits 44(1), 32–48 (2009)
15. Dabiri, F., Nahapetian, A., Massey, T., Potkonjak, M., Sarrafzadeh, M.: General Methodology for Soft-Error-Aware Power Optimization Using Gate Sizing. IEEE Trans. on Computer-Aided Design of Integrated Circuits and Systems 27(10), 1788–1797 (2008)
16. Mitra, S., Seifert, N., Zhang, M., Shi, Q., Kim, K.S.: Robust system design with built-in soft-error resilience. Computer 38(2), 43–52 (2005)
17. Narasimham, B., Bhuva, B.L., Holman, W.T., Schrimpf, R.D., Massengill, L.W., Witulski, A.F., Robinson, W.H.: The Effect of Negative Feedback on Single Event Transient Propagation in Digital Circuits. IEEE Trans. on Nuclear Science 53(6), 3285–3290 (2006)
18. Narasimham, B., Shuler, R.L., Black, J.D., Bhuva, B.L., Schrimpf, R.D., Witulski, A.F., Holman, W.T., Massengill, L.W.: Quantifying the Reduction in Collected Charge and Soft Errors in the Presence of Guard Rings. IEEE Trans. on Device and Materials Reliability 8(1), 203–209 (2008)
19. Stackhouse, B., Bhimji, S., Bostak, C., Bradley, D., Cherkauer, B., Desai, J., Francom, E., Gowan, M., Gronowski, P., Krueger, D., Morganti, C., Troyer, S.: A 65 nm 2-Billion Transistor Quad-Core Itanium Processor. IEEE J. of Solid-State Circuits 44(1), 18–31 (2009)
20. Degalahal, V., Ramanarayanan, R., Vijaykrishnan, N., Xie, Y., Irwin, M.J.: Effect of Power Optimizations on Soft Error Rate. In: IFIP Series on VLSI-SoC, pp. 1–20. Springer, Heidelberg (2006)
21. Oklobdzija, V.G., Stojanovic, V.M., Markovic, D.M., Nedovic, N.: Digital System Clocking: High Performance and Low-Power Aspects. Wiley-IEEE (2005)

Digital Timing Slack Monitors
and Their Specific Insertion Flow
for Adaptive Compensation of Variabilities

Bettina Rebaud[1,2], Marc Belleville[1], Edith Beigné[1], Christian Bernard[1],
Michel Robert[2], Philippe Maurine[2], and Nadine Azemard[2]

[1] CEA, LETI, MINATEC, F38054 Grenoble, France
{firstname.name}@cea.fr
[2] LIRMM-CNRS - Universite Montpellier II,
34392 Montpellier, France
{firstname.name}@lirmm.fr

Abstract. PVT information is mandatory to control specific knobs to compensate the variability effects. In this paper, we propose a new on-chip monitoring system and its associated integration flow, allowing timing failure anticipation in real-time, observing the timing slack of a pre-defined set of observable flip-flops. This system is made of specific structures located nearby the flip-flops, coupled with a detection window generator, embedded within the clock-tree. Validation and performances simulated in a 45 nm technology demonstrate a scalable, low power and low area, fine-grain system. The integration flow results exhibit the weak impact of the insertion of this monitoring system toward the large benefits of tuning the circuit at its optimum working point.

1 Introduction

In order to face PVTA (Process Voltage Temperature Aging) variability issues [1-3], and to reduce design margins due to traditional corner-based methodologies, it is possible to reach the optimal operating point of the manufactured chip and thus, get rid of over-pessimism, in using dynamic adaptation of the circuit performances. This solution requires tunable knobs like programmable supply voltages, body biasing or scalable frequencies. In order to efficiently tune those parameters, a monitoring system, providing a real time and accurate diagnostic of the circuit has to be implemented. Two monitoring means have been proposed: (a) integrating specific non-functional structures or sensors [4-7]. (Those sensors can be difficult to calibrate, and are only sensitive to global variations) and (b) monitoring directly the sampling elements of the chip (Latches or D-type Flip Flop) [8-12] to detect the occurrence of delay faults. Contrary to previous works, the second solution can detect local variations and is much easier to use due to simple binary output data. On the other hand, to obtain good circuit coverage, many sensors have to be inserted. Solutions [8-10] proposed in line with this approach, i.e. solutions aiming at monitoring the critical paths, have several drawbacks like (a) short paths management imposing buffer insertion, (b) need of a replay or correction systems when an error is detected, (c) high timing

J. Monteiro and R. van Leuken (Eds.): PATMOS 2009, LNCS 5953, pp. 266–275, 2010.

sensitivity to voltage or frequency scaling and process variations. [12] removes (a-b) disadvantages in suggesting anticipation before error occurrence. However, the propounded implementation does not fit well with frequency or voltage scaling.

Within this context, the contribution of this work is to propose a new monitoring system in line with critical paths monitoring concept, aiming at improving existing implementations and anticipating timing violations over a wide range of operating conditions. The proposed system monitors locally, at run time, on one or more slow paths, critical timing slacks and discloses their evolution with PVT variations or ageing phenomena. One key feature of the system consists in generating a detection window directly using the clock tree architecture to distribute it efficiently to several sensors.

The paper is organized as follows: Section 2 presents the whole monitoring system features, its insertion close to the flip-flops and the specific structures. In section 3, the specific integration flow is detailed, applied with specific constraints. The section 4 provides simulation results of the whole system, validating the monitoring concept proposed.

2 Monitoring System Proposal

The proposed monitoring system (Fig.1) is composed of two blocks, designed as standard cell library elements: a sensor (Fig. 3) and a specific Clock-tree Cell (CC) (Fig. 4). The sensor is inserted close to the D-type Flip-Flops (DFF) located at the endpoints of critical timing paths of the design while, the CC are inserted within the associated clock leafs. Different cells sizing is proposed within the library allowing, if necessary, fine timing tuning.

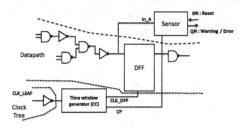

Fig. 1. Proposed monitoring system implemented on a critical path endpoint

As shown Fig.1 and 3, the sensor, acting as a stability checker, is directly connected to a data path output, i.e. to the DFF input. It also receives on one of its input the signal CP periodically provided by CC, which can drive several sensors. Edges of CP signal are in phase with those of the clock. The basic function of the sensor is to detect the occurrence of a full or partial transition of the signal In_A during the detection window (of duration Dpulse) positioned in time by the rising edge of CP as shown Fig. 2. More precisely, this detection window starts at (In-to-CP + CP-to-CLK_DFF) before the rising edge of the clock and ends at (In-to-CP + CP-to-CLK_DFF – Dpulse) due to some timing characteristics of both sensor and CC. A key point here is that (In-to-CP + CP-to-CLK_DFF - Dpulse) must be greater than, or at least equal to, the setup time (Tsetup) of the monitored DFF to detects timing warnings rather than timing errors. In-to-CP is a timing characteristic of the sensor due to its internal inverters [11], and CP-to-CLK_DFF the time interval separating the rising edges of CP and CLK_DFF.

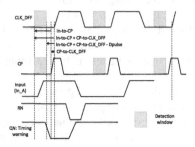

Fig. 2. Transition detection chronogram

If a transition occurs within the detection window, the monitor latches an error signal meaning that, during the last clock cycle, PVT conditions and the data processed by the monitored logic are such that the timing slack (before occurrence of a setup time violation) is lower than Tm = (In-to-CP + CP-to-CLK_DFF - Tsetup). Considering those timing characteristics, sensors are able to warn an imminent system timing failure by detecting the occurrence of a signal transition within the detection window.

To tackle the complexity of actual embedded systems, made of various functional blocks with different levels of timing criticality or working under different operating conditions (Vdd, multiple clock domains), several clock tree cells CC (Fig. 4) generating different time window widths Dpulse and thus, different guard margins Tm must be available in the specific standard cell library.

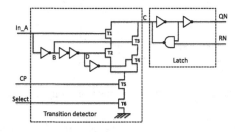

Fig. 3. This one-input sensor works with the load and the discharge of the C node. In order to reduce the area, several transition detectors can share the same latch. In this condition, C is bigger and the structure slower: trade-off has to be made.

Performance and system validation results obtained considering a 45nm Low Power technology are given in [11]. Those results demonstrate that the implemented structures are robust to power supply, frequency and temperature variations. More precisely, it is shown in [11] that:

- the 4-input sensor can detect the occurrence of transitions until 0.6V @ 125C in worst case process, and has low process induced delay variations.
- the clock cell CC provides reliable detection window(s) whatever the environmental conditions are.
- the system can achieve interesting timing margin reduction (w.r.t. to worst case timing conditions).

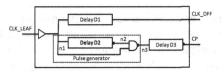

Fig. 4. Example of specific clock cell (CC) implementation

Sensor cells with 1 and up to 4 inputs and a programmable CC with W1 and W2 detection windows have been designed, layout drawn and characterized in 45nm Low Power technology, in order to create a new standard cell library. Sensors were characterized as DFF since their timing behavior is quite similar to that of DFF. The description of CC was done accordingly to the description of any clock buffer.

3 Integration Flow

In order to demonstrate the whole system efficiency, in terms of functionality and integration easiness, a test chip has been designed, and a dedicated digital flow has been studied (Fig. 5). Further details on test chip are given section 4. This section aims at describing this specific flow, and the new timing constraints that must be taken into account for a generic block.

As shown Fig.5, three steps are required to integrate the proposed monitoring system. In a first step, a prototype (a placed and routed design) is obtained in order to identify the critical paths to be monitored, and to get an accurate description of the

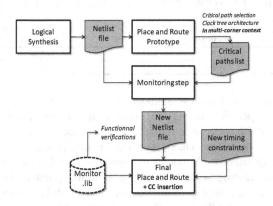

Fig. 5. Flow description to integrate the proposed monitoring system

clock tree. This step achieved, sensors and dummy cells are inserted in the netlist. Then, starting from the prototype results obtained from step 1, final place and route steps are performed, considering additional timing constraints related to CC and sensors insertion. In this last step, balancing the nets between DFF and their associated sensor is a key design guideline.

3.1 Critical Paths Choice

Getting an exhaustive coverage of our test chip is unrealistic as the numbers of sensors will double the occupied area and the power consumed by the sequential elements. Thus, some critical paths to be monitored have to be selected.

One possible solution is to use Statistical Static Timing Analysis [13-14]. SSTA is performed to identify the paths (assuming that these paths are correlated enough) with the highest probabilities of violating the setup time constraint. However, with the decreasing transistor length and the increasing impact of local and random variations, correlations between timing paths shrink, leading to a growing number of paths that have to be monitored to remain sure to detect warning signal before a failure.

Therefore, another selection policy was adopted since our goal was to prevent a system failure before the occurrence of any timing violation (no timing error is allowed in the system). Considering this constraint, our strategy is to impose specific target slack constraints during the synthesis and the place and route steps. More precisely, specific target slack constraints were chosen to create the set of pre-defined critical paths to be monitored. Specifically, we intentionally relax the target slack constraint of a set of critical paths. This set includes the worst critical path which has been identified during synthesis runs at worst case and tight timing constraints.

This results in a timing slack distribution characterized by two distinguishable sets of paths (illustration Table 1). A reduced set of paths characterized by a reduced timing slack forms the set of paths to be monitored, and a huge set of paths characterized by larger timing slacks, and more precisely by slacks 100 ps greater than the most critical path (which is in the first set of paths).

Table 1. Number of critical path endpoints with a delay value lower than that of the worst critical path by less than 100ps (synthesis step at worst timing corner 1,05V, 125°C)

	# critical paths In 100 ps from the WNS	Power (mW)/ Max Freq (ns)
Typical flow	3695	29/1,6
New flow	24	35/1,7

Such timing slack distribution is obtained thanks either to multi-mode capabilities of CAD tools or to specific relaxing tool commands. However, it is of prime importance to warrant that the paths to be monitored are representative of the circuit operating in any possible conditions. Thus a verification step is required in order to fulfill this condition, using either multi-corner or statistical simulations. This specific flow results in over-constraining some paths from a timing point of view that consists mainly in increasing the power consumption as shown Tab.1. However, the overhead is expected to be significantly lower than the gains achieved by applying adaptive voltage, body-biasing and frequency scaling techniques.

3.2   Monitoring Step and Specific Place and Route Constraints

The monitoring phase is performed after the true critical paths identification, in all operating conditions, before the final place and route step. As shown Fig.5, the monitoring phase aims at providing: (a) a new netlist file including dummy cells and sensors, as shown Fig. 6, and (b) a new timing constraints file to guide the place and route step. This step can be fully automated by developing specific scripts to ease the monitor integration. It is also possible to integrate some sensors such as they share several flip-flops; however this is highly dependent on the clock tree structure. As a result, 4 DFF sharing the same sensor has been found as a practical limit in our testcase.

Moreover, Clock Cells (CC) cannot be inserted during the monitoring phase since it would induce some setup and hold timing violations during functional verifications in locally modifying the clock skew. Furthermore, this specific point is highly critical if clock gating is applied to reduce the dynamic power consumption. As a result, the clock cell insertion is pushed to the next step.

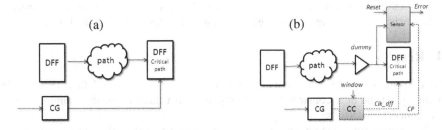

Fig. 6. Critical path before (a) and after (b) the monitoring step. Sensors are added with specific dummy cells allowing an easy place and route. Clock Cells are inserted later.

To ensure that no skew will appear between the event going to the sensor and the same one going to the DFF(s), and thus keep the Tm margin safe, specific timing constraints must fixed in the constraint file considered during the final place and route step. This timing specifications aim at constraining the timing driven place and route tool such as the timing fork between the DFF(s) and the related sensor remains well balanced. This can be done by imposing a specific timing constraint to the dummy cell driving the sensor and its associated DFF. Furthermore, additional hold time issues introduced by the CC detection window (when the window is still open after the rising clock edge) have also to be considered and fixed by adding some specific constraints in the timing constraint file. However, the reduced detection window width (compared to [8-10]) enables to insert a limited number of buffers in short paths.

3.3   Specific Clock Tree Cell Insertion

As the clock tree architecture may be highly sensitive to PVT variations, CC are inserted as close as possible to the monitoring path endpoint (Fig. 7) thanks to the additional timing constraints introduced at the monitoring phase. This method leads to

– reduce the impact of spatial correlations on the timings of the different monitoring elements.
– limit the impact of local voltage drops and temperature gradients on timings.
– reduce the impact on timings of interconnects variability.

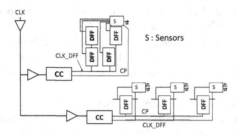

Fig. 7. Final clock tree architecture example with two CC driving 7 DFF and 4 sensors

As a result, Clock Cell insertion is performed at the Place and Route level, after a first clock tree synthesis (CTS). The insertion done, a second CTS is run in order to balance the tree, and minimize the global skew of the design before the final routing.

4 Results

This section describes the main results while using the dedicated flow (Fig. 5), by pointing out the new constraints efficiency and the validation of the monitoring system concept.

The monitoring system has been integrated in an arithmetic and reconfigurable block incorporating: 4 SRAMs, several register banks, and computing elements such as dividers or Multipliers-Accumulators (MAC). This block, inserted in a telecom SoC was considered as an ideal test case because of its timing criticality. Due to the complexity of the considered real time application, no replay of instruction sets was feasible at system level, and timing performances have to be high enough to satisfy a strained real time environment. Designed in 45nm STMicroelectronics Low Power technology, it contains about 13400 flip-flops, which leads to a 606*558 µm² core floorplan implementation. The timing constraint period is 1.5 ns with nominal process libraries, @ 25°C and 1,1V.

Critical path endpoint selection. Applying the specific flow on the placed and routed prototype, a set of 160 critical path endpoints, defining a set of critical paths, situated at the output of the first stage of the pipelined MAC, was isolated. The maximum operating frequency Fmax was characterized in nominal conditions. Values of 1.78 ns and 1.36 ns were estimated as the minimal periods allowing correct timing behaviors of respectively the typical and best endpoints among this set of critical path endpoints.

To reduce the number of endpoints to be monitored we ran a multi-corner analysis to refine our initial selection since the worst endpoint may differ from one PVT conditions to another. To select this reduced set of endpoints to be monitored, we analyzed successively the timing behaviors of the worst, the 10 worst and finally the 50 worst endpoints in nominal conditions (nom 1,1V 25C). Tab 2 gives the obtained simulation results.

The worst endpoint obtained in nominal conditions remains the worst one in most PVT conditions except when the worst case process and voltage corner are considered. Thus monitoring only this endpoint is proved to be deficient to cover the timing behavior of the whole circuit. Considering 10 worst endpoints in nominal corner rather than the worst one improves the results since at least 7 (i.e. 70%) of these endpoints remain among the 10 critical endpoints in all other PVT conditions. We therefore increased the number of considered critical endpoints successfully to 50. The results obtained were similar to the results obtained considering 10 worst endpoints: none of these subsets of endpoints are always the most critical in all PVT conditions.

Table 2. Selecting a reduced set of critical endpoints

	Number (and percentage (%)) of worst endpoints obtained in nominal conditions remaining among the n worst in other PVT conditions					
	Worst endpoint captured (yes or no)					
	bc 1,2V m40C	bc 1,2V 125C	nom 1,1V 25C	wc 1,05V 125C	wc 0,9V 125C	wc 0,9V m40C
The worst endpoint (n=1)	1 (100) yes	1 (100) yes	1 (100) yes	1 (100) yes	0 (0) no	0 (0) No
The 10 worst endpoints (n=10)	8 (80) yes	8 (80) yes	10 (100) yes	8 (80) yes	7 (70) yes	7 (70) Yes
The 25 worst endpoints (n=25)	22 (88) yes	21 (84) yes	25 (100) yes	23 (92) yes	22 (88) yes	22 (88) Yes
The 50 worst endpoints (n=50)	46 (92) yes	45 (90) yes	50 (100) yes	45 (90) yes	45 (88) yes	45 (88) Yes
max frequency (Mhz)	763	735	561	422	270	212
min period (ns)	1,31	1,36	1,78	2,37	3,7	4,7
Greatest Negative Slack obtained considering the 10 worst endpoints (ps)	56	68	60	100	150	190
Greatest Negative Slack obtained considering the 50 worst endpoints (ps)	98	106	164	219	205	297

However, we noticed that the worst endpoint at each considered PVT conditions was always in the sets of 10 and 50 worst endpoints obtained in nominal condition. We thus conclude that monitoring these 10 or 50 worst endpoints instead of 160 was a good warranty to monitor the worst endpoint for all considered PVT conditions (in Tab 2 a 'yes' means that the worst endpoint at the considered PVT conditions is in the n worst endpoint set defined in nominal conditions). We decided to monitor the 50 worst endpoints to cover a larger window of arrival times; as shown Tab 2 the greatest negative slack considering 50 endpoints is roughly 1.3 to 2.7 times larger than the slack obtained considering only 10 paths.

Clock tree architecture, monitoring and CC insertion. Analyzing the clock tree architecture is mandatory to know which standard CC cells have to be used and where they will be inserted. The first clock tree synthesis applied in our specific flow leads to a 15 level clock tree, with 1404 sub trees, monitoring 13400 flip-flops through 530 clock gating elements. The clock tree latency was about 1.19 ns in nominal corner condition, with a skew of 97 ps. These values are given at the end of the place and route prototype. Considering the endpoints to be monitored, the number of inserted sensors in our design was 19 (to monitor the 50 endpoints), with 11 CC (timing pulse 150 ps in nominal corner), with the design policy that close path endpoints are gathered on a same sensor with a limit of 4 paths by sensors, and that each clock cell must be inserted at the clock leaf. After the monitoring step and the second place and route phase (with two clock tree synthesis and new timing constraints), the final clock skew obtained in nominal case was 102 ps with a latency of 1.28 ns. Performing a two back-end run flow in identifying the critical paths during the first run did not imply enough classification changes which can modify the efficiency of the selected set. As a result, we may conclude that the whole monitoring flow is functional and efficient, since (a) the skew has not increased much, (b) the sensors and their related endpoint flip-flops are not physically distant of more than 4 μm (i.e. about 2 standard cell height) and (c) the critical path set is still applicable.

Table 3. FWi/Fmax ratio for a typical process corner

Temp/Power	W1 ratio				W2 ratio			
	0,9	1	1,1	1,2	0,9	1	1,1	1,2
-40	95	93.6	93.9	92.4	92.1	91,2	90,6	89,7
25	92.7	92.5	92.7	92.5	89.8	89,2	89,4	89,9
75	91.8	92.3	90.5	89.8	89.3	89	87,4	87,3
125	92.1	90.5	90.3	90	88.8	87,9	87,2	87,5

Behavior validation and performances. In order to check if the whole system remains functional, we extracted from simulation (a) the maximum operating frequency Fmax of the circuit at different PVT conditions (b) the maximum frequencies FW1 and FW2 at which the monitoring system does not flag any timing warnings or violations, considering respectively two different detection windows W1 and W2; W2 corresponding to the largest detection window. Table 2 gives the simulated results for FW1/Fmax and FW2/Fmax ratios at different VT conditions for a nominal process (other process corners demonstrate similar efficiency):

- FW1/Fmax and FW2/Fmax ratios remain lower than 100% meaning that the monitoring system operates correctly and warns an imminent timing failure, in every PVT conditions.
- Considering the global PVT conditions, the timing margins Tm(W1) and Tm(W2) remain respectively between 80/340 and 120/480 ps when the system operates correctly.

These results demonstrate the efficiency of the monitoring system in making it particularly interesting for adaptation: the circuit can work at roughly 90% of its maximal speed under all PVT conditions and the system is very attractive in nominal and best cases to crop margins or decrease consumption. It can also be favorable to integrate two different detection windows to control the timing margins with accuracy during the voltage scaling.

5 Conclusion

This paper describes a new *in situ* monitoring system, based on the insertion of sensors close to observable flip-flop endpoints, coupled with specific clock tree cells providing detection windows. This system prevents from timing violations rather than detecting an error. Valuable and simulated in a wide range of environmental conditions, this timing slack monitoring system, compact and with little impact on the overall power consumption, can thus be used together with knob-based adaptive solutions.

A dedicated flow based on a standard design flow was described, easing the insertion of the specific detection material and allowing a clear critical path endpoint choice to reduce the number of paths to be monitored. Simulation results demonstrate the efficiency of such a system and its easy integration, making it very attractive to work at the optimal PVT operating point for critical IP blocks in advanced technologies.

References

1. Narayanan, V., et al.: Proc. 18th ACM Great Lakes Symposium on VLSI, Orlando, Florida, USA (2008)
2. Lasbouygues, B., et al.: Temperature- and Voltage-Aware Timing Analysis. IEEE Trans. on CAD of Integrated Circuits and Systems 26(4), 801–815 (2007)
3. Parthasarathy, C., Bravaix, A., Guérin, C., Denais, M., Huard, V.: Design-In Reliability for 90-65nm CMOS Nodes Submitted to Hot-Carriers and NBTI Degradation. In: Azémard, N., Svensson, L. (eds.) PATMOS 2007. LNCS, vol. 4644, pp. 191–200. Springer, Heidelberg (2007)
4. Nourani, M., Radhakrishnan, A.: Testing On-Die Process Variation in Nanometer VLSI. IEEE Design & Test of Computers 23(6), 438–451 (2006)
5. Samaan, S.B.: Parameter Variation Probing Technique: US Patent 6535013 (2003)
6. Persun, M.: Method and apparatus for measuring relative, within-die leakage current and/or providing a temperature variation profile using a leakage inverter and ring oscillators: US Patent 7193427 (2007)
7. Drake, A., et al.: A Distributed Critical Path Timing Monitor for A 65nm High Performance Microprocessor. In: ISSCC, pp. 398–399 (2007)
8. Das, S., et al.: A Self-Tuning DVS Processor Using Delay-Error Detection and Correction. IEEE JSSC 41(4), 792–804 (2006)
9. Blaauw, D., et al.: Razor II: In situ error detection and correction for PVT and SER tolerance. In: ISSCC, pp. 400–401 (2008)
10. Bowman, K.A., et al.: Energy-Efficient and Metastability-Immune Timing-Error Detection and Instruction-Replay-Based Recovery Circuits for Dynamic-Variation Tolerance. In: ISSCC, pp. 402–623 (2008)
11. Rebaud, B., et al.: An Innovative Timing Slack Monitor for Variation Tolerant Circuits. In: ICICDT (2009)
12. Agarwal, M., et al.: Circuit Failure Prediction and Its Application to Transistor Aging. In: Proc. VLSI Test Symposium, pp. 277–286 (2007)
13. Migairou, V., Wilson, R., Engels, S., Wu, Z., Azemard, N., Maurine, P.: A Simple Statistical Timing Analysis Flow and Its Application to Timing Margin Evaluation. In: Azémard, N., Svensson, L. (eds.) PATMOS 2007. LNCS, vol. 4644, pp. 138–147. Springer, Heidelberg (2007)
14. Blaauw, D., et al.: Statistical timing analysis: From basic principles to state of the art. IEEE Trans. on CAD of Integrated Circuits and Systems 27(4), 589–607 (2008)

Quasi-Delay-Insensitive Computing Device: Methodological Aspects and Practical Implementation

Yuri Stepchenkov, Yuri Diachenko, Victor Zakharov,
Yuri Rogdestvenski, Nikolai Morozov, and Dmitri Stepchenkov

Institute of Informatics Problems, Russian Academy of Sciences, Vavilova 44,
build 2, Moscow, 119333 Russia
{YStepchenkov,YDiachenko,VZakharov,YRogdest,
NMorozov,DStepchenkov}@ipiran.ru

Abstract. The approaches to self-timed hardware design are presented. The conditions of intersystem integration of synchronous and self-timed devices are considered through the example of the quasi-delay-insensitive computing device development. This device performs functions of division and square root extraction. It operates with numbers of single and double precisions corresponding to the IEEE 754 standard.

Keywords: Self-timed, quasi-delay-insensitive, division, square root, Radix-2.

1 Introduction

Synchronous, asynchronous and quasi-delay-insensitive (QDI) methodologies are the alternative approaches to the digital hardware design [1]- [3]. Each of them has its advantages and shortages which determine their appropriate applications. At present QDI methodology is used not so widely as traditional synchronous and asynchronous ones due to some reasons, such as relatively higher labor-intensiveness for the design of QDI-circuits and some hardware superfluity.

But it also provides such features as enlargement of the capacity for work area in the range of changing voltage and environment temperature and also stable operation despite any finite delays in elements. This allows them to operate when voltage and environmental conditions are close to the boundary, determined by physical properties of semiconductor active elements [4, 5] - transistors, if this is not critical in respect to the device performance. QDI circuits are correctly operating with the *maximal* possible for current conditions performance. At the same time for a correct operation of synchronized devices, the period of clock signal is chosen taking into account *the worst case* - maximal possible time for the elements switching under unfavorable conditions (supply voltage, temperature, etc.). Thus the price of the correct operation for S-devices is the underexploitation of its abilities regarding performance, compared with a realistically possible one provided by QDI methodology.

J. Monteiro and R. van Leuken (Eds.): PATMOS 2009, LNCS 5953, pp. 276–285, 2010.

The increase in the hardware outlays (number of transistors in the circuit) is especially evident during the implementation of combinative units, but it is graded by the absence of a synchronization circuit and in some practical cases proved to be insignificant (for example, during implementation of sequential devices) [4]. Besides the obtained enlargement of the capacity for work area (at first in voltage) compensates the circuit complication in devices designated for work with a restricted power supply. Modern problems of VLSI-systems design can be more efficiently solved by moving to the synchronous-self-timed style. This style combines the advantages of all three methodologies of digital hardware design.

This paper presents the results of the development of a QDI-device which performs functions of division and square root extraction. It operates with numbers of single and double precision corresponding to the IEEE 754 standard [6]. The calculations are implemented with respect to the standard but with some simplifications:

- only normalized operands arrive to the input of the computing device;
- the result is also a normalized number;
- in case the result cannot be represented as a normalized number, an exceptional situation takes place.

According to the IEEE 754 standard operands are represented as floating point numbers and consist of sign bit, exponent area and mantissa area. The main complexity consists in calculation of the result's mantissa. Later, with the calculation result, we will average its mantissa calculation.

At present, many algorithms for calculating the results of division and square root extractions are known [7]- [13]. But not all of them are suitable for efficient usage of ST-schematics. The proposed computing device provides optimal balance of performance and hardware expenditures with saving all advantages of QDI-circuits.

2   Methodological Aspects

The feature of QDI-circuits - request-acknowledge interaction between blocks, adjacent in the line of information processing - makes multistage implementation of any computational algorithm the most efficient, when the control is transferred from the previous stage to the next one asynchronously, according to the real performance of each stage. The most efficient advantages of QDI-devices is that they show their worth in case of pipeline implementation, and the number of stages in the pipeline should be no less than three. This is determined by the order of QDI-devices operation [3]:

- the presence of two operating phases in each QDI-device: working (active) and spacer (pause);
- the usage of request-acknowledge interactions between adjacent devices in the data processing pipeline.

The first condition is necessary for the successful implementation of absolute control on the termination of transition processes in each device - stage of pipeline. The second condition provides the strict sequence of switches for the adjacent pipeline stages, guarantees trustworthiness of data for the input of each stage at any moment and capacity for work of QDI-circuit with any finite delays of the elements included in the circuit.

According to the principles of self-timing, a QDI-device cannot start switching to the next phase until the previous device reaches a similar phase, and until the next device reaches the opposite phase of operation. The more stages in the pipeline, the less total unproductive time spent when each device in the joint system is standing idle waiting for permission from the adjacent devices to move to the next phase of work. Practically such interaction is implemented by means of hysteretic triggers [3] or C-elements, inputs for them are indication outputs of the previous and next devices, which prove the termination of a corresponding device transition into the next phase of operation.

Taking into account features of pipeline stages operation and QDI-basis for their implementation it is possible to use input control signals as inputs of indicators. Fig.1 illustrates the scheme of interaction of three adjacent stages in QDI-pipeline of the described computing device. The connecting element is C-element. Enable input (E), providing change of operating phases of QDI-device in the i-th stage, is forming by C-element basing on indicative output (I) of the next (i+1)-st stage and control signal from the previous stage. Indicative output I proves the termination of the stage switch to the corresponding operating phase. As the result the strict sequence of adjacent stages switches is provided. In this point the proposed solution differs from similar implementations [12]-[13], where the control signal of the i-th stage ($Reset$) is formed only basing on information about termination of switch to the current operation phase from the next stage. In case of some definite delays of the circuit elements in the different stages such discipline can lead to the wrong operation of the device, for example in the following hypothetic situation: i-th stage terminated switch to the working phase, formed data signals for the (i+1)-st stage and signal $Reset_i$ for (i-1)-st stage, which quickly switches to the spacer phase and then to the working phase, renewing data signals at the inputs of i-th stage. If to that time (i+1)-st stage will not be able to form control signal $Reset_{i+1}$, for the i-th stage, then the data at the output of the i-th stage will be changed, and that can result in the calculation error on (i+1)-st stage. The proposed implementation is free from such shortcoming.

The number of stages in the pipeline implementation of the algorithm can be arbitrary but a theoretical analysis shows [12] that the optimal (in respect to performance) number of stages in such an algorithm is equal to 4 or 5.

In QDI-circuits it is necessary to indicate the termination of each element switch to catch timely the appearance of a fault in the circuit and stop calculations. But practical implementation of the full-scale indication leads to the big overheads - up to 50% of the circuit own complexity. That is why in practice it is usually used the principle "of the expected delays relation for the elements

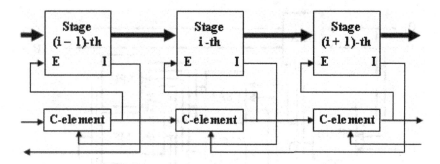

Fig. 1. Arrangement of request-acknowledge interaction between stages of computing device

fabricated on one chip". And only one requirement remains unchanged - implementation of request-acknowledge interaction between adjacent blocks.

The most fast-acting algorithms of division and square root extraction are based on multiplication (for example, the Newton-Raphson method [8]) or on table methods [7]. But they require usage of a multiplier or rather large volumes of ROM, which in the implementation of QDI-circuitry leads to considerable hardware expenditures.

This is why we chose an irretrievable algorithm of division SRT Radix-2 [12, 13] as the basic one. It allows combining functions of division and square root extraction in one unit with minimal additional expenditures.

The QDI-property is brought to the algorithm by the paraphase discipline of all data signals coding, indicating moments of termination of all transition processes and the arrangement of the request-acknowledge interaction between adjacent blocks in a computing device. Similar facilities have been just used in projects [12, 13]. But they did not meet the requirements of QDI methodology; when used, their circuits of request-acknowledge interaction are not figured on the possibility of wide dispersion in the delays of the same type elements due to the degradation of active structure parameters or due to the local deviation of technological parameters.

3   Flow Chart of the Computing Device

Based on the given overall dimension restrictions and requirements to the performance of the computing device we chose the four-stage pipelined variant of its implementation. A flow chart of each stage is presented in Fig. 2.

The stage contains the following main blocks:

- block of the result accumulation (BRA);
- multiplexer of subtrahend in recurrent formula (MSUB);
- Carry-Saved Adders (CSA1, CSA2);
- selector of partial result (SPR);

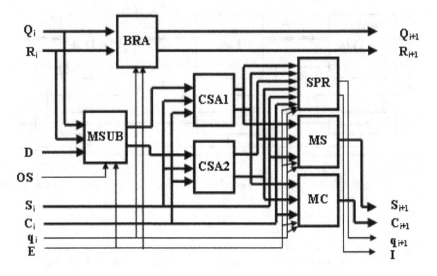

Fig. 2. Flow chart of one stage

- multiplexer of sum (MS);
- multiplexer of carrying (MC).

General flow chart of computing device is represented in Fig. 3. Besides four similar stages ST1 - ST4 it contains also blocks:

- input register of operands and features of operation (IR);
- input multiplexer of operands (MO);
- indication circuit (IC) with control circuit (CC);
- circuit of exponents processing (CEP);
- block of mantissa post processing (PP);
- output register of the result (OR).

Dimensions of operands in Fig. 3 correspond to the asynchronous variant of a computing device implementation. For QDI-variant the dimensions of the external signals remain unchanged as this computing device is designated for work with synchronous environment. The dimensions of the internal buses are increased twice due to the paraphase presentation of the information signals [3]. That allows encoding two working and one space phase for each information signal. Spacer can be zero (00) or one (11). In our device only zero spacer is used for all paraphase signals.

Blocks IR and OR are implementing an asynchronous interface with a synchronous environment. The input signal *Start* is used for the synchronization of writing input data to IR. After termination of forming the result and writing it to OR the ready flag *End* is raised, indicating an availability of the result for synchronous environment.

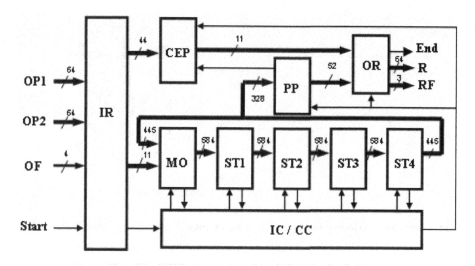

Fig. 3. Flow chart of the computing device

4 Practical Implementation of the Computing Device

One of the problems of multistage calculations is the saving of intermediate result. In synchronous implementations it is traditionally solved using registers separating adjacent stages. In QDI-circuits the problem of intermediate result saving can be solved by using elements with memory. In such case it is efficient to use for the computing device implementation the elements with dynamical logic [12]. Paraphase discipline of information signals simplifies the transition of such elements to the spacer and protects from the appearance on the output false shorttime working states while switching to the working phase.

To implement the divider we used the library of standard elements of Artisan company [14]. It was necessary to additionally design 27 pseudo-dynamic elements, which provide saving of intermediate data, forming of paraphase data signals and simplify indication. The example of pseudo-dynamic element implementing function of the multiplexor 2:1 is presented in Fig. 4(a).

It has paraphase data inputs $\{A, AB\}$, $\{B, BB\}$, inphase select signals EA and EB, inphase control signal E and paraphase output $\{Y, YB\}$. A transition to spacer $\{00\}$ is provided by arriving control signal $E=0$. Weak transistors WT0 and WT1 support spacer state at outputs after rising control signal $(E=1)$, until working combination will arrive to the data inputs and select inputs. Saving of the working state at the outputs is not supported but it corresponds to the zero potential at the inputs of invertors forming multiplexor's outputs and due to the parasitic capacitances can be saved for a rather long time.

Similarly the circuits of other pseudo-dynamic elements are constructed. The usage of control signal E essentially accelerates transition of such element to the spacer state. But in case of multiple-order architecture of computing device they are heavily loaded and require powerful drivers. That is why in some library

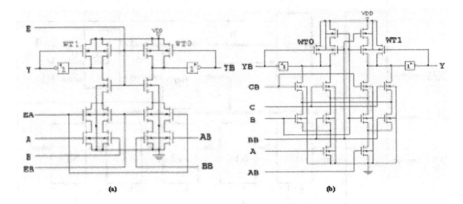

Fig. 4. Schematic diagrams of pseudo-dynamic multiplexor 2:1 (a) and XOR3M (b)

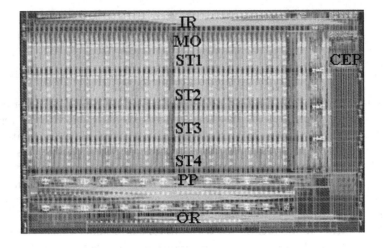

Fig. 5. Topological implementation of computing device

elements, which do not require the alignment of the execution time of similar elements in multiple-order architecture of a computing device, the pseudo-dynamic elements have been used, in which the transition to spacer is implemented by the combination of some input data signals as in XOR3M (see Fig. 4(b)).

QDI computing device have been implemented within test chip with standard 0.18μm CMOS-technology with 6 metal layers [14]. In the result of thorough manual topological design in CAD CADENCE, the block of the divider is formed in a rectangle with an area of 0.33 mm^2 and a ratio of sides 1.4:1 (Fig. 5) that satisfies required specification.

In the Table we represent the averaged data at the time of execution for the operations of division and square root extraction with single and double precision for simulating limited random set of operands and rounding modes. Nevertheless,

Table 1. Result of simulation with Ultrasim

NN	Conditions of simulating, Udd, T°C	Division, ns		Square root, ns	
		single	double	single	double
1	1.98 V, - 60°C, best	20.6	34.7	22.0	36.9
2	1.8 V, + 25°C, typical	28.7	46.7	30.4	49.1
3	1.62 V, + 125°C, worst	38.9	63.9	40.0	70.3
4	0.9 V, + 125°C	139	219	125	199
5	0.8 V, + 125°C	185	300	172	276
6	0.7 V, + 125°C	290	480	265	422
7	0.6 V, + 125°C	536	858	491	775
8	0.5 V, + 125°C	1293	2100	1209	1893
9	0.4 V, + 125°C	4656	7682	4325	6940
10	0.35 V, + 125°C	12920	21705	9142	14440

all complicated cases of the rounding according to the requirements of the IEEE 754 standard, found themselves in this set.

The data in the Table confirms that the times of execution by the computing devices of both operations practically coincide (about 50 ns for typical conditions). It can be seen from the Table that the performance of the computing device within the required specification varies in a wide range. Besides, the computing device, as each QDI-device, is characterized by the steady capacity for work in case of reduced voltage, for example, while falling battery voltage lower than acceptable norms (see lines 4 - 10 of the table).

For those applications where the decisive factor is the keeping capacity for work even owing to the essential falling of the performance, usage QDI-devices becomes of current importance. The results of the computing device measurements within test chip confirmed data obtained while simulating.

Within the test chip, three 64-bit homogeneous devices have been implemented, the described multistage QDI-variant and two synchronous variants. The comparative results of all three variants of computing device testing are presented in Fig. 6.

Presented results regarding performance are obtained for the following conditions:

- the probability of the execution of division and square root extraction operations with single and double precision are the same;
- the number of operations executed in the "best" conditions - 25%, in "typical" conditions - 50%, in "worst" conditions - 25%;
- the set of operands is statistically significant.

At present we are developing the completely QDI-variant of a computing device. In it we obey all principles of QDI-circuits design, which provide the real independence on the elements delay in any conditions of device exploitation and all advantages of QDI-circuits in full volume.

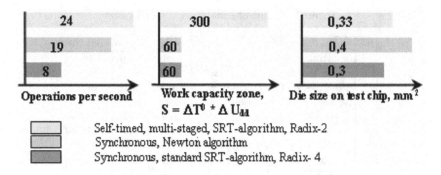

Fig. 6. Results of testing different variants of computing device implementation

5   Summary

The development of QDI computing device for division and square root extraction is demonstrated:

- using the methodology of QDI-circuit design allows obtaining viable and efficient solutions even for a mainly combinative device such as a divider, though traditionally combinational circuits are the least "convenient" for implementation with an QDI-basis;
- the efficient solution of computing devices with QDI-circuits basis is possible only on the base of pipeline organization of a computational path; in our case - using four the same stages, each of them calculates one bit of the result;
- proposed implementation provides the same performance while execution of both operations - division and square root extraction;
- complex comparative parameters: for performance and zone of capacity for work and area occupied on the chip, the presented QDI-variant of the computing device exceeds synchronous analogues.

References

[1] Varshavsky, V.: Time, Timing and Clock in Massively Parallel Computing Systems. In: Proceedings of International Conference Massively Parallel Computing Systems, Colorado Springs, USA, Special Session 2, April 6-9 (1998)
[2] Beerel, P., Cortadella, J., Kondratyev, A.: Bridging the gap between asynchronous design and designers (Tutorial). In: VLSI Design Conference, Mumbai (2004)
[3] Varshavsky, V., Kishinevsky, M., Marakhovsky, V., et al.: Automata Control of Concurrent Processes. In: Varshavsky, V. (ed.) Computers and Discrete Systems, Moscow, Nauka, p. 398 (1986) (in Russian); (English Translation - Self-Timed Control of Concurrent Processes, 428 p. Kluwer Academic Publishes Groop, Dordrecht (1990))
[4] Sokolov, I.A., Stepchenkov, Y.A., Petrukhin, V.S., Djachenko, Y.G., Zakharov, V.N.: Self-Timed Circuitry - Perspective Method of Hardware Development. High Availability Systems 3(1-2), 61–72 (2007)

[5] Plechanov, L., Stepchenkov, Y.: Experimental test of some features of strictly self-synchronized electronic circuits. Annual The Systems and Means of Informatics (16), 445–452 (2006) (in Russian)

[6] IEEE Standard for Binary Floating-Point Arithmetic./IEEE Std. 754. New York ANSI-1985, August

[7] McQuillan, S.E., McCanny, J.V.: Fast VLSI algorithms for division and square root. J. VLSI Signal Processing 8, 151–168 (1994)

[8] Montuschi, P., Ciminiera, L., Guistina, A.: Division unit with Newton-Raphson approximation and digit-by-digit refinement of the quotient. In: IEEE Proceedings: Computers and Digital Techniques, vol. 141, pp. 317–324 (1994)

[9] Lang, T., Montuschi, P.: Very-high radix combined division and square root with prescaling and selection by rounding. In: Proceedings of the 12th IEEE Symposium on Computer Arithmetic, July 1995, pp. 124–131 (1995)

[10] Arjun Prabhu, J., Zyner, G.B.: 167 MHz Radix-8 Divide and Square Root Using Overlapped Radix-2 Stages. In: Proceedings of the 12th Symposium on Computer Arithmetic, pp. 155–162 (1995)

[11] Ajay, N., Atul, D., Warren, J., Debjit, D.S.: 1-GHz HAL SPARC64 Dual Floating Point Unit with RAS Features. In: Proceedings of the 15th IEEE Symposium on Computer Arithmetic (2001)

[12] Williams, T.E., Horowitz, M.A.: A Zero-Overhead Self-Timed 160-ns 54-b CMOS Divider. IEEE Journal of Solid-State Circuits 26(11), 1651–1661 (1991)

[13] Matsubara, G., Ide, N., Tago, H., Suzuki, S., Goto, N.: 30-m 55-b Shared Radix 2 Division and Square Root Using a Self-Timed Circuit. In: Proceedings of the 12th Symposium on Computer Arithmetic, pp. 98–105 (1995)

[14] Chartered Semiconductor 0.18m IB Process 1.8-Volt SAGE-XTM. Standard Cell Library Databook / Artisan Components, Release 1.0 (February 2003)

The Magic Rule of Tiles: Virtual Delay Insensitivity

Delong Shang, Fei Xia, Stanislavs Golubcovs, and Alex Yakovlev

Microelectronic System Design Group, School of EECE, Newcastle University
Newcastle upon Tyne, NE1 7RU, England, United Kingdom
{delong.shang,fei.xia,stanislavs.golubcovs,
alex.yakovlev}@ncl.ac.uk

Abstract. Delay-insensitivity is a theoretically attractive design principle which helps circuits to be resistant to process variations, particularly exhibiting themselves at the system level as delay variations. Unfortunately, delay insensitive (DI) design is impractical for most real systems. Speed independent (SI) design is often used in practice as a *next best* approach. With the scaling of wires becoming more and more difficult compared with logic gates at current and future technology nodes, SI systems are becoming less acceptable as "approximates" for DI systems. This paper proposes an approach based on decomposing complex systems into simple, manageable blocks which can be safely rendered in an SI manner. These blocks are then connected using interconnects which satisfy DI requirements to obtain "virtual DI" behaviour at system level. We demonstrate this approach with a tile-based implementation of a multi-access arbiter.

1 Introduction

VLSI technology scaling has enabled a wide spectrum of applications ranging from high-performance computers to low-power portable devices. The continuation of this scaling process is vital to the future development of the digital industries. The International Technology Roadmap for Semiconductors (ITRS) [1] predicts poorer scaling for wires than transistors in future technology nodes.

The ITRS also predicts that asynchrony will increase with the complexity of on-chip systems. The power, design effort, and reliability cost of global clocks will also make increased asynchrony more attractive. Increasingly complex asynchronous systems or subsystems will thus become more prevalent in future VLSI systems.

The most theoretically sound self-timed or asynchronous systems are DI systems whose operational correctness is not sensitive to the delays of *both* gates *and* wires. Unfortunately, DI design is impractical in most realistic situations, e.g. when circuits are built from standard logic cells [2]. As an approximation to DI, SI design tries to achieve insensitivity to delays across gates, but ignores delays on wires between gates. This method has been widely used with the assumption that wire delays are insignificant compare to gate delays. This is especially relevant in systems of reasonably limited size within which the wire delays can be easily managed through technology and layout awareness. With poorer scaling for wires than transistors (gates) and the increasing size of asynchronous blocks, this kind of assumption is more and more difficult to sustain, thus making SI design less applicable.

J. Monteiro and R. van Leuken (Eds.): PATMOS 2009, LNCS 5953, pp. 286–296, 2010.

With aggressive scaling, logic and interconnects at nanometre-scale are increasingly vulnerable to manufacturing defects, process variability and lifetime degradation [3,4].Impacts of process variation in nanometre CMOS can be divided into three classes, timing, power, and function [3]. In this paper, we only focus on timing variation. Asynchronous techniques have been proposed as a potential solution to the timing problems caused by variations. Intuitively, if these problems caused by aggressive scaling mostly manifest as delay faults, a fully DI system would be completely immune to them naturally. However, an asynchronous design based on an approximation of DI would have reduced tolerance of these faults. The worse the quality of approximation is, the worse the fault tolerance would be.

In this paper we propose a design approach which aims to approximate DI across complex systems of substantial sizes whilst restricting actual system design effort to SI subsystems of small, manageable and safe sizes. This approach advocates the exploitation of regularity, wherever possible of course, so that the eventual system can be based on SI tiles of a limited number of types to reduce the effort of overall system design. By showing the prominent role of the tiling approach, our work for the first time considers the problem of converting SI to DI in the structural domain. It nicely complements the efforts of earlier work [5], which operated in the behavioural domain, where it introduced appropriate transformations (from SI to DI) in the Signal Transition Graph (STG) specifications of control logic blocks.

The rest of this paper is organized as follows: Section 1.1 describes the overall design concept and highlights the problems such a design approach faces. Sections 2 to 4 demonstrate this approach through the design of the central part of a multi-access arbiter, whose simulation verification is described in Section 5. Section 6 gives concluding remarks and lays out our plans for future work.

1.1 Concept of Design Approach

It is not difficult to produce SI designs of small manageable sizes with "virtual DI" behaviour in practical operating conditions. Based on such "SI in the small", we propose this design approach aimed at producing "virtual DI in the large" (Figure 1):

1. Decompose system function into simpler sub-functions implementable with SI blocks, taking care to promote the use of regularity in the decomposition.
2. Derive logic blocks implementing these sub-functions with an SI design process. Regularity in the decomposition in the previous step will help create a design based on tiles of a small number of different types.
3. Connect the SI blocks according to the decomposition information from the first step, making sure that this connecting logic is overall DI between the SI blocks.

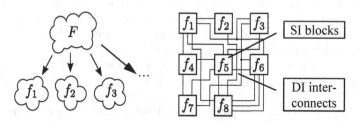

Fig. 1. System decomposition into SI blocks

The main difficulties for this approach are with steps 1 and 3. In the following sections we will try to address some of these concerns using a practical system design example. In the chosen example, the functional decomposition can have very high regularity and the resulting blocks are heavily interconnected. These points help demonstrate the principle of tile-based design exploiting regularity and the techniques of achieving DI across very large numbers of inter-block connections.

The main benefit of this approach is that, by delivering "virtual DI", it allows the designer to take advantage of the inherent resistance to process variations of SI and DI at a much larger scale than before. Our techniques will provide simple and low-cost solutions to the timing closure problems that arise from the poor scaling of wires.

2 Multi-access Arbiters

In complex on-chip systems with multiple computational nodes, there often exists a need to share multiple resources among multiple clients. For this a multi-access arbiter of the general shape shown in Figure 2 would be of good use [6]. Such arbiters need to be implemented in hardware to improve performance and power consumption.

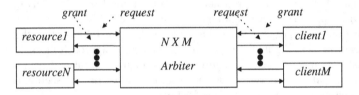

Fig. 2. Synopsis of an arbiter (from [6])

Communications with the arbiter are through request/acknowledgement signal pairs. Regardless of whether the two- or four-phase protocol is used [7] every client needs a way of telling when it needs a resource, and every resource also needs some way of telling when it becomes available for clients. The request part of both resource and client channels can provide additional information, which can be used by the arbiter and can influence its behaviour. For example, these requests can hold information about the priority or the 'quality' of the resource, which may affect arbiter decision among several available grant scenarios.

So far, the majority of existing arbiters assume passive resources where every resource is always available when not used by any of the clients. We consider the general case where resources are active members, similar to clients. The knowledge of a resource's availability is specified explicitly by its request. This allows a resource to not become available immediately after its previous client finishes using it, if it requires a non-specific period of time to become ready again. It also allows any solutions to be readily extendable to non client-resource cases.

Recently, a solution for the active multi-resource arbiter was presented in [8]. The solution uses a regular 2D mesh architecture and it seems easy to build an N×M arbiter based on the method. However, with a large number of clients and resources, the circuit will have big *fan-in/fan-out* problems which will invalidate any DI assumptions.

Here we will use the virtual DI method to derive a true tile-based, scalable solution for the multi-access arbiter and test its variation tolerance with simulations.

3 N×M Arbiter Architecture

The architecture of N×M arbiters proposed in [8] is described in Figure 3. This consists of mutual exclusive arrays whose function is to make sure that at any time no more than one client request and one resource request can be considered by the central computation unit for client-resource pairing.

The N/M-way mutual exclusive (ME) arrays can be implemented in many ways. A simple example 4-input ME is shown in the left hand side of Figure 4. It is assembled from 2-input ME elements. Multi-way ME's following tree, ring, and mesh topologies have been published in the past [7].

The pairing logic consists of a matrix of SI blocks. The block on the ijth pairing junction is shown in Figure 4 (right hand side). The asymmetric C element has N+M inputs and generates an intermediate signal hij. Two inputs Cjg and Rig, from the ME arrays, correspond to the jth client and ith resource. The others are from the *neighbours* of the ijth pairing, all the other pairings

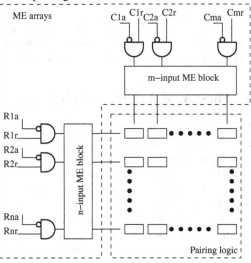

Fig. 3. Block diagram of N×M arbiters

in the ith row and the jth column. The intermediate signal hij, the signals Cjr and Rir are passed by the right C element to generate the final Hij pairing signal.

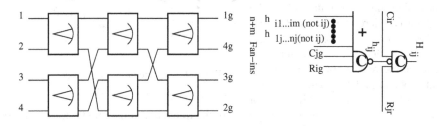

Fig. 4. 4-input arbiter and one so called "tile" for pairing ij

The signals from the neighbours are used to block the Hij signal if an Hxj or Hiy pairing signal in the same row or same column as the ijth pairing has already been generated. Since the ME arrays may be freed at different times in DI behaviour, an old request from one side (which has already achieved a pairing) and a new request from the other could exist simultaneously for a short while. They could erroneously pair in one of the conflicting pairings. This race condition between old and new grant signals on Cjg and Rig (j=0,..,M-1; i=0,..N-1) is eliminated by the disabling (blocking) signal coming from one of the internal pairings, which disables wrong pairings and ensures circuit speed independence (SI).

However, the complexity of such an SI block increases with the numbers N and M. The fan-in/fan-out problem and the large number of long inter-block wires for large N and/or M make it difficult to approximate DI, both within and across blocks. The block circuit also changes with N and M, giving poor scalability.

For good scalability, the blocks need to be true tiles whose internal circuit and interfaces do not change with the size of the tile array. For good approximation of DI within tiles, the SI tile circuit and interfaces need to be simple and well designed. For good approximation of DI across tiles, the inter-tile connections should remain few, simple, without isochronous forks and constant when the size of the matrix changes.

4 Tile-Based Arbiter Solution

In general, small circuits have good tolerance for processing variation. This is because a small circuit can be implemented in a certain small area. This makes it easier to manage the timing variation during circuit design, layout, etc.

Following the approach proposed in Section 1.1, two techniques are used here: 1) decomposition makes each tile small, and 2) maximally SI circuits inside tiles and DI circuits between tiles address variable delays in both gates and wires.

The attempt at decomposition in [8] was based on the natural regularity in the task of pairing individual members of two vectors. However it resulted in the fan-in/fan-out problem indicating poor exploitation of this regularity. Here we use a Petri net (PN) [9] model of the pairing logic, part of which is shown in Figure 5, to analyze the reasons of the fan-in/fan-out problem and find a solution. The figure shows a resource ME array on

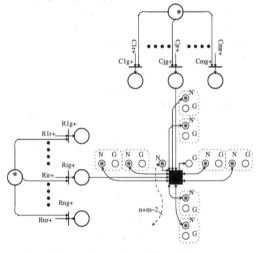

Fig. 5. Part of the arbiter PN model

the left hand side, a client ME array on top, the transition in the middle for the ijth tile and some (N,G) Boolean place pairs (each pair for one tile). These N,G places represent the grant status of the corresponding tile. N indicates no grant and G indicates grant.

The central transition and the N and G places next to it model the same (ijth) tile. The (N,G) pair is connected to the other N+M-2 tiles in its row and column as shown in the figure. The transition firing represents the Hij grant signal being generated, the token in the ijth N place will be moved to the ijth G place, and the tokens in the other N places are referenced through listening arcs. If logic synthesis methods are directly applied on this model, the ijth tile will have one input for each of the transition's input arcs and one output for each of its output arcs. Adding a row or column to this matrix will result in the addition of two extra control signals to each existing tile. This is where the fan-in/fan-out problem comes from.

However, in the matrix architecture, all these (N,G) places are in either the same row or the same column as the ijth tile. This means we can use two group blocking signals to replace all the individual blocking signals. In this case, one is used for the whole ith row and the other for the whole jth column.

An STG [10] specification for generating the Hij grant signal is shown in Figure 6. The part outside the dashed box is the specification of the environment of the corresponding client and resource requests. Here "no blocking at the ith row" and "no blocking at the jth column" are used to replace all N places at the ith row and the jth column, and "blocking (ith row)" and "blocking (jth column)" replace all G places.

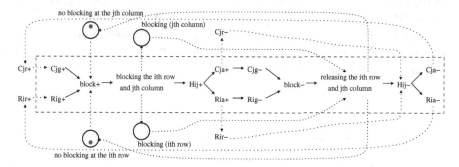

Fig. 6. STG specification of each tile with its environment

This STG specification can be used as input to the Petrify toolkit [11]. However, the generated circuits will not be tile-based. Although all tile-based information is included in this specification, the Petrify toolkit does not support tile-based designs and in any case have poor exploitation of regularity.

We propose to use the following design method to implement such tile circuits:
For each type of tile (usually there is only one type of pairing tile in such arbiters)

1. Derive the pure H pairing specification of the tile by removing inter-tile links;
2. Derive the interface specification of the connections between the pure pairing part of a tile and other tiles;
3. Synthesize the pure pairing part of a tile based on the pure pairing specification using existing toolkits such as Petrify to obtain SI circuits;
4. Design the interface, taking care to achieve virtual DI;
5. Assemble the two parts to obtain complete tiles with interfaces.

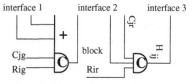

Fig. 7. H tile top-level design

The circuits so obtained, shown in Figure 7, are similar to the circuits from previous work in the right hand side of Figure 4. However the fan-in/fan-out problem is removed. In the circuits in Figure 7, three interfaces are introduced.

Interface 1 is connected to the block signals from other tiles in the ith row and the jth column, in accordance to the specification in Figure 6. The left hand side asymmetric C element is used to generate the *block* signal, used to block the other tiles in the same (ith) row and same (jth) column. The *block* signal is connected to interface 2 which connects to the interface 1's of the other ith row and jth column tiles. According to the specification, only after all other tiles in the ith row and the jth column have been completely blocked, indicated by the confirmation signal coming back from interface 2, the pairing signal Hij can be generated. The right hand side C element is used for this purpose. Hij is connected to interface 3 to generate the acknowledgement signals for the corresponding client and resource requests.

After decomposition and replacing the individual blocking signals, the next step is to design the interfaces. As noted before, at any time, no more than one H grant signal can exist. We can therefore simplify the interfaces by combining the interfaces 1 and 2 of the tiles in a row or column into a single interface using a loop consisting of a series of OR gates. The blocking signal being propagated back through the loop indicates the successful blocking of the entire row or column. The loop, however, forms a memory. So a blocking signal is registered in the loop and will need specific "unblocking" after Hij has been generated.

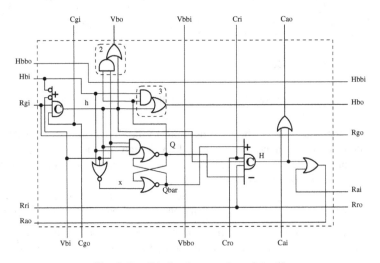

Fig. 8. Possible implementation of the tile

Our solution is to use a loop plus simple control circuits. The solution is shown in Figure 8, and an example of assembled tiles is shown in Figure 9.

The request and grant signals are connected to the first corresponding tile and then propagated to the other tiles in the same row and column. For example, the ith Rr is connected to the Rri pin of the ith tile in the first column and then propagated through Rro to the next tile (the ith tile in the second column). The acknowledgement signals are propagated through the (Cai, Cao) and (Rai, Rao) pairs for client and resource requests respectively. The Rai pins of the tiles at the far right end are connected to logic 0 and so do the Cai pins of the tiles at the bottom. The Hbi, Hbo, Hbbi, Hbbo at the same row form a loop and so do Vbi, Vbo Vbbi, Vbbo at the same column. Figure 9 shows how the run-through Vbbi/o and Hbbi/o signals are used to close the loops across the matrix in a torus fashion.

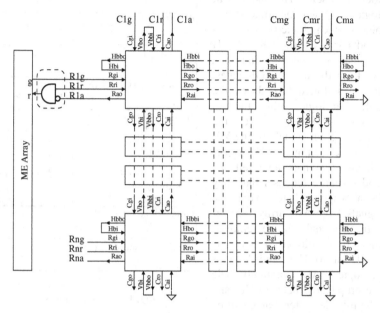

Fig. 9. Block diagram of a 2D tile matrix

The STG specification shown in Figure 10 can help understand how the circuits work. Here we only explain the loop and its control circuits.

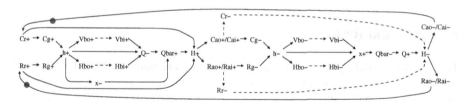

Fig. 10. A complete STG specification of a tile

In order to provide proper reset (unblocking), we use AND-OR gates such as gates 2 and 3 shown in Figure 8 instead of pure OR gates to form a loop for each row and column. An SR flip-flop and some simple logic form the blocking controller for each tile. Initially Q and Qbar are set to logic 1 and 0 respectively, and both Vbi and Hbi are set to logic 0 (not blocking at both row and column). Once Rir and Cjr are granted, if both Hbi and Vbi in the ijth tile are logic 0, the intermediate h signal is generated. The h signal is propagated to Hbo and Vbo through gates 2 and 3. Hbo and Vbo are connected to Hbi and Vbi of the next tiles in the same row and column respectively. As Q is logic 1 in the other tiles, the blocking signal will be propagated, eventually back through Hbi and Vbi of the ijth tile. This indicates that the entire ith row and jth column have been blocked. When h, Hbi and Vbi all go to logic 1, Q will be logic 0 and Qbar logic 1 as x is logic 0. After that as Rir and Cjr are still valid, the H pairing signal is generated and then propagated out through the OR gates. In Figure 9, a dotted box shows the quick releasing logic. When the acknowledgement signals arrive, the corresponding grant signals of the ME arrays will be removed. These acknowledgement signals also tell the client and resource requests that they have been responded to. After the grant signals from ME arrays are removed, the h signal will be removed and logic 0 (unblocking) will be propagated out to Hbo and Vbo as now Q is logic 0. And eventually logic 0 will be propagated back to Hbi and Vbi of the ijth tile. After that x will be

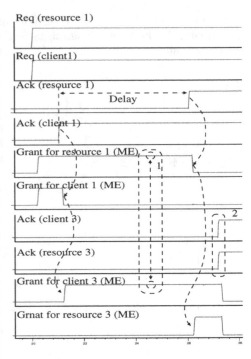

Fig. 11. Simulation waveforms

logic 1 and then Qbar is 0 and Q is 1. Now H is ready to be removed if Rir and Cjr are removed. Only after the removal of H is propagated out to the client and resource, new requests can be issued by this particular client/request pair. On the other hand, when the ijth tile is unblocking its corresponding pair of row and column, other client/request pairs away from these coordinates can be processed concurrently.

5 Simulation Results

Tile-based 4×4 and 10×10 multi-resource arbiters were built in UMC90nm CMOS technology using Cadence toolkits. Figure 11 shows the result from one simulation, in which clients 1 and 3 and resources 1 and 3 issue request signals at the same time. Only one client and one resource requests can go through the ME arrays at any time. In this example, client 1 and resource 1 go through. So H11 is generated and then the acknowledgement signals for them are propagated out. However one Ack signal for resource 1 is artificially delayed (here we want to illustrate the timing robustness of our self-timed solution). This results in the ME grant signal for client 1 being removed and a new ME grant for client 3 being issued but the ME grant for resource 1 not being removed at the same time. Now the grant signals for client 3 and resource 1 exist at the same time. However they are not paired (dashed box 1), where the effect of blocking is manifested. Client 3 is waiting for a new grant signal for one of the resources. In this example, only after the grant signal for resource 1 has been removed and resource 3 has passed through the ME, H33 can be generated (dashed box 2).

Table 1. Arbiter latency performances

Cg+&Rg+ → H+	Best	Average	Worst
4×4 [8]	0.29n	0.29n	0.29n
Our 4×4	0.79n	0.86n	0.92n
Our 10×10	1.43n	1.65n	1.83n

We inserted arbitrary delays at all tile interfaces in both the 4×4 and 10×10 cases, with the circuits always working correctly. We also implemented a 4×4 arbiter based on the design in [8] and studied the overall gate delays of that design and the new designs (Table 1). Our new 4×4 tile-based design, with more gates in the signal path, pays a latency penalty compared with the design using techniques from [8], but this older design method cannot deal with arbitrary inter-block delays and is unsuitable for extending beyond 4×4 size. The average delays of the new 10×10 and 4×4 tile-based designs indicate linear latency scaling from the new method. The new designs have variable Cg/Rg→H delays depending on the values of i and j, because the Cg signal must pass through j-1 columns and Rg must pass through i-1 tiles to reach the ijth tile. The overall delay for the ijth tile from Cg/Rg to H is therefore

$$\text{Delay}_{ij} = \max\{(j-1) \times T_{\text{row}}, (i-1) \times T_{\text{col}}\} + T_{\text{block}} + T_{\text{gen}},$$

where T_{row} is the time for Rg to pass through a tile along a row, T_{col} is the time for Cg to pass through a tile along a column, T_{block} is the time for the blocking signal to complete the loops and T_{gen} is the time needed to generate H in a tile upon satisfaction of all conditions. The last two delays are constant with respect to the coordinates.

6   Conclusions and Future Work

We propose a general approach of designing asynchronous systems of substantial size by combining small manageable SI logic blocks with DI inter-block connections. This avoids the twin problems of theoretically rigorous self-timed system design: that it is impractical to design DI systems for real applications and that it is impossible to design large-sized SI systems which can retain a reasonable degree of DI approximation. Our approach produces virtual DI systems which will provide good tolerance for process variability and other adverse effects of aggressive VLSI scaling, especially those manifesting as latency unpredictability.

This approach also advocates the maximum exploitation of regularity, generating tile-based designs with true tiles of simple and regular structures to enhance scalability and better approximation of DI.

We demonstrate the validity of this method by deriving a tile-based design of multi-access arbiters by rigorously following the steps of the method. The inherent regularity of this system allows us to showcase the advantages of designs based on true tiles, and its large number of interconnects across function blocks makes it possible for us to demonstrate the simplicity and effectiveness of inter-block DI connection design.

Two examples (4×4 and 10×10 arbiters) are implemented in UMC 90nm CMOS technology. Simulation results show the circuits implemented using the method working as expected under delay uncertainty but we have yet to conduct theoretical verification. For arbiters of this type with large N and M the ME arrays will become more of a bottleneck. We plan to investigate these issues in the future.

We believe the virtual DI approach has significance in a much wider scope than arbiters whose functions can be decomposed into regular matrixes. With this first study completed, we plan to start investigating the wider implications of the method.

Acknowledgements. This work is supported by the EPSRC, Project STEP (EP/E044662/1) at Newcastle University. The authors would like to thank Andrey Mokhov for fruitful discussions.

References

[1] International Technology Roadmap for Semiconductors,
http://public.itrs.net/

[2] Martin, A.J.: The limitations to delay-insensitivity in asynchronous circuits. In: Dally, W.J. (ed.) Advanced Research in VLSI, pp. 263–278. MIT Press, Cambridge (1990)

[3] Sylvester, D., Agarwal, K., Shah, S.: Variability in nanometer CMOS: Impact, analysis, and minimization. Integration the VLSI Journal 41, 319–339 (2008)

[4] Roy, S., et al.: Impact of intrinsic parameter fluctuations in nano-CMOS devices on circuits and systems. In: Ryzhii, M., Ryzhii, V. (eds.) Physics and Modeling of Tera- and Nano-Devices. World Scientific, NY (2008)

[5] Saito, H., Kondratyev, A., Cortadella, J., Lavagno, L., Yakovlev, A.: What is the cost of delay insensitivity? In: Proc. ICCAD 1999, San Jose, CA, November 1999, pp. 316–323 (1999)

[6] Patil, S.S.: Forward acting nXm arbiter, Computation structures group memo No. 67, Massachusetts Institute of Technology (April 1972)

[7] Kinniment, D.J.: Synchronization and arbitration in digital systems. John Wiley, Chichester (2007)

[8] Golubcovs, S., Shang, D., Xia, F., Mokhov, A., Yakovlev, A.: Modular approach to multi-resource arbiter design. In: Proc. of ASYNC 2009, Chapel Hill, North Carolina, USA, May 2009, pp. 107–116 (2009)

[9] Peterson, J.L.: Petri net theory and the modelling of systems. Prentice-Hall, Englewood Cliffs (1981)

[10] Rosenblum, L.Y., Yakovlev, A.: Signal graphs: from self-timed to timed ones. In: Proc. of international workshop on timed Petri nets, Torino, Italy, July 1985, pp. 199–207 (1985)

[11] http://www.lsi.upc.es/~jordic/petrify

Analysis of Power Consumption Using a New Methodology for the Capacitance Modeling of Complex Logic Gates

Sidinei Ghissoni[1,4], Joao Batista dos Santos Martins[2],
Ricardo Augusto da Luz Reis[1], and Jose Carlos Monteiro[3]

[1] PGMICRO-UFRGS, Porto Alegre, RS-Brazil
`{sghissoni,reis}@inf.ufrgs.br`
[2] PPGEE-UFSM, Santa Maria –RS-Brazil
`batista@inf.ufrgs.br`
[3] INESC-IST, Lisboa, Portugal
`jcm@inesc-id.pt`
[4] UNIPAMPA-Alegrete, RS, Brazil
`Sidinei.Ghissoni@unipampa.edu.br`

Abstract. This paper proposes a new approach for the analysis of the power consumption at the logic level of complex static CMOS gates. A new methodology for the capacitance modeling is described, which considers a mathematic model of equivalent concentrated capacitance at each external node of the gate. To generate this model, all the possible combinations of input vectors transitions and their capacitive effects are analyzed. A set of complex gates is modeled and the dissipated power is estimated with 100 input vectors. The results are compared with electric level simulation, using the Hspice tool of the Synopsys, and logic level, with Prime Power. A maximum error of 6.7% for a complex logic gate (OAI321) is found. Furthermore, to validate the method, power estimation of circuits composed essentially of complex gates was obtained and the maximum error found in this case was 6.2%. The main advantage of the method is the estimation time, which can be up to 160 times faster.

Keywords: Power estimation; Complex logic gates; Capacitance modeling.

1 Introduction

The implementation of integrated digital circuits of great complexity makes the power estimation in the electric level not practical. The use of complex static CMOS gates (SCCG) in logic circuits allows for the reduction of both occupied area and power consumption.

Power estimates at the logic level give a prediction of consumption before the generation of layout. This makes possible the application of specific techniques [1], preventing the re-design if the initial specifications are not met.

J. Monteiro and R. van Leuken (Eds.): PATMOS 2009, LNCS 5953, pp. 297–306, 2010.

In the last years, many researchers have developed several techniques and tools that estimate the power consumption quickly. The PowerTheater tool [2] is a commercial tool capable of performing the estimate of power consumption in different levels of abstraction, with focus on power consumption at RTL level. This tool presents high level of precision for the simulations of SoC (System-on-Chip) designs. The XPower tool [3] is another commercial tool that evaluates the dissipation power for programmable logic devices. It is enclosed in all the configurations of the ISE/Xilinx and allows analyzing the total or partial power consumption of a device. The XPower estimates the power of a circuit at system level, through the use of VHDL description language. PrimePower [4] is a tool for power analysis at the logical level in the Synopsys Environment [6], offering a high degree of precision associated with short time of simulation. The analysis of the power consumed by the circuit is performed considering the impedance and glitching of the circuit.

This paper proposes the analysis of the power consumption, especially dynamic power, in complex logic gates (SCCG) of static CMOS circuits at the logic level, by means of using a new methodology of capacitance modeling. This methodology considers a mathematic model of equivalent concentrated capacitance in each external node of the gate. This model analyzes all the possible combinations of transitions at the gate inputs and their capacitive effects. In the present work, the capacitances of interconnections and crosstalk have not yet been considered.

This paper is organized in the following way: in Section 2 we present the set of complex logic gates used for modeling. In Section 3, the new methodology proposed for SCCGs is illustrated for a complex gate (AOI21). In Section 4, this methodology is validated by a set of circuits with SCCG. Finally, in Section 5, the conclusions are presented.

2 Proposed Methodology

The model proposed for the power estimation of complex logic gates estimates the intrinsic capacitances of each transistor through the linear model and dimensions of design: width (W) and length (L) of the channel. These capacitances are concentrated in the external nodes of the logic gate, being computed using a mathematical model that considers the effect of all possible transitions of input vectors for the considered input.

The dynamic power of static CMOS circuits is defined in equation (1) as:

$$P_{dyn} = \frac{1}{2} \cdot f_c \cdot V_{dd}^2 \cdot \sum_{i=1}^{n} C_i \cdot \alpha_i \tag{1}$$

where P_{dyn} is the dynamic power consumed by the circuit, f_c the clock frequency, V_{dd} is the voltage of the circuit, n the total number of gates of the circuit, C_i the equivalent capacitance of node i and α_i the switching activity of each gate.

The models of transistors are considered linear. The complex gates that will be analyzed, are the following: AOI21, AOI22, AOI221, AOI222, AOI32, AOI321, AOI33, OAI21, OAI22, OAI221, OAI222, OAI32, OAI32 and OAI33.

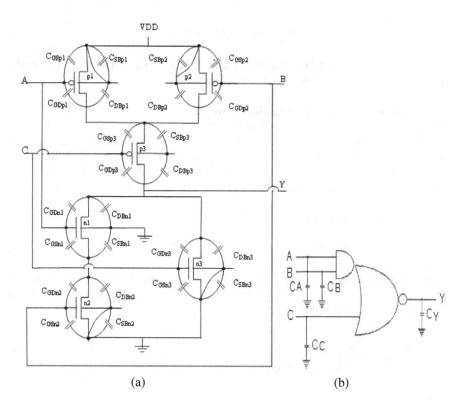

Fig. 1. Complex gate AOI21: a) Model with intrinsic capacitances; b) Logic model with con-centrated capacitances

2.1 Modeling of Complex Gate AOI21

The complex logic gate AOI21 that realizes the logical function of equation (2), has 6 external nodes and 2 internal nodes, as depicted in Figure 1(a).

$$Y = \overline{AB + C} \qquad (2)$$

In this figure, $C_{GD(n,p)}$, $C_{DB(n,p)}$, $C_{GS(n,p)}$ and $C_{S,B(n,p)}$ are defined respectively as gate-drain capacitance, drain-bulk capacitance, gate-source capacitance and source-bulk capacitance of the transistor $n(p)$.

The three inputs of the gate allow the pairwise combination of input vectors **000, 001, 010, 011, 100, 101, 110** and **111** and that they act in the transistors switching PMOS and NMOS, resulting in the equivalent capacitance. However, the equivalent capacitance of each internal node is determined by the effect of the transition of the signals (external and internal) related to the node analyzed; the number of capacitive components is equal to the number of analyzed vectors. In this way, the number of components is reduced to 4, as in equation (3):

$$C_n = C_1 + C_2 + C_3 + C_4 \tag{3}$$

where C_n is the equivalent capacitance of the node being analyzed and $C_1....C_4$, are the capacitances due to the transition of the input states.

2.1.1 Equivalent Capacitance Model for Input A

In the analysis of the equivalent capacitance of the input A of the SCCG AOI21, the transition of inputs B and C are verified. From Equation (3) above, the C_1 component is the capacitance due to the combination of input signals 0**00** and 1**00**, C_2 is the resulting capacitive component of the transition of signals 0**01** and 1**01**, C_3 is the capacitive component which had signals 0**10** and 1**10** and C_4 resulting of signals 1**11** and 0**11** is the capacitive component.

Therefore, C_A is given by:

$$C_A = C_{AX1} + C_{AX2} + C_{AX3} + C_{AX4} \tag{4}$$

C_{AX1} corresponds to the signals of input 0**00** and 1**00** where the transistors $n2$ and $n3$ of Figure 1, are in the OFF state, whereas the transistors type $p2$ and $p3$ are ON. In such a way C_{AX1} is obtained with:

$$C_{Ax1} = 0.25 \left(\frac{C_{GSn1}.C_{TAx1}}{C_{GSn1} + C_{TAx1}} + C_{GDn1} + C_{GDp1} + C_{GSp1} \right) \tag{5}$$

and C_{TAx1} is:

$$C_{TAx1} = C_{GDn2} + C_{DBn2} + C_{SBn1} \tag{6}$$

C_{AX2} corresponds to the input signals 0**01** and 1**01** where the transistors $n2$ and $p3$ are in the OFF state, and the transistors $n3$ and $p2$ are ON, which results in the capacitive part of C_{AX2}:

$$C_{Ax2} = 0.25 \left(\frac{C_{GSn1}.C_{TAx2}}{C_{GSn1} + C_{TAx2}} + C_{GDn1} + C_{GSp1} + \frac{C_{GDp1}.C_{TAX2}}{C_{GDp1} + C_{TAX2}} \right) \tag{7}$$

and C_{TA21} is:

$$C_{TAx2} = C_{SBp3} + C_{GDp3} + C_{SBp1} \tag{8}$$

Transistors $n2$ and $p3$ are in the ON state and transistors $p2$ and $n3$ in the OFF state for the transition of inputs 1**10** and 0**10**. Thus the capacitive component for these vectors of input results in C_{AX3}:

$$C_{Ax3} = 0.25 \left(C_{GSn1} + C_{GDn1} + C_{GDp1} + C_{GSp1} \right) \tag{9}$$

Finally, when the signals switch from $0\underline{11}$ to $1\underline{11}$, transistors $n2$ and $n3$ are ON and transistors $p2$ and $p3$ enter the OFF state, which results in C_{AX4} being given by:

$$C_{Ax4} = 0.25\left(\frac{C_{GDp1}\cdot C_{TAx4}}{C_{GDp1}+C_{TAx4}} + C_{GDn1} + C_{GSn1} + C_{GSp1}\right) \tag{10}$$

and C_{Tax4} is:

$$C_{TAx4} = C_{GDp2} + C_{DBp1} + C_{SBp3} + C_{DBp3} + C_{GDp2} \tag{11}$$

2.1.2 Equivalent Capacitance Model for Input B

For input B, the same analysis is made in terms of the influence for the input combinations on the transistors. The input is composed of 4 capacitive components.

$$C_B = C_{BX1} + C_{BX2} + C_{B2X3} + C_{BX4} \tag{12}$$

Analyzing the signal of input $\underline{000}$ and $\underline{010}$, it is verified that the net of transistors PMOS is saturated, whereas the net of transistors NMOS is in the OFF state. Therefore the capacitance of this part will be:

$$C_{Bx1} = 0.25\left(\frac{C_{GDn2}\cdot C_{TBx1}}{C_{GDn2}\cdot C_{TBx1}} + C_{GDp2} + C_{GSp2} + C_{GSn2}\right) \tag{13}$$

and C_{TBX1} is:

$$C_{TBx1} = C_{GSn1} + C_{SBn1} + C_{DBn2} \tag{14}$$

Continuing the analysis, when the input vectors are $\underline{001}$ and $\underline{011}$, transistors $n3$ and $sp1$ are in the ON state; transistors $n1$ and $p3$ are in the OFF state. In this way, the resulting capacitance will be:

$$C_{Bx2} = 0.25\left(\frac{C_{GDn2}\cdot C_{TBx1}}{C_{GDn2}+C_{TBx1}} + C_{GSn2} + C_{GDp2} + C_{GSp2}\right) \tag{15}$$

The transistors $p1$ and $n3$ are in OFF and the transistors $p3$ and $n1$ conducting when the input transitions assume values $\underline{100}$ and $\underline{110}$. In this way, the capacitive component result is:

$$C_{Bx3} = 0.25\left(C_{GDn2} + C_{GDp2} + C_{GSp2} + C_{GSn2}\right) \tag{16}$$

Under input transition $\underline{101}$ and $\underline{111}$, the net of NMOS transistors is ON and the net of transistors PMOS enters the OFF state. Therefore, the resulting capacitance will be:

$$C_{Bx4} = 0.25 \left(C_{GDn2} + \frac{C_{GDp2} \cdot C_{TBx2}}{C_{Gpn2} + C_{TBx2}} + C_{GSp2} + C_{GSn2} \right) \tag{17}$$

and C_{TBx2} is:

$$C_{TBx2} = C_{DBp2} + C_{DBp1} + C_{GDp1} + C_{SBp3} + C_{GDp3} \tag{18}$$

2.1.3 Equivalent Capacitance Model for Input C

The same procedure adopted for inputs A and B is adopted for input C. Thus, the equivalent capacitance of input C will be:

$$C_C = C_{CX1} + C_{CX2} + C_{CX3} + C_{CX4} \tag{19}$$

With the combinations of vectors **00**1 and **00**0, applied in the input of the gate, transistors *n1* and *n2* are in the OFF state, and the transistors of net PMOS are ON. Then the resultant capacitive parcel is given by:

$$C_{CX1} = 0.25 \left(C_{GDn3} + C_{DBn3} + C_{GDp3} + C_{GSp3} \right) \tag{20}$$

In the analysis of the capacitive load for the transition **01**0 and **01**1, we observe that the transistors *n1* and *p2* are OFF and transistors *n2* and *p1* are ON, leading to:

$$C_{CX2} = 0.25 \left(C_{GDp3} + C_{GDn3} + C_{GSp3} + C_{GSn3} \right) \tag{21}$$

In 25% of the cases, that is, when the input signals assume **10**0 and **10**1, the transistors *n1* and *p2* are ON, and the transistors *n2* and *p1* in the OFF state. Thus the partial capacitance results in:

$$C_{CX3} = 0.25 \left(C_{GDp3} + C_{GDn3} + C_{GSp3} + C_{GSn3} \right) \tag{22}$$

Finally, for the input transition **11**0 and **11**1, transistors *n1* and *n2* are ON and transistors *p1* and *p2* in the OFF state. In this way, the resulting capacitance of this part will be:

$$C_{CX4} = 0.25 \left(C_{GDp3} + C_{DBn3} + \frac{C_{GSp3} \cdot C_{TCX1}}{C_{GSp3} + C_{TCX1}} + C_{GSn3} \right) \tag{23}$$

and C_{TCX3} is:

$$C_{TCX1} = C_{GDp1} + C_{DBp1} + C_{SBp3} + C_{GDp2} + C_{DBp2} \tag{24}$$

2.1.4 Equivalent Capacitance Model for Output Y

The output capacitance Y is obtained applying the *Thevénin Theorem*, that is, when observed from the output to the inputs all the voltages are grounded, resulting in:

$$C_Y = C_{GDp3} + C_{DBp3} + C_{GDn1} + C_{DBn1} + C_{GDn3} + C_{DBn3} \tag{25}$$

3 Simulation Experiments and Analysis of Results

This section presents the simulations with results of the power consumption and the CPU time, using the proposed methodology, integrated into the SIS tools [5]. The results of power consumption estimation at logical level are compared against electric level power estimates through Hspice of Synopsys [6]. All the simulations have been performed in a PC Pentium IV, 3 GHz processor and 1GB of RAM. The parameters of technology used were from AMS08. The circuits were simulated assuming 5V supply voltage, an operation frequency of 20MHz and using 100 input vectors.

Figure 2 presents the flow of analysis for simulation:

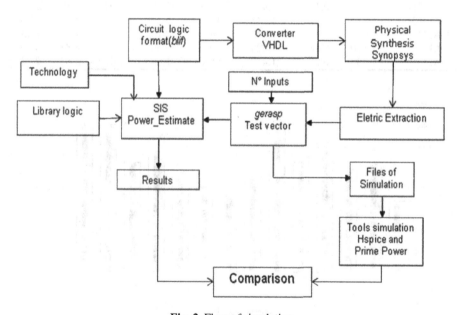

Fig. 2. Flow of simulation

Table 1 presents the results of power estimation between the logic level and the electric level. The errors obtained are between 0.1% (OAI32) and 6.5% (OAI321) when compared with the Hspice tool of the Synopsys, and the errors when compared with Prime Power tool are between 0.75% (OAI22) and 6.66% (OAI321). In Figure 3, we present a comparison through a graph of the different simulations. In terms of processing time, the complex gate with larger error in the estimation presents a CPU time faster than the electric (80x).

Table 1. Power consumption estimation of SCCGs with electric parameters from AMS08 tested using 100 random input vectors

Complex Logic Gates	Power SIS (µW)	CPU (s)	Power Hspice (µW)	CPU (s)	Error HSpice/ SIS %	Power Prime Power (µW)	CPU (s)	Error Prime Power SIS %
AOI21	0.690	0.14	0.691	10.6	0.14	0.677	4.32	1.92
AOI22	1.039	0.15	1.028	11.4	1.07	1.019	4.21	1.96
AOI221	0.983	0.17	0.987	12.7	0.41	0.997	4.34	1.40
AOI222	1.239	0.18	1.203	14.6	2.99	1.253	4.69	1.11
AOI32	1.104	0.18	1.071	13.2	3.08	1.055	4.68	4.65
AOI321	1.427	0.20	1.365	15.4	4.54	1.342	4.83	6.34
AOI33	0.956	0.17	0.921	15.2	3.80	0.908	4.83	5.29
OAI21	0.760	0.15	0.735	11.1	3.40	0.728	4.37	4.39
OAI22	0.813	0.15	0.817	10.8	0.49	0.807	4.31	0.75
OAI221	0.965	0.17	0.952	13.6	1.38	0.946	4.59	2.00
OAI222	1.315	0.17	1.243	14.8	5.79	1.256	4.77	4.70
OAI32	1.048	0.19	1.049	14.6	0.10	1.061	4.71	1.23
OAI321	1.410	0.18	1.324	16.2	6.50	1.322	4.83	6.66
OAI33	1.432	0.20	1.418	15.1	1.08	1.402	4.81	2.14

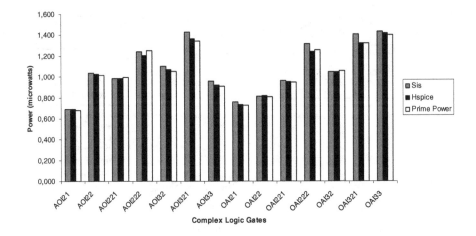

Fig. 3. Comparison of power consumption between electric and logic levels

To further validate the method, some circuits composed of complex gates were simulated. The characteristics of these circuits are presented in Table 2 and in Table 3 the results of the power estimation at the logic level versus power at the electric simulation are presented.

Table 2. Characteristics of the circuits with complex gates

Circuits	Transistors	Complex Logic Gates
Comp_sd1	20	$\overline{A.B+C}+\overline{A.B+C}+\overline{(A+B).(C+D)}$ [AOI21+AOI21+OAI22]
Comp_sd2	30	$\overline{A.B+C.D}+\overline{(A+B).(C+D)}++\overline{(A+B).(C+D)}+\overline{A.B+D}$ [AOI22+OAI22+OAI22+AOI21]
Comp_sd3	38	$\overline{A.B+C.D}+\overline{(A+B).C}+\overline{A.B+C}+$ $+\overline{(A+B).(C+D)}+\overline{(A+B).(C+D).E}$ [AOI22+OAI21+AOI21+OAI22+OAI221]
Comp_sd4	60	$\overline{A.B.C+D.E}+\overline{(A+B).(C+D)}+\overline{A.B+C}+$ $+\overline{(A+B).(C+D)}+\overline{(A+B).(C+D)}+$ $+\overline{A.B+C}+\overline{(A+B).(C+D)}+\overline{(A+B).C}$ [AOI32+OAI22+AOI21+OAI22+OAI22 +AOI21+ OAI22+OAI21]
Comp_sd5	68	$\overline{A.B+C.D}+\overline{(A+B).(C+D)}+\overline{A.B+C}+$ $+\overline{(A+B).C}+\overline{(A+B+C).(D+E)}+\overline{A.B+C}+$ $+\overline{(A+B).(C+D)}+\overline{(A+B).C}+\overline{(A+B).(C+D)}$ [AOI22+OAI22+AOI21+OAI21+OAI32 +AOI21+ OAI22+OAI21+OAI22]
Comp_sd6	74	$\overline{A.B+C.D}+\overline{(A+B).(C+D)}+\overline{A.B+C}+$ $+\overline{(A+B).(C+D)}+\overline{(A+B).(C+D).E}+$ $+\overline{A.B+C}+\overline{(A+B).(C+D)}+\overline{(A+B).C}+$ $+\overline{(A+B).(C+D)}+\overline{(A+B).C}$ [AOI22+OAI22+AOI21+OAI22+OAI221 +AOI21+OAI22+OAI21+OAI22+OAI21]
Comp_sd7	34	$\overline{A.B+C}+\overline{(A+B).C}+\overline{A.B+C}++\overline{(A+B).(C+D)}+\overline{A.B+C.D}$ [AOI21+OAI21+AOI21+OAI22+AOI22]
Comp_sd8	88	$\overline{A.B+C.D}+\overline{A.B+C}+\overline{(A+B).(C+D)}+$ $+\overline{A.B+C.D}+\overline{A.B+C}+\overline{A.B.C.+D.E+F)}+$ $\overline{A.B+C}+\overline{A.B+C}+\overline{A.B+C}+\overline{A.B+C}+$ $+\overline{A.B+C}+\overline{(A+B).(C+D)}+\overline{A.B+C.D}$ [AOI22+AOI21+OAI22+AOI22+AOI21 +OAI321+AOI21+AOI21+AOI21+AOI21 +OAI22+AOI22]
Comp_sd9	26	$\overline{A.B+C.D}+\overline{(A+B).C}+\overline{A.B+C}+\overline{(A+B).C}$ [AOI22+OAI21+AOI21+OAI21]
Comp_sd10	24	$\overline{A.B.C+D.E}+\overline{(A+B).(C+D)}+\overline{A.B+C}$ [AOI32+OAI22+AOI21]

In Table 3 we observe that the Comp_sd6 circuit presents the largest error when comparing the logical level power with the electric simulation (6,2%), however the processing time is around 130 times faster. Therefore, the method presented very satisfactory results for modeling of complex gates.

Table 3. Power consumption of circuits that use only complex logic gates with electric parameters AMS08 tested using 100 random input vectors

Circuits	Power SIS (μW)	CPU (sec)	Power Hspice (μW)	CPU (s)	Error (%)
Comp_sd1	2.413	0.79	2.298	55.2	4.77
Comp_sd2	1.766	0.80	1.714	68.4	2.94
Comp_sd3	4.364	1.08	4.357	88.1	0.16
Comp_sd4	2.972	1.43	2.796	23.1	5.92
Comp_sd5	2.951	1.96	2.862	187.4	3.02
Comp_sd6	3.564	2.51	3.343	324.9	6.20
Comp_sd7	1.848	1.12	1.783	71.4	3.52
Comp_sd8	5.384	3.77	5.240	395.1	2.67
Comp_sd9	2.347	0.91	2.284	395.1	2.68
Comp_sd10	2.367	0.82	2.297	32.1	2.96

4 Conclusions and Future Work

The method of power consumption estimation using the modeling of the capacitance that computes the equivalent concentrated capacitance to external nodes of each logic gate obtained in the logical level presents an error smaller than 6.20% in comparison to the ones obtained in the electric level for the considered circuits, with the advantage of the simulations being much faster. For the complex gates was obtained an error smaller than 6.66% in comparison com Prime Power tool. Considering the analysis of the proposed method, which does not consider information of interconnection capacitances and crosstalk, the results were quite satisfactory.

The next step is to test others circuits and different technologies including in the model, the effects of interconnections, crosstalk capacitances, glitch and static power.

Acknowledgments. The authors would like to thank the FINEP, CNPQ and CAPES.

References

1. Rabaey, J.M.: Digital Integrated Circuits: A Design Perspective. Prentice-Hall, New Jersey (1996)
2. PowerTheater - Low Power Design & Power Analysis For Nanometer System-on-Chip Design. Disponívelem, http://www.sequencedesign.com/2_solutions/2b_power_theater.html
3. Xpower Data sheet, http://www.xilinx.com/xlnx/xebiz/designResources
4. PrimePower Full-Chip Dynamic Power Analysis for Multimillion-Gate Designs Data sheet, http://www.synopsys.com/galaxypower
5. Sentovich, E.M., et al.: SIS: A System for Sequential Circuit Synthesis. Electronics Research Lab. University of California, Berkeley (1992)
6. Synopsys University Program, http://www.synopsys.com

A New Methodology for Power-Aware Transistor Sizing: Free Power Recovery (FPR)

Milena Vratonjić[1], Matthew Ziegler[2], George D. Gristede[2], Victor Zyuban[2], Thomas Mitchell[3], Ee Cho[4], Chandu Visweswariah[2], and Vojin G. Oklobdzija[5]

[1] University of California Davis, Davis, CA
milena@ucdavis.edu
[2] IBM T. J. Watson Research Center, Yorktown Heights, NY
{zieglerm,gristede,zyuban,chandu}@us.ibm.com
[3] IBM Electronic Design Automation, Burlington, VT
tmitch@us.ibm.com
[4] IBM Electronic Design Automation, Poughkeepsie, NY
cho@us.ibm.com
[5] University of Texas at Dallas, Dallas, TX
vojin@acsel-lab.com

Abstract. In this paper we present a new transistor sizing methodology called Free Power Recovery (FPR) for low power circuit design. The objective of this methodology is to minimize the total power of a circuit by accounting for node switching activities and leakage duty cycles (LDC). The methodology has been incorporated into the EinsTuner circuit tuning tool. EinsTuner automates the tuning process using state-of-the-art non-linear optimization solvers and fast circuit simulators. Node switching activities and LDC are integrated into the EinsTuner framework as parameter inputs to the FPR tuning mode. In FPR mode, the power is minimized using gate width reduction with respect to power properties of the node. The FPR methodology is evaluated on next generation microprocessor circuit designs. Power reduction results are compared with the results from the existing EinsTuner tuning methodology. The results show improvement in power reduction with the FPR optimization mode.

Keywords: Low-power, Optimization.

1 Introduction

Power dissipation remains one of the critical challenges in microprocessor design. It requires innovation at all design levels to sustain performance scaling [1],[2]. Designers rely on the use of automated circuit design tools to provide low power and high performance circuits. However, existing automated circuit design tools focus solely on minimizing total device width under the constraint of critical path delay [3]. These tools do not consider the impact of circuit properties such as switching activities and leakage duty cycles at each circuit node. Minimization of the total device width, without accounting for these circuit properties

J. Monteiro and R. van Leuken (Eds.): PATMOS 2009, LNCS 5953, pp. 307–316, 2010.

that determine the power consumption, does not guarantee that the optimized
(tuned) circuit will operate under minimum power consumption.

EinsTuner can operate under a variety of tuning modes, some of which are:
area minimization, Free Area Recovery (FAR), delay minimization, etc. For example, area minimization has the goal of reducing the total device width of
the circuit under the timing constraint given by the specified slack[1] threshold
value. Another EinsTuner tuning mode known as Free Area Recovery (FAR)
[4] attempts to reduce the total device width without degrading the slack of
the critical path. FAR is a variation of the area minimization method discussed
above and it also requires a slack threshold specification. However, the slack
threshold parameter for the area minimization and FAR tuning modes has two
very different meanings.

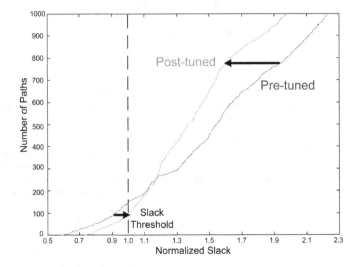

Fig. 1. Example of a slack histogram for which the worst slack is smaller then the slack
threshold

In the area minimization tuning mode, the slack threshold is a constraint and
has to be satisfied or the optimization problem is infeasible and the tuned circuit is suboptimal. In the FAR mode, the slack threshold is used to specify the
criticality boundary. When tuning in the FAR mode, any slack that is smaller
(worse than) the specified slack threshold is guaranteed to either improve or
remain constant after tuning (it will not get any worse). However, this does not
imply that the devices along the paths that have slacks below the threshold
slack are excluded from the tunable pool of devices. All devices are subjected to
optimization in the mathematical tuning problem formulation. This means that

---

[1] Slack is a timing characteristic associated with each timing point of the design and
represents the difference in arrival time versus required arrival time.

all device widths can be modified, provided that the modification of the widths
of the devices on the critical path does not cause the slack to fall below the
threshold or initial slack value, depending on which value is smaller. An example is a circuit in which the critical path slack is smaller than the specified slack
threshold, i.e. the worst case slack is considered to be negative. The representative slack histogram of a circuit with such timing characteristics is shown in
Figure 1. We cannot tune such a circuit in the area minimization mode since the
slack threshold constraint is not satisfied, but we can perform the circuit optimization using the FAR mode. Even though the worst case slack of the circuit is
negative, the circuit contains many other non-critical paths that satisfy timing
requirements and have positive slacks. Note that the worst case slack can also
improve after tuning since off-path capacitive loading is reduced, as shown in
this example for the post-tuned timing histogram in Figure 1. Unlike in the area
minimization tuning mode, the slack threshold value specified in the FAR tuning
mode will not cause infeasible problems. The FAR tuning mode can therefore
be applied to any circuit with either positive or negative critical (worst) slack.

The ideal case is to have the circuit that is delay optimized such that further
delay improvement cannot be obtained from delay-based tuning (delay minimization mode in EinsTuner) for a given circuit topology. Usually, such a circuit
is said to be "fast" but it is not necessarily power optimized. To minimize the
power of the circuit without degrading the critical path delay, we need a follow-
up optimization step for circuit power reduction. In this paper, we propose a
new tuning step for power reduction, Free Power Recovery (FPR), which will
provide power reduction while maintaining circuit delay performance. The result
of FPR as the second optimization step is a fast and minimum-power circuit.

2   Free Power Recovery

FPR (Free Power Recovery) is a variation of the FAR (Free Area Recovery) tuning mode. The optimization objective of the FPR tuning mode is to minimize the
total power of a circuit instead of the circuit area, as done in Free Area Recovery
(FAR) and in area minimization modes. The area of a circuit is represented as
the total device width (1).

$$Area = \sum_{i=1}^{N} W_i \tag{1}$$

The FPR mode takes the switching activity and leakage information to formulate
the total power as an objective of the optimization problem. The optimization
problem is then presented to the non-linear solver under the constraint that
circuit timing cannot degrade on the paths which have slack below the threshold.

The total power P of a circuit is the sum of dynamic power ($P_{dynamic}$) and
leakage power ($P_{leakage}$) components:

$$P = P_{dynamic} + P_{leakage} \tag{2}$$

Dynamic power of a circuit can be represented as the sum of dynamic power contributions from each of the N devices as given by

$$P_{dynamic} = \frac{1}{2} f V_{dd}^2 c_g \sum_{i=1}^{N} \alpha_i W_i \tag{3}$$

where c_g represents the gate capacitance per unit gate width and α_i is the device switching factor. We only model dynamic power component associated with device switching which is directly affected by transistor sizing; therefore, dynamic power due to switching wire capacitance is not included in the model but it is accounted for in the total power reported in the results.

Leakage power can be expressed as

$$P_{leakage} = \sum_{i=1}^{N} p_i^{leakage} \delta_i W_i \tag{4}$$

where δ_i stands for *Leakage Duty Cycle (LDC)* of the ith device and $p_i^{leakage}$ is the leakage power per device width $[\mu W/\mu m]$ which depends on the operating voltage supply V_{dd}, polarity of a device ($nFET$, $pFET$) and the device threshold voltage V_t (low LV_t, regular RV_t, high HV_t, and super-high SV_t threshold voltage).

Leakage Duty Cycle accounts for the probability of the input pattern for which the device is in the leaking state. It also evaluates the reduction of leakage current in transistor stacks with one or more *off* devices. State dependent calculation of leakage duty cycles for a two-input NAND gate example is summarized in Table 1. The transistor stacking effect (DIBL) [5] of two devices that are *off* is incorporated in the calculation and reduces the leakage current when compared to a single *off* device by a factor of 10, depending on the technology [6]. The source-follower effect is also taken into account with 30% leakage reduction for the nFET device at the bottom of the stack, when the top device in the stack is *on*.

Table 1. State dependent leakage LDC calculation for the two-input NAND gate example with transistor B at the bottom of the stack

a	b	State Probability	N_a	N_b	P_a	P_b
0	0	p_{00}	0.1	0.1	0	0
0	1	p_{01}	1	0	0	0
1	0	p_{10}	0	0.7	0	0
1	1	p_{11}	0	0	1	1

LDC for each device in the two-input NAND gate is calculated as follows:

$$\delta_{N_a} = p_{00}(0.1) + p_{01}(1) + p_{10}(0) + p_{11}(0) \tag{5}$$

$$\delta_{N_b} = p_{00}(0.1) + p_{01}(0) + p_{10}(0.7) + p_{11}(0) \tag{6}$$

$$\delta_{P_a} = p_{00}(0) + p_{01}(0) + p_{10}(0) + p_{11}(1) \tag{7}$$

$$\delta_{P_b} = p_{00}(0) + p_{01}(0) + p_{10}(0) + p_{11}(1) \tag{8}$$

Assuming that all states for the two-input NAND gate example are equally probable, we obtain the following values of *Leakage Duty Cycles* for each of four devices:

$$\delta_{N_a} = 0.275, \delta_{N_b} = 0.2, \delta_{P_a} = \delta_{P_b} = 0.25 \tag{9}$$

Taking equations for dynamic power (3) and leakage power (4) components, the total power (2) of a circuit can be rewritten as:

$$P = \sum_{i=1}^{N} t_i W_i \tag{10}$$

where the *weight factors* for device width in the power equation (10) are computed as:

$$t_i = \frac{1}{2} f V_{dd}^2 c_g \alpha_i + p_i^{leakage} \delta_i \tag{11}$$

Previously, we had the area of a circuit as the sum of equally weighted device widths (1). A comparison of the equations for total area (1) and total power (10) shows that the total power is proportional to the weighted sum of the gate widths, where the weight factors correspond to the t_i factors as defined in equation (11). Therefore, minimizing the total area of a circuit is <u>not</u> equivalent to minimizing its total power.

The FPR tuning mode properly accounts for the dynamic power of a circuit because it considers only those devices that are switching (see Figure 2). On the other hand, the area minimization and FAR modes consider all devices equally in the optimization, irrespective of switching activity.

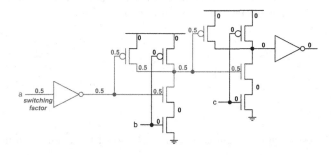

Fig. 2. Example of propagation of switching factors in a circuit

3   FPR vs. FAR

Figure 3 depicts the results we expect from tuning a circuit in FAR and FPR modes. The left-hand side of the figure shows power and timing characteristics of a pre-tuned and post-tuned circuit in both modes. The right-hand side shows area and timing characteristics of these circuits. The pre-tuned design point is delay optimized. Starting from this point and applying both FAR and FPR tuning, we expect FAR mode to achieve minimum area, and FPR mode to achieve minimum power.

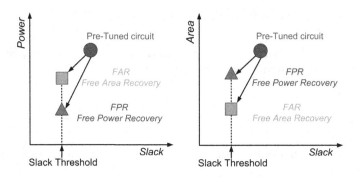

Fig. 3. Expected results for FAR and FPR optimizations

As an example, we have applied both our new FPR tuning methodology and the existing FAR tuning mode on the tiny test circuit chosen for illustration purposes only and shown in Figure 4. In particular, we compare the results of power reduction obtained with the FPR with the results of power reduction obtained with the FAR tuning mode.

We divide the test circuit into two parts: one part that is switching all the time ($\alpha = 1$) and the other part that is not switching at all ($\alpha = 0$). The main purpose of this example is to exaggerate the effects of input pattern dependency on power-aware tuning and to identify which devices are targeted for optimization when using different optimization modes. We expect that FPR mode will focus only on the part of the circuit that is switching, whereas the FAR mode will target every device equally whether it is switching or not.

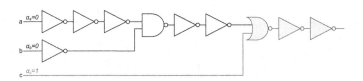

Fig. 4. Test circuit for comparison of FAR and FPR optimization modes

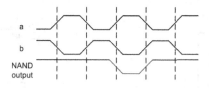

Fig. 5. Glitch-aware tuning

In this example, the results from the test circuit match our expectations. Specifically, Figure 6 shows the timing, power and area comparison of the initial pre-tuned test circuit and both FAR and FPR post-tuned results. Results from both the new and existing tuning methodologies were obtained and verified using existing timing and power tools. Figure 6 shows that the FPR mode was more successful than the FAR mode at minimizing the circuit power and the FAR mode achieved the minimum area as expected (see Figure 3).

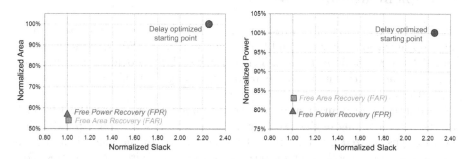

Fig. 6. Power recovery improvement and area comparison of pre-tuned and post-tuned results with FPR over FAR shown for the test circuit from Figure 4

To analyze how the devices were tuned differently in the FAR and FPR tuning modes, we plotted the area comparison of the circuit blocks in Figure 7. A comparison of total device width is plotted for the part of the circuit that is not switching versus the part that is fully-switching. When tuning in the FAR mode, the ratio of total device width of the circuit block that is switching versus the one that is not switching stayed constant as compared to the ratio of respective circuit blocks in the pre-tuned (initial) circuit. As seen from the comparison, the FPR tuning mode properly accounts for the circuit power because it considers only those devices that are switching. The area of the circuit that is not switching ($\alpha = 0$) is allowed to increase and the area of the circuit that is switching ($\alpha = 1$) is reduced in order to simultaneously minimize the power and satisfy the timing requirements. Of course, other constraints keep this from shrinking to zero.

Figure 5 shows that glitch events must also be considered as part of node switching activity in order to correctly account for associated power consumption. In the FPR framework, switching activity accounts for both true and spurious (glitch) transitions, thereby allowing for both power- and glitch-aware circuit tuning.

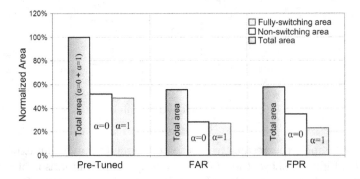

Fig. 7. Comparison of total area and areas of non-switching and fully-switching circuit blocks (marked with $\alpha = 0$ and $\alpha = 1$, respectively) for pre-tuned and post-tuned test circuit from Figure 4 using FAR and FPR optimization modes

4   Implementation Flow

The EinsTuner tool [3] automates the tuning process using state-of-the-art non-linear optimization solvers [7] and fast circuit simulators. We have incorporated the FPR tuning mode in the EinsTuner framework by providing switching activities for each circuit node and their corresponding Leakage Duty Cycle values as inputs to EinsTuner as shown in Figure 8.

We obtain timing information of the pre-tuned circuit using the EinsTLT transistor level timing engine [8]. Our framework includes a power profiler that generates customized input patterns for each circuit. In the analysis and optimization we use several input patterns with different switching activities. Formation of customized input patterns is a complex and effort-intensive process. Good coverage for circuit devices that are switching is also addressed in the pattern formation process. For each input pattern, we use logic simulator and leakage analysis tools [9] [10] to obtain switching activities and LDC information for every device in the circuit.

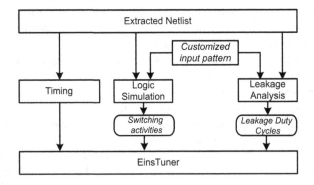

Fig. 8. Tuning implementation flow

5   Results

Our new power-aware tuning methodology (FPR) was applied to the post-layout optimization of an arithmetic block. Maintaining the constant number of fingers was the constraint in our optimization. Even though our analysis was performed to the post-layout optimization, we were able to achieve more than 10% power reduction. Input data patterns with switching activity of 50% were applied. We performed both FAR and FPR tuning optimizations on the test circuit and we compared the optimization results in terms of achieved power reduction. For a given delay target, we performed FAR optimization first and then we performed FPR power-aware tuning. We also analyzed how optimization results varied with and without clock-gating. Note that latches are non-tunable objects and the relative improvement in power reduction is higher in clock-gated runs. The results of FPR vs. FAR tuning for the adder with an input data pattern with 50% switching activity are shown in Figure 9. In both free and clock-gated optimization runs, FPR achieved lowest power consumption at the same delay target. In terms of dynamic (AC) power, FPR was able to achieve 2% more in power reduction when comparing to FAR optimization. In terms of leakage (DC) power, FPR tuning achieved 4% more in power reduction.

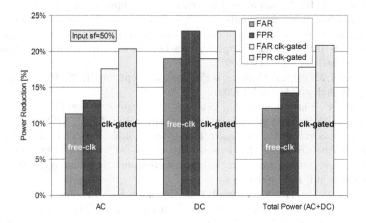

Fig. 9. FAR vs. FPR power reduction comparison on the adder example for an input data pattern with 50% switching activity

6   Conclusion

A new power-aware tuning methodology, Free Power Recovery (FPR), has been introduced. Its application and demonstrated power reduction potential has been evaluated on both a simple example and complex microprocessor circuits. The methodology takes into account switching activities and state-dependent leakage duty cycle properties to tune a design. The goal is to minimize the total power consumption of a circuit without degrading its delay performance. The FPR optimization mode has been incorporated into the EinsTuner circuit tuning tool. Results from both the new and existing tuning methodologies were obtained and verified using existing timing and power tools. The FPR optimization mode was found to be better at reducing power as compared with the existing optimization modes (such as FAR). The FPR mode appears to be particularly effective for non-symmetrical circuits. Power and timing results of pre-tuned and post-tuned designs were used as comparison criteria.

References

1. Horowitz, M., Stark, D., Alon, E.: Digital Circuit Design Trends. IEEE Journal of Solid-State Circuits 43(4), 757–761 (2008)
2. Oklobdzija, V.G., Krishnamurthy, R.K.: High-Performance Energy-Efficient Microprocessor Design. Series on Integrated Circuits and Systems. Springer-Verlag New York, Inc., Secaucus (2006)
3. Conn, A.R., Elfadel, I.M., Molzen, W.W., O'Brien, P.R., Strenski, P.N., Visweswariah, C., Whan, C.B.: Gradient-Based Optimization of Custom Circuits Using a Static-Timing Formulation. In: DAC, pp. 452–459 (1999)
4. Berridge, R., et al.: IBM POWER6 Microprocessor Physical Design and Design Methodology. IBM Journal of Research and Development 51(6), 685–714 (2007)
5. Narendra, S., De, V., Antoniadis, D., Chandrakasan, A., Borkar, S.: Scaling of Stack Effect and its Application for Leakage Reduction. In: ISLPED 2001: Proceedings of the 2001 International Symposium on Low Power Electronics and Design, pp. 195–200. ACM, New York (2001)
6. BSIM 4.2.1 MOSFET Model: User's Manual, Dept. of EECS, University of California, Berkeley, CA, USA (2002)
7. Wächter, A., Visweswariah, C., Conn, A.R.: Large-Scale Nonlinear Optimization in Circuit Tuning. Future Generation Computer Syst. 21(8), 1251–1262 (2005)
8. Rao, V.B., Soreff, J.P., Brodnax, T.B., Mains, R.E.: EinsTLT: Transistor-Level Timing with EinsTimer. In: Proceedings of the ACM/IEEE 1999 International Workshop on Timing Issues in the Specification and Synthesis of Digital Systems (Tau 1999), pp. 1–6 (1999)
9. Bard, K., et al.: Transistor-Level Tools for High-End Processor Custom Circuit Design at IBM. Proceedings of the IEEE, invited paper (March 2007)
10. Neely, J.S., et al.: CPAM: A Common Power Analysis Methodology for High-Performance VLSI Design. In: IEEE Conf. Electrical Performance of Electronic Packaging, pp. 303–306. IEEE Press, Los Alamitos (2000)

Routing Resistance Influence in Loading Effect on Leakage Analysis

Paulo F. Butzen, André I. Reis, Renato P. Ribas

PGMICRO – UFRGS
{pbutzen,andreis,rpribas}@inf.ufrgs.br

Abstract. Leakage currents represent emergent design parameters in nanometer CMOS technologies. Leakage mechanisms interact with each other at device level (through device geometry and doping profile), at gate level (through intra-cell node voltage) and at circuit level (through inter-cell node voltages). In this paper, the impact of loading effect in the standby power consumption is evaluated in relation to the gate oxide leakage magnitude and the routing resistivity. Simulation results, considering a 32nm technology node, have demonstrated an increase of up to 15% in the total circuit leakage dissipation due to the loading effect influenced by wire resistance.

Keywords: Loading effect, subthreshold leakage, gate tunneling leakage, routing resistance.

1 Introduction

Leakage currents are one of the major design concerns in deep submicron technologies due to the aggressive scaling of MOS device [1-2]. Supply voltage has been reduced to keep the power consumption under control. As a consequence, the transistor threshold voltage is also scaled down to maintain the drive current capacity and achieve performance improvement. However, it increases the subthreshold current exponentially. Moreover, short channel effects, such as drain-induced barrier lowering (DIBL), are being reinforced when the technology shrinking is experienced. Hence, oxide thickness (t_{ox}) has to follow this reduction but at expense of significant gate oxide tunneling. Furthermore, the higher doping profile results in increasing reverse-biased junction band-to-band tunneling (BTBT) leakage mechanism, though it is expected to be relevant for technologies bellow 25nm [3].

Subthreshold leakage current occurs in off-devices, presenting relevant values in transistor with channel length shorter than 180nm [4]. In terms of subthreshold leakage saving techniques and estimation models, the *'stack effect'* represents the principal factor to be taken into account [5]. Gate oxide leakage, in turn, is verified in both on- and off-transistor when different potentials are applied between drain/source and gate terminals [6]. Sub-100nm processes, whose t_{ox} is smaller than 16Å, tends to present subthreshold and gate leakages at the same order of magnitude [7]. In this sense, high-K dielectrics are been considered as an efficient way to mitigate gate leakage at process level [8].

J. Monteiro and R. van Leuken (Eds.): PATMOS 2009, LNCS 5953, pp. 317–325, 2010.

Since a certain leakage mechanism cannot be considered as dominant, the interaction among them should not be neglected. In [9], the interaction between leakage currents in logic cells has been accurately modeled. However, in nanometer technologies, the total standby power consumption of a circuit cannot be estimated just by summing individual leakages from logic cells, since leakage currents of distinct cells interact with each other through internal circuit nodes (inter-cell connectivity). Such interaction is known as *'loading effect'*. In [10] and [11], the impact of loading effect in total leakage estimation is analyzed. Those works claims the loading effect modifies the leakage of logic gates by approximately 5% to 8%.

In this work, two important aspects are carefully taken into account in such a kind of evaluation. At first, the gate oxide leakage magnitudes to attain the relevant impact suggested in [10]. Secondly, the influence of routing resistance in loading effect, not mentioned in previous works [10-11].

2 Loading Effect

In logic circuits, different leakage currents, in particular gate oxide leakages, from distinct logic cells interact with each other through the internal circuit node voltages. Such interaction modifies the inter-cell node potentials, changing thus the total leakage of individual logic gates connected at this node. The loading effect can either increase or decrease the static currents of cells. For an easier comprehension of loading effect analysis, fig. 1 illustrates the leakage currents of two cascaded CMOS inverters. Considering input logic value equal to '0' (0V), all leakage currents (subthreshold, gate oxide, BTBT) on the first inverter, and the gate leakage currents of second inverter contribute to decrease the voltage at intermediate voltage V_i (ideally in V_{dd} – power supply voltage). Such potential reduction, on the other hand, tends to reduce those leakage components directly associated to this node. However, the voltage reduction in V_i changes the gate-source potential (V_{gs}) at PMOS on the second inverter, increasing significantly its subthreshold current (exponentially dependent of V_{gs}). BTBT leakage on the second inverter is not affected. Similar analysis is easily done considering the input logic value of the inverter chain equal to '1' (V_{dd}).

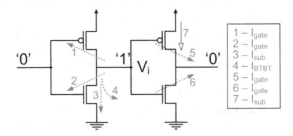

Fig. 1. Leakage currents illustration associated to the intermediate node potential V_i (loading effect) in two cascaded CMOS inverters

Based on the analysis above, it is possible to conclude:

- Gate leakage is the main leakage mechanism responsible for loading effect. In the given example, four from six leakage components that affect the node potential V_i are gate oxide leakage currents.
- Loading effect reduces all currents directly linked to the evaluation node.
- Loading effect increases significantly the subthreshold leakage on the next stage. It is due to the increasing in gate-to-source potential, creating a conducting channel in an original turned off transistor.

2.1 Routing Resistance Influence

In previous section, the connection wire resistance between two logic cells is neglected in the analysis.

In [12] is presented the evaluation of routing wire characteristics in nanometer technologies, and the authors concluded that the wire resistance (per unit length) grows under scaling. From data presented on that work, the resistance of equivalent wire segments increases around 10% to 15% for each technology node. Simulation results have showed a routing resistance varies from units of ohms until kilohms for an 8 bit processor designed using FreePDK technology [13]. In the same manner, gate oxide leakage, which represents the major contributor of loading effect, is predicted to increase at a rate of more than 3X per technology generation [11].

Fig. 2 shows the circuit used to investigate the influence of routing resistance in loading effect analysis. In Fig. 2, a resistor representing the routing resistance has been included in the circuit discussed in previous section (see Fig. 1). By doing so, the logic cells do not have a common node anymore. There are two distinct potentials, the output voltage of first stage (V_1) and the input voltage of second one (V_2). From Kirchhoff's Current Law (KCL), it can be verified that, for the steady state condition defined in Fig. 2:

- V_1 is larger than V_i.
- V_2 is smaller than V_i.

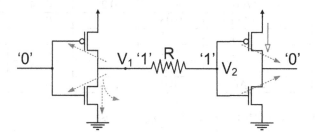

Fig. 2. Evaluation of routing resistance in the loading effect

Similar analysis can be done by considering the opposite logic static condition. Thus, the influence of routing resistance in loading effect analysis can be summarized as:

- Leakage currents on the first cell do not reduce as much as when routing resistance is ignore, because V_1 is larger than V_i.
- Gate oxide leakage current on the second cell reduces even more by taking into account the routing resistance, once V_2 is smaller than V_i.
- Subthreshold current on the second cell increases significantly due to the routing resistance influence, again because V_2 is smaller than V_i.

3 Simulation Results

Electrical simulations were carried out in order to validate the assumptions outlined in previous sections. Experiments were divided in three different goals. First of all, four technology processes have been characterized in terms of NMOS and PMOS transistor current values, to be used as reference in the proposed investigation. At second, the relevance of gate oxide leakage current magnitude on the loading effect has been verified, without considering the routing wire parasitic influence. Such routing resistance has been taken into account in the last set of simulations.

3.1 Technology Characterization

Table 1 presents device characteristics of four Berkeley Predictive BSIM4 models [14], obtained through HSPICE simulations. Those processes represent CMOS technologies from 90 nm down to 32 nm, with specific gate oxide thickness (t_{ox}) values. The current components characterized for each transistor type in each technology node were: subthreshold leakage current (I_{sub}); and gate oxide leakage currents (I_{gate}) for turned on and turned off devices, i.e. I_{gate_ON} and I_{gate_OFF}, respectively.

Table 1. Devices current characterization for different PTM CMOS processes

Transistor Type	Technology Node	90nm	65nm	45nm	32nm
	t_{ox} (Å)	17	15	13	11
NMOS	I_{sub} (A/m)	0.16	0.24	0.44	0.89
	I_{gate_ON} (A/m)	0.05	0.19	0.71	2.90
	I_{gate_OFF} (A/m)	0.01	0.05	0.19	0.86
PMOS	I_{sub} (A/m)	0.11	0.16	0.26	0.77
	I_{gate_ON} (A/m)	< 0.01	< 0.01	0.03	0.16
	I_{gate_OFF} (A/m)	< 0.01	< 0.01	0.01	0.08

3.2 Loading Effect in Different Technology Process

Table 2 presents DC simulation results performed by considering the circuit depicted in Fig. 3. CMOS inverters present the same sizing, that is, NMOS transistor width equal to 1.0 μm and PMOS transistor width equal to 2.0 μm, keeping transistor length at minimum dimension allowed at process node. This table provides the comparison between the four different devices models, described in Table 1. The voltage at node

N and the total leakage currents in cells *G0* and *G1* are given. Cells *G2* and *G3* have the same total leakage of cell *G1*.

By evaluating the data from Table 2, one is possible to conclude that the loading effect influences the leakage analysis when the gate leakage current achieves similar magnitude of subthreshold leakage. Different loading effect contribution in total cell leakage is also verified, observing the reduction of total leakage in cell *G0*, while it increases in cells *G1*, *G2* and *G3*.

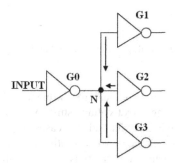

Fig. 3. Circuit for loading effect evaluation at node *N*

Table 2. Loading voltage at node *N* in circuit from Fig. 3, and the total leakage currents in cells *G0* and *G1*, for different processes presented in Table 1

CMOS PROCESS	V(N) (V)		I_{Leak} (G0) (µA)		I_{Leak} (G1) (µA)	
	NLE *	LE **	NLE *	LE **	NLE *	LE **
INPUT = '0' (low logic value)						
90 nm	1.00	0.999	0.17	0.17	0.27	0.28
65 nm	1.00	0.999	0.29	0.29	0.51	0.52
45 nm	1.00	0.998	0.68	0.68	1.25	1.27
32 nm	1.00	0.991	2.07	2.00	4.60	4.78
INPUT = '1' (high logic value)						
90 nm	0.00	< 0.001	0.27	0.27	0.17	0.17
65 nm	0.00	< 0.001	0.51	0.51	0.29	0.29
45 nm	0.00	0.001	1.25	1.25	0.68	0.69
32 nm	0.00	0.002	4.60	4.58	2.07	2.09

* NLE = No Loading Effect ** LE = Considering Loading Effect.

3.3 Routing Resistance Influence

In Table 3, in turn, DC simulation results for circuit depicted in Fig. 4 are given. The resistance value is equal to 2kΩ and CMOS inverters keep the same sizing from previous analysis. The voltages at node *N0* and *N1*, in Fig. 4, area provided, as well as the total leakage current in cells *G0* and *G1*. The cells *G2* and *G3* present the same leakage value of cell *G1*.

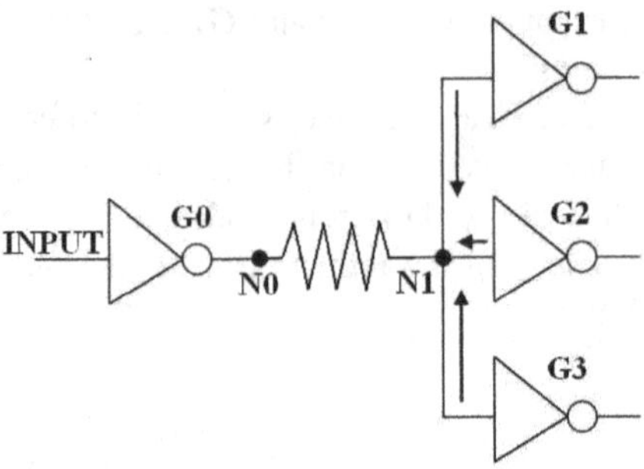

Fig. 4. Circuit for loading effect evaluation at node *N0* and *N1*, according to the influence of connection resistance

When compared to Table 2, it is clear the influence of routing resistance in the leakage current through loading effect voltage shift. As mentioned before, the loading effect increases some leakage currents and decreases other ones. However, the total leakage in circuit cells becomes worst when routing resistance is taken into account. The decrement of some leakage components is not as significant while the increment in other leakages is more severe. The loading effect, when routing resistance is considered, modifies the total leakage of a logic cell up to 15%, while with no routing resistance influence it is changed up to 4%. Fig. 5 compares the total leakage current in cells *G0* and *G1* when routing resistance is considered (LE + R) in the loading effect analysis.

The influence of routing resistance in loading effect analysis can also be observed in Table 4. In this experiment, the resistor depicted in Fig. 4 varies from 10 Ω to 10 kΩ. The voltage at nodes *N0* and *N1*, as well as the total leakage current in cells *G0* and *G1* are obtained, while the cells *G2* and *G3* present the same leakage value of cell *G1*.

Table 3. Considering routing resistance in the loading voltage at nodes *N0* and *N1*, and the total leakage currents in cells *G0* and *G1* (as illustrated in Fig. 4), for different processes presented in Table 1

CMOS PROCESS	V(N0) (V)	V(N1) (V)	I_{Leak} (G0) (μA)	I_{Leak} (G1) (μA)
INPUT = '0' (low logic value)				
90 nm	0.999	0.999	0.17	0.28
65 nm	0.999	0.998	0.29	0.53
45 nm	0.998	0.993	0.68	1.31
32 nm	0.992	0.975	2.01	5.28
INPUT = '1' (high logic value)				
90 nm	< 0.001	0.000	0.27	0.17
65 nm	0.000	0.001	0.51	0.30
45 nm	0.001	0.002	1.25	0.70
32 nm	0.002	0.009	4.59	2.20

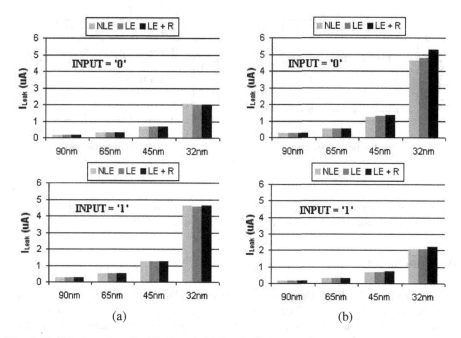

Fig. 5. Total leakage in cells *G0* (a) and *G1* (b), from circuit in Fig. 4, for different processes: 'NLE' – without loading effect influence; 'LE' – considering loading affect but no wire resistance; and 'LE+R' – including the routing resistance in analysis

Fig. 6 shows the total leakage current in cells *G0* and *G1* according the results presented used in Table 4. The graphics show more clearly the huge increment in total leakage current due to routing resistance influence in loading effect. The voltage difference created by the resistance increases significantly the subthreshold current of subsequent cells connected to evaluation node.

Table 4. Routing resistance influence at nodes N0 and N1, and the total leakage currents in cells G0 and G1 (illustrated in Fig. 4) for different resistance values, considering the 32 nm technology model

RESISTANCE (Ω)	V(N0) (V)	V(N1) (V)	I_{Leak} (G0) (μA)	I_{Leak} (G1) (μA)
INPUT = '0' (low logic value)				
10	0.991	0.991	2.00	4.78
100	0.991	0.990	2.01	4.81
1000	0.992	0.983	2.01	5.01
10000	0.993	0.927	2.02	8.59
INPUT = '1' (high logic value)				
10	0.002	0.002	4.58	2.09
100	0.002	0.002	4.58	2.09
1000	0.002	0.005	4.58	2.14
10000	0.002	0.033	4.59	2.76

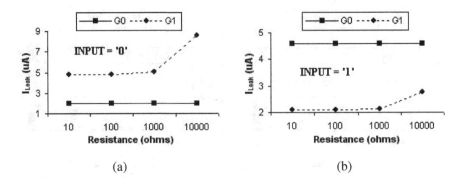

Fig. 6. Total leakage in cells G0 and G1 (see Fig. 4) for a resistance variation range from 1 Ω to 10 kΩ, in 32 nm process node, when input = '0' (a) and input = '1' (b)

4 Conclusions

In this paper the loading effect has been reviewed. The direct relation to gate oxide leakage current has been reinforced, and the influence of routing wire resistance, not mentioned in previous works reported in the literature, have been analyzed. The first evaluation shows that the loading effect starts to modify the leakage analysis only when the gate leakage current achieves the same magnitude of subthreshold leakage. In the second analysis, where the influence of the routing resistance in the loading effect is investigated, experimental results show that the loading effect modifies the total leakage of a logic cell up to 15%, instead of 4% when routing resistance is ignored.

References

1. Semiconductor Industry Association, International Roadmap for Semiconductor (2006), http://public.itrs.net
2. Roy, K., et al.: Leakage Current Mechanisms and Leakage Reduction Techniques in Deep-submicron CMOS Circuits. Proc. IEEE 91(2), 305–327 (2003)
3. Agarwal, et al.: Leakage Power Analysis and Reduction: Models, Estimation and Tools. IEE Proceedings – Computers and Digital Techniques 152(3), 353–368 (2005)
4. Narendra, S., et al.: Full-Chip Subthreshold Leakage Power Prediction and Reduction Techniques for Sub-0.18um CMOS. IEEE Journal of Solid-State Circuits 39(3), 501–510 (2004)
5. Cheng, Z., et al.: Estimation of Standby Leakage Power in CMOS Circuits Considering Accurate Modeling of Transistor Stacks. In: Proc. Int. Symposium Low Power Electronics and Design, pp. 239–244 (1998)
6. Rao, R.M., et al.: Efficient Techniques for Gate Leakage Estimation. In: Proc. Int. Symposium Low Power Electronics and Design, pp. 100–103 (2003)
7. Ono, et al.: A 100nm Node CMOS Technology for Practical SOC Application Requirement. Tech. Digest of IEDM, pp. 511–514 (2001)

8. Gusev, E., et al.: Ultrathin High-k Gate Stacks for Advanced CMOS Devices. Tech. Digest of IEDM, pp. 451–454 (2001)
9. Butzen, P.F., et al.: Simple and Accurate Method for Fast Static Current Estimation in CMOS Complex Gates with Interaction of Leakage Mechanisms. In: Proceedings Great Lakes Symposium on VLSI, pp. 407–410 (2008)
10. Mukhopadhyay, S., Bhunia, S., Roy, K.: Modeling and Analysis of Loading Effect on Leakage of Nanoscaled Bulk-CMOS Logic Circuits. IEEE Trans. on CAD of Integrated Circuits and Systems 25(8), 1486–1495 (2006)
11. Rastogi, W., Chen, S.: On Estimating Impact of Loading Effect on Leakage Current in Sub-65nm Scaled CMOS Circuit Based on Newton-Raphson Method. In: Proc. of Design Automation Conf., pp. 712–715 (2007)
12. Horowitz, M.A., Ho, R., Mai, K.: The Future of Wires. Proceedings of the IEEE 89(4), 490–504 (2001)
13. Nangate FreePDK45 Generic Open Cell Library (2009),
    http://www.si2.org/openeda.si2.org/projects/nangatelib
14. Zhao, W., Cao, Y.: New generation of Predictive Technology Model for sub-45nm early design exploration. IEEE Transactions on Electron Devices 53(11), 2816–2823 (2006)

Processor Customization for Software Implementation of the AES Algorithm for Wireless Sensor Networks

Néstor Suárez[1], Gustavo M. Callicó[1], Roberto Sarmiento[1],
Octavio Santana[2], and Anteneh A. Abbo[2]

[1] IUMA, Institute for Applied Microelectronics
ULPGC, University of Las Palmas of G.C., Spain
{nsuarez,gustavo,roberto}@iuma.ulpgc.es
[2] Philips Research Eindhoven,
High Tech Campus, The Netherlands
{octavio.santana,anteneh.a.abbo}@philips.com

Abstract. The Advanced Encryption Algorithm (AES) has been the most widely used symmetric block cipher technique for providing security to applications adopting Wireless Sensor Networks (WSN). In this paper, an efficient software implementation of the AES algorithm is described running on an application specific processor (ASIP) platform that has been developed for use in low-power wireless sensor node designs with low memory requirements. Experimental results show that up to 46.3% reduction in cycle count is achievable through extensive code optimization. Hardware customization are proposed to the ASIP template to further improve the code performance. The gains include cycle count reductions of 33.1% and 45.2% for encryption and decryption, respectively and 21.6% reduction in code memory.

Keywords: Advanced Encryption Standard (AES), Wireless Sensor Networks (WSN), application-specific integrated circuits (ASIP), code optimization, processor customization.

1 Introduction

Recent technological advances in device miniaturization and cost reductions have led to the development of wireless sensor nodes – small autonomous devices that combine sensing, computing, and wireless communication capabilities. These nodes are the building blocks of wireless sensor networks that serve a wide range of applications, such as, industrial, scientific and military [1].

Each sensor node is inherently resource constrained, i.e., has limited processing power, storage capacity, communication bandwidth and energy supply. Due to the wireless communication, which simplifies sensor node deployment, WSNs are more susceptible to attacks than the wired counterpart. Consequently, cryptographic techniques are an essential part of the security architecture of sensor

J. Monteiro and R. van Leuken (Eds.): PATMOS 2009, LNCS 5953, pp. 326–335, 2010.

nodes; the most widely used approach being symmetric encryption of data using the AES algorithm [2], [3], [4].

Following the AES standardization, hardware implementation of AES has been the most common approach in the form of cryptographic coprocessors or ASICs. In applications where high data throughput is of prime importance, this approach is the most practical one, specially with regard to power consumption. On the other hand, recent works have demonstrated that it is also possible to realize AES in software when the desired performance can be achieved with small overhead [5], [6], [7]. An efficient software AES implementation implies resource sharing that avoids the need for dedicated hardware resources. Publicly reported software approaches cover a variety of compute platforms ranging from implementations on 32-bits and 64-bits desktop computers to tiny 8-bits microcontrollers.

When optimizing wireless sensor nodes for low-power, application-specific processors play an important role since the architecture can be customized according to the functional requirements. Since the ASIPs are programmable, they could be used to run the AES code besides normal sensor operations. Moreover, an ASIP implementation will avoid the leakage power and the area of an AES coprocessor that are increasingly important in low-power devices.

In this paper, we examine this approach based on an ASIP platform called PEARL [8] chosen by the company, Philips Research. First, we apply well-known software optimization techniques to improve the performance of a reference code. Next, we investigate the performance gain by introducing hardware functional units (FUs) to accelerate critical code sections.

The paper is organized as follows. In Section 2, essential features of the AES algorithm are described. This is followed by a discussion on the ASIP architecture in Section 3. The AES software optimization and hardware customization steps are explained in Sections 4 and 5, respectively. In Section 6, experimental results are discussed followed by concluding remarks in Section 7.

2   Advanced Encryption Standard (AES)

AES is a symmetric block-cipher algorithm that operates with 128-bit blocks of data and supports keys of 128, 192, 256 bits of length. The input block is arranged in a 4x4 matrix of bytes called *state* and the different transformations operate on the intermediate result. The key is used to generate a number of *round keys*.

An AES encryption process consists of a number of encryption rounds (N_r) that depend on the length of the cipher key. Each round is composed of four transformations that operate on the *state* matrix:

- **SubBytes**: a byte substitution process using a table called *S-Box*.
- **ShiftRows**: changes the order of bytes in every row of *state*.
- **MixColumns**: multiplies *state* by a fixed polynomial.
- **AddRoundKey**: XORing of each column of *state* with four round keys.

For ciphering a message of arbitrary length, a mechanism to partition the message into packets of standard length is needed. The *Block Cipher Mode* is one such approach which uses a symmetric key block cipher algorithm to provide confidentiality or authentication. There are five different block cipher modes (ECB, CBC, CFB, OFB, CTR) described in the AES standard [9], [10] that exhibit different characteristics.

3   Application Specific Processor for WSN

Figure 1 shows composition of a wireless sensor node that is capable of getting information from the physical medium, performing some data processing, collecting all the information and communicating with other connected nodes in the network. Since the sensor node has to operate on a tight energy budget in most use cases, the components have to consume as small power as possible [11].

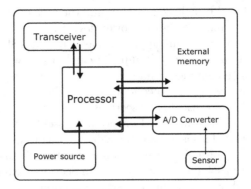

Fig. 1. Sensor node architecture

There are different architectural alternatives for the sensor node implementation. The choice depends on the speed-power-cost and design time trade-offs in relation to the design requirements. Application-specific processors (ASIPs) are a cost-effective trade-off between dedicated hardware implementations and general purpose processors. ASIPs are programmable devices that have been tailored to a specific application domain or task using custom functional units and instructions. The short time-to-market combined with extensive tool-support makes ASIPs an attractive alternative.

The ASIP chosen in this work is shown in Figure 2. Basically, it is a 2-issue slot very long instruction word (VLIW) processor with the possibility of customizing the on-chip memories (data and program), register files, functional units and their connectivity. The customization depends on the sensor node processing requirements and involves design space exploration guided by the code profiling tools.

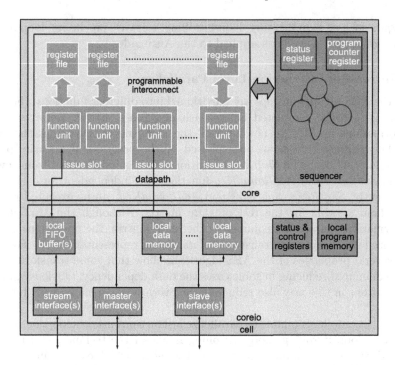

Fig. 2. The PEARL processor template from Silicon Hive [8]

4   AES Code Optimization

Although compilers do a good job in code optimization, they are not able to exploit the full potential of the processor especially with regard to ASIPs which have special architectural features. In such circumstances, the programmer must guide the compiler by rewriting critical code sections that are identified with the help of code profiling tools.

The optimization should reduce the execution time (cycles), memory usage, bandwidth, or some other resource. In general, those objectives can be mutually exclusive, and require a trade-off decision. Our principal objective is minimizing the number of cycles while maintaining low memory usage. The optimization process was accomplished in two phases: data format manipulation and instruction flow scheduling.

Applying data format manipulation implies rearranging the processed data taking into account the processor architecture. All AES byte transformations are clustered as 32-bit transformations using techniques specified in [12] since the chosen ASIP has a 32-bit data path.

In case of VLIW architectures, optimization via instruction flow scheduling targets at increasing the instruction-level parallelism (ILP) thereby maximizing issue slot utilization. In general, this is an intractable problem and programmers must help the compiler by rewriting parts of the source code. Well-known techniques such as loop merging, loop unrolling, software pipelining, loop invariant extraction, etc. have been applied to the AES code.

4.1   Increasing Instruction-Level Parallelism

When the AES algorithm steps are partitioned into different functions, the *state* matrix needs to be completed before each new function call. However, some transformations in AES do not need all the *state* matrix entries at the same time. This characteristics can be exploited by the processor to identify parallelizable instructions. The *ShiftRows* transformation is independent from row to row and *SubBytes* and *AddRoundKey* functions are independent for each byte. Consequently, *ShiftRows*, *SubBytes* and *AddRoundKey* can be executed row by row without waiting for the rest of *state* matrix. Although the *MixColumns* transformation operates on columns of the *state* matrix, the operations can be parallelized when using the transposed *state* matrix representation [12]. Furthermore, several properties of the AES algorithm allow that some transformations can be commuted reducing in some cases the data dependency. Obviously, merging operations in this way also reduces cycle overheads associated with function calls.

Since the compiler is unable to parallelize instructions inside a loop, one option is applying loop unrolling. Loop unrolling is one of the techniques to increase ILP by decreasing the number of control statements which execute in one loop. There is a decreasing return from excessive unrolling, and other issues concerning register file size and instruction buffer size need to be considered as well. This technique is applied for each row of the *state* matrix because operations for doing conditional evaluation have significant overhead compared to the repetition of each line of code.

4.2   Reducing Memory Access

Since memory accesses (loads and stores) are costly in terms of cycle count and energy consumption, a great deal of our work has focused on techniques for an effective use of memory. In the chosen ASIP template, only one issue slot has access to the data memory and each access to memory requires two clock cycles. For the AES algorithm, the *state* matrix is the most frequently used entity and should be stored in the register files between transformations to increase the performance of code.

When memory is accessed consecutively, post-increment and post-decrement operators are frequently used to update the pointer. When using these operators, the processor has to wait for access to memory before starting computing the next address. Programmers can force the compiler not to use these operators by specifying the offset with a constant number that is coded inside each instruction.

4.3   Optimization of Critical Kernels

In AES, many of the operations applied involve the Galois field $GF(2^8)$. The byte $(b_7 b_6 b_5 b_4 b_3 b_2 b_1 b_0)$ is considered as a polynomial with coefficients in $\{0,1\}$.

In this case, polynomial addition and subtraction are realized as bitwise xor ($\oplus$) operations. Multiplication of polynomials in *MixColumns* is more complex and involves modulo operations with an irreducible polynomial of degree 8 (in hexadecimal, {0x11B}).

An operation called *xtime* is defined to represent a special case of polynomial multiplication by x ={0x02}. Multiplications with higher powers of x are computed by iterating *xtime* operation and accumulating intermediate results. The *xtime* operation is realized as a simple left shift (<<) followed by a conditional XOR with {0x11B} and truncating the result to 8 bits.

In 32-bit architectures, the *xtime* operation is likely to be executed in parallel on four bytes at the same time. This can be achieved using a mask that changes its value as a function of the most significant bit for each byte. This is shown in Table 1 where four *xtime* operations are executed in six instructions, much less than operating on a byte at a time. This function is coded in-line by using macros at the cost of small increase in code size. As a result of *xtime* optimization, the reduction in cycles count was 48%. Despite the use of in-line coding using function macros, the code size was slightly reduced due to multi-byte based computation. The instruction in time equal 2, issue slot 1, is a multiplication with a constant which replaces the conditional XOR operation which would otherwise have to be done per byte. The argument here is that the ASIP already has a multiplier which could be reused, hence no extra hardware cost.

Table 1. XTIMEx4 logic operations

Time	issue slot 1	issue slot 2
1	mask = in & 0x80808080	temp = in & 0x7F7F7F7F
2	mask = mask 7 >>	temp = temp 1 <<
3	mask = mask * 0x1B	
4	out = temp $\oplus$ mask	

4.4   Storing Partial Results

Sometimes, a program can be accelerated by increasing the use of memory, saving results instead of computing them again. In case of AES, some partial results are stored in *look-up* tables. For instance, *SubBytes* transformation replaces each byte in the *state* matrix by its substitute in a *S-Box* table that comprises a composition of two transformations: a Galois field inverse function and an affine transformation. Instead of executing these operations, very expensive in software, the results are stored in two tables, one for the direct and other for inverse transformation. Other approaches include techniques to combine the two tables [13] or adopt an ASIC implementation [14].

In 32-bit processors, the SubBytes, ShiftRows and MixColumns operations can be combined in a single set of table look-ups as it is described in AES proposal [15] and implemented in paper [16]. The 4-Kbytes of data memory needed for these look-up tables is not available in PEARL processor, because of that we discarded this option.

5   Hardware Customization

In order to improve the performance of the optimized code further, some hardware modifications are applied. Two functional units are developed, at small hardware overhead, to accelerate *MixColumns* and *SubBytes* transformations. These transformations represent the 72.58% and 77.82% of encryption and decryption operations respectively. Due to their overhead, we decided to improve the performance of these transformations implementing the critical kernel of them. Corresponding to the processor customizations, the AES code is modified by making explicit reference to the new instruction.

5.1   XTIMEx4 Functional Unit

This module and the associated instruction replace the operations listed in Table 1 to speed up the *MixColumns* transformations. Architecture of the XTIMEx4 FU is shown in Figure 3, in which four basic *xtime* operations are executed on 4 bytes in parallel. Unlike the software approach, no real hardware multiplication is implemented; instead, four conditional byte-level XOR functions are used keeping the hardware overhead small.

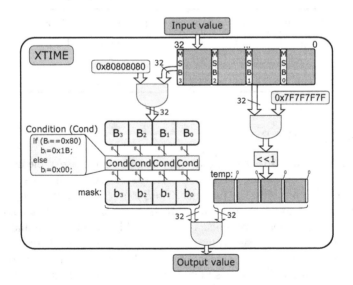

Fig. 3. Architecture of the XTIMEx4 functional unit

5.2   XBYTE Functional Unit

The *SubBytes* transformation, which is called 160 times for each encryption or decryption of process constitutes a considerable part of the execution cycle count. Since the transformation is byte-level substitution, it can not be fully parallelized on 4-byte words. The primary task of the XBYTE FU (shown in Figure 4) is fast extraction of bytes out of a 32-bit word. This is done with two combined operations: byte selection followed by logical AND with a constant mask of {0x000000FF}.

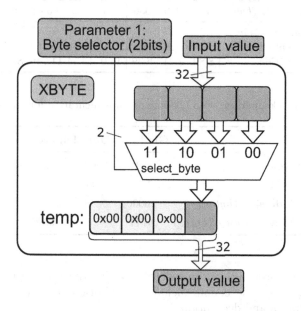

Fig. 4. Architecture of the XBYTE functional unit

6   Results

A summary of the experimental results on AES software optimization are in Table 2. The hardware customization improves the AES code performance significantly in terms of cycle count and program memory usage. The improvements are depicted as performance changes averaged over the three AES key sizes and indicate the expected improvement. The encryption/decryption throughput, excluding overhead associated with *Key Expansion* and block cipher modes, is given for a processor running at 100 MHz. Hardware customization represents an increase in the number of LUTs of 0.46%, with respect to our processor size over a Xilinx XC4VLX160. It is demonstrated that the two functional units have an acceptable overhead for our processor.

For comparison purposes, a 32-bit version of Gladman's reference code [17] is executed on the PEARL processor. Table 3 shows the relative performance

Table 2. Optimized AES code Performance

Processor	PEARL			PEARL + FUs			Average
Key size *(bits)*	128	192	256	128	192	256	Change
Cycles count *(cycles)*							
Encryption	916	1082	1248	614	724	833	-33.1%
Decryption	1451	1727	2003	800	945	1090	-45.2%
Key Schedule	537	808	622	537	808	622	0%
Program size *(bytes)*	5048	6328	5576	3816	5128	4376	-21.6%
Data memory *(bytes)*	624	640	656	624	640	656	0%
Throughput *(Mbps)*							
Encryption	13.97	11.82	10.25	20.84	17.68	15.36	+49.53%
Decryption	8.82	7.41	6.39	16.0	13.54	11.74	+82.61%

Table 3. Comparison with Gladman's implementation for AES-128

	Gladman	Ours	Difference
Cycles	6534	3507	-46.3%
IPC	1.40	1.44	+2.8%
Code size (*bytes*)	20000	5048	-74.7%
Data memory (*bytes*)	4744	624	-86.8%

advantage of the proposed optimized solution for the case without hardware customization. The cycle counts include contributions of key expansion runs both for encryption and decryption.

The work reported in [18], based on a 32-bit StrongARM SA-1100 processor, is a good benchmark to compare with since it has an application scope similar to the wireless sensor networks discussed here. The encryption and decryption cycle counts are lower by, respectively, 60% and 50% in favour of our proposal.

7   Conclusions and Future Work

In this paper, an efficient software implementation of the AES algorithm for wireless sensor nodes is presented. This implementation is optimized in code size, execution cycle count and memory usage. Based on an application-specific processor template, the code optimization is further improved by introducing functional units that accelerate critical code section with small hardware overhead. The combined code and functional unit optimization yields results that show significant improvement over state-of-the art software AES implementations. Although, dedicated hardware AES implementations set the record in terms of data throughput, the adopted ASIP based software implementation is a serious candidate when considering low data rate sensor nodes consisting sufficient compute power to also run the encryption/decryption tasks.

References

1. Hof, H.J.: Applications of Sensor Networks. In: Wagner, D., Wattenhofer, R. (eds.) Algorithms for Sensor and Ad Hoc Networks. LNCS, vol. 4621, pp. 1–20. Springer, Heidelberg (2007)
2. National Institute of Standards and Technology: Report on the development of the Advanced Encryption Standard (AES) (October 2000)
3. Institute of Electrical, Electronics Engineers (IEEE): IEEE 802.15.4-2006, Revision of IEEE 802.15.4-2003 (2006)
4. ZigBee Alliance, http://www.zigbee.org/
5. Perrig, A., Stankovic, J., Wagner, D.: Security in wireless sensor networks. Commun. ACM 47(6), 53–57 (2004)
6. Law, Y.W., Doumen, J., Hartel, P.: Survey and benchmark of block ciphers for wireless sensor networks. ACM Trans. Sen. Netw. 2(1), 65–93 (2006)
7. Karlof, C., Sastry, N., Wagner, D.: Tinysec: A link layer security architecture for wireless sensor networks. In: SenSys 2004, Baltimore, November 2004, pp. 162–175 (2004)
8. Silicon Hive's website, http://www.siliconhive.com/
9. International Organization for Standardization: ISO/IEC 10116, Information technology – Security techniques – Modes of operation for an n-bit block cipher (2006)
10. Dworkin, M.: Recommendation for block cipher modes of operation: Methods and techniques. NIST Special Publication 800-38A (2001)
11. Simunic, T., Benini, L., Micheli, G.D.: Energy-efficient design of battery-powered embedded systems. In: ISLPED 1999, pp. 212–217. ACM, New York (1999)
12. Bertoni, G., Breveglieri, L., Fragneto, P., Macchetti, M., Marchesin, S.: Efficient software implementation of AES on 32-bit platforms. In: Kaliski Jr., B.S., Koç, Ç.K., Paar, C. (eds.) CHES 2002. LNCS, vol. 2523, pp. 159–171. Springer, Heidelberg (2003)
13. Rijmen, V.: Efficient implementation of the rijndael S-Box
14. Lamberger, M., Oswald, E., Wolkerstorfer, J.: An ASIC Implementation of the AES SBoxes. In: Preneel, B. (ed.) CT-RSA 2002. LNCS, vol. 2271, p. 67. Springer, Heidelberg (2002)
15. Daemen, J., Rijmen, V.: Aes proposal: Rijndael
16. Bernstein, D.J., Schwabe, P.: New AES software speed records. In: Chowdhury, D.R., Rijmen, V., Das, A. (eds.) INDOCRYPT 2008. LNCS, vol. 5365, pp. 322–336. Springer, Heidelberg (2008)
17. Gladman, B.: Reference code, http://www.gladman.me.uk/
18. Schädl, J.G., Tillich, S., Rechberger, C., Hofmann, M., Medwed, M.: Energy evaluation of software implementations of block ciphers under memory constraints. In: DATE 2007, pp. 1110–1115 (2007)

An On-Chip Multi-mode Buck DC-DC Converter for Fine-Grain DVS on a Multi-power Domain SoC Using a 65-nm Standard CMOS Logic Process

Motoi Ichihashi[1], Hélène Lhermet[1], Edith Beigné[1], Frédéric Rothan[1], Marc Belleville[1], and Amara Amara[2]

[1] CEA-Léti, MINATEC, F38054 Grenoble, France
[2] ISEP (Institut Supérieur d'Electronique de Paris), Paris, France

Abstract. In this paper, we propose an on-chip dc-dc buck converter for fine-grain dynamic voltage scaling (DVS) on a multi-power domain SoC. The proposed circuit converts from the I/O voltage to the required core operating voltage. This regulator is equipped with the programmable output buffer and the switching signal modulator according to the module operating condition. The proposed converter is fabricated with a 65-nm standard CMOS logic process within the area of 5 bonding pads. The maximum power efficiency is over 88%, and the leakage current in the deep stand-by mode is measured only 19 nA.

1 Introduction

As the transistor size decreases [1], a number of logic modules can be implemented on one chip, called "System on Chip (SoC)". Nowadays, some chip including over 10 power domains has been already proposed [2]. Each module is assigned to a specific and independent power domain through power switch transistors. On the other hand, the "Dynamic Voltage Scaling (DVS)" technique has been also proposed [3] to achieve higher efficiency of energy use, and a number of chip-level implementation examples have been reported [4] [5]. In the previous report [6], one chip containing a number of logic modules based on the global asynchronous local synchronous (GALS) structure has been proposed. Though the GALS structure, each module can operate with different operating voltage according to the required performance. In other words, each power domain can take its own operating voltage, then voltage tuning at module-level can be done. Corresponding to this situation, on-chip dc-dc converters, which supply the operating voltage to each module, have to operate independently.

Beyond a 90-nm technology, the leakage current of a transistor is now the emergent challenge towards future device process [7]. When a logic module does not operate, the corresponding power supply within a given power domain should be turned off by cutting-off the power switch transistors [8] [9]. It has been demonstrated that super cut off technique [10] is one of the techniques used to reduce drastically the leakage current by using a power switch transistor supplied independently using a charge pump. Due to the presence already of on-chip buck

J. Monteiro and R. van Leuken (Eds.): PATMOS 2009, LNCS 5953, pp. 336–346, 2010.

converters in our approach, it could be judicious to combine the power switch of the regulator and the power switch of the super cut off technique in one transistor. The equivalent leakage suppression technique is then more efficient.

2   Logic Module Operation

Picking up a 65-nm technology SoC based on an asynchronous Network on Chip (NoC) [11], the power consumption of a logic module was analyzed. Fig. 1 shows the analysis results of power consumption.

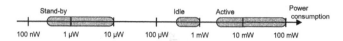

Fig. 1. Power consumption of a logic module on a 65-nm technology [11]

Each logic module has 3 operation modes: Stand-by mode, Idle mode, Active mode. Operating condition on those modes is summarized in Table 1.

Table 1. Operation mode of a logic module

	Mode name		
	Stand-by	Idle	Active
Supply voltage	N/A or 0 V	0.6 V	0.8 ∼ 1.2 V
Stored data	Flushed	Hold	Active
Clock	N/A	Stop	Active

In the stand-by mode, all the operation is stopped to reduce the power consumption. Thus, the stored data in the memory or flip-flop is not maintained. At this moment, the leakage current is the dominant factor of the power consumption. Therefore, the power supply is not needed and the primary objective is to suppress the leakage current. In the idle mode, all stored data in flip-flops and memories have to be maintained while reducing the power consumption. Thus the lowest operating voltage is supplied to maintain the data. The minimum retention voltage is 0.6 V and the output current varies from a few hundreds μA to 1 mA. In the active mode, various operating voltage level can be chosen to achieve the module-level DVS. Current consumption range is from a few mA to 100 mA. With only one on-chip dc-dc converter, it is required to cover the wide output current range including the idle mode and the active mode with high power efficiency. The maximum power efficiency of an ideal linear regulator converting from 2.5 V to 1.2 V is 48% excluding the controller power consumption. The power efficiency of an inductive buck converter should have a better value, higher than 48%.

3   Design Specification

On the conventional SoC design, two power rails are usually needed for one chip. One is the core power supply and the other is the I/O power supply. A typical example is shown in Fig. 3(a). The I/O power supply, for example: 3.3 V, 2.5 V and 1.8 V are always used for the interface circuits that allow the communication between LSIs. For example, the operating frequency of memory interface, like DDR-SDRAM and so on, is now over 200 MHz. Thus, the height of the I/O ring is determined by that of I/O cell including a large size output buffer [12] to operate at such a high frequency.

A basic structure of an inductive buck converter needs one inductor and one capacitor as shown in Fig. 2. When the core voltage can be supplied from the I/O voltage, only one power rail is necessary for one chip, and this situation results in an easy printed circuit board (PCB) design.

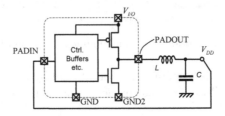

Fig. 2. Minimum number of bonding pad for an inductive dc-dc converter

In our case, and as shown in Fig. 2, 5 pads are required: $V_{I/O}$, GND, GND2, PADOUT and PADIN. $V_{I/O}$ is the I/O power supply voltage and GND is the common ground level. The final buffer transistors are the biggest size in the converter. When those transistors are toggled, large rush current is occurred. Thus, the ground level of the final buffer is separated and is named GND2. PADOUT is the output node of the output buffer and PADIN is the monitor node for the requested voltage. Using off-chip passive devices, the proposed converter is integrated within the area of 5 bonding pad with ESD protection circuits. The converter can be treated as an I/O cell-like design. Fig. 3(b) presents the placement of proposed converter.

Comparing Fig. 3(a) and 3(b), the drawback is that our proposed converter has one additional internal bonding pad. Each converter requires only two

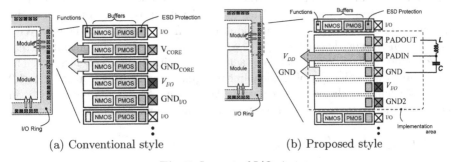

(a) Conventional style   (b) Proposed style

Fig. 3. Layout of I/O ring

external passive components: one capacitor and one inductor. The discrete devices can be implemented like multi-chip module (MCM), System-on-Package (SoP) or 3-D stack techniques. Thus, using these techniques, one external package pin can be saved. As a result, seeing from the external of the chip, there is only one power rail of the I/O power supply.

4   Circuit Design

4.1   Overview

Fig. 4 shows a block diagram of the proposed dc-dc converter.

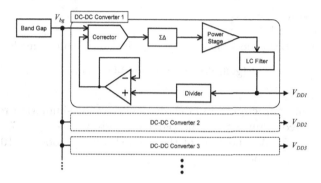

Fig. 4. Block diagram

According to the required performance of the logic module, the proposed dc-dc converter enables each logic module to operate at the required operating voltage in a multi-power domain SoC. Considering the power consumption and occupied area in a chip, the reference voltage generator, band gap circuit, should be shared with all dc-dc converters implemented in the chip. A number of dc-dc converters share one band gap circuit as their reference voltage. As far as using this structure, each dc-dc converter can operate independently and supply the corresponding operating voltage.

The proposed dc-dc converter consists of five main components as shown in Fig. 5: divider, source follower amplifier, corrector, sigma delta ($\Sigma\Delta$) and power stage circuits.

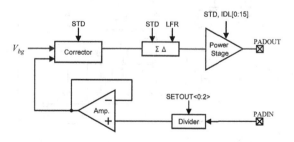

Fig. 5. Circuit diagram of dc-dc converter

When one logic module is set to the stand-by mode, the state of the corresponding dc-dc converter can also enter into the stand-by mode. At this moment, the band gap circuit, however, can not enter into the stand-by mode if just one dc-dc converter operates as shown in Fig. 6(a). When all dc-dc converters are switched to the stand-by mode, the band gap circuit can enter into the stand-by mode as shown in Fig. 6(b).

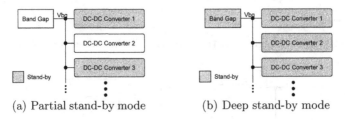

(a) Partial stand-by mode   (b) Deep stand-by mode

Fig. 6. State of the stand-by mode

With one band gap circuit and one dc-dc converter, simulation results show that the power consumption of the partial stand-by mode is 8.7 μW (2.5 V operation with 3.5 μA) and that of the deep stand-by mode is 210 nW (with 84 nA) on a typical condition.

4.2 Circuit Implementation

The $\Sigma\Delta$ circuit generates the driver switching signal of this dc-dc converter. The input voltage bias determines the switching frequency and the duty cycle. Implemented circuit schematic is described in Fig. 7. This circuit itself enables to create the switching signal with no external signal.

This circuit also corresponds to "stand-by mode" and "low frequency mode". In the stand-by mode, STD is high and the input voltage bias is $V_{I/O}$, which is

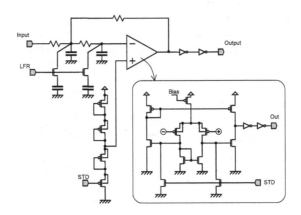

Fig. 7. $\Sigma\Delta$ circuit

derived from the previous stage, corrector. Thus, the circuit stops its operation and there is no pass-through current path. At this moment, the output voltage is $V_{I/O}$. The duty cycle enough covers from 0.2 to 0.8, and the switching frequency is from 7 MHz to 11 MHz according to the simulation results. When the output load of dc-dc converter is low, the switching power of the final transistor gates dominates the power loss on a dc-dc converter. LFR signal enables that the switching frequency becomes lower to reduce the switching power. The duty cycle also enough covers from 0.2 to 0.8, and the switching frequency is lower than the normal operation and the range is from 5 MHz to 8 MHz. The low frequency mode means that this LFR signal is activated.

The largest transistors in dc-dc converter are designed in the final power stage buffer. Moreover, its output node is connected to a LC filter to supply the required output voltage towards a logic module as an output load. As shown in Fig. 8, proposed power stage involves some technique corresponding to the state of logic module. In the stand-by mode, STD signal is high and the entire final transistor is off then high impedance seeing from the output node. The leakage current of I/O transistor is quite smaller than that of core transistor, thus this realizes that the power consumption can be drastically reduced regardless of the connected load module.

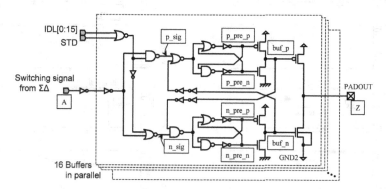

Fig. 8. Power switch circuit corresponding to 3 modes

In general, the power efficiency curve versus the output current describes a mountain curve. As the output current becomes larger beyond its peak, the efficiency decreases due to the power loss on parasitic resistances. On the other hand, as the output current becomes smaller before the peak of the efficiency, the operating power consumption of the converter itself degrades the efficiency. The final output buffers on the power stage are the largest transistors on a converter. Thus, the on-off switching power of those transistors dominates the operating power consumption of an inductive converter. This technique can obtain higher power efficiency according to the output current and effectively contribute the power tracking to the efficiency optimization in the active mode.

This power stage contains 16 buffer fingers in parallel. One finger has final buffers and pre buffers, which take a nesting style on pre buffers and final buffers to be no-overlap driver in order to avoid creating pass through current. Fig. 9 shows signal waveforms from simulation results. With this nesting style, gate signals of pMOS transistor always rise up faster than those of nMOS transistor. In reverse, gate signals of pMOS transistor always fall down faster than these of nMOS transistor. When the rise up time or fall down time is too short, some spike current occurs between the power supply nodes as if a pass through current due to the capacitance coupling. In final buffer transistors, therefore, the rise time of nMOS transistor gate node (buf_n) and the fall down time of pMOS transistor gate node (buf_p) is quite long comparing to the opposite edge.

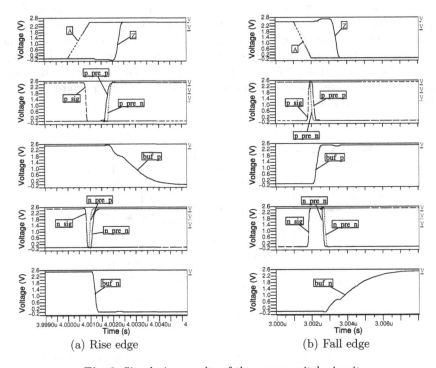

(a) Rise edge   (b) Fall edge

Fig. 9. Simulation results of the power switch circuit

The number of operation finger is changeable according to IDL signals. When the output load is large like as the active mode, all the fingers should be used to reduce the parasitic resistance on the final output buffers. On the other hand, a few fingers should operate to reduce the switching power consumption in the final buffer transistors for higher power efficiency when the output load is small, for example in the idle mode. When the IDL[x] is high, the corresponding finger stops its operation.

5 Measurement Result

Fig. 10(a) shows the test chip fabricated in an ST 65-nm process. The design summary and measurement results are described in Table 2. The proposed dc-dc converter is intended to place under bonding pads. The designed layout is successfully drawn within the area of 5 bonding pads where the bonding pitch is 50 μm. A standard telecom FHT digital block is used as a load. This module can be supplied by any of the two embedded dc-dc converters: one is implemented under the pads to demonstrate the compatibility with the I/O cells and the other is placed in the core for test purposes. Fig. 10(b) shows a photograph of the first demonstration board. The designed chip is packaged with a JLCC (J-Leaded Chip Carrier) 68 pins. The packaged chip, which is represented with DUT in Fig. 10(b), is mounted on the package socket in the center of the test board. In the test measurement, the discrete devices are implemented on the board for the test purpose instead of the in-package implementation as mentioned before. Thus the parasitic resistance is larger than the ideal condition. In the stand-by

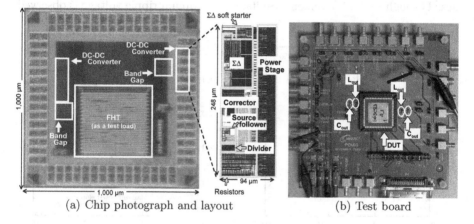

(a) Chip photograph and layout   (b) Test board

Fig. 10. Test chip design

Table 2. Design summary & measurement results

Technology	ST 65 nm CMOS (LSTP)
Circuit area	$248 \times 94\ \mu m^2$: DC-DC converter
	$137 \times 134\ \mu m^2$: Band gap
Supplied voltage	2.5 V
Output set point	1.2 / 1.0 / 0.8 / 0.6 V
Maximum output load	100 mA
Switching frequency	4~18 MHz
Inductor diameter	10 μH (size: 1608)
Decoupling capacitance	0.47 μF (size: 0603)
Voltage ripple	~10 mV

mode, the measured current dissipation is only 19 nA regardless of the connected load module on a pair of one dc-dc converter and one band gap circuit, where the simulation result demonstrated it down to 84 nA.

Fig. 11(a) demonstrates the measurement results of the power efficiency where the set point is 1.2 V. Even though the test chip operates with larger parasitic resistance, the peak power efficiency exceeds 88% whereas the transistor simulation demonstrates it over 90% with less parasitic resistance. As explained in section 4, when the number of active buffer finger is small, the power efficiency is higher for low output power. This trend is visible in Fig. 11(a) comparing the power efficiency obtained with 1 and 16 fingers in the power stage. In the low switching mode of the $\Sigma\Delta$ circuit, the power consumption on the power stage is smaller increasing the power efficiency at low output loads. The theoretical maximum power efficiency of a linear regulator is 48% and 24% converted from 2.5 V to 1.2 V and 0.6 V respectively. As shown in Fig. 11(b), the proposed dc-dc converter demonstrates clearly higher power efficiency than that of a linear regulator in the active operation range of the output load.

Fig. 12 shows one-shot measured waveforms of 1.2 V and 0.6 V output voltages. Through the measurement results, the maximum ripple voltage is observed

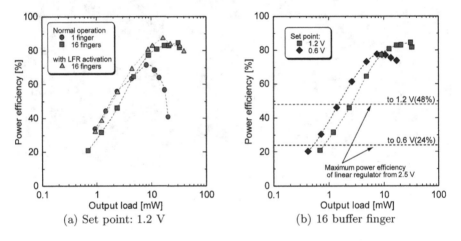

(a) Set point: 1.2 V

(b) 16 buffer finger

Fig. 11. Measurement result of power efficiency

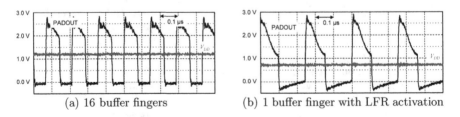

(a) 16 buffer fingers

(b) 1 buffer finger with LFR activation

Fig. 12. Measured waveform of the test chip (Output load: 5 mA)

under 10 mV. The designed test chip has the test mode operation where only power stage buffer can run according to the supplied switching signal from the external pulse generator. When the test chip is forced to operate with a switching frequency of 0.5 MHz, the output ripple voltage of 58 mV and 92 mV is measured with the number of buffer finger of 1 and 16 respectively.

6 Conclusion

Proposed dc-dc converter enables that the leakage current in the stand-by mode can be drastically reduced and the DVS technique is easily available for each module on a multi-power domain SoC. The measured leakage current in the deep stand-by mode is only 19 nA on the first test chip where the simulation demonstrates it down to 84 nA. The layout of the test chip is well drawn within the area of 5 bonding pads with 2 external discrete devices. The fabricated test chip with an ST 65-nm CMOS technology also demonstrates the power efficiency of over 88%.

References

1. The International Technology Roadmap for Semiconductors: Process integration, devices, and structures. 2006 Update (2006)
2. Hattori, T., Irita, T., Ito, M., Yamamoto, E., Kato, H., Sado, G., Yamada, T., Nishiyama, K., Yagi, H., Koike, T., Tsuchihashi, Y., Higashida, M., Asano, H., Hayashibara, I., Tatezawa, K., Shimazaki, Y., Morino, N., Hirose, K., Tamaki, S., Yoshioka, S., Tsuchihashi, R., Arai, N., Akiyama, T., Ohno, K.: A power management scheme controlling 20 power domains for a single-chip mobile processor. In: ISSCC (IEEE International Solid-State Circuit Conference) (February 2006)
3. Burd, T.D., Brodersen, R.W.: Energy efficient cmos microprocessor design. In: Proc. 28th Hawaii International Conference of System Sciences (January 1995)
4. Kuroda, T., Fujita, T., Mita, S., Nagamatu, T., Yoshioka, S., Sano, F., Norishima, M., Murota, M., Kako, M., Kinugawa, M., Kakumu, M., Sakurai, T.: A 0.9v 150mhz 10mw 4mm^2 2-d discrete cosine transform core processor with variable-threshold-voltage scheme. In: ISSCC (IEEE International Solid-State Circuit Conference) Feburuary (1996)
5. Nowka, K.J., Carpenter, G.D., MacDonald, E.W., Ngo, H.C., Brock, B.C., Ishii, K., Nguyen, T.Y., Burns, J.L.: A 32-bit powerpc system-on-a-chip with support for dynamic voltage scaling and dynamic frequency scaling. IEEE J. Solid-State Circuits (November 2002)
6. Lattard, D., Beigné, E., Bernard, C., Bour, C., Fabien Clermidy, Y.D., Durupt, J., Varreau, D., Vivet, P., Pénard, P., Bouttier, A., Berrens, F.: A telecom baseband circuit based on an asynchronous network-on-chip. In: ISSCC (IEEE International Solid-State Circuit Conference) (Feburuary (2007)
7. Roy, K., Mukhopadhyay, S., Mahmoodi-Meimand, H.: Leakage current mechanisms and leakage reduction techniques in deep-submicrometer cmos circuits. Proceedings of the IEEE (Feburuary 2003)
8. Mutoh, S., Douseki, T., Matsuya, Y., Aoki, T.: Satoshi, Shigematsu, Yamada, J.: 1-v power supply high-speed digital circuit technology with multithreshold-voltage cmos. IEEE J. Solid-State Circuits (August 1995)

9. Valentian, A., Beigné, E.: Automatic gate biasing of an sccmos power switch achieving maximum leakage reduction and lowering leakage current variability. IEEE J. Solid-State Circuits (July 2008)
10. Valentian, A., Beigné, E.: Gate bias circuit for an sccmos power switch achieving maximum leakage reduction. In: ESSCIRC (European Solid-State Circuits Conference) (September 2007)
11. Beigné, E., Clermidy, F., Durupt, J., Lhermet, H., Miermont, S., Thonnart, Y., Xuan, T.T., Valentian, A., Varreau, D., Vivet, P.: An asynchronous power aware and adaptive noc based circuit. In: IEEE Symposium on VLSI Circuits (June 2008)
12. Hiraki, M., Ito, T., Fujiwara, A., Ohashi, T., Hamano, T., Noda, T.: A 63-μw standby power microcontroller with on-chip hybrid regulator scheme. IEEE J. Solid-State Circuits (May 2002)

Energy Dissipation Reduction of a Cardiac Event Detector in the Sub-V_t Domain By Architectural Folding

Joachim Neves Rodrigues[1], Omer Can Akgun[2], Puneet Acharya[1],
Adolfo de la Calle[1], Yusuf Leblebici[2], and Viktor Öwall[1]

[1] EIT, Lund University, Box 118, 22100 Lund, Sweden
joachim.rodrigues@eit.lth.se, puneet.acharya@gmail.com,
adolfinguer@gmail.com, viktor.owall@eit.lth.se
[2] EPFL, STI-IEL-LSM, 1015, Lausanne, Switzerland
omercan.akgun@epfl.ch, yusuf.leblebici@epfl.ch
http://www.eit.lth.se

Abstract. This manuscript presents the digital hardware realization of a wavelet based event detector for cardiac pacemaker applications. The architecture of the detector is partially folded to minimize hardware cost. An energy model is applied to evaluate the energy efficiency in the sub-threshold (sub-V_T) domain. The design is synthesized in 65 nm low leakage-high threshold CMOS technology, and it is shown that folding reduces the area cost by 30.6 %. Folding decreases energy dissipation of the circuit by 14.4 % in the sub-V_T regime, where the circuit dissipates 3.3 pJ per sample at V_{DD}=0.26 V.

Keywords: Cardiac pacemaker, QRS detection, wavelet filterbank, folding, time-multiplexing, sub-threshold, energy model.

1 Introduction

The application of implantable biomedical appliances has tremendously progressed during the last decades due to advances in CMOS technology scaling. The functionality of cardiac pacemakers has evolved from the steady-rate pacing in 1958, to programmable rate-responsive operation [5]. Traditionally, sensing, amplification and filtering of cardiac activity in the μV signal range is performed in the analog domain, before the signal is digitized [5,11]. However, pacemaker functionality may be enhanced by performing signal processing in the digital domain, with the advantage of deploying more advanced algorithms.

The application of digital CMOS for cardiac event detection in favour of analog circuitry has previously been discarded because of the constraint on energy dissipation [5]. Technology scaling reduces dynamic power consumption due to smaller capacitive parasitics. However, disadvantageously leakage current has emerged as a major design constraint. Thus, leakage dissipation is seen as the major barrier, if targeting smaller technology nodes. However, if leakage is aggressively addressed, the overall energy dissipation may be competitive to analog circuitry.

J. Monteiro and R. van Leuken (Eds.): PATMOS 2009, LNCS 5953, pp. 347–356, 2010.

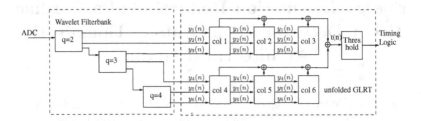

Fig. 1. Parallel architecture of the wavelet filterbank and GLRT

An effective approach to minimize leakage is reduction of the gate count. This may be attained by hardware re-use, realized by time-multiplexing or folding. A folded architecture experiences an increased latency and needs to be triggered by a faster clock. However, gate count may be decreased if the overhead for extra registers and control logic does not eat up the gate reduction attained by folding. Moreover, in sub-threshold (sub-V_T) operation mode, power consumption is decreased significantly by aggressive supply voltage scaling.

Several successful implementations of digital circuits operating in the sub-threshold regime are available in the literature [6,10]. Circuits operating at these extreme low supply voltages work at much lower speeds, i. e., the FFT processor presented in [10] has a maximum clock frequency of 10 kHz with a power supply of 350 mV. Their extreme low power consumption results in excellent power delay product, making such circuits very interesting candidates for ultra-low power applications which do not have very high processing requirements.

The proposed architecture of a 3-scaled wavelet filterbank that feeds a generalized likelihood ratio test (GLRT), is optimized by folding the GLRT. The architecture is synthesized with 65 nm low leakage-high threshold (LL-HVT) CMOS technology. Energy efficiency is evaluated by deploying a SPICE-accurate energy model on the gate-level netlists [1]. These simulations require only a fraction of SPICE simulation time, and compute the supply voltage for the energy optimal operation point, maximum frequency, as well as dynamic and leakage dissipation.

In Sec. 2 the folding scheme of the cardiac event detector is presented. The energy model is presented in Sec. 3. In Sec. 4 the results of the energy dissipation reduction are discussed. Finally, conclusions are presented in Sec. 5.

2   Digital Hardware Implementation

This section presents the theory and architecture of a 3-scaled wavelet filterbank, that scales and conditions the signal for hypothesis testing in the GLRT, see Fig. 1. Furthermore, event detection efficiency is discussed.

2.1   Implementation of the R-Wave Detector

To achieve a power-efficient hardware mapping, short filters with integer values are chosen, i.e., first order difference, and the impulse response was chosen as a

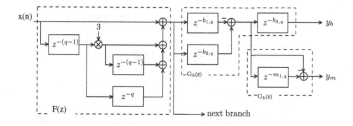

Fig. 2. Data flow diagram of the first wavelet filterbank branch using Mallat's algorithm, $(q = 2)$

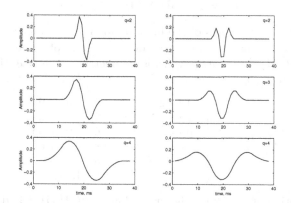

Fig. 3. Impulse responses of the wavelet filterbank. The biphasic impulse responses $y_{b,k}(n)$ for $q = 2, 3, 4$ are displayed in the left panel and the monophasic impulse responses $y_{m,k}(n)$ in the right panel

third order binomial function. A more detailed description of the wavelet filterbank and the GLRT is found in [2]. The implemented wavelet filterbank consist of three branches, $q = 2, 3, 4$, that scale and filter the signal $x(n)$ from the analog-to-digital converter, see Fig. 1 and 2. The first biphasic branch realizes a straight-forward implementation as

$$F(z) = 1 + 3z^{-(q-1)} + 3z^{-(2q-2)} + z^{-(2q-1)} \tag{1}$$

and

$$G_b(z) = -1 + z^{-q}. \tag{2}$$

Reusing $G_b(z)$ implements the monophasic filterbank using a single branch for one scale factor and realizes the output of the filterbank. However, in order to center the functions to the longest propagation delay in the third branch, it is necessary to introduce additional delays in $G_b(z)$, see Fig. 2. The impulse responses of the filterbank are presented in Fig. 3. It can be observed that the wavelet-based structure offers a high flexibility for various cardiac morphologies.

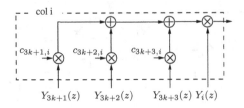

Fig. 4. Data flow diagram of a unfolded block in the GLRT.

The decision signal $T(n)$ is computed by the GLRT as

$$T(n) = \mathbf{x}^T(n)\mathbf{H}(\mathbf{H}^T\mathbf{H})^{-1}\mathbf{H}^T\mathbf{x}(n), \tag{3}$$

where $\mathbf{H}$ holds the coefficients of the bi- and mono-phasic filter functions. Since $\mathbf{x}^T(n)\mathbf{H} = \mathbf{H}^T\mathbf{x}(n)$, the remaining part of (3) to be implemented is the multiplication by $(\mathbf{H}^T\mathbf{H})^{-1}$, a matrix which is symmetric and sparse with half of its elements equal to zero,

$$(\mathbf{H}^T\mathbf{H})^{-1} = \begin{bmatrix} 4.3 & -2.8 & 0.7 & 0 & 0 & 0 \\ -2.8 & 4.5 & -1.8 & 0 & 0 & 0 \\ 0.7 & -1.8 & 1.5 & 0 & 0 & 0 \\ 0 & 0 & 0 & 4.8 & -2.3 & 0.6 \\ 0 & 0 & 0 & -2.3 & 4.2 & -1.4 \\ 0 & 0 & 0 & 0.6 & -1.4 & 1.7 \end{bmatrix}. \tag{4}$$

The multiplication of $\mathbf{y}(n)$ with the first column of $(\mathbf{H}^T\mathbf{H})^{-1}$ and the first element of $\mathbf{H}^T\mathbf{x}(n)$ is carried out as depicted in Fig. 4, where $c_{3k+j,i}$ are elements of $(\mathbf{H}^T\mathbf{H})^{-1}$ and $y_{3k+j}(n)$ the output of the filterbank, with $k = 0, 1$ and $j = 1, 2, 3$.

2.2 Unfolded Architecture

The unfolded architecture of a wavelet scale and GLRT is mapped as illustrated in Fig. 2 and 4, respectively. Three elements of the wavelet scale are cascaded to realize the scaling factors $q = [2, 3, 4]$ of the wavelet filterbank. The schematic in Fig. 4 represents the block referred to as *col i* in Fig. 1, which needs to be replicated six times to realize the multiplication with the columns of the matrix $(H^TH)^{-1}$ in (4). To simplify the implementation the matrix coefficients $c_{i,i} \cdots c_{i,i+2}$ are replaced with rounded integer values, which does not degrade performance. Thus, the multiplications are realized by *shift-add* instructions. Hence, the unfolded realization of the GLRT requires six generic multipliers and 35 adders. Furthermore, the architecture is optimized by register minimization, numerical strength reduction, and internal word-length optimization, which, in turn, results in narrower adders and multipliers in the following GLRT.

2.3 Architectural Folding

Initially, both the wavelet filterbank and the GLRT, see Fig. 1, were folded. However, for the wavelet filterbank it turned out that the controller and register

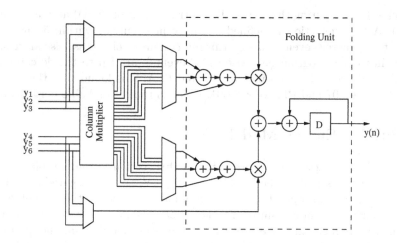

Fig. 5. Folded by three architecture of the GLRT

overhead were larger than savings achieved by reusing the adders. Consequently, only the GLRT is mapped as a by three and six folded architecture, i.e., the unfolded GLRT in Fig. 1 is replaced by the architecture in Fig. 5. In Fig. 5 folding by three is illustrated. The output $y_1 \cdots y_6$ of the wavelet filterbank is subjected to a block called *Column Multiplier* (CM). This block realizes concurrently the multiplications by $c_{i,i} \cdots c_{i,i+2}$, and holds the products for several clock cycles until processed by the *folding unit*. Folding of CM would lead to an area overhead since the coefficients are integer values. The de-multiplexers receive a control signal from a controller and switch the products to the adders, and switches $y_1 \cdots y_6$, correspondingly. The arrangement in Fig. 5 realizes the unfolded structure presented in Fig. 1 and 4. The HW cost of the folded architectures are listed with the unfolded realization in Table 1. The numbers show clearly the gain in area, i.e., the area cost for GLRT in PF3 and PF6 is reduced by 42 % and 49 % respectively. To maintain throughput the folded GLRT needs to be clocked three or six times higher than the wavelet filterbank.

2.4   Detector Performance

The detector implemented in this study qualifies for pacemaker applications with reliable detection performance in noisy environments, validated on cardiograms digitally recorded during pacemaker implantation [8]. Detection performance is

Table 1. HW cost of a by three (PF3) and six (PF6) folded GLRT

	Add	Mult	GLRT Area [μm^2]
Unfolded	35	6	6793
PF3	25	2	3912
PF6	21	1	3436

measured by computing the probability of true detections (PD) and false alarms (PFA). A true detection is defined as an event occurring within 50 ms of the annotation, whereas events outside this interval are declared as false alarms. All signals in the electrogram database (3200 events), are fed to the detector, and the detected events are classified as PD and PFA. It is found that the detector has a PD of 0.997 and PFA of < 0.001, which is rated as reliable performance.

3   Sub-V_T Energy Model

The energy dissipation model presented in this section is comparable to other sub-V_T energy dissipation models [9,12,3]. In [9] Vittoz investigated and proved the energy-minimum operation property of sub-V_T logic. In this model, an expression for energy minimum operating voltage (EMV) is not derived, but determined by numerically inverting the duty factor for minimum energy. In [12] occurrence of the EMV is shown, but the corresponding equation is solved by curve fitting. In [3] sub-V_T EMV is solved analytically, where the model average switched capacitance and leakage current parameters are extracted from SPICE level simulation results.

As shown in this section, the model employed in this study uses parameters derived from high level simulations. The proposed model delivers SPICE-accurate data, but requires only a fraction of SPICE simulation runtime to obtain the internal energy dissipation of a single inverter equivalent capacitance value, which is not directly available in the synthesis library.

The total energy dissipation of static CMOS digital circuits is given by the following well-known equation:

$$E_{total} = \underbrace{\alpha C_{tot} V_{DD}{}^2}_{E_{dyn}} + \underbrace{I_{leak} V_{DD} T_{clk}}_{E_{leak}} + \underbrace{I_{peak} t_{sc} V_{DD}}_{E_{sc}}, \tag{5}$$

where E_{dyn} and E_{leak} are the average switching and leakage energy dissipated during a clock cycle T_{clk}, respectively. The contribution of short circuit energy (E_{sc}) in the sub-V_T regime is neglected, as it is known to contribute only a small share of the overall energy dissipation [9]. In (5), E_{dyn} during one clock period is specified by the switching activity factor (α), and the maximum possible switched capacitance of the circuit (C_{tot}). The total capacitance C_{tot} is normalized in terms of total inverter capacitance using a capacitance scaling factor k_{cap} as $C_{tot} = k_{cap} C_{inv}$, where C_{inv} is the switched capacitance of an inverter. To calculate k_{cap}, the total capacitance obtained by the synthesis is normalized by the gate capacitance value of an inverter from the synthesis library. The leakage energy dissipation during a clock period T_{clk} is defined as

$$E_{leak} = k_{leak} I_0 V_{DD} T_{clk}, \tag{6}$$

where k_{leak} and I_0 are the average leakage scaling factor of the circuit and the average leakage current of a single inverter, respectively. The value for k_{leak} is obtained from the synthesis results by summing the individual average leakage currents of the gates, where the average leakage current is the mean of the leakage current for all the combinations of input vectors applied to the logic gate, and normalizing the result to the average leakage current of a single inverter.

The critical path that constraints the maximum clock frequency is specified as

$$T_{clk} = k_{crit}T_{sw\_inv}, \tag{7}$$

where k_{crit} is a coefficient that defines the critical path delay of the circuit in terms of the inverter delay T_{sw_inv}. The parameter k_{crit} is calculated by dividing the critical path from the synthesis results by the average delay of the inverter while operating at nominal supply.

The delay of an inverter operating in the sub-V_T regime is given in [9] as

$$T_{sw\_inv} = \frac{C_{inv}V_{DD}}{I_0 e^{V_{DD}/(nU_t)}}. \tag{8}$$

By introducing (8) into (7), the clock period is specified as

$$T_{clk} = k_{crit}\frac{C_{inv}V_{DD}}{I_0 e^{V_{DD}/(nU_t)}}, \tag{9}$$

and by combining (5), (6) and (9), the final total energy dissipation while working at the maximum clock frequency is specified as

$$E_T = C_{inv}V_{DD}^2\left[\alpha k_{cap} + k_{crit}k_{leak}e^{-V_{DD}/(nU_t)}\right]. \tag{10}$$

EMV is found by taking the derivative of (10) with respect to V_{DD}. Thus, EMV is specified as

$$V_{opt-sync} = 2nU_t - nU_tW_{-1}\left[-\frac{2e^2\alpha k_{cap}}{k_{crit}k_{leak}}\right], \tag{11}$$

where W_{-1} is the -1 branch of the LambertW function [4], which confirms [3]. All k-parameters in (10) and (11) are obtained from synthesis results, and the switching activity factor α is calculated after running gate level simulations where toggle information is generated from real data [8]. Hence, the total simulation time to characterize sub-V_T performance is highly reduced compared to the SPICE-level simulations. The only parameters that need to be extracted from SPICE simulations for numerical calculations are the slope factor n and the switched inverter capacitance C_{inv}. The accuracy of the model is checked with respect to the SPICE level simulations using the ISCAS85 benchmark circuits and the first quantile of error of the energy dissipation model is found to be below 6% with a mean error of 0.61% in the sub-V_T regime.

4   Sub-V_T Operation Mode

This section presents the energy dissipation results of the unfolded (UF), and by three (PF3) and six (PF6) folded architectures. Static noise margin (SNM)

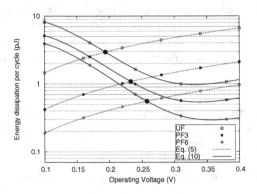

Fig. 6. Sub-threshold energy dissipation curves of different architectures

failure rates are taken into consideration to find an optimal operation point. Table 2 shows the circuit parameters of the synthesized architectures. By employing a higher folding factor the total gate count of the circuit is reduced. This results in lower leakage energy dissipation for the same amount of operation time. The data is fed to the cardiac event detector at a speed of 1 kHz, and in order to maintain throughput, the GLRT operation frequency in UF, PF3 and PF6 architectures needs to be 1, 3 and 6 kHz, respectively. Fig. 6 shows the sub-V_T energy dissipation curves for one clock cycle. The continuous lines show the energy dissipation while working at the speed of the critical path, i. e., minimum leakage time, and the dashed lines show the dissipation while working with a fixed clock. The circuits need to be operated at least at a V_{DD} value that meets the requirement on the maximum clock frequency, i.e., 3 and 6 kHz, indicated by the black dots, which are lower than the EMV values. If V_{DD} is raised higher than indicated by the black dots while working at an externally set speed, E_{total} from (5) will increase (dashed lines). The higher achievable clock frequency at EMV due to a higher V_{DD}, hence lower leakage time, can not be utilized since the clock speed constraint is external. Thus, if the circuit need operate at an external throughput constraint, i.e., fixed clock, then, working at a V_{DD} higher than the value that satisfies the speed requirement results in energy overhead. A technique to operate at EMV with external speed requirements lower than the operating speed at EMV, is power-shut off (PSO), which is not investigated in this paper. It should be noted that although PSO and working at EMV will reduce the energy dissipation, it will introduce energy overhead and a more complicated design process.

Table 2. Composition properties of the synthesized circuits

Architecture	k_{cap}	k_{leak}	k_{crit}	EMV (V)
Unfolded	17820	13358	608.051	0.33
PF3	12550	10991	463.259	0.34
PF6	10303	9794	396.805	0.36

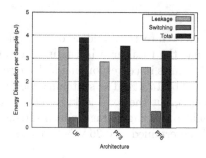

Fig. 7. Energy dissipation components of different architectures

Theoretically, the supply voltage of sub-V_T circuits can be reduced down to 50 mV [9], in practice at such voltage values functional failures occur due to the process variations. Thus, circuits need to be checked for failure rates while operating at extremely low voltages. In this paper the static noise margin (SNM) failure rates of the gates are extracted from 5k-point Monte Carlo analysis, which follows the methodology in [7]. It is found that the supply voltage value which realizes operation with less than 0.001 failure rate for a 65 nm process is 0.25V and this value is taken as the minimum reliable operating voltage (ROV). This results in UF and PF3 operating voltages rising to 0.25V, causing energy dissipation overhead. The PF6 architecture still operates at 0.26V as in Fig. 6 to satisfy the speed requirement. From now on, the mentioned supply voltages will be taken as the operating voltages of different architectures.

To sustain throughput in a folded architecture, the computation of one sample requires 3 and 6 clock cycles for PF3 and PF6, respectively. Therefore, the switching energy per cycle for the folded architectures should be multiplied by their respective folding factors to obtain the switching energy per sample. Moreover, since the idle part of the circuitry leaks during the calculation, the total leakage time of all the architectures is the same and is 1 ms per sample. Thus, it is necessary to multiply leakage energy per clock cycle by the applied folding factor. Since the throughput is an external speed constraint, all the architectures process the data at the same amount of time. Gate count reduction minimizes leakage energy, and hence the average leakage scaling factor (k_{leak}) of the circuit. Fig. 7 shows the energy dissipation components of the designed architectures per sample. Since all circuits need to be supplied with a voltage lower than EMV, they will operate in the leakage dominated region. From Fig. 7, it is seen that by increasing the folding factor, the switching energy increases. This is due to the increase in the complexity of the control circuit. However, although the switching energy increases, it is offset by the reduction in the leakage energy, which in turn reduces overall energy dissipation. By going from the UF architecture to the PF6 architecture, the overall energy dissipation per sample point is reduced by 14.4%.

356   J. Neves Rodrigues et al.

5 Conclusions

This manuscript presents architectural folding of a wavelet based cardiac event detector. It is shown that the total area in the most optimized architecture is reduced by 31 %, which results in corresponding leakage reduction. Thereby, energy dissipation is reduced by 14.4 %. The switching energy due to controller and register overhead increases, but the total leakage reduction offsets this increase in energy dissipation. The operating voltage, which satisfies both speed and failure rate requirement, is determined as 0.26 V, where the circuit dissipates 3.3 pJ per sample.

References

1. Akgun, O., Leblebici, Y.: Energy Efficiency Comparison of Asynchronous and Synchronous Circuits Operating in the Sub-Threshold Regime. J. Low Power Electronics 3(3), 320–336 (2008)
2. Åström, M., Olmos, S., Sörnmo, L.: Wavelet-based event detection in implantable cardiac rhythm management devices. IEEE Trans. Biomed. Eng. 53(3) (March 2006)
3. Calhoun, B., Wang, A., Chandrakasan, A.: Modeling and sizing for minimum energy operation in subthreshold circuits. IEEE Journal of Solid-State Circuits 40(9), 1778–1786 (2005)
4. Corless, R., Gonnet, G., Hare, D., Jeffrey, D., Knuth, D.: On the LambertW function. Advances in Computational Mathematics 5(1), 329–359 (1996)
5. Haddad, S., Houben, R., Serdijn, W.: The evolution of pacemakers. IEEE Engineering in Medicine and Biology Magazine 25(3), 38–48 (2006)
6. Kulkarni, J.P., Kim, K., Roy, K.: A 160 mV robust schmitt trigger based subthreshold SRAM. IEEE Journal of Solid-State Circuits 42(10) (2007)
7. Kwong, J., Chandrakasan, A.: Variation-driven device sizing for minimum energy sub-threshold circuits. In: Proceedings of the 2006 international symposium on Low power electronics and design, pp. 8–13. ACM, New York (2006)
8. Rodrigues, J., Olsson, L., Sörnmo, T., Öwall, V.: Digital implementation of a wavelet-based event detector for cardiac pacemakers. IEEE Transactions on Circuits and Systems I: Regular Papers 52(12), 2686–2698 (2005)
9. Vittoz, E.: Low-Power Electronics Design, ch. 16. CRC Press LLC, Boca Raton (2004)
10. Wang, A., Chandrakasan, A.: A 180-mV subthreshold FFT processor using a minimum energy design methodology. IEEE Journal of Solid-State Circuits 40(1), 310–319 (2005)
11. Wong, L., Hossain, S., Ta, A., Edvinsson, J., Rivas, D., Naas, H.: A very low-power cmos mixed-signal ic for implantable pacemaker applications. IEEE Journal of Solid-State Circuits 39(12), 2446–2456 (2004)
12. Zhai, B., Blaauw, D., Sylvester, D., Flautner, K.: Theoretical and practical limits of dynamic voltage scaling. In: Proceedings of the 41st Annual Conference on Design Automation, pp. 868–873. ACM, New York (2004)

A New Optimized High-Speed Low-Power Data-Driven Dynamic (D3L) 32-Bit Kogge-Stone Adder

Fabio Frustaci and Marco Lanuzza

Department of Electronics, Computer Science and Systems
University of Calabria, Arcavacata di Rende - 87036
Rende (CS) Italy

Abstract. Data Driven Dynamic Logic (D3L) achieves a considerably energy saving, over conventional Domino Logic, by removing the clock signal: the control of the precharge and evaluation phases is managed only by input data. Unfortunately, this advantage is typically obtained at the expense of speed performances and consequently affecting the Energy-Delay Product (EDP). This paper presents a novel technique to design D3L parallel prefix adders considerably reducing speed penalties. Moreover, a new design style, named Splith-Path D3L, is introduced to overcome the limits of standard D3L. When applied to a 32-bit Kogge-Stone adder realized with the STMicroelectronics 65nm 1V CMOS technology, the proposed technique leads to an EDP 25% and 20% lower than the standard Domino Logic and the conventional D3L counterparts, respectively.

Keywords: data pre-charged dynamic logic, D3L, parallel prefix adder.

1 Introduction

Digital adders are crucial components in any digital system because they can significantly influence the overall achievable performances [1]. For this reason, novel high-speed adders are highly desirable.

Speed performances of an adder can be improved optimizing both the top-level architecture and the circuit implementation. For example, parallel prefix adder topologies, such as the Kogge-Stone, assure a low computation delay. Moreover, using fast design logic style, such as Domino Logic, can further improve the adder speed. However, despite the high speed reached by a Domino Logic parallel prefix adder, such a circuit dissipates a large amount of energy due to the presence of the clock distribution tree which inputs the clock signal to all the logic gates. As demonstrated in [2], the power dissipation owing to the clock distribution network in a dynamic system can range from 20% up to 45% of the overall consumed power. This prevents from exploiting Domino Logic when achieving low-power dissipation is a primary issue.

In order to reduce the power consumption of Domino circuits, Data-Driven Dynamic Logic (D3L) was recently proposed in [3]. The clock distribution network is eliminated and the precharge function of the clock signal is carried out by the input

J. Monteiro and R. van Leuken (Eds.): PATMOS 2009, LNCS 5953, pp. 357–366, 2010.
© Springer-Verlag Berlin Heidelberg 2010

signals. As a consequence, the power consumption is significantly reduced at the expense of a non-negligible penalty in terms of speed performances [4].

This paper presents a new technique for exploiting the energy-saving advantages offered by D3L without paying significant performance penalty with respect to the conventional Domino Logic. A fast and low-power 32-bit Kogge-Stone parallel prefix adder is described. The novel circuit exploits a parallel-prefix tree structure implemented by a new optimized D3L design. When realized with the STMicroelectronics 65nm 1V CMOS technology, the novel adder exhibits an Energy-Delay Product 25% and 20% lower than the standard clock precharged Domino Logic and the conventional D3L implementations, respectively.

Moreover, the proposed adder results to be more tolerant to random process variations than Domino and standard D3L designs demonstrating its effectiveness for very scaled technologies.

The paper is organized as follows: in Section 2 an overview of Dynamic Domino and D3L is furnished; in Section 3 the design of a Domino and D3L 32-bit Kogge-Stone is described; the new data-precharged parallel prefix structure and the novel optimized D3L design style are described in Section4; in Section 5 obtained results are presented and finally conclusions are given.

2 Dynamic Domino Logic and D3L

Domino gates operate using a sequence of precharge and evaluation phases on the basis of a clock input. During the precharge phase, the output signal is forced to a pre-defined value, independently of input data. On the contrary, during the evaluation phase, the output signal does not depend on the clock but it may eventually switch according to the received inputs. An n-type (p-type) Domino gate executes its precharge phase when the clock signal is low (high), whereas it performs the evaluation phase when the clock is high (low). Fig. 1.a illustrates the generic n-type Domino gate. The clocked-PMOS transistor M1 is on during the precharge phase and it sets the dynamic node to the logic value 1. During the evaluation phase, M1 is off whereas the clocked-NMOS transistor M2 (the so-called footer transistor) is on providing the evaluation network with a path to ground.

A new dynamic logic, called Data-Driven Dynamic Logic (D3L), has been recently introduced in [3] in order to eliminate the clock distribution tree. In an n-type (p-type) D3L gate, the clocked precharging PMOS (NMOS) transistor employed in Domino Logic is replaced by a Pull-up PMOS (Pull-Down NMOS) network, which receives a subset of the input data signals (the so-called *pre-charge inputs*) instead of the clock

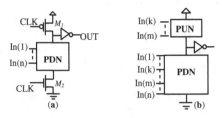

Fig. 1. The generic n-type (a) Domino and (b) D3L gate

signal. The evaluation network of the gate remains unchanged, with respect to the equivalent Domino gate, and the clocked NMOS (PMOS) foot transistor is avoided. Fig. 1.b depicts the generic n-type D3L gate. It can be observed that the precharge inputs *In(k)...In(m)* need to satisfy the following conditions: 1) during the precharge phase, the Pull-Down network (PDN) is OFF, the Pull-Up network (PUN) is certainly turned ON and the output node is charged to *Vdd*; 2) during the evaluation phase, the output node is eventually discharged to 0 by the PDN without any contention with the PUN.

D3L achieves two main advantages: the energy reduction owing to the elimination of the clock distribution network and the decrease of the evaluation path delay owing to the elimination of the clocked NMOS (PMOS) transistor. Unfortunately, the absence of a global clock signal, which simultaneously synchronizes all the gates, involves the existence of a precharge propagation path [4]. In order to keep high speed performances, the precharge path needs to be not slower than the evaluation path by opportunely increasing the PMOS (NMOS) transistors size of the precharging PUNs (PDNs). As a consequence, the precharge inputs have to drive a larger load capacitance and the dynamic energy consumption increases. This may limit the advantages offered by D3L making its effectiveness dependent on the specific application.

In the following, the design of a fast adder is presented as a case study where the limits of D3L are evident. The choice of this circuit comes from its crucial importance in determining the computational speed of the most of digital systems.

3   Domino and D3L High-Speed Adder Designs

As it is well known, logarithmic parallel prefix adders are the most widely used for reaching high-speed [5, 6]. The addition of two operands $A = a_{n-1}...a_0$ and $B = b_{n-1}...b_0$ is performed through a three-stage operation: the pre-processing stage computes the *generate* $g_i = a_i \cdot b_i$ and *propagate* signals $p_i = a_i \oplus b_i$ for each bit position *i*; the carry-propagation stage, organized in a logarithm tree of "dot" operators, produces the *grouped-generate* $G_{i:j}$ and *grouped-propagate* $P_{i:j}$ signals; the final stage performs the calculation of the sum bits. The generic signal $G_{i:j}$ indicates a carry bit generation between the bit positions i and j (j<i) whereas the generic signal $P_{i:j}$ indicates the propagation of a carry signal, previously generated, from the position j to i. Their logical equations are given in (1) with k<j:

$$G_{i,j} = g_i + g_{i-1} \cdot p_i + ... + g_j \cdot p_i \cdot p_{i-1} \cdots p_{j+1}$$
$$P_{i,j} = p_i \cdots p_j \tag{1}$$

$$(G_{i,k}, P_{i,k}) = (G_{i,j}, P_{i,j}) \bullet (G_{j-1,k}, P_{j-1,k}) =$$
$$= (G_{i,j} + P_{i,j} \cdot G_{j-1,k}, P_{i,j} \cdot P_{j-1,k}) \tag{2}$$

In the past, several parallel-prefix adder topologies have been developed which differ for the connections of the dot operators within the carry-propagation stage [7-9]. Each of them has its own advantages and drawbacks in terms of speed, energy dissipation and hardware complexity. Among the existing adder topologies, the Kogge-Stone structure represents a worthwhile choice for its very regular structure with the minimum logic depth and the minimum fan-out [7]. The logical equations of the generic Kogge-Stone dot operator are described in (3):

$$G_{i,j}^m = G_{i,k}^{m-1} + P_{i,k}^{m-1} \cdot G_{k-1,j}^{m-1} \qquad G_{i,j}^0 = g_i$$
$$P_{i,j}^m = P_{i,k}^{m-1} \cdot P_{k-1,j}^{m-1} \qquad P_{i,j}^0 = p_i$$

(3)

with $\quad m = 1,...,\lceil \log_2 n \rceil, \quad i \geq 2^{m-1}, \quad k = i - 2^{m-1} + 1$

$$j = \begin{cases} i - 2^m + 1 & \text{when } i > 2^m - 1 \\ 0 & \text{else} \end{cases}$$

where m indicates the row index of the adder tree (i.e. the depth level), and i represents the column index. Fig 2 depicts the structure of a 32-bit Kogge-Stone adder.

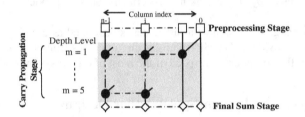

Fig. 2. The 32-bit Kogge-Stone adder

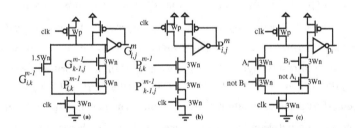

Fig. 3. Domino gates: Grouped Generate (a); Grouped Propagate (b); propagate (c)

Obviously, the design style chosen to implement the dot operator has a crucial impact on the energy and speed performances of the whole adder. Figs. 3 and 4 show the Domino and D3L implementations of the dot operator and the XOR gate performing $p_i = a_i \oplus b_i$, respectively.

According to (3), the signals $G_{i,k}^{m-1}$ and $P_{i,k}^{m-1}$ can be exploited as precharge inputs in the D3L realization of the dot operators. As shown in Fig. 4, the main disadvantage of the grouped-generate D3L gate is the need to have two precharging series-connected PMOS devices. This causes a slow-down of the precharge phase of the gate, so the width of the series-connected PMOS transistors has to be properly sized in order to make the precharge phase not slower than the evaluation one. As a result, the transistors width may assume a large value and the load capacitance driven by the signals $G_{i,k}^{m-1}$ and $P_{i,k}^{m-1}$ may excessively increase, resulting in an increasing of the energy consumption of the gate.

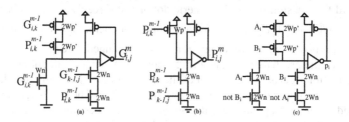

Fig. 4. D3L gates: Grouped Generate (a); Grouped Propagate (b); propagate (c)

4 Proposed Optimized D3L Kogge-Stone Adder

A new technique is here proposed that emphasizes the advantages of the conventional D3L over Domino Logic, avoiding the energy-related drawbacks coming from the high input capacitance driven by the precharge inputs. As it will be discussed in the following, the new adder benefits by an optimization of the Kogge-Stone carry propagation tree and a more efficient implementation of the dot operator and XOR gate.

4.1 Optimized Kogge-Stone Carry Propagation Tree

The proposed carry-propagation tree exploits the possibility to use, as the precharge inputs, signals that are not inputted to the corresponding evaluation network of the gate [4]. From equations (3), the expressions (4) can be derived for the signals $G_{i,k}^{m-1}$ and $P_{i,k}^{m-1}$:

$$G_{i,j}^m = G_{i,k}^{m-1} + P_{i,k}^{m-1} \cdot G_{k-1,j}^{m-1} =$$
$$= \left(G_{i,x}^{m-2} + P_{i,x}^{m-2} \cdot G_{x-1,k}^{m-2} \right) + P_{i,x}^{m-2} \cdot P_{x-1,k}^{m-2} \cdot \left(G_{k-1,y}^{m-2} + P_{k-1,y}^{m-2} \cdot G_{y-1,j}^{m-2} \right) =$$
$$\vdots$$
$$= g_i + p_i \cdot g_{i-1} + p_i \cdot p_{i-1} \cdot g_{i-2} + ... + p_i \cdot p_{i-1} \cdot\cdot\cdot p_{j+1} \cdot g_j \tag{4}$$
$$P_{i,j}^m = P_{i,k}^{m-1} \cdot P_{k-1,j}^{m-1} = P_{i,x}^{m-2} \cdot P_{x-1,k}^{m-2} \cdot P_{k-1,y}^{m-2} \cdot P_{y-1,j}^{m-2} =$$
$$\vdots$$
$$= p_i \cdot p_{i-1} \cdot\cdot\cdot p_{j+1} \cdot p_j$$

where x, k and y are three intermediate bit positions between i and j, with $j<y<k<x<i$ and $x = i - 2^{m-2} + 1$. It follows that the generic gate computing the signal $G_{i,j}^m$ can

receive, as its precharge inputs, the signals $G_{i,x}^{m-2}$ and $P_{i,x}^{m-2}$. In fact, it can be easily verified that these signals satisfy the two conditions of a generic precharge signal described in Section 2. As a consequence, the generic dot operator belonging to the m-th row of the carry propagation tree receives, as its precharge inputs, two signals coming from dot operators belonging to the $(m-2)$-th row. It follows that the propagation path occurring during the precharge phase is halved with respect to the standard D3L design where the generic dot operator receives, as precharge inputs, the signals $G_{i,k}^{m-1}$ and $P_{i,k}^{m-1}$ coming from dot operators belonging to the $(m-1)$-th row.

So, the proposed adder topology remains unchanged except for the physical distribution of the precharge signals. Fig. 5 depicts the generic i-th column of the new carry propagation tree and D3L design of the dot operators. The latter are classified as "*odd*" and "*even*" nodes depending on their depth level m. The precharge inputs of the generic odd (even) dot operator are the outputs of the preceding odd (even) operator. It follows that the generic dot operator belonging to the m-th row receives its precharge inputs from the $(m-2)$-th level whereas its input signals come from the $(m-1)$-th level. For the first node in the column, the precharge inputs and the evaluation inputs are the same: g_i and p_i.

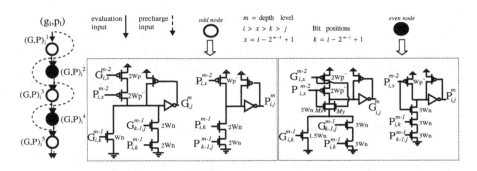

Fig. 5. The generic column of the proposed tree structure

An important issue arises for the implementation of the dot operators: since the precharge and the input signal are different, a contention between the PUN and PDN can occur during the precharge phase. This has to be prevented in order to avoid a high shot-circuit energy dissipation. The gate level implementation of a generic odd dot operator can be designed in standard D3L without incurring in such a case. In fact, for an odd dot operator, during the precharge phase, the input and precharge signals arrives simultaneously since they both have a propagation path of $m-2$ depth levels: this eliminates a possible DC contention. On the contrary, for a generic even dot operator, during the precharge phase, the input signals have a propagation path of $m/2$ level whereas the precharge signals are formed through $(m/2)-1$ depth levels. In this way, the PDN can be turned ON before the PUN is turned OFF, thus generating a DC path from supply to ground. To avoid such a case, the PDN of the even node contains extra NMOS transistors driven by the precharge signals (Mx and My).

It is then clear that the proposed carry-propagation stage structure is able to half the propagation path during the precharge phase. As a consequence, the constraint of setting the width of the precharging PMOS devices to a value high enough to guarantee a fast propagation phase can be relaxed: this means smaller PMOS transistors width, smaller input capacitance of the gates and, consequently, smaller dynamic energy consumption and computation delay.

4.2 Split-Path Gate Level Implementation of the Dot Operators

The above described optimized carry-propagation tree structure allows the width of the PMOS precharging transistors of D3L dot operators to be reduced. However, it does not eliminate the need for two series-connected PMOS devices in the PUN which is the main reason of a slow precharge propagation path. To this aim, an optimized gate level implementation of the dot operators is here presented. The proposed design style, named *split-path* D3L, consists in splitting the PDN of the D3L gate into sub-networks. In this way, the number of series-connected precharging transistors and the gate input capacitance are minimized with remarkable benefits in terms of dynamic energy dissipation and computation speed. As a further advantage, the split of the PDN also causes the split of the parasitic capacitance of the dynamic node, thus increasing the gate speed [10]. Fig. 6.a shows the new *split-path* D3L grouped-generate gate of a even dot operator.

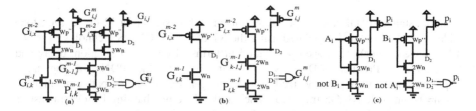

Fig. 6. Split-Path D3L Gates: Grouped Generate (a); Grouped Propagate (b); propagate (c)

The original PDN is split into two evaluating sub-networks each of them requiring only one precharging PMOS. As a result, the width of the precharging PMOS can be reduced with respect to the precharging devices of the D3L implementation. In order to correctly evaluate the logic function, a static 2-input NAND gate replaces the final static inverter used in Domino and D3L gates. Also the keeper transistor is split into two keeper PMOS devices, each of them related to one evaluating sub-network. Since there is only one leakage path for each PDN, the width of each keeper can be scaled down by a factor of 2. Thanks to this, the DC contention between the keeper and the related PDN during the gate switching is mitigated and the energy dissipation and delay are further reduced. The only drawback of the proposed split-path D3L gate is the two series-connected NMOS devices of the final static NAND. The width of these transistors is doubled with respect to the single NMOS device of the final static inverter in Domino and D3L implementation, leading to an increase of the parasitic capacitance of the two dynamic nodes D1 and D2. However, this negative effect is well counterbalanced by the reduced parasitic capacitances of the smaller keepers and of the smaller PMOSs in the PUNs.

For what it concerns about the grouped-propagate gate of the dot operator, the new design style is inapplicable since there is only one path in the PDN.

It is worth noting that the proposed *split-path* D3L design style is completely compatible with the new optimized carry-propagation tree structure described in Sub-Section 4.1: they both concur to decrease the width of the precharging PMOS transistors.

Unfortunately, the *split-path* design style can not be applied also to the grouped-generate gate of odd dot operators. Fig. 6.b depicts the split-path D3L version of an odd dot operator. It can be easily verified that the following case may occur: the signal $G_{i,x}^{m-2}$ is low whereas the signal $G_{i,k}^{m-1}$ is high. As a consequence, a DC path between supply and ground is established and the gate dissipates a high short-circuit energy. For such a reason, the odd dot operators of the proposed adder were implemented in standard D3L.

Finally, the proposed split-path D3L style can be applied to the design of the XOR gates of the pre-processing stage. The new gate computing the propagate signal $p_i = a_i \oplus b_i$ is depicted in Fig. 6.c.

5   32-Bit Kogge-Stone Implementation and Comparison Results

Domino, standard D3L and proposed optimized D3L designs of a 32-bit Kogge-Stone adder were laid out and simulated using the ST 65nm 1V CMOS technology (@27°, TT process corner). They were compared in terms of energy dissipation, delay and Energy-Delay Product (EDP). NMOS transistors in the PDNs of the three implementations were equally sized to make the generic evaluation path equivalent to a Wn=0.6um wide NMOS transistor. The width of the precharging PMOS transistors were accurately chosen so that the precharge phase of the adder is not larger than the evaluation phase. Parametric simulations were performed and the resulting sizing was the following: Wp=0.12um, Wp'=0.8um and Wp''=0.6 (the definitions of such parameters are given in Figs. 3-6). Skewed static inverters and NAND gates with a skew ratio (PUN equivalent width - PDN equivalent width ratio) equal to 4 were exploited in order to assure high speed performances [11]. For the Domino design, the two-level clock buffer tree depicted in Fig. 7 was purposely designed according to the logical effort method [12]: the capacitances of the static buffers Cg_{1-4} were calculated taking into account the values of the load capacitances C_L^{1-5}. Finally, each output node of the adder was loaded with a 1.1fF capacitance (i.e. the input capacitance of a X9 D-type Flip-Flop [13]). Results reported in Table 1 show that the proposed adder exhibits an energy dissipation 5% and 30% lower than the conventional D3L and the Domino implementation, respectively. The Domino adder shows the highest energy dissipation owing to the clock distribution network, which dissipates roughly 25% of the overall consumed energy.

From Table 1, it is easy to verify that the evaluation delay of the proposed adder is 15% lower than the conventional D3L, whereas it is slightly higher (roughly 6%) with respect to the Domino adder.

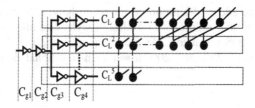

Fig. 7. The clock buffer tree used in the domino implementation

Table 1. Comparison results

	Precharge delay [ps]	Evaluation delay [ps]	Total Energy[1] [pJ]	Energy of the clock buffer [pJ]	EDP [nJ*ps]
Domino	325	320	8.86	2.3	2.88
D3L	408	400	6.56	0	2.67
New	340	335	6.24	0	2.12

[1]Average value over 100 random input pattern

As expected, the D3L implementation consumes less energy than the Domino adder. However, this advantage is obtained at the expense of the computational delay and, as a result, the EDP is only 7% lower with respect to the Domino design. On the contrary, the proposed optimized adder exhibits a very slight speed penalty leading to a significant reduction of the EDP that is 20% and 25% lower than the conventional D3L and Domino designs, respectively.

The exploited scaled technology has required also a study of the adders performance under random process variations. The latter are well known to be one of the most important sources of delay variability in nanometer digital ICs [14, 15]. Table 2 reports the mean (μ), standard deviation (σ) and the relative (σ/μ) delay variation obtained by MonteCarlo simulations. Obtained results reveal that the proposed design has the lowest σ/μ value so resulting more tolerant to random process variation. This means that the proposed optimized design can be efficiently exploited also in more scaled technology.

Table 2. Mean, standard deviation and relative variation of the adder delay

	μ [ps]	σ [ps]	σ/μ
Domino	324	44	0.14
D3L	405	48.6	0.12
New	343	34	0.1

6 Conclusion

In this paper, a new parallel-prefix structure is presented to efficiently exploit Data Driven Dynamic Logic (D3L) in the design of low-power high-performance adders. Moreover, a new dynamic design style, named Split-Path D3L, is proposed to overcome the speed limitations of traditional D3L. When applied to the design of a

32-bit Kogge-Stone adder, the proposed approach halves the precharge propagation path with respect to the traditional D3L design style, and allows a smaller sizing of the precharging PMOS transistors. As a consequence, the new technique leads to an Energy-Delay Product 25% and 20% lower than traditional domino and D3L logic styles.

References

[1] Shalem, R., John, E., John, L.K.: A novel low power energy recovery full adder cell. In: Proceedings of the 9th Great Lakes Symposium on VLSI, Ypsilanti, Michigan (USA), March 4-6, pp. 380–383 (1999)

[2] Kawaguchi, H., Sakurai, T.: A reduced clock-swing flip-flop (RCSFF) for 63% power reduction. IEEE J. Solid-State Circuits 33(5), 807–811 (1998)

[3] Rafati, R., Fakhraie, S.M., Smith, K.C.: A 16-Bit Barrel-Shifter Implemented in Data-Driven Dynamic Logic (D3L). IEEE Transaction on Circuits and Systems I 53(10), 2194–2202 (2006)

[4] Frustaci, F., Lanuzza, M., Zicari, P., Perri, S., Corsonello, P.: Designing High Speed Adders in Power-Constrained Environments. IEEE Transaction on Circuits and Systems. II. Express Brief 56(2), 172–176 (2009)

[5] Kim, J., Lee, K., Yoo, H.-J.: A 372ps 64-bit Adder using Fast Pull-up Logic in 0.18-um CMOS. In: Proceedings of the 2006 IEEE International Symposium on Circuits and Systems (ISCAS 2006), Island of KOS, Greece, May 21-24, pp. 13–16 (2006)

[6] Kao, S., Zlatanovici, R., Nikolic, B.: A 240ps 64b Carry-Lookahead Adder in 90nm CMOS. In: Proceedings of the2006 IEEE International Solid-State Circuits Conference, San Francisco, California, USA, February 6-9, pp. 1735–1744 (2006)

[7] Kogge, P.M., Stone, H.S.: A parallel algorithm for the efficient solution of a general class of recurrence equations. IEEE Transactions on Computers 22, 786–793 (1973)

[8] Brent, R.P., Kung, H.T.: A Regular Layout for Parallel Adders. IEEE Transactions on Computers C-31, 260–264 (1982)

[9] Knowles, S.: A family of adders. In: Proceedings of the 15th IEEE Symposium on Computer Arithmetic, Vail, Colorado (USA), June 11-13, pp. 277–281 (2001)

[10] Elgebaly, M., Sachdev, M.: A leakage tolerant energy efficient wide domino circuit technique. In: Proceedings of the 45th Midwest Symposium on Circuits and Systems, Tulsa, Oklaomah (USA), August 4-7, vol. 1, pp. 487–490 (2002)

[11] Solomatnikov, A., Somasekhar, D., Roy, K., Koh, C.-K.: Skewed CMOS: Noise-Immune High-Performance Low-Power Static Circuit Family. IEEE Transactions on Very Large Scale Integration (VLSI) Systems 10(4), 469–476 (2002)

[12] Sutherland, I., Sproull, R., Harris, D.: Logical Effort. Morgan Kaufmann Publishers, San Francisco (1999)

[13] STMicroelectronics CORE65LPSVT_1.00V 4.0 Standard Cell Library User Manual & Data Book

[14] Croon, J.A., Sansen, W., Maes, H.E.: Matching Properties of Deep Sub-Micron MOS Transistors. Springer, Heidelberg (2005)

[15] Srivasta, A., Sylvester, D., Blaauw, D.: Statistical Analysis and Optimization for VLSI: Timing and Power. Springer, Heidelberg (2005)

Author Index